THE EARLIER EPISTLES OF ST. PAUL

THE

EARLIER EPISTLES OF ST. PAUL

THEIR MOTIVE AND ORIGIN

BY

KIRSOPP LAKE

Wipf & Stock
PUBLISHERS
Eugene, Oregon

Wipf and Stock Publishers
199 West 8th Avenue, Suite 3
Eugene, Oregon 97401

The Earlier Epistles of St. Paul
Their Motive and Origin
By Lake, Kirsopp
ISBN: 1-59244-700-7
Publication date 5/19/2004
Previously published by Rivingtons, 1911

TO

THE SENATUS ACADEMICUS

OF THE

UNIVERSITY OF ST. ANDREWS

PREFACE

THE difficulty which undoubtedly attends any attempt to understand the Epistles of St. Paul is largely due to the fact that they are letters; for the writer of a letter assumes the knowledge of a whole series of facts, which are, as he is quite aware, equally familiar to his correspondent and to himself. But as time goes on this knowledge is gradually forgotten, and what was originally quite plain becomes difficult and obscure; it has to be rediscovered from stray hints and from other documents by a process of laborious research, before it is possible for the letters to be read with anything approaching to the ease and intelligence possessed by those to whom they were originally sent. It is necessary to reconstruct the story of the motive and origin of the letters, and create a picture of the background of thought and practice against which they were set in the beginning.

The following pages are an attempt to do this for the earlier Epistles of St. Paul. I have not tried to give a description of St. Paul's own thoughts—I trust that I may attempt this task later—but to reconstruct the background, a knowledge of which renders it possible to read the Epistles with intelligence; and for this purpose two main types of problems have been attacked.

In the first place, an effort has been made to deal with the literary and critical questions introductory to these letters, concerning their integrity, destination, and history. These problems are often somewhat tedious, but they acquire interest if they are seriously studied, and in any case they cannot be neglected by those who desire to have a real grasp of the nature of early Christian literature.

Secondly, attention has been given to the intricate question of the world of religious thought to which the earliest Gentile Christians belonged—the world of the Hellenistic Mystery Religions. This is much more difficult, and much more important, but has as yet been much less adequately studied than the more purely literary questions. Students of the New Testament have been somewhat slow to grasp its importance, or to make use of the rich material which has been given by classical and archaeological scholars, such as (if I may mention two names out of a great number) Cumont and Reitzenstein.

Nevertheless, I have no fear but that the immediate future will make good the remissness of the past. The study of the religious life of the Graeco-Roman world as a whole is now fully recognized to be absolutely necessary if we do not wish our notions about early Christianity to be a mere caricature of the truth.

There is, however, one subsidiary point to which I have drawn attention in more than one chapter, and desire to emphasize once more,—the psychological aspect of religion. To understand the history of religions we must understand the psychology of religious men. I have endeavoured in the following pages to use what knowledge of psychology I possess, but I am confident that this method ought to be extended far more widely. The difficulty is due to our ignorance of co-ordinated facts, and this again is partly caused by the unnatural limitation of the modern study of theology.

We desire to arrive at an intelligent understanding of religion; we grow old and weary in the study of texts and inscriptions, and we do well, for they have much to teach us; but we forget that religion is to be found in men, not in manuscripts, and we need to take a lesson from our brothers the doctors. They are the students of the body, as we are of the soul; they make the centre of their work the study of the body as it is found here and now, and their use of the books of past generations is always subsidiary to that study. It is the fatal mistake of the theologian to think that he can do otherwise, and understand the soul from the study of ancient books. Our great need at present is the study of the living soul, and I venture to say this, because it is, among other more important things, very necessary for the study of those Epistles on which I am writing.

KIRSOPP LAKE.

LEIDEN, *September*, 1911.

CONTENTS

CHAPTER I

THE OUTLINE GIVEN IN ACTS OF EVENTS IN ST. PAUL'S LIFE

IT needs no argument to show that the problems concerning the Pauline Epistles can only be stated, much less solved, in connection with the evidence of the Acts. In the Acts we have not, indeed, any attempt to give an account of all St. Paul's work, but we have an outline of a great part of it, and in some places detailed information as to his journeys, which it is impossible to overvalue. This outline of the course of events is the necessary basis of any attempt to reconstruct the background of the Epistles. Fortunately, it is quite easy to follow, and presents in itself hardly any serious difficulties. The writer of Acts takes us from city to city with St. Paul, and often gives us some indication of the time spent in each, so that with surprisingly few exceptions we can reconstruct St. Paul's route, and (though here the degree of certainty is markedly less) the duration of his work in various districts.

Nevertheless, the matter is occasionally complicated by a series of critical questions, some of which in turn depend on the Epistles. Therefore we are to some extent dealing, in connection with St. Paul, with a problem involving two factors, one of which must always be assumed as certain when the other is under discussion, though neither can really be finally treated as possessing its assumed stability. Ideally the proper method is first to assume one factor, and afterwards to consider the necessary correction to be allowed for, owing to the possible range of error in the assumption. But in practice certain limitations can be usefully observed in carrying out such a plan. It is neither necessary nor desirable to fight all over again the battle of the Acts in the spirit of Zeller, or of his immediate opponents. Zeller[1] is still worth reading, but even though half a century of criticism has not been able to settle all the problems which have been raised in connection with the Acts, it has gone some way towards reducing them to manageable dimensions, so that for the purpose of the present book, which is concerned primarily with the Epistles, it is possible within very short limits to present a sufficient statement of the subject, showing the points on which there is especial room for doubt, and the general position which most commends itself to those who have fully investigated the Acts.

It would be generally admitted that the central point of all study of the Acts is the "we-clauses," in which the writer speaks of himself and St. Paul in the first person plural. These clauses, by an almost unanimous consent, are regarded as the work of a companion of St. Paul; and there is scarcely less agreement in tracing most of the important facts of the "Pauline" half of Acts to the same source. The contentious points are concerned with the relation of this writer to the redactor, and with the earlier or "Petrine" half of the book. Many critics, by no means

[1] *Die Apostelgeschichte nach ihrem Inhalt und Ursprung kritisch untersucht*, 1854. Published in English by Williams and Norgate in 1875 as *The Contents and Origin of the Acts of the Apostles.*

belonging to an extreme school, think that the "we-clauses" and the source to which they belong—which is very commonly recognized to have been the work of St. Luke, the friend of St. Paul—ought to be distinguished from the final redactor, who may have lived in the last days of the first century, and have compiled the Third Gospel and Acts from earlier documents. Others think that the writer of the "we-clauses" was himself the redactor, whom they identify with St. Luke, and consider that he used the first person in order to indicate the occasions on which he had been actually present at the incidents described. Professor Harnack's studies on the question[1] have done much to commend the latter opinion, but he has not yet succeeded in obtaining such a measure of agreement as to justify a writer on the Epistles in disregarding the alternative view.[2] This question is not, however, of the first importance for the present subject, as there is in any case something approaching unanimity in assigning a high value to the "Pauline" half of Acts, though its accuracy is still questioned on some individual details; these will be considered, so far as is necessary, when they are met with in discussing the Epistles. Far more serious is the problem raised by the "Petrine" half of the Acts Here it is conceded generally that the redactor, whether he was St.

[1] *Untersuchungen zu den Schriften des Lukas*, Hinrichs, 1906–8. These studies were originally published in three volumes, under the titles of *Lukas der Arzt*, *Sprüche und Reden Jesu*, and *Die Apostelgeschichte*. They have been published in English by Williams and Norgate, as *Luke the Physician*, *The Sayings and Words of Jesus*, and *The Acts of the Apostles*.

[2] No special book more recent than Harnack can be cited; but very important articles will be found in the *Theol. Literaturzeitung*, vol. xxxiii. pp. 172–6, by Schürer; in the *Theologische Rundschau*, vol. xi. pp. 185–205, by Bousset; in the *American Journal of Theology*, vol. xi. pp. 454–474, by Bacon; and in the *Zeitschrift für wiss. Theologie*, vol. l. pp. 176–214, by Hilgenfeld. Bousset's article gives a full account of all recent studies of the Acts of any importance.

Luke or a later writer, was using various sources ; but there is no agreement as to whether these sources were written or oral, or, if they were written, Greek or Aramaic. It is also generally conceded that these sources were not all of equal value, and that some difficulties in the opening narratives can best be explained on the hypothesis that the redactor, or one of his sources, had misunderstood the narrative. The importance of this fact for the Pauline Epistles is chiefly in connection with the Judaistic controversy. If, for instance, we assume that the redactor of Acts, as redactors are wont to do, made two incidents out of two narratives of the same incident, we have to face the possibility that Acts has multiplied the visits of St. Paul to Jerusalem, and this is an important factor in considering the problem of the relation between the visit mentioned in Gal. ii. and the Apostolic Council.

It will be seen that it will be necessary in the end to consider several points of this nature in relation to the Epistles ; but the clearest method seems unquestionably to be found in starting with the narrative of Acts as we have in the ordinary Greek text, using this as the working hypothesis from which a study of the historical side of the Epistles must begin, and taking into consideration in the course of this study the modifications rendered possible by the criticism of the Acts. The narrative of the Acts, which it is proposed to use in this way, is familiar to every one, but for convenience it is perhaps not superfluous to state in the shortest possible summary the facts which it contains relating to St. Paul.

The Acts describe St. Paul as a Roman citizen,[1] a Jew of

[1] Acts xxii. 25–29.

Tarsus,[1] called Saul in Jewish circles, who had been educated in Jerusalem under the guidance of Gamaliel.[2] He was a zealous defender of a strict Pharisaic Judaism,[3] and took part in the persecution of Christians.[4] He was at his own request employed in this connection by the High Priest to go to Damascus in the interests of the anti-Christian Jewish propaganda,[5] but on the way to that city he was suddenly converted by a vision of the risen Lord to believe the doctrine, which he had hitherto repudiated, that the Messiah was Jesus, and became as zealous a defender of Christianity, as he had previously been a persecutor of it.[6]

After his conversion he went first to Damascus,[7] where he was cured of the temporary blindness which had befallen him, and was baptized by Ananias, a Christian of Damascus,[8] who had been told in a vision to do this. Here he stayed for some time, preaching Christianity in the Jewish synagogues, but when the Jews became enraged at his gospel[9] he escaped to Jerusalem, where the disciples were at first afraid of him, but afterwards accepted him on the recommendation of St. Barnabas.[10] He then spent some time in Jerusalem arguing with the Greek-speaking Jews, but when a plot was formed to kill him the disciples sent him to Caesarea and thence to Tarsus.[11] How long he stayed in Tarsus is not stated: but it is probable that he spent his time in energetically preaching the gospel, for the next that is heard of him is that St. Barnabas, who had been sent from Jerusalem to Antioch to investigate and

[1] Acts xxi. 39; 22–3. [2] xxii. 3. [3] xxii. 3; xxiii. 6.
[4] vii. 58; viii. 3; xxvi. 9–10. [5] ix. 1–2; xxii. 5; xxvi. 12.
[6] ix. 3–8; xxii. 6–10; xxvi. 13–19. [7] ix. 8.
[8] ix. 10–19. [9] ix. 19–25. [10] ix. 26–27.
[11] ix. 28–30.

supervise the growing Christian community in that city, fetched St. Paul from Tarsus to assist him.[1]

From this point onwards our information becomes much fuller. The first important incident was the sending of St. Paul and St. Barnabas from Antioch to Jerusalem in order to bring help in the time of the famine.[2] This is the second visit of St. Paul to Jerusalem that is mentioned in the Acts: what happened beyond the distribution of alms is not stated, and when it was finished St. Paul and St. Barnabas returned to Antioch.[3]

At Antioch the Church decided to take the important step of sending St. Barnabas and St. Paul, accompanied by John Mark, on a missionary expedition outside the province Syria Cilicia in which they had hitherto worked.[4] They first went to Cyprus,[5] and then crossed over to Perga in Pamphylia, where John Mark appears to have been reluctant to go any further and returned to Jerusalem.[6] From Perga St. Barnabas and St. Paul went to Antioch in Pisidia,[7] Iconium,[8] Lystra,[9] and Derbe,[10] passing in this way from the province of Pamphylia to that of Galatia, which is, however, not actually mentioned by name, and then retraced their steps to Perga.[11] From Perga they went to the neighbouring port of Attalia, and thence sailed to Antioch in Syria, whence they had started.[12]

In Antioch they found that the peace of the community was disturbed by the arrival of members of the Church at Jerusalem who insisted on the necessity of circumcision,[13] and in order to settle the disputes which arose it was arranged that St. Paul and St. Barnabas should go up to

[1] Acts xi. 22–26. [2] xi. 27–30. [3] xii. 25.
[4] xiii. 1–3, 5. [5] xiii. 4-12. [6] xiii. 13.
[7] xiii. 14–50. [8] xiii. 51—xiv. 5. [9] xiv. 6–20. [10] xiv. 20–21.
[11] xiv. 21-25. [12] xiv. 25-26. [13] xv. 1.

Jerusalem to confer with the Apostles and elders, and represent the Antiochene point of view.[1] The result was the famous "Council of Jerusalem" which decided, after hearing St. Paul and St. Barnabas, various Christians of the Pharisaic party, and finally St. Peter and St. James, that circumcision ought not to be demanded from Gentile Christians, but that they should be exhorted to keep themselves from "the pollutions of idols, and from fornication, [and from things strangled], and from blood."[2] This decision, the text of which is doubtful (see pp. 48 ff.), was made the substance of a letter to the Christians of Antioch and its Province, Syria Cilicia, and entrusted to Judas Barsabbas and Silas to take to Antioch, whither St. Paul and St. Barnabas also returned.[3]

In Antioch they remained for some time; after which St. Paul and St. Barnabas formed the plan of revisiting the communities which they had established already. But as St. Paul would not agree to take again John Mark, who had turned back on the first journey, they separated, and St. Barnabas went to Cyprus, while St. Paul went with Silas through Syria Cilicia, and ultimately reached Derbe, Lystra (in which Timothy joined them), and Iconium.[4] What next happened is a matter of dispute. The text of Acts says: "And they went through the Phrygian and Galatian Region (τὴν Φρυγίαν καὶ Γαλατικὴν χώραν) having been prevented by the Holy Spirit from speaking the word in Asia, and when they were come over against Mysia, they assayed to go into Bithynia, and the Spirit of Jesus suffered them not, and passing by Mysia, they came down to Troas,"[5] but exactly what this means is not quite certain, and, as

[1] Acts xv. 2. [2] xv. 4–21. [3] xv. 22–32. [4] xv. 36; xvi. 2. [5] xvi. 6–8.

it has some bearing on the Epistle to the Galatians, it will be discussed later in connection with that Epistle (see Chap. V.).

In any case, whatever route St. Paul may have followed, in the end he reached Troas and thence went to Neapolis (the modern Cavalla), Philippi, where he was imprisoned and beaten,[1] Thessalonica,[2] and Beroea,[3] (in both of which Jewish opposition put an end to his work,) and thus founded the Christian Churches of the Province of Macedonia. From Beroea, leaving Timothy and Silas behind, he went, partly by sea, to Athens[4] and then to Corinth where Timothy and Silas rejoined him. Here he stayed a year and six months, and founded the Church in that city, living with Aquila and Priscilla, Jews of Pontus who had recently come from Rome, and teaching first in the synagogue, and afterwards in the house of Titus[5] Justus who lived next to it. He was here also brought before the Roman magistrate, Gallio, but acquitted.[6]

From Corinth he went for a short time to Ephesus, and then returned, possibly after a short visit to Jerusalem, to Antioch. This is generally regarded as the end of the second missionary journey.[7]

After an interval, spent in Antioch, St. Paul started on his third missionary journey, returning through the "Galatic Region and Phrygia," along the hill country of the province of Asia, to Ephesus.[8] In Ephesus he preached for three months in the synagogue, and afterwards for two years in the "school of Tyrannus," with the result, according to St. Luke, that "all they which dwelt in Asia heard the

[1] Acts xvi. 11–40. [2] xvii. 1–9. [3] xvii. 10–14.
[4] xvii. 15–34. [5] Or Titius; the text is doubtful.
[6] xviii. 1–17. [7] xviii. 18–22. [8] xviii. 23.

word of the Lord, both Jews and Greeks."[1] Towards the end of the period St. Paul formed the plan of going to Jerusalem, after paying a visit to his converts in Macedonia and Achaia, and then extending his field of preaching to Rome.[2] It would also seem, from an allusion in his speech before Felix, that the reason for his desire to visit Jerusalem was the bringing of alms to the poor of the community.[3] As a preliminary to this journey he sent Timothy and Erastus into Macedonia shortly before the time when he intended to leave Ephesus.[4] His last days in Ephesus were rendered unpleasant by a riot raised against him by Demetrius, a silversmith, and worshipper of Artemis, who thought that St. Paul's teaching was derogatory to his goddess, and harmful to his trade.[5]

After the agitation raised by Demetrius had died down, St. Paul went through Macedonia to Achaia[6]—probably Corinth is intended—and formed the plan of sailing direct to Syria, but finding a plot among the Jews, changed his mind and returned over land through Macedonia to Philippi,[7] whence after the Passover he crossed, in the company of the writer of the we-clauses, to Troas, where Sopater, Aristarchus, Secundus, Gaius of Derbe, Timothy, Tychicus, and Trophimus joined him.[8] Here they waited seven days, and the main body of the party then went in a coasting vessel to Assos, where St. Paul, who had gone by road, was again taken up.[9] From Assos they sailed in stages to Mitylene, Chios, Samos, and Miletus, where St. Paul bade farewell to the Ephesian Presbyters, who came to see him.[10] From Miletus they sailed to Cos, Rhodes, and

[1] Acts xix. 1–10. [2] xix. 21. [3] xxiv. 17. [4] xix. 22. [5] xix. 23–41. [6] xx. 1–2. [7] xx. 3–6. [8] xx. 4–6. [9] xx. 6, 13. [10] xx. 14–38.

Patara, and then changing ships sailed south of Cyprus to Tyre, where the ship stopped seven days, thence to Ptolemais, and Caesarea.[1]

In Caesarea they stayed for some time with Philip the Evangelist, who, it is mentioned, had four prophetess daughters,[2] and during this stay Agabus prophesied that St. Paul would be imprisoned by the Jews, in Jerusalem.[3] This made both his own party, and also the Caesarean community, urge him not to go to Jerusalem; but he held to his plan and insisted on going.[4]

On his arrival at Jerusalem St. Paul was received by St. James,[5] who told him that the Jews regarded him as a renegade who preached to the Jews of the Diaspora that they should not circumcise their children nor "walk after the customs." He suggested, therefore, that St. Paul should show his respect for the Jewish law by taking part in a vow which four men of the community had taken, and by paying their expenses.[6] St. Paul agreed to do this, but before the week of the vow was completed Jews from Asia saw him in the temple and raised a tumult by accusing him of teaching against the law and of introducing Greeks into the temple.[7] He was violently turned out of the temple, and only saved from being lynched by the interposition of Lysias, the *tribunus militum* in charge of the Roman garrison at Jerusalem, who arrested him.[8]

This arrest was the beginning of a long imprisonment. St. Paul was tried four times without any decisive verdict being given. (1) By the Sanhedrim in Jerusalem.[9] (2) By the Governor Felix in Caesarea, where he had been

[1] Acts xxi. 1–8. [2] xxi. 8–9. [3] xxi. 10–11.
[4] xxi. 12–14. [5] xxi. 18. [6] xxi. 19–24.
[7] xxi. 25-29. [8] xxi. 33; xxiii. 26. [9] xxii. 30; xxiii. 10.

sent by Lysias in consequence of a Jewish plot which rendered it unsafe to keep him in Jerusalem.[1] (3) After two years, when Felix was succeeded by Porcius Festus, St. Paul was brought before Festus, who proposed that he should go to Jerusalem and there be tried. St. Paul, however, stood on his rights and demanded to be tried by Caesar's tribunal, and Festus determined to send him to Rome.[2] (4) A short time after this Herod Agrippa II. was staying in Caesarea, and Festus brought St. Paul before him. The result of this trial before Agrippa was favourable to St. Paul, but having appealed to Caesar (whose representative Agrippa was not) he could not be released,[3] and soon afterwards was sent off by sea, accompanied, it would seem, by St. Luke and by Aristarchus of Thessalonica.[4] Thus ended the first period of imprisonment, at Caesarea, which seems to have lasted rather more than two years.[5]

St. Paul's voyage to Rome was adventurous: he started from Caesarea in a ship of Adramyttium which was going to the coast of the Province of Asia. After touching at Sidon they sailed across, leeward of Cyprus, to Myra.[6] Here they changed into a ship of Alexandria, bound for Italy, and made their way with difficulty to Fair Havens, near Lasea in Crete. It was now the late autumn, and sailing became dangerous, but the captain tried to push on, and being caught in a strong north-easterly wind was wrecked on the island of Malta.[7] Here St. Paul, his friends, and escort spent the winter,[8] and after three months sailed in another Alexandrian ship, called the Dioscuri, to Syracuse, Rhegium, and

[1] Acts xxiii. 12–27. [2] xxv. 1–12. [3] xxv. 13; xxvi. 32.
[4] xxvii. 1–2. [5] xxiv. 27. [6] xxvii. 2–5.
[7] xxvii. 6–44. It is sometimes disputed if the island was really Malta, but the point is immaterial for the present purpose.
[8] xxviii. 1–10.

finally Puteoli,[1] where they landed, and, after a week's rest, made their way to Rome, being met at Appii Forum and Three Taverns by members of the Christian community at Rome.[2]

On his arrival, St. Paul was lodged by himself, possibly in an inn[3] (cf. *ξενίαν*, xxviii. 23), in the custody of a soldier.[4] After three days he summoned the Jews to hear him, and on two separate occasions they came. On the first the main issue of the meeting was the charges brought against him: of these the Jews professed complete ignorance, and said that no instruction had reached them from Jerusalem.[5] On the second occasion St. Paul explained his teaching, and when the Jews, with some exceptions, would not believe, he announced to them, with a quotation from Isaiah, his intention of preaching to the Gentiles.[6]

At this point the narrative in Acts is closed by the statement "And he abode two full years in his own hired dwelling, and received all that went in unto him, preaching the kingdom of God, and teaching the things concerning the Lord Jesus Christ with all boldness, none forbidding him,"[7] a curious and enigmatic conclusion, which has often been discussed, and leaves us doubtful whether St. Paul was acquitted, condemned, or dismissed for lack of evidence.[8]

Such is the sequence of events with which the Acts provide us. For the present purpose it is invaluable as affording the outline of the missionary activity of St. Paul

[1] Acts xxviii. 11–13. [2] xxviii. 14–15.

[3] This is the traditional view; but the evidence of the Papyri points to the probability that *ξενία* means "hospitality"; see Moulton and Milligan in the *Expositor*, March, 1910, p. 286, who regard this view as "practically certain."

[4] xxviii. 16. [5] xxviii. 17–22. [6] xxviii. 23–28. [7] xxviii. 30–31.

[8] In favour of the view that the trial was quashed because no hostile witnesses appeared, see *Interpreter*, 1909, pp. 147 ff. and 438 f., *What was the end of St. Paul's trial?*

which is one of the chief features in that background of the Epistles which it is proposed to reconstruct. It is no doubt imperfect; St. Paul must have done much more than St. Luke recorded, and, therefore, the mention in the Epistles of events which find no place in the Acts is not surprising. But, imperfect though it be, it covers most fully precisely that period to which all the Epistles, except the Pastorals, belong. As will be seen, we are able to fix with tolerable certainty the time when the Epistles were written, even though the degree of certainty is by no means always the same, and this result is chiefly owing to the record of the sequence of events in the Acts. It is, of course, obvious that the statements in the Acts are not always plain, and so far as this is the case they will be discussed fully in connection with the Epistles on which they have a bearing, but on the whole, and considering the character of the book, Acts is a first-rate historical document, and singularly easy to understand, so far as the mere enumeration of events is concerned.

The enumeration of events, however, is only the beginning of historical research, and it is far more difficult, as well as more important, to discover from the Acts that development of tendencies and ideas which produced the controversies and problems that called forth the Pauline Epistles. For this purpose it will be necessary to consider the real meaning of the Judaistic controversy, of which the Council at Jerusalem was the culminating point, but by no means the end, and the results which sprang from the ensuing propagation of Christianity in the Graeco-Roman world.

CHAPTER II

THE JUDAISTIC CONTROVERSY, THE GENTILE CONVERTS, AND THE BACKGROUND OF GENTILE CHRISTIANITY.

THE earliest Christian community was in Jerusalem: the fact that it was here and not in Galilee is perhaps a curious problem, but it cannot be denied. Moreover it was a community within the limits of Judaism rather than one clearly separated from it. The disciples frequented the Temple, observed the Jewish Law, and believed all the articles of the Jewish faith. That which distinguished them from other Jews was that to the usual Pharisaic belief that in the last days the Messiah—the Lord's Anointed—would appear on earth, to break the powers of evil and to establish the kingdom of God, they added the assurance that they knew who the Messiah was. He was Jesus, who had appeared already as Son of man—that is, as Messiah in personality, but not yet in function,[1]—had been crucified and buried, and had been raised again by God to the glorified existence of the heavenly Messiah who would soon come in the clouds of heaven to inaugurate in power that Kingdom of God of which He was already the proleptic[2] head, and

[1] This fact is to be found most clearly expressed in Professor Burkitt's *The Earliest Sources for the Life of Jesus*, p. 66.

[2] The use of this technical term of the grammarians may be excused by the difficulty of finding any expression to convey the required meaning. The point

the Christians were already the proleptic members, and as such had received the Holy Spirit which was to be given in the "last days." This was the point on which Jews and Christians differed,—the identification or the non-identification of the Messiah, whom they both expected, with Jesus; and they found their common ground for argument in the Law and in the Prophets, which each regarded as the infallibly inspired word of God. Probably there was a dispute between them as to the interpretation of the Old Testament, for it is likely[1] that the Christians explained passages such as Isaiah liii., in which allusion is made to a suffering servant of Jahweh, in relation to the Messiah, while such a view did not obtain among the Jews. Nevertheless, this was relatively a matter of domestic difference of opinion, and could scarcely be regarded, except in the heat of controversy, as unfaithfulness to the hope of Israel. Christians in no sense felt that they had ceased to be Jews, and the question of the admission of the Gentiles was not raised. It is true that there had been an open rupture between Jesus and the Galilaean synagogues, and that the Priests had conspired to put Him to death, but the disciples clung to the Temple, and never accepted the situation. Perhaps the most instructive parallel to their position (though of course only in this respect) is afforded by that of Catholic Modernists, who have been frequently

is that the kingdom was not yet come, and therefore there could not yet be any king; but it was quite certain that it was coming, and that Jesus would be the King. Thus Christians lived in a constant anticipation of the future, a "prolepsis" of things to come.

[1] The point is, however, not quite certain; see H. Gressmann, *Der Ursprung der Israelitisch-jüdischen Eschatologie*. References to other books on the subject are given by Bousset, *Religion des Judentums*, p. 266. The most important authority for the view taken above is Dalman, *Der leidende und sterbende Messias der Synagoge*.

disavowed by Catholic authority, yet have never accepted the situation.

That there was more or less severe, but probably intermittent rather than continuous persecution of the Christians by the Jews is probable in itself, and corroborated by the accounts in Acts iv. and v.[1] But there is no suggestion that either the Jews or the Christians felt that the latter were in any way outside the Jewish Church.[2] The Christians held that the crucifixion of their leader had been a crime, and the Jews believed that it was a necessary incident in the development of political life, but the former did not think themselves outside the covenant or the service of the Temple, and the latter were not prepared to drive out those whose only fault was an erroneous belief that they knew who the Messiah was, for it must be remembered that the strong eschatological and Messianic belief of the Christians was—apart from the question of the identity of the Messiah—shared by many of the Jews, and especially by those who were most enthusiastic for the "Hope of Israel").[3]

Nevertheless, looking back on history, it is clear that this situation could not last. If Christianity had remained unchanged it would have died out, as indeed it did among the Jews, so soon as the eschatological expectation was clearly falsified, for to the Jews—who had already

[1] It seems unnecessary to discuss Harnack's suggestion that these two accounts may be "doublet" narratives of one event. Possibly he is right; (see his *Apostelgeschichte*, chap. v.), but it is also possible that there were two attempts by the Jews to suppress Christianity. What is here important is merely the fact that the attempts (or attempt) were unsuccessful and not vigorously carried out.

[2] Jewish "Church" is of course an anachronism, but it is too convenient a phrase to abandon.

[3] Cf. Acts xxiii. 6. The Pharisees immediately accepted St. Paul's statement that "for 'Hope' and a resurrection of the dead am I being judged."

a divinely instituted Church—it was impossible to adopt the point of view which identified or confused the Kingdom with the Church, and put into the background the expectation of the Parousia. It was impossible for Christianity to flourish for long within the limits of the Judaism of Jerusalem. But already partially distinct from the Judaism of Jerusalem there was a Judaism in the Diaspora which offered a far more hopeful prospect, and from the beginning it was the Hellenistic Jews belonging to this who were attracted. Apart altogether from questions as to the accuracy of the account given in Acts of the day of Pentecost, it is clear that the point which St. Luke wishes to emphasize, in addition to the inspiration of the Church, is the Hellenistic character of the converts. They were Jews, but they were Jews of the Diaspora, "Jews, devout men . . . Parthians, and Medes, and Elamites"—and St. Luke exhausts language in his attempt to make plain their diversity of nationality.[1]

The introduction of this new element could not but profoundly affect the development of the community. The first sign which we find of its influence is in Acts vi. 1–7, which describes how there was friction between the Hellenist and Palestinian Christians as to the distribution of alms among their "widows." The result of this was the introduction into the community of a new element of organization. Up till now the leaders had been "the Twelve." They had been promised by Jesus positions of authority in the Kingdom, and were to be the Judges over the twelve tribes of Israel.[2] Among other

[1] Just as a Jew of to-day can call himself an Englishman or a German, a Jew of the first century could call himself a Parthian, a Mede, or even a Roman—if he were fortunate enough to possess the right to do so, as St. Paul did.

[2] This statement belongs to the oldest stratum of the Gospels. It is

things they had apparently undertaken various social and financial arrangements which at the least were regular and organized charity, at the most, something approaching communism—it is probably impossible to define them more accurately. But now a great part, or perhaps all, of this work was handed over to "the Seven," who seem mostly to have belonged to the Hellenist section.[1] According to St. Luke, then, the duties of "the Seven" were primarily practical and internal to the community; but they also seem to have attracted attention by their development of certain lines of thought which were probably present in the teaching of Jesus Himself, but were not taken up by the original Jerusalem community. These lines were concerned with the Temple and the official class connected with it, which was treated by St. Stephen in a manner which seems to find no parallel in the teaching of the Twelve, and certainly not in that of other Jewish Christians.

This new development of Christianity met with active hostility from the orthodox Hellenists in Jerusalem; St. Stephen was summoned before the Sanhedrin, and stoned to death, while other Hellenists were forced to leave Jerusalem. It appears, however, that this persecution did not extend

found in Matt. xix. 28 and Luke xxii. 30, and probably no one would dispute that it belongs to Q.

[1] Harnack thinks that they were in some sense rivals of the Twelve. The evidence for this view is small, but if one does not regard rivals as implying an unfriendly attitude there is something to be said for it (see Harnack's *Kirchenverfassung*, p. 23). The whole question of "The Seven" is obscure, and we have no sufficient evidence to help much in dealing with it. The point is that we need some explanation of the fact that those who were appointed in order to relieve the Twelve from the practical and charitable side of their work, and to set them free to preach, nevertheless only appear in the capacity of missionaries and controversalists, and as such seem to have attracted more attention than the "Twelve."

to the original disciples, for St. Luke expressly excepts the Apostles, by which he probably means the Twelve. Probably, therefore, we ought to consider that the persecution connected with the death of St. Stephen was primarily a persecution of Hellenists by Hellenists, and did not largely affect the original Palestinian Christians.

The Christian Hellenists scattered ; St. Philip among others preached in Samaria, and on one occasion returning to Judaea converted an Ethiopian—probably a proselyte. Ultimately he went farther north, and settled in Caesarea. Thus a Christian propaganda began to spread among the Hellenist Jews outside Jerusalem. What form their teaching took we do not know in any detail, but we may be sure that it varied to some extent from that of the original disciples, and the account given in the Acts of the teaching of St. Stephen seems to show that it was perceptibly less attached to the Temple and to the Law, an attitude which was probably not uncommon among Hellenists entirely apart from Christianity. In answer to this propaganda a persecution was instituted among the orthodox Hellenists, with the support of the priests at Jerusalem, and among those who took part in it was Saul of Tarsus.

Obviously the original Jewish community could not stand entirely outside this movement. Possibly some of its members doubted whether it ought to meet with approbation. At all events, some of the leaders felt compelled to investigate it ; among them St. Peter and St. John the son of Zebedee, who went to Samaria where Philip had been preaching. What they saw led them to approve, so that they joined in the work of evangelization outside Jerusalem, and thus began careers which ultimately led both of them[1] far afield into the Roman Empire.

The result of this development was that the history of the Church began to divide into two branches. On the one hand, there was the propaganda of the Hellenists, ever spreading further and further from the centre; and on the other, the preaching of the members of the Jerusalem community, for the time, at least, confined to a circle of a smaller radius.

Turning first to the Jerusalem community, two facts are of outstanding importance. The absence of St. Peter, and probably of other members of the "Twelve" led to a change in organization. Instead of the Twelve being the rulers, we find James, the brother of the Lord, apparently becoming the head of the community. Whether this took place[2] in consequence of a definite arrangement, or more or less imperceptibly in consequence of the absence of the Twelve, we do not know, but it probably marks the acceptance of the δεσπόσυνοι—the family of the Lord—as having in some sense a claim to the headship of the community in Jerusalem. St. James appears to have belonged to the original type of Christianity, and was for many years unharmed; indeed, tradition represents him as enjoying the general respect of the Jews.[3] Thus a conservative

[1] If tradition may be trusted, St. Peter went to Rome and St. John to Ephesus. But, of course, there is considerable doubt as to this. The evidence in neither case is quite convincing, and in the case of St. John there is some evidence (that of Papias—but in a doubtful passage) that he was put to death by the Jews. See Schwartz, *Über den Tod der Söhne Zebedaei*, and Sanday, *The Criticism of the Fourth Gospel*, pp. 103 ff.

[2] Tradition says that it took place twelve years after the Ascension, *i.e.* *c.* 42. It may have been connected with the persecution of the Christians under Herod; but I think it was more probably the result of the absence of the Twelve.

[3] See Eusebius, *Hist. Eccl.* ii. 23, for a long account of St. James, taken from Hegesippus.

and essentially Jewish type of Christianity became fixed in Jerusalem.

On the other hand, St. Peter, the leader of the Twelve, was induced to take a new and profoundly important step, which he was successful in commending at all events to the theoretical approbation of the Christians in Jerusalem. This was the conversion of Cornelius.[1] Cornelius was a centurion stationed in Caesarea, not a proselyte but a "God-fearer" who desired to hear the teaching of St. Peter. St. Peter hesitated whether he might go to a Gentile, but was convinced by a vision that he ought to do so, and after hearing his gospel Cornelius visibly received the gift of the Spirit.

St. Peter interpreted this fact to mean that he might at once be formally admitted by Baptism into the Christian community. It is important here to notice how central was the belief that Christians were men who were inspired with a Holy Spirit: there are many problems in connection with this fact—for instance, its relation to Baptism—but as to the fact itself there can be no doubt. When, therefore, St. Peter found that Cornelius and his household presented all the signs of being "filled with the Spirit," he naturally was forced to the conclusion that Cornelius, Gentile though he was, had been placed within the Christian Community.

The great importance of this decision of St. Peter was that it forced him, and the Church of Jerusalem with him, to acknowledge that it was both theoretically and practically possible for a Gentile to become a Christian, or in other words, a proleptic member of the Messianic Kingdom. It did not, however, settle the further question,

[1] Acts x. For the importance of the God-fearers, see pp. 37 ff.

which was sure to arise, whether Gentiles who became Christians were free from the obligation of the Jewish Law. St. Peter himself does not seem at the moment to have seen clearly that this question must arise, and his action in baptizing Cornelius was to some extent a confusion of thought. Before the incident of Cornelius he had held that the Christian community was open to Jews only, and that the method of entry was Baptism. From the gift of the Spirit he concluded that Cornelius had been divinely admitted into the Church, and therefore that the limitation of Church membership to Jews was untenable. By a strict parity of reasoning he ought to have decided that it also proved that Baptism was not the only method of entry into the Church, for Cornelius was, by the evidence of the Spirit, among its members, though he had never been baptized. But this reasoning was not followed by St. Peter, who baptized Cornelius, opening, as it were, the door after the guest was already in the house. It was therefore possible for the Jewish Christians to argue that even if Gentiles had been admitted into the Church, they ought to be circumcised as well as baptized. If they followed the reasoning which led St. Peter to admit Gentiles, and to reject the limitation to Jews because of the evidence of the Spirit, naturally they would not require circumcision; but if they followed the reasoning which led him in spite of that evidence to baptize Cornelius, they would logically demand circumcision as well. That this attitude was actually adopted is clear from the course of events, though it is not actually stated in connection with the case of Cornelius.

Thus the result of the incident of Cornelius may be stated to have been that the Christians in Jerusalem and Palestine generally recognized the admission of Gentiles to the Christian Church, but that the exact conditions imposed on them remained undetermined.

Meanwhile events of equal importance had happened in the circle of the Hellenists. St. Paul, the enthusiast for orthodoxy had seen a vision on the road to Damascus, had joined the ranks of the Hellenist Christians whom he had previously persecuted, and was engaged in preaching in Cilicia in the district of which Tarsus, his native city, was the centre. Moreover, some of the Hellenists who had been driven out of Jerusalem—according to St. Luke they were Cypriotes and Cyrenaeans—had settled in Antioch, and had taken the epoch-making step of preaching to the Gentiles, no doubt chiefly among the God-fearers, with immediate and great success, without insisting on their adopting the Law or practices of Judaism.[1] Obviously this raised in an acute form the same question as the incident of Cornelius, and it was impossible here to regard the circumstances as exceptional—they represented a fixed policy.

The Church at Jerusalem therefore decided to send St. Barnabas to investigate the situation. He was admirably fitted for the task, for he was himself a Hellenist from Cyprus, but had always belonged to the Jerusalem community, and had relations in the city.

St. Barnabas was completely persuaded, by the facts which he saw, that the new movement was desirable, threw himself into the work, and called St. Paul from Tarsus to help him. In this way a vigorous Christianity grew up among the Gentiles, which recognized neither the circumcision nor the ceremonial law of the Jews.

If this had been a wholly new doctrine in Judaism it

[1] This is not stated in Acts, but is clear from the context of the events implied by the Council, see Acts xv.

would be almost inconceivable that St. Paul and St. Barnabas would have started it without further discussion, but, as a matter of fact, they were only following a line of thought which had already found supporters among a minority of the Jews, not only in the Diaspora, but even in Jerusalem. It is, for instance, related by Josephus that when Izates, King of Adiabene, was converted to Judaism, the merchant Ananias[1] whom he consulted urged him not to be circumcised, because of the offence which he would give to his subjects, but to content himself with a general observance of the Jewish Law, and adherence to the Jewish creed. This was almost exactly contemporaneous with the teaching of St. Barnabas and St. Paul in Antioch. But perhaps the most important witness to the existence of a "liberal" school among the Jews of the first century is Philo. In his book *De Migratione Abrahami*,[2] he refers definitely to a class of Jews who attached only a symbolic importance to the Law. "There are persons," he says, "who regard the traditional law as a symbol of spiritual life; the symbolic meaning they seek with every care, but despise the literal meaning. Such laxness I can only deprecate. They ought to be zealous for both,—both the exact search for the hidden meaning as well as the punctilious observance of the literal sense. . . . Although it be true that the law of the Sabbath contains the deeper meaning that the Creator (τὸ ἀγένητον) is active and the Creation (τὸ γενητόν) is passive, we have no right to ignore the command to

[1] The words of Ananias are important enough to be quoted:— . . . δυνάμενον δ' αὐτὸν, ἔφη, καὶ χωρὶς τῆς περιτομῆς τὸ θεῖον σέβειν, εἴγε πάντως κέκρικε ξηλοῦν τὰ πάτρια τῶν Ἰουδαίων τοῦτ' εἶναι κυριώτερον τοῦ περιτέμνεσθαι . . . Ultimately, however, Izates listened to his other Jewish adviser, Eleazar, and was circumcised. See Josephus, *Antiquit.*, xx. 2. 4.

[2] Ed. Mangey, I. 450, and Cohn and Wendland, II. p. 285 ff.

keep it holy. . . . Even though the Feast is a symbol of the joy of the soul and of thankfulness to God, we have no right to give up the annual festivities, and though the circumcision signifies the cutting away of every passion and lust, and the destruction of all godless thoughts . . . we are still not justified in departing from the law of circumcision which was laid upon us."

It is plain that Philo, who, of course, fully accepted the symbolic or allegorical meaning of the law, was acquainted with Jews who went further than he did, and regarded this not as the hidden meaning, but as the only valid meaning, so that they abandoned Circumcision, Sabbath, Feasting and Fasting, and, in a word, the whole of the ceremonial law.

If Jews were inclined in Alexandria to doubt in this manner whether the law was, in its literal sense, really valid for themselves, it is not surprising that some of them did not insist on its observance by Gentiles who desired not to be excluded from the Kingdom of God. Thus we find a few years later than Philo that the Jewish writer of the fourth book of the *Oracula Sibyllina*[1] promised entry into

[1] The Oracula Sibyllina are a curious collection of Jewish and Christian verse, written in a bad imitation of Homeric Greek, giving a series of Apocalyptic prophecies. They vary in date from the first century before Christ to the third century after Christ. The best text is that of Geffcken in the Berlin edition of *Die griechischen christlichen Schriftsteller der ersten drei Jahrhunderte.* The best introductions are probably those of Alexandre (the first edition, of 1841–56, not the second of 1869, which is less valuable), and of Geffcken, *Komposition und Enstehungszeit der Oracula Sibyllina* in *Texte und Untersuchungen*, xxiii. 1; but sufficient for all except special purposes will be found in Schürer's *Geschichte des Jüdischen Volkes*, ed. 4, iii. pp. 555–592. This is one of the places in which Schürer's fourth edition is considerably fuller than the third.

In the fourth book the Sibyl is supposed to be speaking to the first generation of mankind, and gives a prophetic sketch of the successive dominations of Assyrians, Medes, Persians, Greeks, and Romans, up to the flight of Nero and the destruction of Jerusalem, and apparently mentioning the eruption of Vesuvius in 79 A.D. It then goes on to foretell that Nero will return from the East, and

the Messianic kingdom to all of the heathen who accept the true God, abandon idolatry, murder, theft, fornication, and sodomy, generally lead a good life, and are baptized.[1] Nothing whatever is said of circumcision or the Jewish Law.

Less well attested, and much less important, is the story of the Babylonian Talmud (*Yebhamoth, f.* 46*a*) that in the first century Rabbi Joshua maintained that Baptism without circumcision was sufficient for the admission of a proselyte, and was opposed by Rabbi Eliezer who argued in favour of circumcision without Baptism. Thus the more advanced position held among the Christians at Antioch as to the method by which a Gentile might be admitted was only the continuation of a discussion which had already arisen among the Jews. Neither the admission of Gentiles, nor omission of circumcision were quite new things in the history of Judaism, but both represented the adhesion of the Christians at Antioch to the more liberal principles of a minority, probably found chiefly in the Diaspora, and the rejection of the narrower and stricter point of view which was dominant in Jerusalem.

Moreover, this latter view was dominant not only among the Jews but also among many of the Christians at Jerusalem, who probably still held fast to their original point of view, and had not grasped the importance of the incident

history will close with the judgment, resurrection, and establishment of the righteous.

It is clear from this summary that the book was written during the time after the fall of Nero when his death was still doubted and his return expected at the head of a Parthian army. This might be at any time after the death of Nero, and before about 90 A.D. (the last false Nero appeared in 88), but the reference to Vesuvius narrows the range of possible dates to 79–90 A.D.

[1] The important passages are *Or. Sib.*, iv. 24–33 and 162–170. The text is quoted on pp. 56–7.

of Cornelius, so that in this way Antioch became in a few years the centre of a type of Christianity which really differed from that in Jerusalem, and was adopted chiefly by Gentiles rather than by Jews. The importance of it was that, although it may possibly have been the view of St. Barnabas and St. Paul that their converts were made members of the true Jewish Church by their Baptism, this rapidly ceased to be true of the Gentile Christians themselves. They had accepted much of the Jewish theology, and especially the doctrine of the Messiah, but the community which they desired to enter was the Messianic kingdom, not the Jewish Church, and to their mind it was plain that membership in this kingdom was the privilege of those who accepted the Messiah, and was independent of the Law, which was an exclusively Jewish possession. Let the Jews keep their own Law, they were themselves free. Either they argued like this, or else they accepted the teaching of the liberal Jews, whom Philo reprobated, to the effect that the Law had only a symbolical meaning. We find, for instance, that the writer of the Epistle of Barnabas, who may have lived in the first century, took exactly this standpoint, and regarded a literal exegesis of the Old Testament as the invention of an Evil Angel.[2]

We cannot reconstruct the precise standpoint of the Gentile converts,—indeed, we may be certain that they had more than one—but it is at any rate plain that under the leadership of St. Barnabas and St. Paul the new type of Christianity which rejected the Law for Gentile Christians

[1] The probable range of date is about 90–135.

[2] Cf. Barn. ix. 4, περιτομὴν γὰρ εἴρηκεν οὐ σαρκὸς γενηθῆναι· ἀλλὰ παρέβησαν, ὅτι ἄγγελος πονηρὸς ἐσόφιζεν αὐτούς.

grew rapidly. It was clearly inevitable that it should come into collision with the older type at Jerusalem; sooner or later, if the unity of Christians was to be preserved, some sort of an agreement had to be reached as to the conditions of membership to be demanded from Gentile Christians; and any occasion on which the representatives of Jerusalem were brought into close relations with those of Antioch was likely to give rise to discussion on this point.

Of such occasions we have in the Acts several good examples, and the effect of what may be called the Antiochene movement is quite plain. The first is the mission of St. Barnabas and St. Paul from Antioch to Jerusalem with assistance for the sufferers in the time of the famine. The writer of Acts somewhat exaggerates the universality of this famine, but it was undoubtedly widespread and particularly severe in Jerusalem.[1] It is impossible to fix the date with absolute certainty, but 45 A.D. is not probably more than one year wrong in either direction. In Acts it is not stated that St. Barnabas and St. Paul discussed the treatment of the Gentile converts, or even that they saw the leaders of the Jerusalem Church, but it is improbable that at such a time St. James would have left Jerusalem (the question of St. Peter is more complicated (see Chap. V.), though one would be inclined to think that the need of the community would be the best reason for bringing him back to Jerusalem, if he had left it already), and just as a mission of help from Antioch to Jerusalem was an unsuitable opportunity for any public

[1] For this we have the evidence of Josephus, who narrates that Queen Helena, the mother of Izates, was in Jerusalem at the time, and endeavoured to relieve the distress by distributing corn and figs among the poor, and that Izates himself sent money to Jerusalem for the same purpose; see Josephus, *Antiquit.*, xx. 2. 5.

discussion as to the Antiochene movement, so it was admirably fitted for a private and friendly discussion among the leaders, and for a spirit of general concession on both sides. One of the main problems in connection with the Epistle to the Galatians is whether the meeting described in Galatians ii. may not in reality refer to some such meeting at this time, but even if this view be rejected, it still remains *à priori* probable that St. Peter and St. James were in Jerusalem, and that they talked with St. Barnabas and St. Paul about the question of Gentile converts and their desirability.

Probably partly as a result of their intercourse with the Church at Jerusalem, in any case immediately after it, St. Barnabas and St. Paul undertook their first missionary journey. This was so successful that the question of Gentile Christians obtained increased importance, and the Jerusalem Church took fright at a movement the true significance of which was perhaps now for the first time fully realized, and sent out a rival mission, to which reference is made both in Acts and in Galatians,[1] in order to convince Christians of Gentile origin that circumcision and the Law were binding on them.

The result of this conflict of propaganda was, according to the Acts, the Council at Jerusalem, which was practically a meeting between representatives of the Antiochene Church and the Jerusalem leaders.

According to St. Luke's account, speeches were made by St. Barnabas and by St. Paul representing Antioch, and afterwards by St. Peter and St. James representing Jerusalem. St. Peter and St. James recognized the force of the Antiochene arguments, and the latter proposed an *eirenicon*, which was

[1] Acts xv. 1; Gal. ii. 12.

drawn up in writing and circulated among the Gentile Churches by St. Barnabas, St. Paul, Silas, and Judas.[1]

As to the historical value of this narrative opinions differ widely. What may be called the extreme right wing of criticism treats it as if it were a stenographic report, while the extreme left regards it as the purely imaginary product of the writer of Acts. Probably both extremes are wrong; there seems no good reason to suppose that the exact form of the speeches of St. Peter and St. James is anything more than St. Luke's view of the way in which they would naturally have spoken, though the substances of what they said may very probably have been communicated to him by St. Paul or Silas, or some other of those present.[2] Similarly the decrees have a distinct *à priori* probability if the Lucan authorship of Acts be accepted, and it may be said with apparent reasonableness that it is far more probable that St. Luke was in a position to give the actual words of a document than of a speech. It is, of course, by no means impossible that St. Luke had heard that there was such a document, and in the usual manner of historians of his day, gave a reconstruction of it when modern writers would have been content with a description; but it is also quite possible that he may have seen a copy of it. Unless one disputes the Lucan authorship of Acts, or the general historical value

[1] Silas ultimately joined the Antiochene mission, but Judas returned to Jerusalem, if the Bezan text of Acts xv. 34 be trusted.

[2] In speaking in this way I am assuming that the Acts were probably written by St. Luke the companion of St. Paul. In so doing I am certainly open to the accusation of arguing in a circle. But it is unfortunately almost always necessary to start by assuming something. In this case my position is that if we assume the Lucan authorship there is nothing in Acts xv. which he would not have known on good authority, and that if we turn round and treat the Lucan authorship as the question to be discussed, there is also nothing in Acts xv. which he could not have written,—though this is disputed by many critics.

of the book, every *à priori* probability is in favour of the view that a decision was come to, and issued by the Council at Jerusalem in the form, or very nearly in the form, given in Acts xv. If there is nothing wholly unacceptable in the account given by St. Luke, we ought to follow it. Is there anything of this kind? In attempting to answer this question we are faced with one of those complexes of historical and textual difficulties which can only be discussed profitably at some length. To do so at this point would cause too great a break in the narrative, and the detailed consideration has therefore been postponed to an appendix (pp. 48 ff.). The main points are these. The ordinary text of the Acts says that the letter of the Apostles demanded that the Gentiles should keep themselves from "things offered to idols, from blood, from things strangled, and from fornication." Now, it is said, this is a food law, and was a compromise between the two parties: why is it never referred to in the Pauline Epistles? The answers which have been given are manifold, but they may be divided into two main classes. On the one hand, it is said that St. Paul never mentions the compromise because it was a failure from the beginning,[1] or was only intended for the Churches of Syria Cilicia.[2]

[1] So Sanday, *The Apostolic Decree* (published by Deichert in Leipzig, 1908), p. 15 f. The objection to this view is that it makes it an insoluble mystery why St. Luke writing twenty years later, should have made such a "dead letter" (to use Dr. Sanday's expression) as the decrees had become, into a document of such importance. Surely St. Luke was too good a historian to make so wrong a selection of facts.

[2] So Lightfoot, *Galatians*, p. 127. There is less to be said against this view, but it is improbable because—on the theory that the decree was a compromise—it was not a question of geography but of nationality, and was just the same in Galatia as it was in Syria. Besides, on the South Galatian hypothesis (Chap. V.) the decrees were actually delivered to the Galatians (Acts xvi. 4). A third view is that the decrees are genuine but antedated by St. Luke. This view was formerly held by Harnack, and is to be found (in various forms)

On the other hand, it is argued that it is inconceivable that the decrees should not be mentioned by St. Paul, and therefore the account in Acts must be abandoned as unhistorical. So the matter stood for a long time, more or less at a deadlock, for the explanations given of St. Paul's silence were quite unsatisfactory, and the abandonment of the narrative in Acts as unhistorical seemed to be insufficiently justified. Recently, however, a third view has been propounded, to the effect that the whole difficulty may be solved by textual and historical criticism, which shows that the words "things strangled" are a gloss, and that the decree was not a food law.[1] It is discussed at length in the Appendix on pp. 48 ff.

This last view is, I believe, correct. It seems to me to be the only solution enabling us to hold the accuracy of the Lucan account, and at the same time to explain St. Paul's silence, which is perfectly intelligible if the decrees were not a compromise but a victory for his party. For with this text of the Acts—"that they should abstain from things offered to idols, from blood, and from fornication"—there was no compromise, but the decrees were the concession by the Jerusalem party of the main contention of the Antiochene movement—that converts ought to be admitted to Christianity without being compelled to observe the Jewish Law as to circumcision and ritual observances. It was not a compromise, for in a compromise each party concedes something, and if the Apostolic decrees be not a food law, but moral requirements, the Antiochene party had conceded nothing—to abstain from idolatry in any

in Weizsacker, *Das apostolische Zeitalter*, p. 180 f.; McGiffert, *Apostolic Age*, p. 213 f.; and v. Dobschütz, *Die urchristlichen Gemeinden*, p. 274.

[1] G. Resch, *Das Aposteldecret*, and Harnack's chapter on *Das Aposteldecret* in his *Die Apostelgeschichte*, pp. 188–198.

form, or from idolatry, murder, and fornication, was not a concession.[1]

We ought thus to regard the result of the Apostolic Council as the decision of the leaders of the Church at Jerusalem to admit the contention of the Antiochene movement, and to accept Gentile converts to Christianity without the condition of observing the Jewish Law. It was not a compromise, it was a triumph—a triumph of the most far-reaching consequences for Christianity, and Judaism. For the success of Christianity and the failure of Judaism in their attempts to conquer the Roman Empire largely depended on it. Christianity had been originally a part of Judaism, and in selecting a method for carrying its propaganda among the Gentiles it had, along with the other sects of Judaism, to choose between the liberal spirit of the Diaspora—represented by Antioch—and the strictness of the dominant school of Jerusalem. Christianity at the Council of Jerusalem chose aright. Judaism both then, and after the fall of Jerusalem, chose wrongly, for though the Sibylline oracles bear witness to the survival of the broader spirit in Judaism, it was only found in a small minority, never became typically Jewish, and soon disappeared, just as the narrower spirit survived in some parts of Jewish Christianity, but never became dominant, and ultimately died out. The result was that Christianity gained all those of the Graeco-Roman world who had felt the attraction of Jewish monotheism, Jewish ethics, and Jewish eschatological hope, while Judaism failed to do so.

It is now necessary to ask what was the general effect

[1] It is doubtful whether "*εἰδωλόθυτα*, *αἷμα*, and *πορνεία*" means "idolatry, murder, and fornication," or "sacrificial food, sacrificial blood, and fornication in connection with worship"; but in neither case does it imply a compromise.

of this Antiochene triumph. That it was not the end of the Judaistic controversy need scarcely be said; in such a struggle the minority is defeated without being either convinced or destroyed. Even if we had no proof we should be justified in assuming that there remained a party which continued to unite Christian propaganda with a strict adhesion to the Jewish Law, and regarded the Council as a lamentable mistake. Moreover, it is obvious that the Jews would regard this new development of Christianity with increased dislike: for it was no longer merely the identification of the Messiah with Jesus, but a definite denial of the universal validity of the Jewish Law and cultus—the participation by the Christians, already heretical enough, in the dangerous latitudinarianism which Ananias had so lamentably suggested to Izates, and the Jews of the Diaspora had occasionally been so weak as to encourage. At the other end of the scale, also, human nature suggests the probability that some of the Antiochene Christians, or their converts, would rush to extremes and introduce a dangerous antinomianism in the name of liberty, and force the Antiochene leaders to protest, and to contend against extravagant perversions of their teaching.

It is therefore natural to expect to find that the Jerusalem propaganda continued among Christians, though now rather as a protesting and reactionary conservatism; that the opposition of the Jews to Christianity was strengthened and embittered; and that a new school of thought soon arose which exaggerated the plea for liberty which had been so successfully put forward by Antioch, and threatened to convert liberty into libertinism. As a matter of fact, the two first of these phenomena can be traced in the Acts, in the events of St. Paul's final visit to Jerusalem, and the last, though it can scarcely be found in the Acts, can clearly be traced in several of the Pauline Epistles.

On the occasion of St. Paul's visit to Jerusalem, St. James, while reaffirming his acceptance of the Apostolic Decrees, emphasized the existence of "many myriads" of Christian Jews, who were all zealous for the Law and were afraid that St. Paul was not content with absolving the heathen who became Christians from the obligation of the Law, but was also teaching the Jews that it was no longer binding on them and their children. It is for our purpose immaterial whether this be accepted as really an utterance of St. James, or as representing St. Luke's idea of the attitude of the Jewish Christians and of their leader. In either case, it is good evidence of the Jewish Christians' position, and of their attitude towards St. Paul and the Antiochene movement generally. Equally instructive is St. Paul's conduct: he at once agreed to show by his actions that he recognized the validity of the Law for Jews. The Jewish Christians honestly believed that the direct result of his writing and preaching must be the abandonment of the Law even by Jews; and St. Paul's action was intended to convince them that, although the observance of the Law was not demanded from Gentiles, it was nevertheless recognized as binding on Jewish Christians. At the same time, the seriousness with which both St. James and St. Paul faced the situation suggests that some of St. Paul's adherents were pushing his principles further, and denying that circumcision and the Law were binding on any one. We may also assume with much probability that this question was connected with a certain vagueness as to whether it was possible to say that the Messiah was already come or not. The original position was no doubt that Jesus was the Messiah, but it was equally clearly held that He had not yet come as Messiah. The Parousia—which means "coming," not "return"—was still future, and the Messianic kingdom did not yet exist, except in a certain proleptic sense. But until the Messiah came—not until it was known who He was—the Law was binding. This was probably the original position, so far as it was consciously thought out at all, but almost from the first amongst Gentile Christians the "proleptic" element began to be forgotten, more and more importance came to be given to the actual work of Jesus, His life to be regarded as really a "coming" of the Messiah, and the concept of the Kingdom to gain a somewhat different meaning. With such a position the Law naturally seemed to be entirely superseded. Over against this extreme Gentile position stood the mass of Jewish Christians, who were zealous for the Law, had not St. James's personal knowledge of St. Paul, but identified him with the extreme position of some of his followers, and so came more and more to stand aloof, and to dislike the whole Antiochene movement.

The increased hostility of the non-Christian Jews is equally well shown by the Pauline Epistles and by the Acts. According to these, St. Paul's most determined enemies were the Jews. In Galatia, Asia, Macedonia; and Achaia Jewish hostility was strong and irreconcileable, and in Jerusalem it was the direct cause of his imprisonment. It is clear that the Jews in the capital tolerated St. James and his party, even though their toleration was tempered with contempt and dislike: after all, they seem to have argued, though these people have foolish ideas as to the identity of the Messiah, they nevertheless observe the Law, and are otherwise orthodox.

But for St. Paul nothing was bad enough—he was a renegade and a traitor, and as such worthy of death.

Moreover, this Jewish hatred of St. Paul was especially stimulated by a fact which also was prominent in producing the antinomian extremists, and later on in introducing other problems into the life of the Gentile Churches. This fact was the existence in the Graeco-Roman world of the class of "God-fearers" whom the synagogue had attracted towards itself by much careful preparation, and hoped ultimately to convert into proselytes. This class is often mentioned in the New Testament,[1] and a more accurate understanding of its position is one of the great steps forward which have been made of recent years in the interpretation of early Christianity. The source of most statements on the subject was formerly the essay of Deyling, *De Σεβομένοις τὸν Θεόν* in his *Observationes Sacrae*, ii. pp. 462–69, in which he identified them with the "proselytes of the gate" mentioned in the Talmud. On this view the theory was based that the Jews recognized two sorts of proselytes—those "of the gate" and those "of righteousness," of whom the former stood in a less close relation to the Jews than the latter—and that "God-fearers" is a synonym for the former. This view will be found expressed at length in the first edition of Schürer's *Geschichte des jüdischen Volkes in Zeitalter Jesu Christi*, and it was long the dominant opinion. But, in the light of further study, in his third, and still more completely in his fourth edition (1909), Schürer completely gave up this theory, and showed convincingly

[1] They are referred to in the following places:—as "*φοβούμενοι τὸν Θεόν*," in Acts x. 2, 22, 35; xiii. 16, 26; as "*σεβόμενοι τὸν Θεόν*," Acts xvi. 14; xviii. 7; as "*σεβόμενοι*" in Acts xiii. 50; xvii. 4, 17; and as "*σεβόμενοι προσήλυτοι*" in Acts xiii. 43. Cf. Josephus, *Antiquit.*, xiv. 7. 2.

that "proselyte of the gate" is a purely mediaeval term, of which the meaning is doubtful, but probably is "Gentiles living among Jews," and that the God-fearers were not proselytes at all. His conclusion is based on inscriptions, both in Latin and Greek,[1] and is that "Almost everywhere in the Diaspora there was a fringe of 'God-fearing' heathen round the Jewish Church. They adopted the Jewish form of worship, with its monotheism and absence of images, and frequented the Jewish synagogues, but confined themselves with regard to the ceremonial law to certain cardinal points, and thus could not be reckoned as actually belonging to the Jewish Church. . . . When we ask which points of the ceremonial law were thus observed, the clearest indications are afforded by Josephus, Juvenal, and Tertullian.[2] These three all agree that it was especially

[1] Cf. especially, *C.I.L.*, v. 1, *n.* 88. *Ephem.Epigr.*, iv. 1881, p. 291, *n.* 838; *C.I.L.*, vi. *n.* 29759, 29760, and 29763. Deissmann, *Licht vom Osten*, 326 f. Schürer, *Die Juden im bosporanischen Reiche und die Genossenschaften der σεβόμενοι Θεὸν ὕψιστον ebendaselbst* (*Sitzungsberichte der königl. preussischen Academie zu Berlin*, 1897); and F. Cumont, *Hypsistos* in the *Supplément* to the *Revue de l'instruction publique en Belgique*, 1897.

[2] The passages indicated are the following: Jos., *Contra Ap.*, ii. 39: "καὶ πλήθεσιν ἤδη πολὺς ζῆλος γέγονεν ἐκ μακροῦ τῆς ἡμετέρας εὐσεβείας, οὐδ' ἔστιν οὐ πόλις Ἑλλήνων οὐδητισοῦν οὐδὲ βάρβαρον οὐδὲ ἓν ἔθνος, ἔνθα μὴ τὸ τῆς ἑβδομάδος, ἣν ἀργοῦμεν ἡμεῖς, τὸ ἔθος [δὲ] διεπεφοίτηκεν καὶ αἱ νηστεῖαι καὶ λύχνων ἀνακαύσεις καὶ πολλὰ τῶν εἰς βρῶσιν ἡμῖν οὐ νενομισμένων παρατετήρηται." Tertullian, *Ad Nationes*, i. 13: "Vos certe estis, qui etiam in laterculum septem dierum solem recepistis, et ex diebus ipso priorem praelegistis, quo die lavacrum subtrahatis aut in vesperam differatis, aut otium et prandium curetis. Quod quidem facitis exorbitantes et ipsi a vestris ad alienas religiones. Judaei enim festi sabbata et coena pura et Judaici ritus lucernarum et jejunia cum azymis et orationes litorales, quae utique aliena sunt a diis vestris." Juvenal, *Sat.*, xiv. 96–106—

"Quidam sortiti metuentem sabbata patrem
nil praeter nubes et caeli numen adorant,
nec distare putant humana carne suillam
qua pater abstinuit; mox et praeputia ponunt.
Romanas autem soliti contemnere leges
Judaicum ediscunt et servant ac metuunt jus

the observance of the Sabbath, and the food law which most generally obtained in these circles. . . . Their adherence would vary in degree, and it is improbable that there were fixed limits."[1] To this statement of Schürer's no exception can be taken on the ground of what it says, but it ought to be added that the evidence of Philo shows that there were Jews who regarded the Law as merely allegorical, and that the *Sibylline Oracles* (see pp. 25 f. and 56 f.) show that there were also circles among the God-fearers in which the food law and even the sabbath were disregarded, and that monotheism and the moral law alone were observed. This would no doubt vary in different places, and would be influenced by the type of Judaism which was dominant: in places, for instance, where the extreme allegorizing party had representatives, and the Law was explained in the manner which the Epistle of Barnabas tried to popularize among Christians, the observance of the ceremonial law would naturally sink into the background among the God-fearers.

It does not need the testimony of Juvenal to convince us that it was from this circle of God-fearers that the Jews drew their proselytes, and the Acts give us superabundant proof that it was in the same circle that St. Paul met with the greatest success in making converts; it is therefore easy to understand the bitterness of Jewish feeling against St. Paul and other Christians of the Antiochene school, for it is not in human nature to regard with equanimity the sight

tradidit arcano quodcunque volumine Moses:
non monstrare vias eadem nisi sacra colenti
quaesitum ad fontem solos deducere verpos.
Sed pater in causa cui septima cuique fuit lux
ignava et partem vitae non attigit ullam."

[1] *Geschichte des jüdischen Volkes*, ed. 4, iii. 173 ff.

of heretics successfully reaping a harvest which the orthodox had sown, had seen grow up, and had expected to gather, and the rapid passing over of God-fearers to the ranks of the Christians was in the eyes of the orthodox Jews a triumph for heresy as bitter as it was unexpected.

In this way the existence of the God-fearers helps to explain the increased hatred of the Jews; it also explains the existence of the extreme antinomian party of which Acts tells us nothing, but the Epistles more than a little. For the God-fearers brought Christianity into the troubled world of thought of the Roman Empire. They represent to a large extent the general attitude of the "religious man" of the first century. He was, as a rule, dissatisfied with the ancestral forms of culture, as well as with the traditional theology. It was an age of religious unrest and theological inquiry. The propaganda of Judaism and Christianity were only two of the many efforts which were being made to answer this intellectual curiosity and to satisfy the yearnings of unhappy souls, and, on the whole, we can distinguish two main currents to one or the other of which these efforts usually belonged. Those whose interest was primarily intellectual, or, at all events, demanded a theology which was intellectually acceptable, were strongly influenced by the metaphysics of the Neo-Platonists, and the ethics of the Stoics. In them they seemed to find a reasonable explanation of the universe, a "weltanschauung" which corresponded to facts, and a rule of life which satisfied the conscience and seemed to offer a lasting happiness. On the other hand, those whose interest was chiefly religious, in the narrower sense of the word, were attracted by the Oriental "Mystery Religions," so diverse in detail, yet so similar in essentials, which held out the offer of happiness in this world and salvation in the next to all who by initiation into their sacraments joined in the risen life of a redeemer God, and thus secured a knowledge of the great secret, which would guard the traveller when he passed hence through the gate of death on his long and dangerous journey, and bring him safely to the eternal life which he desired. Finally, we can see in such a man as Plutarch the curious combination of these two currents which fully accepted all these mysteries, but by a vigorous use of allegory and symbolism brought them in agreement with philosophy, and felt that whether the God whom they celebrated was called Isis, or Attis, or Mithras, or any other name, it was, nevertheless, the divine Logos, "the Word," who was working in them all—the Logos who is the source of all life and all wisdom, though he be called by different names in different lands.

Plutarch was, we may be sure, no exception, save in so far as he was of exceptional ability, and doubtless there were many in the Roman Empire who, in some such way as he had done, united the practice of the mysteries with the philosophy of the Stoics or Platonists. But in the lower and less educated classes this syncretism must have been less common. Men felt that spiritually they were ill, and needed a physician, nor were they able to see, as Plutarch did, that all the physicians offered the same prescription, though they varied the exact form of its composition. No doubt, they had their own syncretism, but it was not the philosophic syncretism of Plutarch, but rather a tendency to modify the practices of the various cults, to borrow attractive features from others, and to give up objectionable even though characteristic customs.

This influence of the Oriental "Mystery Religions" was increased by the fact that not only the Jews, but every

Eastern nation had its "Diaspora" in the Roman Empire. We are apt to overlook this because, for obvious reasons, it is the Jewish Diaspora of which we hear most, but after all it was the Orontes, not the Jordan, which seemed to the Roman eye to be flowing into the Tiber, and we ought to remember that just as there was a Jewish Diaspora, with its proselytizing propaganda, there were Egyptian, Syrian, Persian, and other Diasporae, in which the various cults were taught, though each probably with more or less pronounced variations from the native type.

Each Diaspora of this kind was a centre for a wider circle, corresponding to the God-fearers of the Jewish community, composed of those who were interested in what they saw and heard, but were only prepared to accept the cult partially, eclectically, and in combination with features taken from other cults, of which they had obtained knowledge in a similar way. An excellent example of this type of syncretism is to be found in the cults,[1] found in Asia Minor, which combined Judaism with the worship of Zeus Hypsistos and of Attis the Phrygian Redeemer-God whose worship united an originally local cult with that of the Magna Mater and her mysteries.[2] But it is safe to assume that for one form of eclecticism which endured long enough to crystallize into a definite shape there must have been many which were purely ephemeral, or, even if they lasted longer, failed to be preserved in any inscription or literary reference which has survived.

[1] See F. Cumont's *Hypsistos*, in the *Supplément* to the *Revue de l'instruction publique en Belgique.* 1897.

[2] For a further description reference may be made to F. Cumont's *Les Religions orientales dans le Paganisme romain.* This book affords an indispensable introduction to the study of the Oriental side of the background of early Christianity. It has, also, the advantage of being more easily intelligible and more interesting than most works of fiction.

It is easy to see how these influences must have worked in the case of those who were brought into contact with Judaism as well as with the "Mystery Religions." In the Jewish theology they found a monotheism which satisfied their intellects. The Messianic expectation presented no difficulties to those who, since the time of Augustus, had learnt to believe that the world-cycle was approaching its completion, and that a Deliverer[1] would soon appear to lead mankind into the glories of the golden age of which the poets sang and the Sibyl prophesied.[2] In the deeply ethical and spiritual austerity of the synagogue they found a satisfaction and a stimulus for their religious life.[3] Some of them also appreciated the moral and practical value of the observance of the sabbath, and felt that there was an element of truth in the distinction between clean and unclean foods—a distinction which is, indeed, more obviously valuable in hot climates than in Northern Europe. But the rest of the ceremonial law, circumcision, and the national pretensions of the Jew to the especial favour of God, had no value in their eyes, so that they either rejected them, or accepted the position which changed their meaning by allegory and symbolism. But they were very unlikely to stop at this point; the metaphysics of the Neo-Platonists, and the ethics of the Stoics agreed with and supplemented the teaching of the Old Testament and the

[1] It is remarkable that the title of Σωτήρ was actually given to Augustus; Cf. Deissman, *Licht vom Ocsten*, p. 248.

[2] Cf. Bousset, *Religion des Judentums*, p. 576; and Wendland, *Die Hellenistisch-Römische Kultur*, pp. 87 f.

[3] That this was the strength of Judaism has often been unfairly overlooked by Christian writers, who have judged Judaism by the polemics of early Christian literature and the subtleties of the Talmud, rather than by the ethical spirit of, for instance, the *Testaments of the Twelve Patriarchs*, or the many noble sayings of Philo.

synagogue, while the "Mystery Religions," with their elaborate and impressive ritual, made a reiterated appeal to the sympathy of those who found in the stern and cold worship of the Jews, bracing though its atmosphere might be, insufficient scope for the permanent satisfaction of an aesthetic and mystical imagination.

Such must have been the result of the contact of this type of eclectic mind with Judaism—a result which doubtless caused the synagogue to ponder long and anxiously over the problem of such God-fearers—but what kind of impression must have been made by Christianity on those who belonged to such a circle?

They must have been but little attracted by Christianity of the original Jerusalem school, except in so far as it accentuated the doctrine of the Messiah and His kingdom, and introduced an element of superior certainty by being able to give the name of the Messiah, nor, as a matter of fact, is there any evidence to show that the Jerusalem school ever obtained any very important or permanent hold in the Graeco-Roman world. It was very different with the Antiochene movement. In this the eclectic Gentile found all the features which he most admired in Judaism, set free from the ceremonial law and from the custom of circumcision which had repelled him. But he saw more than this: in the teaching of St. Paul as to the meaning of the death of Jesus he saw every reason for equating the Lord with the Redeemer-God of the Mystery Religions, with the advantage that this Redeemer possessed an historic character which could scarcely be claimed for Attis or Mithras. Similarly in Baptism and in the Eucharist he found "mysteries" which could immediately be equated with the other "mysteries," offering eternal life to those who partook of them. In other words, many of the Greeks must have regarded Christianity as a superior form of "Mystery Religion."

The importance of this fact is not easily exhausted; it will be found to be one of the most important elements in the situation at Corinth, which led to the Epistles, and in the wider sphere of the history of doctrine it can scarcely be over-estimated. It is, for instance, of enormous importance in considering the course of the development of Christian doctrine from the belief that the Messiah was Jesus, and that He was speedily coming to set up the Kingdom of God, to the creed in which the original meaning of the word "Messiah," or "Christ," was almost wholly forgotten, Jesus was regarded as a Redeemer-God, and the Sacraments became the real centre of Christianity. That we find one type dominant in Jerusalem in the middle of the first century, and the other type dominant in Rome in the middle of the second seems incontrovertible, but the exact course of the development is outside the present purpose: it is sufficient to call attention to the fact that the existence of the eclectic type of God-fearer is an extremely important factor in the situation.

Or, again, the existence of this type is of enormous importance in considering the origin of Gnosticism. Formerly it was the custom to regard Gnosticism as a development from Christianity under the influence of Greek thought. We have now, however, learnt[1] that it was in basis neither Christian nor Hellenic, but eclectic and Oriental. It comprised an almost infinite variety of sects which combined parts of various Oriental religions, including Christianity, and united the fragments by the application of a more or less intelligent application of philosophy. It

[1] See especially Bousset's *Hauptprobleme der Gnosis.*

will be seen that such a movement was independent of Christianity, and this point is of importance because it used to be argued that documents—such as some of the Pauline Epistles—which imply a point of view similar to that of the Gnostics, must be late, because time must be allowed for the development of Gnostic "heresy" from Christianity. The argument is unsound: Gnostic ideas are earlier, not later, than Christianity, and to prove that any given document is engaged in controverting a Gnostic point of view, shows merely that it was addressed to the eclectic circles described in the preceding paragraphs—it has no necessary bearing on the question of date.

Putting aside, however, these larger questions it is clear that the attitude which regarded Christianity as a "Mystery Religion" inevitably must have led men to exaggerate and misinterpret the Pauline doctrine of freedom, to regard the cleansing from sin gained by the Christian as giving him permission henceforth to do as he liked without incurring guilt, and to consider Baptism as an *opus operatum* which secured his admission into the Kingdom apart from the character of his future conduct. Thus there was from the beginning an antinomian and unethical spirit which offered the most difficult problem for St. Paul and other Christians, who would naturally reject with horror this licentious liberty of conduct so different from the ethical standards of Judaism, and we can imagine—though I do not know that there is any extant example of it—that it was often flung by the Jewish Christians in the face of the Pauline school of Christianity as the natural result of its mistaken freedom.

Such are the main characteristics of the background which we must expect to find in the Pauline Epistles. The chief feature is the large confused mass of unsatisfied seekers after religious truth, who were testing all the various offers made to them by the preachers of diverse cults, and were inclined to combine select features of them all in a strange medley of ritual and doctrine. And emerging from the struggle fully to convert this class—a struggle in which convinced Jews, Christians of Jerusalem, Christians of Antioch, worshippers of Isis and other Oriental cults, magicians, astrologers, and wizards jostled each other in a theological confusion to which no parallel can be found—we can distinguish the endeavours of St. Paul to preach freedom without libertinism, and his constant efforts against the hatred of the Jew for a renegade Rabbi, against the scarcely less fierce opposition of Christians who held firmly to the principles of the stiffly conservative party at Jerusalem, and against the even more serious danger of a tendency to misunderstand his teaching of Christian freedom, to misinterpret the nature of Christianity, and to regard him as a narrow-minded preacher, who had little appreciation of the mysteries of the spirit, and was scarcely better than the Jews whom he had deserted.

It will be one of the tasks of the following chapters to trace more fully the details of this background in connection with each of the Epistles, so as to render it possible for them to be read with a somewhat better appreciation of the circumstances which caused them to be written.

LITERATURE.—Besides the references which have been for special points, the following books will be found generally valuable: E. Schürer, *Geschichte des jüdischen Volkes* (ed. 4), vol. iii., *Das Judentum in der Zerstreuung und die jüdische Literatur*. W. Bousset, *Die Religion des Judentums* (ed. 2). W. M. Ramsay, *The Church in the Roman Empire*, and *St. Paul the Traveller and Roman Citizen*. R. Reitzenstein, *Die hellenistischen Mysterienreligionen, ihre Grundgedanken und Wirkungen*. J. Harrison, *Prolegomena to the Study of Greek Religion*, chap. x., *The Orphic Mysteries*. L. R. Farnell, *Cults of the Greek States*, vol. v. chap. v. *Dionysiac ritual*. T. R. Glover, *The Conflict of Religions in the Early Roman Empire*. F. Cumont, *Les Religions orientales dans le Paganisme romain*.

APPENDIX

THE TEXT OF THE APOSTOLIC DECREES

THE textual variants in the Apostolic Decrees are numerous and complicated: they can be found most fully in G. Resch's *Das Aposteldecret*, pp. 7–17, and the material in the later Greek MSS. will no doubt be increased when von Soden's new critical edition is published. But for the purposes of all except students of the later history of the text the facts may be stated as follows:—

The text of all the manuscripts which represent the dominant Greek tradition—ℵABCP, etc.—supported by the Alexandrian Fathers Clement and Origen, states that the Apostles told the Gentile converts to keep themselves from things offered to idols, from blood, from things strangled, and from fornication. Thus there is a four-clause text of which the first three clauses seem, when united in this way, to give a food law,[1] to fix, as it were, the conditions of intercourse between Jewish and Gentile Christians, while the last clause—against fornication—seems to have nothing to do with food, but to belong to a different category altogether.

Over against this reading is the evidence of D, the Latin version, Irenaeus (in Greek as well as in the Latin translation),

[1] For a different interpretation, see p. 60.

Tertullian, Cyprian, and other Latin writers, who omit "things strangled," generally [1] insert after the reference to fornication, "and do not do to others what you would not that they should do to you," and at the end of all add, "Ye shall do well, being carried along by the Holy Spirit." Thus it is plain that a widely received text of the decrees ran somewhat as follows: ἀπέχεσθαι εἰδωλοθύτων καὶ αἵματος καὶ πορνείας, καὶ ὅσα μὴ θέλετε ἑαυτοῖς γίνεσθαι ἑτέρῳ μὴ ποιεῖν· ἀφ' ὧν διατηροῦντες εὖ πράξετε [or πράξατε?] φερόμενοι ἐν τῷ ἁγίῳ πνεύματι, and was opposed, ultimately successfully, by a rival form which ran ἀπέχεσθαι εἰδωλοθύτων καὶ αἵματος καὶ πνικτῶν καὶ πορνείας· ἐξ ὧν διατηροῦντες ἑαυτοὺς εὖ πράξετε.

Now, the evidence of Irenaeus and Tertullian on the one hand, and of Clement on the other, shows that both these readings are very old. Moreover, the history of exegesis confirms them. For in Alexandria the Apostolic Decrees were always interpreted as a food law, but in Africa (up to the time of Augustine) and in Europe as referring to the three deadly sins. Irenaeus and Tertullian were, it is true, acquainted with a food law, but they did not connect it with the Apostolic Decrees.

Nevertheless, the three-clause text, in its entirety, cannot be maintained. Among modern critics there is an almost complete [2] agreement that the additions of the negative form of the golden rule, and the reference to the Spirit cannot be original: partly because the former introduces a very harsh parenthesis or change of thought,[3] but chiefly

[1] Tertullian is the extremely important exception.

[2] G. Resch, whose work on the subject entitles him to great respect, is the most important exception.

[3] "From which if ye keep yourselves ye shall do well," reads awkwardly after the golden rule.

because if the golden rule had been in the text from the beginning, the interpretation of the decrees as a food law would have been impossible. This consensus of opinion has prejudiced critics against the omission of "things strangled," which is supported by much the same witnesses, and Dr. Sanday in particular has argued that as D and Irenaeus have made a mistake in adding the golden rule, they ought not to be trusted where they omit "things strangled." His view is that the same people left out "things strangled" and inserted the golden rule in order to change a food law into a moral enactment.

Against this argument serious objections can be brought. In the first place, it is not the case that the evidence for the golden rule is quite the same as that for the omission of "things strangled"; Tertullian omits "things strangled," but does not insert the golden rule. There is, therefore, important if not extensive evidence that the two readings are independent of each other. In the second place, there is no historical evidence whatever that the circles which can be shown to have read a text which omitted "things strangled" had any objection to a food law. On the contrary, in the second century Gaul, in which Irenaeus lived, observed a food law, and Tertullian, the other earlier witness for the omission, observed a food law which actually mentioned "things strangled" (*suffocatis*).[1] Thus there is no possibility of alleging any motive for the change of text. Finally, it is difficult to suppose that any scribe of Acts in the second century *deliberately* changed the obvious meaning of an important passage. No doubt redactors may have treated their sources in this way, but the scribes who copied the Gospels and Acts confined themselves to elucidating the

[1] See p. 58.

meaning of the text. They made additions, alterations, and omissions, but their intention was to explain, not to alter. Of course they made many lamentable mistakes, but where is the evidence that they consciously set to work to change the manifest meaning of the text which they read? Whenever, therefore, we find a considerable variety of readings, we ought, if possible, to look for an original text offering some ambiguity which scribes would seek to clear up, first by notes in the margin, and afterwards by their insertion in the text.

Such a text would be excellently provided by the reading of Tertullian, which omits "things strangled," but does not insert the golden rule.[1] This three-clause text presents just the ambiguity necessary to account for the early diversity both of text and of exegesis.

The first clause (εἰδωλόθυτα) means "things offered to idols," and may be as well taken in a narrow sense, a literal command not to eat that sort of food (which was often sold in the market), as in the wider sense of a synonym for idolatry.[2] In the former case it is a food law, in the latter it is a moral or ethical rule. The next clause "from blood,"

[1] The insertion of the reference to the Spirit in the last clause seems to have no bearing on the question. Supposing it to be (as I am inclined to believe) an insertion, it neither negatives nor affirms the other readings. To be "carried along by the Holy Spirit" was a general characteristic of the early Christians.

[2] 1 Cor. x. 14 ff. is an instructive commentary on the word. It is part of the answer to the question of the Corinthians περὶ εἰδωλοθύτων. In the first half (vv. 14–22) of the passage, εἰδωλόθυτον is treated as an act of idolatry, the actual sacrifice to a false god, and is forbidden: in the second half (vv. 23–33) it is treated in the sense of merely food which, after having been used in sacrifice, was sold in the shops and used for an ordinary meal, and this is in principle allowed, though St. Paul makes practical reservations because of the chance of giving offence to the weaker brethren. It is clear that in this chapter, St. Paul is either deliberately ignoring the Apostolic Decrees, or interpreting them as forbidding idolatry, not as establishing a food law. Cf. G. Resch, *Aposteldecret*, p. 21.

(*αἵματος*), is equally ambiguous, and was probably the cause of the later confusion. To any one who had already interpreted the first clause in the sense of an ethical forbidding of idolatry it would either mean "murder,"[1] or possibly blood as used ritually in sacrifices in the temples (see p. 60), but if the first clause were taken in the stricter sense of a literal command not to eat that sort of food, the second would naturally be interpreted as a reference to the Jewish objection to the use of blood as food. It is plain that the tendency of scribes would be to clear up this ambiguity, and in some way to indicate which interpretation was correct. Those who favoured the sense of a food law made it clear by adding "things strangled"—first perhaps as a gloss in the margin, afterwards in the text itself—thus explaining blood as "meat in which the blood had been retained," "*sanguine suffocato*" as the Vulgate (in some manuscripts) puts it.[2] Those, on the other hand, who regarded the decrees as a moral law made their meaning plain by adding the negative form of the golden rule. It is possible that the addition of the reference to the Spirit was made at the same time, and for the same purpose, but the evidence of Tertullian (who has it, but has not yet adopted the golden rule) suggests that it is an earlier interpolation, and probably has nothing to do with the addition of the golden rule, or

[1] Probably few will doubt that *αἷμα* can be used in the sense of murder—blood-guiltiness—but G. Resch has met any such objection by a convincing list of quotations in his *Aposteldecret*, p. 42. The passages he quotes are: Lev. xvii. 4; Num. xxxv. 27; Eccles. xxxiv. 21; Matt. xxiii. 30; Rev. vi. 10. Demosthenes, *In Meidiam*, 548; Pausanias, v. 1, 6; Æschylus, *Eumen.*, 203. Plato, *Laws*, 872, DE, and others of less importance.

[2] It is significant also that Origen (*In Matthaeum*, ii. 837), though he seems to have known the ordinary four-clause text, also quotes the decrees in a three-clause form with *πνικτοῦ instead of αἷματος*. Methodius, too, has the same curious text. This may be a slip, or may be an instance of the gloss replacing the word glossed.

the omission of "things strangled," but is merely one of the edifying remarks which the early scribes loved and sometimes allowed to pass into the text.

Each of these two ways of altering the text rendered the meaning unmistakable—that is exactly the reason why neither can be original. But the short three-clause text used by Tertullian is ambiguous; it adequately explains the origin of both readings, and is implicitly borne witness to by both of them. It would no doubt be foolish to claim that the textual question can be solved with certainty; there must be an element of doubt in a text on which second-century evidence—two hundred years before our best manuscripts—was sharply divided, but reflection is likely to convince all who concede that our most famous uncials only represent an Alexandrian recension of the third or fourth century, that the argument on purely textual grounds is against the four-clause text, and in favour of the shorter form.

To the textual argument can be added a far stronger historical argument, to show that the Apostolic Decrees were originally of the nature of moral requirements rather than a food law. This historical argument is contained in the answers given to the questions: Which is really more likely to have been the decision of the Council? Which is more consistent with the subsequent course of events? Which is implied more probably by the Pauline Epistles?

Taking the two last questions first, the superiority of the three-clause form of the decree is as follows: (1) It removes the obvious difficulties of the sudden association of a food law with fornication; (2) the absolute silence of St. Paul on the decrees in 1 Cor. x., when he is discussing "things offered to idols," and in Rom. xiv., when he is discussing food in general, is almost unintelligible if we suppose that the decrees were a food law. Even more difficult is the statement in Gal. ii. 6, that the Jerusalem Apostles added nothing (οὐδὲν προσανέθεντο) to St. Paul, that is to say, made no additions to his gospel. If we suppose[1] that Gal. ii. refers to the Apostolic Council, and that the Council enacted a food law, it would be hard for St. Paul to say that the Apostles had made no additions to his gospel: for it is plain from all his Epistles that a food law was widely removed from his thoughts. On the other hand, it would be quite true if the decrees were merely a moral requirement to abstain from idolatry, murder, and fornication. There is no evidence that St. Paul ever condoned these offences or needed an Apostolic Decree to persuade him to require his converts to abstain from them.

The remaining question—which form of decree is in itself more likely to have been adopted by the Council? —is more difficult to answer, but again there is a decided balance of argument in favour of the three-clause text. Generally speaking, commentators have been inclined to argue that a food law is a probable decree, because the Jews placed so much importance on such regulations. It is probably true that this argument is partly based on the very unfair attitude which so many Christian theologians have adopted towards Jewish religion—always emphasizing the ritual and legalist elements in it, and ignoring the ethical and religious basis. Still, when all possible allowance has been made for this factor, it remains true that the outward side of religious life had great importance for the Jews of the first century. So much must be admitted.

[1] Personally I do not think so (see Chap. V.), but in deference to a widely spread opinion I adopt the view for the moment.

But when one goes on to ask for proof that "things strangled" was a point on which the Jewish element in the Christian Church at Jerusalem would probably have laid stress, it is simply not forthcoming. There is no evidence earlier than the fifth century after Christ that the Jews regarded the command not to eat blood as meaning more than that they were not to collect and use for cooking blood which was shed in the act of slaughtering an animal.[1] Even if we concede that in some circles the Jews had this custom in the first century, and that this is the origin of the later Christian practice, it is at least obvious that this rule was not likely to have been so crucial a point at the Jerusalem Council, that the Jewish party would have given way on the question of circumcision, but have held firm on the question of extracting blood from slaughtered animals. Moreover, the suggestion which is sometimes made that the Apostolic Decrees correspond to the so-called Noachic regulations, which on the basis of Gen. ix. 4 were supposed to be binding on Gentiles living in Palestine, is unfortunately negatived by a comparison of the seven Noachic commands with the Apostolic Decrees. The seven commands[2] were: (1) on the foundation of courts (*Beth din*); (2) against blasphemy; (3) against idolatry; (4) against shedding of blood; (5) against incest; (6) against robbery; (7) against cutting flesh from a living

[1] Once more reference must be made to Resch, who collects all the evidence (*Das Aposteldecret*, pp. 21 ff.). It would seem that the present Jewish custom of extracting all blood from meat (the "Kosher" meat) can only be traced back to the tractate *Chullim* of the fifth or sixth century. The matter is, of course, one on which only Rabbinical scholars have a right to speak, but I do not gather that Resch's view is disputed by them.

[2] Sanhedrin, 56 a. ff. I am indebted to my friend Prof. Oort for the verification, and correction, of the reference. Cf. Schürer, *Geschichte des jüdischen Volkes* (Fourth Edition), III. p. 178, note 77 (Third Edition, p. 128).

animal. It is also said [1] that the last of these commands is a later addition. It is clear that there is here if anything a closer resemblance to the three-clause than to the four-clause form of the Apostolic Decrees.[2]

Thus there is no reason to think that the Jewish feeling of the first century would have been inclined to accept a food law as the basis of a compromise with the Antiochene movement. On the other hand, it is undeniable that the evidence of the advice given to King Izates, the statement of Philo (see above, pp. 24–26), and the fourth book of the Sibylline Oracles are the proof that the requirement of the moral law alone would have been nothing unique in the history of Judaism. Moreover, a comparison of the text of the Sibyllines raises the question whether the actual formula of the three-clause text of Acts xv. does not go back to some Jewish form of which there is also a trace in the Oracles.

The two passages which are important are as follows:—

(1) *Or. Sib.*, iv. 24–34—

ὄλβιοι ἀνθρώπων κεῖνοι κατὰ γαῖαν ἔσονται,
ὅσσοι δὴ στέρξουσι μέγαν θεὸν εὐλογέοντες
πρὶν πιέειν φαγέειν τε πεποιθότες εὐσεβίῃσιν·
οἳ νηοὺς μὲν ἅπαντας ἀπαρνήσονται ἰδόντες
καὶ βωμούς, εἰκαῖα λίθων ἀφιδρύματα κωφῶν,
αἵμασιν ἐμψύχων μεμιασμένα καὶ θυσίῃσιν
τετραπόδων· λεύσουσι δ' ἑνὸς θεοῦ εἰς μέγα κῦδος
οὔτε φόνον ῥέξαντες ἀτάσθαλον οὔτε κλοπαῖον
κέρδος ἀπεμπολέοντες, ἃ δὴ ῥίγιστα τέτυκται,

[1] By Hamburger, *Realencyclopaedie*, in the article on "Noachiden."

[2] The fact probably is that the Noachian rules are a later crystallization of the primarily moral requirements of the early Jewish Propaganda in the Diaspora.

οὐδ' ἄρ' ἐπ' ἀλλοτρίῃ κοίτῃ πόθον αἰσχρὸν ἔχοντες,
οὐδ' ἐπ' ἄρσενος ὕβριν ἀπεχθέα τε στυγερήν τε.[1]

(2) *Or. Sib.*, iv. 162–170—

ἆ μέλεοι, μετάθεσθε, βρότοι, τάδε, μηδὲ πρὸς ὀργήν
παντοίην ἀγάγητε θεὸν μέγαν, ἀλλὰ μεθέντες
φάσγανα καὶ στοναχὰς ἀνδροκτασίας τε καὶ ὕβρεις
ἐν ποταμοῖς λούσασθε ὅλον δέμας ἀενάοισιν,
χεῖράς τ' ἐκτανύσαντες ἐς αἰθέρα τῶν πάρος ἔργων
συγγνώμην αἰτεῖσθε καὶ εὐλογίαις ἀσέβειαν
πικρὰν ἱλάσκεσθε· θεὸς δώσει μετάνοιαν
οὐδ' ὀλέσει· παύσει δὲ χόλον πάλιν, ἤνπερ ἅπαντες
εὐσεβίην περίτιμον ἐνὶ φρεσὶν ἀσκήσητε·

It is surely very remarkable that here, as in the Apostolic Decrees, if the three-clause text be followed, abstinence from idolatry, blood-shedding, and immorality (it is highly probable that ὕβρεις in l. 164 has a sexual significance, cf. l. 33) should be selected as the characteristics of a good life. It is very unlikely that there is any literary connection between the Oracles and the Acts, and the only possible suggestion seems to be that both are to be traced back to antecedent Jewish expression.

So far, therefore, there is a decided balance of argument in favour of the three-clause form of the Apostolic Decrees. The one argument which at first seems seriously to weigh against it on historical grounds is that there existed at the end of the second century in the Christian Church a food law which certainly did refer to meat with the blood in it. The earliest evidence for this is probably the letter of the Churches of Lyons and Vienne (A.D. 178), in which Biblis, one of the martyrs, is stated to have refuted the accusation

[1] Geffcken rejects this line, as the construction is harsh, and it is not found in the Ω recension. But it is doubtful whether this is sufficient reason.

of cannibalism by saying, "Those who are not allowed to eat the blood of irrational animals, how should they eat children?"[1] A little later in his *Apology*[2] and elsewhere Tertullian refers to the food law of the Christians as commanding them to abstain from "suffocatis"; and Clement of Alexandria[3] also bears witness to the same practice. This seems certainly strong evidence that "things strangled" were forbidden by a Christian food law. But it is weakened to unimportance by the fact that none of these writers except Clement connect the custom with the Apostolic Decrees. For Irenaeus (who even if not the writer of the letter of Lyons and Vienne, was the bearer of the letter to Rome, and was afterwards Bishop of Lyons[4]) used the three-clause text of the decrees, and Tertullian not only used the three-clause text, but explained it as a reference to the three deadly sins. Moreover, writers earlier than the end of the second century say nothing of any food law, and mention "things offered to idols" in the same way as St. Paul, as an incident in idolatry and communion with demons,[5] while the *Didache*[6] knows so little of a food law that it says, "Concerning food, bear what thou canst, but keep strictly from idol-sacrifice (εἰδωλοθύτου), for it is the service of dead gods."

[1] Eus., *H. E.*, v. 1. 26 (ed. Schwartz, p. 412). The Latin of Rufinus has "flesh" instead of "blood," but the Greek is probably right.

[2] "Erubescat error vester Christianis, qui ne animalium quidem sanguinem in epulis esculentis habemus, qui propterea suffocatis quoque et morticinis abstinemus, ne quo modo sanguine contaminemur vel intra viscera sepulto." *Apol.*, 9; cf. also *de Monogam*, 5; *de Jejun*, 4 and 15; *de Spect.* 13; and see Resch. *op. cit.*, p. 148, where these passages are collected.

[3] *Paed.*, 2, 7; *Strom.*, 4, 15.

[4] One copy went to Asia, another to Rome; cf. Harnack, *Die altchristliche Literatur*, p. 262; and *Chronologie*, pp. 315 f. 323.

[5] Aristides, *Apol.*, 15; Justin, *Dial. c. Tryph.*, 35.

[6] *Did.*, 6.

Thus while there is evidence for a Christian food law before the end of the second century, it is not certain that it existed earlier, and it is in no case, except in Alexandria, connected with the Apostolic Decrees.

Hence the evidence to be derived from the early Christian food law is really in favour of the three-clause text. The theory that the four-clause text is original, and refers to a food law, necessitates the hypothesis that it was altered to the three-clause form because a food law had become repugnant or obsolete. When we find, therefore, that the writers who quote the decrees as a moral requirement, nevertheless did possess exactly the food law which the four-clause form represents, and that it was neither obsolete or offensive to them, we are debarred from accepting this hypothesis. There is clearly no reason whatever why they should have changed the decrees from a food law, if they had ever known them as such ; or, in other words, the three-clause form is presumably primitive, and the existence of the four-clause form is due to the reaction of the food law in Alexandria, first on the exegesis and afterwards on the text of the decrees. It is natural that this corruption should have taken place in Alexandria, because the text in that Church, although sometimes corrupt, escaped the great inundation of glosses—one might almost say commentary—which overwhelmed the text of Acts elsewhere. It was, therefore, free from that addition of the golden rule, which, though textually corrupt, was exegetically not far from the truth, and protected the text elsewhere from the smaller but more pernicious gloss of "things strangled," which by so small an addition converted moral requirements into a food law.

There is one point more to be considered. So far it has

been more or less assumed that the choice must necessarily be between a food law and moral requirement illustrated by abstention from idolatry, murder, and fornication. Perhaps this is correct, but a few scholars[1] take a different position. They explain all the clauses of the decrees as references to various forms of idolatry. They have thus taken "things strangled" as meaning sacrifices in which there was no shedding of blood. It is, however, obvious that the same exegesis could be applied to the three-clause text. The advantage of this line of interpretation is that it avoids the historical and critical difficulties connected with the view that the decrees were a food law, and this argument ought to weigh heavily with those who, on textual grounds, are reluctant to accept the three-clause text. Moreover, as applied to the three-clause text, it avoids explaining blood as meaning murder, and brings it into connection with idolatry. The disadvantage is that there is no trace in early Christian literature that this interpretation was ever adopted. It is, however, not necessary to discuss this point further, as, whichever view of the meaning of the three-clause text be taken, it does not affect the general view which has to be held of the position of the decrees in the Judaistic controversy.

[1] The best statement of their case may be found in Prof. H. Oort's *Het besluit der Apostelsynode*, in the *Theologisch Tijdschrift*, vol. 40, pp. 97 ff. *Cf.* also Sanday, *The Apostolic Decrees*, p. 11.

CHAPTER III

THE EPISTLES TO THE THESSALONIANS

THE chronological position of the First Epistle to the Thessalonians is indicated by St. Paul's reference to Athens in 1 Thess. iii. 1 ff. in which he states that he had sent Timothy to Thessalonica, and was writing to his converts in consequence of the report which Timothy had brought back. It is thus plain that the letter was written during St. Paul's stay in Achaia on his second missionary journey. Moreover, though 2 Thessalonians contains no similar reference to a fixed point of chronology, it so closely resembles 1 Thessalonians that it is usually conceded to be indisputable that, if it be genuine, it must have been written at the same time as, or immediately after the former Epistle. There is, however, some legitimate room for doubt whether it ought to be accepted as authentic.

These facts define the points which require treatment for the historical introduction to the Epistles. It is necessary to consider the narrative in the Acts which describes the doings of St. Paul at Thessalonica together with the parallel passages in the Epistles, and the light which is thrown on the movements of Timothy before he delivered his report to St. Paul. After this an attempt must be made to reconstruct from the Epistles Timothy's report, and, as a necessary preliminary to this attempt, the question must be faced whether 2 Thessalonians may be legitimately used for the purposes of this reconstruction.

I. St. Paul at Thessalonica.

When St. Paul and his companions left Philippi they took the Via Egnatia, which led through Amphipolis and Apollonia to Thessalonica.[1] It is usually thought that the text—διοδεύσαντες δὲ τὴν Ἀμφίπολιν καὶ τὴν Ἀπολλωνίαν—implies that Amphipolis and Apollonia were the two stages at which he broke his journey. But the distance from Philippi to Amphipolis is thirty-three Roman miles;[2] from thence to Apollonia is thirty miles; and the final stage is thirty-seven miles. This, while not physically impossible, would be extraordinarily rapid travelling; if it be accepted as the meaning of Acts, it must be taken to imply that St. Paul was able and willing to pay well for exceptional speed.[3] Therefore, it is quite probable that διοδεύσαντες ought to be taken as meaning that St. Paul broke his journey at Amphipolis and Apollonia in order to preach in those towns, though St. Luke knew of no incidents worth recording in connection with this work. This use of διοδεύειν is parallel to the constant use of διέρχεσθαι, which almost always means "to make a missionary journey," and it is to some extent covered by Luke viii. 1—διώδευεν κατὰ πόλιν καὶ κώμην κηρύσσων, κ.τ.λ. The same comments apply with even more force to the Bezan text of Acts xvii. 1—διοδεύσαντες δὲ τὴν Ἀμφίπολιν [καὶ] κατῆλθον

[1] Acts xvii. 1.

[2] Slightly less than English miles.

[3] Conditions are no doubt worse now in Macedonia than they were in the first century, but the difference for travelling cannot be very great, and nothing would induce me to attempt such a pace, unless life and death depended.

εἰς Ἀπολλωνίδα κἀκεῖθεν εἰς Θεσσαλονίκην. Either this text means, "They made a missionary journey to Amphipolis, came down to Apollonia, and thence to Thessalonica," or it means something impossible—that is, that St. Paul went from Philippi to Thessalonica in two stages, "passing through" Amphipolis.[1]

However this may be, the important point of the narrative both to St. Luke and ourselves is the arrival of St. Paul and his companions at Thessalonica. It is not quite clear who ought to be reckoned as certainly among the latter. In Philippi St. Paul had been accompanied by Silas, who had come with him from Antioch, presumably by Timothy, whom he had brought from Lystra,[2] and—according to the implicit testimony of the "we-sections"—by St. Luke. Of these St. Luke—according to the same implicit testimony—remained in Philippi, and Silas, according to Acts xvii. 4, came on with St. Paul. The case of Timothy is more doubtful: he is not directly mentioned in Acts between Philippi and Beroea, but in the latter place he is spoken of as though his presence was natural, so that he probably came with St. Paul to Thessalonica.[3]

[1] It seems to me to be probable that the Bezan text is here clearly secondary. The redactor thought that διοδεύειν meant "to pass through," and altered the text to bring out this meaning. As a matter of fact, the emphasis is not on the διὰ but on the ὁδὸς implied in the verb. I suspect that St. Luke used διοδεύειν here instead of διέρχεσθαι because he wished to indicate that St. Paul went along the great ὁδός, the Via Egnatia, and that a similar shade of meaning can be traced in Luke viii. 1.

[2] Acts xvi. 1-3.

[3] The comment of von Dobschütz is here very much to the point. "To conclude from Acts xvii. 4 that Timothy did not come to Thessalonica with St. Paul, as has often been done, is to ignore the fact that Timothy is not mentioned in Philippi, where, however, he must have been (so also John Mark in xiii. 7), and is alluded to in xvii. 14 (Beroea) only because the narrative is here concerned with the party of travellers, not with the mission as such" (p. 8, note 3).

The procedure of the missionaries and its result is described in Acts xvii. 1–10: "Now when they had passed through Amphipolis and Apollonia, they came to Thessalonica, where was a synagogue of the Jews: and Paul, as his manner was, went in unto them, and three sabbath days reasoned with them out of the scriptures, opening and alleging, that the Messiah must needs have suffered, and risen again from the dead; and that the Messiah is this Jesus, whom I preach unto you. And some of them believed, and consorted with Paul and Silas; and of the 'God-fearing' Greeks a great multitude, and of the chief women not a few."

The obvious meaning of this passage is that St. Paul preached for three weeks in the synagogue and among those who congregated in the synagogue, *i.e.* the Jews and the "God-fearers." Whether the words *τρία σάββατα* ought to be translated "three weeks" or "three sabbath days," is for this purpose unimportant. Similarly it is really not important whether the ordinary text be read or the Bezan text which distinguishes between the "God-fearers" and the "Greeks."[1] It is, however, to be noted that this distinction is precisely one of the points in which the Bezan text most clearly fails to commend itself, for the "God-fearers" were "Greeks" in any case, and it seems as though, in this respect, the Bezan text was so far removed from the spirit of the first century as not to recognize this fact.

If, then, we follow the plain meaning of the Acts, we must suppose that St. Paul's activity in Thessalonica lasted three weeks, and the result was a few Jewish converts, and a great success among the God-fearers. It is,

[1] It reads: *καὶ προσεκληρώθησαν τῷ Παύλῳ καὶ τῷ Σιλαίᾳ τῇ διδαχῇ πολλοὶ τῶν σεβομένων καὶ Ἑλλήνων, καὶ γυναῖκες τῶν πρώτων οὐκ ὀλίγαι.*

however, argued by many commentators that 1 Thessalonians implies a degree of success which is incompatible with so short a period of preaching. They therefore consider that St. Paul must have spent a much longer time in Thessalonica than the three weeks mentioned in Acts, and that the truth must be that he gave up three sabbaths to the synagogue, after which there was an unrecorded quarrel with the Jews, followed by a longer period, probably some months, of preaching outside the synagogue to the God-fearers and possibly to others. There is, of course, no reason to suppose that St. Luke is infallible ; in other places he has certainly omitted incidents. But here the suggestion of a more prolonged preaching in Thessalonica seems psychologically as unnecessary as it is certainly historically unvouched for. Christianity did not succeed through the slow and laborious efforts of hard-working missionaries, but by the contagion of an enthusiasm which spread from St. Paul to his hearers. St. Paul and Silas must not be compared to men who preach to a heathen population tolerably well satisfied with its creed, or seek to convince minds which are not especially interested, and do not share in the general point of view of the missionaries, but rather to "revival preachers" such as Wesley or Whitefield, who understood and were understood by their hearers, and had a definite message for a clearly felt want. For such men three weeks is long enough for anything; certainly it is long enough to create a considerable body of fervent believers among men who are dissatisfied with their own position—and that is exactly what the God-fearers were. Furthermore, although it is possible that St. Luke accidentally omitted any reference to the preaching outside the synagogue, which is supposed to be necessary, it is remarkable that in Corinth, Ephesus, and Rome St. Luke is careful to mention the conditions of St. Paul's preaching, and to indicate with some precision the point at which he broke with the Jews. Probably, therefore, there is insufficient reason for deserting the testimony of Acts, and we ought to conclude (though with considerable reserve) that St. Paul's visit to Thessalonica was only three weeks[1] or, more accurately, only included three sabbaths, during which he met with some slight success among the Jews, and great success among the God-fearers. As was pointed out on pp. 37 ff., this was exactly what was to be expected; the God-fearers provided, as it were, soil specially fitted for the sowers of the Christian word.

Here is also, perhaps, the best place to draw attention to a small side-light on St. Paul's life in Thessalonica given by the Epistles. In 1 Thess. ii. 9 he says that he supported himself by working night and day, but it would seem that this was not his only source of livelihood, for in Phil. iv. 16 he mentions that the Philippians more than once sent help to him at Thessalonica, and this point may fairly be used by those who think that St. Paul's preaching in Thessalonica must have lasted longer than

[1] *Σάββατα* in xvii. 2, is taken by Zahn (*Einl.*, p. 152) to mean weeks rather than sabbaths. Of course, three Sabbaths imply three weeks, more or less, but I do not think *τρία σάββατα* is likely to mean anything except "three sabbaths." St. Luke uses the plural in Luke iv. 31; vi. 2; xiii. 10, each time in the sense of "sabbath day." At the same time, the point is far from certain, for the genitive, either singular or plural, is used, with a numeral prefixed, to give the days of the week. It is possible that an extension of this use gave the meaning of week to *σάββατον*, but I know no evidence in favour of this (generally accepted) view. *Δὶς τοῦ σαββάτου* is the nearest approach, but here also it is the genitive. See E. Schürer, *Die Siebentätige Woche* in the *Zeitschrift für die neutestamentliche Wissenschaft*, vi. (1905) p. 8.

three weeks, for it is possible to argue with much plausibility that the Philippians are not likely to have sent more than once in so short a time.

The names of some of the converts at Thessalonica have been preserved. Jason seems to have been the host of St. Paul and Silas in Thessalonica, and in Acts xx. 4 Aristarchus and Secundus are mentioned as two of the Thessalonians who went with St. Paul to Jerusalem on his journey with alms for the poor. To these some editors add a fourth—Gaius. Their method of reaching this result is as follows: in Acts xix. 29 in the scene in the theatre at Ephesus we are told that the crowd seized "Gaius and Aristarchus, Macedonians, comrades of Paul (Γ. καὶ 'Α. Μακεδόνας, συνεκδήμους Παύλου), and it is thought that this Gaius ought to be identical with the Gaius in Acts xx. 4. The difficulty is that in xx. 4 Gaius is described as a native of Derbe, and therefore Blass emends the text from καὶ Γαίος Δερβαῖος, καὶ Τιμόθεος into καὶ Γαίος, Δερβαῖος δὲ Τιμόθεος. If this were correct, Gaius was a Thessalonian, for the preceding words are, "And of the Thessalonians, Aristarchus and Secundus," to which would now be added—"and Gaius, and the man of Derbe, Timotheus." The objection to this is that in Acts xvi. 1 Timothy seems to be a Lystran. It is therefore probably better either to make the neat emendation (which is actually found in some MSS.) in xix. 29 of Μακεδόνα for Μακεδόνας, explaining the usual reading as a dittography of the initial σ in συνεκδήμους, in which case it would be possible to regard Gaius in xix. 29 as identical with the Gaius of Derbe in xx. 4, or merely to accept the view that there was a Gaius in Macedonia as well as in Derbe. This latter view has no more difficulty than there is in thinking that there is a Smith in London as well as in Glasgow, and seems to gain in probability if we remember that there was in any case another Gaius at Corinth (1 Cor. i. 14 and Rom. xvi. 23). If this be so, and Gaius was a Macedonian, it is, of course, possible that he was a Thessalonian, though the epithet "Macedonian" may refer to some other town. It is not possible to say with any degree of certainty whether these converts were all of them drawn from the ranks of the God-fearers, or belonged to the Jewish element; but Jason is at all events a name often used by Jews, and in Col. iv. 10 St. Paul speaks of an Aristarchus as belonging to the circumcision, and he may quite well be the Thessalonian who had gone with St. Paul to Jerusalem.

Further tradition as to these Thessalonians is probably valueless, though the Synaxarion and similar works have various details. Jason, for instance, is identified with the Jason of Rom. xvi. 21. His further labours are placed in Tarsus or in Thessalonica, and he is described as bishop of both these places in various sources. According to Clement of Alexandria, he was the protagonist in the Dialogue between Jason and Papiscus. Aristarchus is sometimes described as suffering martyrdom together with St. Paul, sometimes as Bishop of Apamea, sometimes of Lydda or Diospolis in Syria. Secundus seems not to be noticed. Gaius was, according to Origen (*In Rom.* xvi. 23), the first Bishop of Thessalonica; according to the Apostolic Constitutions (vii. 46, 9), Bishop of Pergamum; and according to other tradition, either Bishop of Ephesus or a martyr in the neighbourhood of Antioch.

None of these traditions seem to be valuable. Full references will be found in Th. Schermann's *Propheten- und*

Apostellegenden in *Texte und Untersuchungen*, xxxi. 3, and the same writer's *Prophetarum Vitae Fabulosae* in Teubner's *Bibliotheca Scriptorum Graecorum et Romanorum.*

It is not surprising to find that St. Paul's success aroused the enmity of the members of the synagogue who saw those who were reckoned as already half converted being led astray to a sect of which they profoundly disapproved, and the form which they gave to their resentment is shown in the next paragraph of the Acts,—xvii. 5–10: "But the Jews which believed not, moved with envy, took unto them certain agitators[1] of bad character, and gathered a company, and set all the city on an uproar, and assaulted the house of Jason, and sought to bring them out to the crowd. And when they found them not, they drew Jason and certain brethren unto the Politarchs, crying, These that have turned the world upside down are come hither also; whom Jason hath received: and these all do contrary to the decrees of Caesar, saying that there is another Emperor, Jesus. And they troubled the people and the Politarchs, when they heard these things. And when they had taken security of Jason, and of the others, they let them go. But the brethren immediately sent away Paul and Silas by night unto Beroea: who coming thither went into the synagogue of the Jews."

This account is tolerably plain, but a few points call for some comment. It is not possible at present to be certain what was the exact nature of the crowd in xvii. 5 (*τὸν δῆμον*), though we may guess that it practically amounted to something like an "indignation meeting."[2]

[1] The Greek is *ἀγοραίων*. That it means "agitators" and not "loafers," is probably shown by Plutarch, *Aemil. Paul.*, 38, *ἀνθρώπους ἀγεννεῖς καὶ δεδουλευκότας, ἀγοραίους δὲ καὶ δυναμένους ὄχλον συναγαγεῖν, κ.τ.λ.*

[2] I cannot help thinking that it is possible to read too much into this phrase. Surely the *δῆμος* here is not a special juridical body, but merely the meeting or

In this case it is easy to understand that St. Paul and Silas were prudent in avoiding such an ordeal, for what began as an indignation meeting might easily end as a lynching party. At the same time, their absence had its drawback: it meant that the Jews could bring the case at once before the Politarchs, who were the local, not the Imperial magistrates, and formulate a charge of the greatest gravity, for which colourable evidence could be produced, and that the absence of the defendants appeared conclusive proof of their guilt. The result was —so Acts certainly implies—that judgment went against St. Paul by default, security was taken from Jason not to harbour these suspected persons, and—most important of all—legal ground was afforded for presuming Christianity to be a punishable offence. Fortunately, however, the jurisdiction of the Politarchs[1] was only local, so that their decision did not form an Imperial precedent, and that is probably the reason why St. Luke is careful to mention their exact title; it was essential to the apologetic side of the Acts that he should point out that the Imperial authorities, when they understood the facts, always acquitted St. Paul—in Philippi, Corinth, and Caesarea—and that when he was condemned or punished it was either by a local magistrate, imperially unimportant, as at Thessalonica, or through a mistake which was afterwards rectified, as at Philippi.

Thus St. Paul and his companions had remained in hiding; but after the decision of the Politarchs it was

crowd, whichever we may choose to name it, which had been called into existence by the γοραῖοι.

[1] For the epigraphic evidence for the title, see de Witt Burton, in the *American Journal of Theology* for 1898, pp. 598–632.

necessary for them to escape. They were therefore sent off by their friends to Beroea under cover of night.

In Beroea, according to Acts xvii. 10 ff., St. Paul and Silas again began to preach in the synagogue of the Jews, and at first met with a better reception than in Thessalonica, for "they received the word with all readiness, searching the Scriptures to see if these things were so." Thus many Jews believed, "and of Greek ladies of position and men,[1] not a few." But when the report of this success reached Thessalonica, the Jews there sent to Beroea and broke up the Mission. The result was that it was decided that St. Paul must leave Beroea,[2] and some of the Christians undertook to accompany him to the coast, where he would be able to sail to Athens. Temporarily, however, Silas and Timothy were left behind.

If we may press the exact words of the Acts, when Beroea was left, the plans of St. Paul and his friends were uncertain. Ultimately they went with him as far as Athens, presumably by sea. In this way Thessaly was passed over and St. Paul went directly from Macedonia to Achaia. Probably the reason for this omission is that at this time Thessaly belonged to Macedonia.[3] No doubt the Politarchs' decision was only valid in Thessalonica, but it would probably be known to and have influence with the Imperial authorities. Events at Beroea had shown

[1] Or possibly "of their husbands."

[2] Is it possible that the local authorities in Thessalonica had some power of fetching him to their jurisdiction?

[3] This is probable but not certain. Ptolemy regards Thessaly as Macedonian, and possibly Strabo does so also (this is Mommsen's view, but the point is doubtful). There is, however, no doubt but that it was formerly Achaean. Ramsay thinks it was given to Macedonia in 44. Others suggest a later date, which, if true, is of course fatal to the suggestion made above. (See Ramsay, *St. Paul the Traveller*, p. 234.)

that St. Paul was a marked man in Macedonia, and if Thessaly was part of the province it was wiser not to touch it, but to pass on to Achaia.

The omission to preach in Thessaly has made its mark on the text. Codex Bezae adds to v. 15: "But he passed by Thessaly, for he was prevented from preaching the word to them."[1] Prof. Zahn thinks that this is part of the original text, and moreover deduces from the verb "passed by" (παρῆλθεν) that St. Paul went from Beroea to Athens by land, for he argues, that had he gone by sea, St. Luke would have written "sailed past" (παρέπλευσεν). This argument is, however, not very probable. It is far more likely that the reading of Codex Bezae is merely the comment of some early reader who was struck by the omission of Thessaly. It may be noted that a similar gloss is found in the Armenian catena on the Acts,[2] which reads, "But the Holy Spirit prevented him from preaching, lest they should slay him." In any case, St. Paul and the Beroeans reached Athens, and the latter then returned home, taking a message to Silas and Timothy to join their leader as soon as possible.

It is not necessary for the present purpose to follow the details of the history of St. Paul in Athens. He was not especially successful, and after a time went on to Corinth. Still he was presumably a week or ten days in Athens, and we should expect to find that Silas and Timothy had joined him before he left, but as a matter of fact, we hear nothing more of them in Acts, until in xviii. 5, when St. Paul is in Corinth, we are told that "Silas and Timothy came down from Macedonia."

[1] παρῆλθεν δὲ τὴν Θεσσαλίαν ἐκωλύθη γὰρ εἰς αὐτοὺς κηρῦξαι τὸν λόγον.

[2] See Rendel Harris, *Four Lectures on the Western Text*, p. 47.

It is at this point that it is possible to turn to the Epistles to the Thessalonians and begin to consider the problem of fitting the historical information which they supply into the frame-work of the narrative in the Acts.

This information is contained in two passages in 1 Thessalonians. In the first (1 Thess. iii. 1–2, 5) St. Paul says: "Wherefore when we could no longer forbear, we thought it good to be left at Athens alone; and sent Timotheus, our brother, and minister of God, and our fellow-labourer in the gospel of Christ, to establish you, and to comfort you concerning your faith: for this cause, when I could no longer forbear, I sent to know your faith, lest by some means the tempter had tempted you, and our labour be in vain."

It is tolerably plain that here St. Paul is referring to the same incident in both verses, but in vv. 2 and 3 he speaks in the plural and in v. 5 in the singular. It is, therefore, impossible to be certain whether any use ought to be made of the plural as a proof that Silas and Timothy were present when the decision was arrived at, and that Silas also went away to some unmentioned destination. Usually, however, it is argued that the passage proves that Silas and Timothy did, as a matter of fact, join St. Paul while he was in Athens,—an incident of which there is no mention in Acts. As 1 Thessalonians goes on in iii. 6,[1] to narrate Timothy's return with good news from Thessalonica, it is usually supposed that this verse corresponds to Acts xviii. 5, which describes the coming of Timothy and Silas to join St. Paul in Corinth, and from this the

[1] "But now when Timotheus came from you unto us, and brought us good tidings of your faith and charity, and that ye have good remembrance of us always, desiring greatly to see us, as we also to see you."

conclusion is drawn that I Thessalonians, which was clearly written directly after Timothy's return, was sent from Corinth. According to this theory, St. Luke entirely omitted to mention that Timothy and Silas joined St. Paul at Athens, and that Timothy was sent thence to Thessalonica, and only narrates his return, not to Athens, but to Corinth. From the fact that Acts says that Silas and Timothy, not Timothy only, returned to Corinth, it is also generally thought that Silas must have been sent to some town in Macedonia, probably to Philippi. Thus according to this view the table of events can be drawn up as follows:

1. St. Paul leaves Silas and Timothy in Beroea and goes to Athens, sending a message back to them to join him at once. Acts xvii. 14 f.

2. Silas and Timothy join St. Paul in Athens. Implied by I Thess. iii. 1, not in Acts.

3. St. Paul sends Timothy to Thessalonica [and Silas elsewhere]. I Thess. iii. 1–5, not in Acts.

4. St. Paul goes to Corinth. Acts xviii. 1, not in I Thess.

5. [Silas and] Timothy return from Macedonia to Corinth. Acts xviii. 5; I Thess. iii. 6.

6. St. Paul writes to the Thessalonians from Corinth.

This theory has the advantage of combining both Acts and I Thessalonians without doing violence to either. At the same time, interpretations are probably to be deprecated which attempt to maintain that this is what St. Luke meant, and that he intentionally omitted the arrival of Silas and Timothy at Athens. It is undeniable that a cursory reading of Acts xvii. 14–18 creates not merely the impression that St. Luke omits the return of Silas and Timothy, but also that his narrative definitely implies that their arrival at Corinth is the fulfilment of St. Paul's command, sent to them at Beroea, and if this be so it is difficult to avoid the conclusion that St. Luke is here inaccurate in his account, and that he has confused the arrival of Silas and Timothy from Beroea—which was really at Athens—with the return of Timothy from Thessalonica. Personally, I am inclined to think that this much ought to be conceded, but the point is not of very great importance for the study of the Epistle, as in any case the fact remains apparently certain that it was to Corinth that Timothy returned, and therefore from Corinth that the Epistle was written. It is surely gratuitous to suppose that St. Luke made the further mistake of saying Corinth instead of Athens, and that the Epistle was really written from Athens.[1] The fact that St. Paul says that he was willing to remain alone in Athens is no decisive evidence that he was or was not still there when he wrote, though it makes it slightly more probable that he was elsewhere.[2]

Whatever view may be taken of this complicated little problem, the fact stands out undisputed that Timothy was sent to Thessalonica. Apart from his general desire to know something of the development of his converts, St.

[1] Though this view is not inconceivable, it ought not to be forgotten that the view that Thessalonians was sent from Corinth depends on the theory that "Corinth" in Acts is correct; probably it is—but it is only one word, and no one can be trusted not to go wrong on these details.

[2] It need scarcely be said that there have been many other attempts to solve this problem of the difference between Acts and 1 Thessalonians. For instance, it has been suggested that St. Paul returned to Athens for a short time after he had gone to Corinth, intending to go to Thessalonica; or, that Timothy never reached Athens because St. Paul sent a message to tell him to go first to Thessalonica (so von Dobschütz). Of all these it can be said that they are not impossible, but they seem more complicated and less probable than the usual view. The whole problem defies a final decision, because we have not sufficient data, and opinions are likely to continue to differ as to the greater or less probability of various not impossible solutions.

Paul had a special reason for anxiety in their case. When he and Silas left Thessalonica without appearing before the Politarchs he no doubt took the wisest course ; but he also incurred the disadvantage that he allowed the question of the treasonable nature of his preaching—that is, of Christianity—to be settled against him by default. It is obvious that as neither he nor Silas appeared, the Politarchs were forced to decide between the conflicting accounts of Jason and of the Jews, and the failure to appear of the parties chiefly implicated must have been used with unanswerable effect by the Jews to show that they were right, and that Christianity was a treasonable movement. That was a serious matter for every Christian in Thessalonica, and St. Paul must have known that it was so ; it meant that the Jews had succeeded, for the time at least, in persuading the Greeks to persecute the Christians. Therefore, St. Paul was naturally anxious for his converts, and wished to know in the first place whether, as there was every reason to fear, they were suffering persecution, and in the second place whether, if that were the case, they were remaining steadfast. This is exactly what we find stated in 1 Thess. iii. 2 f. "We sent Timothy, our brother, and God's minister in the gospel of Christ, to establish you, and to comfort you concerning your faith ; that no man be moved by these afflictions. . . . For this cause I also, when I could no longer forbear, sent that I might know your faith, lest by any means the tempter had tempted you, and our labour should be in vain." It is plain that St. Paul foresaw that there must be persecution ; he was anxious to know to what extent it would be pushed, and how far the Christians would stand firm.

Under these circumstances, then, Timothy went to Thessalonica. What report did he bring back? That question can only be answered by reconstructing his report from the hints given in the Epistles, and it is, therefore, first necessary to face the problem of the authenticity of 2 Thessalonians, in order to see whether we are justified in using it, as well as 1 Thessalonians, for this purpose.

II. The Authenticity of 2 Thessalonians.

Ever since the modern criticism of the Pauline Epistles began, this letter has been one of those as to the authenticity of which it has been most generally conceded by impartial scholars that there is legitimate room for doubt, and though the tide of opinion has ebbed and flowed, there has never been any practical unanimity, such as has been reached in favour of 1 Thessalonians. A good account of the various writers who have contributed to the discussion of the question may be found in von Dobschütz's Commentary, pp. 32–36, but the main arguments against the Pauline authorship may be reduced to two: (1) the view that the Apocalyptic passage in the second chapter refers to events later than the life of St. Paul, or is inconsistent with the eschatological teaching of 1 Thessalonians; (2) a comparison with 1 Thessalonians as to literary style, and as to the general characteristics of the community implied by the Epistles.

The argument derived from the Apocalyptic section in 2 Thessalonians has taken, in the main, two forms.

(*a*) It has been said, in the first place, that it is, whatever it means, irreconcilable with 1 Thessalonians. In the first Epistle St. Paul describes the Parousia as imminent; in the second he protests against those who maintain that the day of the Lord "ἐνέστηκε," and says that it will not come before the revelation of the "Man of Lawlessness." Moreover, in 1 Thessalonians St. Paul, though speaking of the Parousia as imminent, says that it will come as a thief in the night,—*i.e.* suddenly and unexpectedly—whereas in 2 Thessalonians he says that he had told the Thessalonians of the Apostasy, and the revelation of the Man of Lawlessness which would be the signs of the Parousia.

These arguments do not seem to bear investigation. It is true that in 1 Thessalonians St. Paul implies that the day of the Parousia is imminent, but 2 Thessalonians does not contradict this; ἐνέστηκε does not mean "is imminent," but "has come," and St. Paul never meant that the day of the Lord was not future, to however close a future he might assign it.

(*b*) In the second place, some critics have maintained that this passage contains the so-called Nero Saga, which is of course later than St. Paul. The main points of this legend are well known: when the Emperor died in A.D. 68, the first feeling of the populace was joy at their deliverance from the tyrant, but in a short time doubts began to arise as to whether the report of his death was not a piece of news too good to be true. The result was that pretenders appeared who gave themselves out as Nero. The first of these appeared in 69, and was speedily destroyed. Another eleven years later, in the reign of Titus, was, according to Zonaras, recognized as Nero by Artabanus, the King of the Parthians; and still later in 88 another impostor almost succeeded in raising the Parthians in revolt against Domitian. After 88 the fact of Nero's death was recognized: but a belief arose that he would rise from the dead and lead the armies of the East against Rome.[1] Finally,

[1] For the history of the Nero Saga in its early stages the main source is

the figure of Nero himself became obscure, and there remained that of a partly human, partly diabolic Antichrist.

It used frequently to be thought that the Nero Saga was in this way the source of the whole Antichrist legend, and it was argued that in this case 2 Thessalonians, which shows clear traces of the Antichrist legend, cannot be earlier than the death of Nero, and therefore cannot have been written by St. Paul. This argument, or something like it, certainly played a great part in the commentaries on 2 Thessalonians in the nineteenth century. But it is unnecessary to discuss it in detail, because W. Bousset to his many services to the study of the New Testament has added this, that he has shown the true history of the Antichrist legend to be independent of the Nero Saga, and far older than the time of St. Paul.

The history of the Antichrist legend is far too complicated to be dealt with here: the main outlines alone can be given. There seems to have been current among the Jews, and among other Eastern peoples, the belief that the "end shall be as the beginning." The sign that the New Age is near at hand will be the repetition of the events preceding the creation. Now, these events comprised a struggle between God and a daemonic being who strove to take the place of God. This is the old Babylonian myth of the strife between Marduk and Tiamat, of which there

Tacitus, *Hist.*, ii. 8 f.; Suetonius, *Nero*, 40; 47; 57. Zonaras, XI 15; 18. (Dio Cassius, LXIV); for the later stage of the belief in Nero redivivus the *Oracula Sibyllina*, books IV and V, and the canonical Apocalypse of St. John. The chief modern literature on the subject is T. Zahn, *Apokalyptische Studien III.* in the *Zeitschrift für kirchliche Wissenschaft*, 1886; Geffcken, *Studien zur älteren Nerosage*, in the *Nachrichten von der königl. Ges. d. Wiss. zu Göttingen*, 1899; and Bousset's commentary on the Apocalypse, in Meyer's *Kritischexegetischer Komm. ü. d. N. T.*, 6th ed., 1906, pp. 411 ff.

are many traces in the Old Testament. It was believed that at the end of this age the struggle would again be renewed, and the victory of God would be the inauguration of a New Age, as it had formerly been of the Creation. Thus we find in Jewish and in Early Christian sources a certain amount of confusion of thought as to whether the Antichrist would be a human or a daemonic figure, and sometimes even a duplication in which a human Antichrist is accompanied or followed by a still more terrible supernatural apparition.[1]

So much is now generally accepted: it still leaves almost as difficult as ever the problems connected with the exact exegesis of St. Paul's words. We are still incapable of giving a decisive answer to the questions whether St. Paul expected a Jewish or a Gentile "Man of Lawlessness," and whether "he that letteth" (ὁ κατέχων) was a supernatural being or the Roman Empire. But these problems may be left on one side for the present purpose. What is important is that the result of the last fifteen years of research is decisively to remove the eschatological argument from the list of possible objections to the authenticity of 2 Thessalonians.

It is, therefore, not surprising that there was in the last years of the nineteenth century a strong reaction in favour of 2 Thessalonians. In 1903, however, this reaction was checked and reversed by the extremely able monograph of the late Prof. Wrede, *Die Echtheit des zweiten*

[1] The two really indispensable books on this subject are Gunkel's *Schöpfung und Chaos* and W. Bousset's *Der Antichrist Legende*, translated by A. H. Keane, *The Antichrist Legend.* The latter book gives very full references to the scattered and confused sources from which the outlines of the myth can be built up. Much the same ground is covered, in a more compressed form, by the article by Bousset on "Antichrist" in the *Encyclopædia Biblica.*

Thessalonicherbriefs.[1] In this it was freely admitted that the apocalyptic section could not be used as the basis of any discussion either of the date or of the authenticity of the Epistle, but the attention of scholars was recalled to the literary problem afforded by the comparison of 1 and 2 Thessalonians. This may shortly be described as a remarkable combination of similarity and difference: the language is largely the same—so much so that it would, if found in two writers, completely justify the theory of literary dependence—but the general tone is quite different—so that no one would, apart from the tradition, ever have suggested that both letters were written by the same author to the same community. The extent of this similarity, which is at once felt on reading the Epistles rapidly through one after the other, may be seen best in the tables given by Wrede[2] (*op. cit.*, pp. 3–36). The dissimilarity can also be felt on a cursory reading of both Epistles, though it is more difficult to analyze, but the main points are: (1) 1 Thessalonians is full of the deepest and most heartfelt sympathy and friendship, but 2 Thessalonians is much cooler, and, as it were, official in tone; (2) 1 Thessalonians seems to imply a purely Gentile community, while 2 Thessalonians shows no trace of Gentile thought, and contains no reference to anything implying Gentile origin, but, on the contrary, shows a strongly Jewish colouring, with—in spite of the absence of definite quotations[3]—perhaps a more strongly marked

[1] In *Texte und Untersuchungen*, N. F. ix. 2. (der ganzen Reihe xxiv. 2).

[2] Holtzmann considers that the only passages in 2 Thessalonians for which no parallel can be found in 1 Thessalonians are 2 Thess. i. 5, 6, 9, 12; ii. 2–9, 11, 12, 15; iii. 2, 13, 14, 17 (*Einleitung in das Neue Testament*, p. 214).

[3] It should be noted that St. Paul's quotations from the Old Testament are

resemblance to the thought and language of the Old Testament than any book in the New Testament except the Apocalypse.[1] There are other points in which a contrast can be observed,[2] but these are the most noticeable, and are the main reasons for the difficulty, so ably expressed by Wrede, of believing that the two Epistles could have been written by the same writer, to the same community, at the same time. If both had been written by the same writer, and the identity of language were explained merely as due to the fact that the same ideas were in his mind when he wrote both letters, it would be almost impossible to doubt that they were written at the same or almost the same time. But the community cannot have changed from Gentile to Jewish, and it is very improbable that St. Paul's tone can have so suddenly altered ; if therefore, so Wrede argued, we accept the tradition connecting the Second Epistle with Thessalonica, we are bound to doubt the Pauline authorship. It is then important to notice that the one passage which presents no parallelism to the First Epistle is the apocalyptic section. Wrede, therefore, suggested that we ought to regard the Second Epistle as the work of some unknown writer, who found that the Thessalonians were too much imbued with an immediate expectation of the Parousia, and therefore wrote a warning that the Parousia could not come before the Antichrist, of whom, it is implied, no sign has yet been seen, while in order to secure attention for his warning

mostly in his polemical passages, and are not due to the nationality of his readers, but to the character of his letters.

[1] Bornemann, in his commentary (p. 461), adds the Epistle of St. James.

[2] See especially the list of twelve points given by Harnack in his *Das Problem des zweiten Thessalonicherbriefs*, in the *Sitzungsberichte der kön. preus. Akademie*, 1910, p. 562 f.

he surrounded it in a mosaic of Pauline phraseology from 1 Thessalonians, and issued it as an Epistle of St. Paul.

This theory of Wrede, set out, as it was, in his own clear and most attractive style, immediately met with a friendly reception, and swung the pendulum back again against the authenticity of 2 Thessalonians. Nor was it for a long time satisfactorily answered: even von Dobschütz, in the 7th edition of Meyer's commentary (1909), did not really make any decisive reply, though he emphasized with truth the strange fact that it is only because we possess 1 Thessalonians that any one doubts the authenticity of the Second Epistle, for there is nothing un-Pauline in it, and the only reason for disputing its authorship is the difficulty of finding room for it alongside of 1 Thessalonians. This may be described as a plea which is perhaps sufficient for a stay of execution, but scarcely adequate for a reversal of judgment.

Recently, however, Prof. Harnack has read a paper to the Berlin Academy which throws a new light on the question. He does not dispute Wrede's contention that 2 Thessalonians cannot have been written at the same time, by the same writer, to the same community as 1 Thessalonians, but, instead of solving the problem by denying the identity of the writer, he does it by a closer consideration of the circumstances of the Church at Thessalonica, and by the suggestion that alongside of the Gentile community implied by the First Epistle there was a smaller and earlier Jewish community to which the Second Epistle was directed.

It is, of course, plain that this suggestion takes the force out of most of the objections to the authenticity of the Epistle, and Harnack's reconstruction of the circumstances which led up to its being sent is extremely attractive. St. Paul ends the First Epistle by adjuring its recipients to see that it was read by all the Christians; and in the immediately preceding verse there seems to be a similar emphasis on the idea of *all* the brethren. It would therefore seem that he was aware of a division at Thessalonica which justified the fear that his letter would not be read to all the community unless he insisted on it. In view of the obviously Gentile character of those whom he is addressing in I Thessalonians, the only probable view as to the minority whom he wished to reach is that they were Jewish Christians. But, suggests Harnack, there is nothing in I Thessalonians which would be especially agreeable to Jewish Christians, and several points which might be obnoxious to them. Therefore, immediately after the First Epistle the Second was despatched for the benefit of the Jewish Christians. In support of this theory one other piece of corroborative evidence can be alleged, though the point is complicated a little by the uncertainty of the text. In 2 Thess. ii. 13 St. Paul says that he is bound to thank God ὅτι εἵλατο ὑμᾶς ὁ Θεὸς ἀπαρχὴν εἰς σωτηρίαν, if we follow the text of BFGP 17 al f vg syr^{hl} Did. Dam. Amb., etc., or ὅτι . . . ἀπ' ἀρχῆς εἰς σωτηρίαν if we follow ℵDEKL al pler. d e g syr^{pesh} boh. arm. aeth. Chr., etc. Merely as a matter of textual criticism, there is about as much to be said for the one reading as the other—probably, if it were merely a question of evidence and lexical probability, most critics would choose ἀπαρχὴν, because it is the more Pauline expression (see Lightfoot's note *ad loc.*), but in practice ἀπ' ἀρχῆς has been followed because of the difficulty of giving an adequate meaning to ἀπαρχήν—"God chose you as a first-fruit,"—for in what sense could the Thessalonians be regarded as first-fruits? The expression seemed not to be true to history in any sense, for they were neither St. Paul's earliest converts, nor were they the first in Macedonia. Therefore interpreters have preferred to think that the passage is a reference to predestination rather than to the facts of history, and to read ἀπ' ἀρχῆς. If, however, Harnack's suggestion be followed, the matter appears in a new light, for the Jewish Christians in Thessalonica were, according to the Acts, the first-fruits of St. Paul's preaching in that city, though they were soon surpassed in numbers by the Gentile converts.

The obvious objection to which this theory is liable is that the address given in 2 Thess. i. 1 is "To the Church of the Thessalonians," just as it is in 1 Thess. i. 1, and Harnack suggests that we ought to regard this as probably not original. He points out that the address of Ephesians, (and, it might be added, of Romans) shows signs of having been tampered with, and that that of the Epistle to the Hebrews has been wholly lost. He thinks that the original address may have been τῇ ἐκκλησίᾳ τῶν Θεσσαλονικέων τῶν ἐκ τῆς περιτομῆς, and that the last four words dropped out early in the tradition of the Epistle. An alternative suggestion might be that the bearers of the Epistle were given special instructions, or that the name of the individual to whom it was sent secured that it would reach the Jewish Christians; it may have been inexpedient in the letter itself to emphasize the difference between the two classes of Christians.

As Harnack himself admits, his theory is open to some objections, but on the whole it seems to be far more acceptable than any other which has yet been put forward, and whereas before its publication the balance of argument seemed to be in favour of some such hypothesis as that of Wrede, and against the authenticity of 2 Thessalonians, the situation is now reversed, and there is sufficient justification for accepting the Epistle as a genuine document belonging, together with 1 Thessalonians, even if not so certainly, to the earliest period of Christian life in Thessalonica. In any case, however, the point which it is most desirable to emphasize is that the main argument against the Epistle is the difficulty of imagining circumstances to account for its curious combination of likeness to and difference from the First Epistle—and such an argument is too negative to be ever quite decisive; while, on the other hand, the main argument in favour of it is traditional ascription, which, however highly it be valued, is insufficient to give absolute confidence, if it be impossible to present a probable reconstruction of the circumstances under which the letter was written. Harnack has succeeded in producing a reconstruction which is, at the least, not impossible, and therefore we are justified in using 2 Thessalonians in reconstructing Timothy's report, even though it must be conceded that points derived exclusively from it have not the same certainty as those derived from the First Epistle.

III. The Report brought by Timothy from Thessalonica.

It is very probable, on general grounds, that Timothy brought back with him a letter from Thessalonica to St. Paul, and that 1 Thessalonians is in part an answer to it. Nor are hints wanting in the Epistle that this was actually the case. Far the most cogent of these is the expression in 1 Thess. ii. 13—διὰ τοῦτο καὶ ἡμεῖς εὐχαριστοῦμεν—in which the proper force of the καὶ ἡμεῖς can be given only if we assume that St. Paul means, "we give thanks just as you say that you do." Besides this the analogy of 1 Corinthians (see p. 136) suggests that the paragraphs beginning, οὐ θέλομεν δὲ ὑμᾶς ἀγνοεῖν, ἀδελφοί, περὶ τῶν κοιμωμένων, κ.τ.λ. (1 Thess. iv. 13), and περὶ δὲ τῶν χρόνων καὶ τῶν καιρῶν, κ.τ.λ. (1 Thess. v. 1), may be direct references to questions in a letter.[1] Thus it is probable that Timothy's verbal report was supplemented by a letter from the Thessalonians, though it is clearly impossible—and fortunately not very important—to distinguish with any certainty between items derived from the various sources of information with which St. Paul was thus supplied.

On the subject of persecution and the attitude of the Christians it proved that St. Paul's forebodings were correct. The persecution had been serious, so that it could fairly be compared to that of the prophets of old,[2] and of the Christians in Palestine. "For ye, brethren," is St. Paul's comment[3] on, or, one might almost say, quotation from the report, "became imitators of the Churches of God which are in Judaea in Christ Jesus, for ye also suffered the same things of your own countrymen as they did of the Jews, who both killed the Lord Jesus, and the prophets, and drove out us, and please not God, and are contrary to all men." It is clear from this passage that St. Paul is addressing

[1] The most complete exploitation of this theory will be found in Dr. Rendel Harris's article, "A Study in Letter-writing," in the *Expositor* for September, 1898.

[2] I am not sure that this is a right interpretation; the "prophets" may refer to Christian prophets, such as St. James the son of Zebedee, or St. Stephen.

[3] 1 Thess. ii. 14 f.

a Gentile community, and that they were suffering persecution from their fellow Greeks, even though the burst of indignation against the Jews shows that St. Paul recognized that the latter were—as Acts explains—ultimately responsible. Probably we shall not be wrong if we go a step further, and say that this persecution had already led to the martyrdom of some Christians. This is certainly suggested by the reference to the death "of the Lord Jesus and of the prophets," and perhaps also by the difficult expression in 1 Thess. iv. 13, τοὺς κοιμηθέντας διὰ τοῦ Ἰησοῦ. It is extremely probable that here διὰ τοῦ Ἰησοῦ ought to be taken closely with κοιμηθέντας, but it is less certain (though, on the whole, I believe it to be probable) that it means martyrdom rather than (as the R.V. takes it) a natural death in the faith of Jesus.[1]

So far the news brought back by Timothy was distressing enough; but it was partly compensated for by the fact that the Christians were standing firm, so that their constancy under persecution was famous among all the brethren in Macedonia and Achaia (1 Thess. i. 2–8, which describes, not only the original conversion of the Thessalonians, but also the permanent effects of it, up to the time when the Epistle was written).

1 Thessalonians is primarily comment on and answer to Timothy's report as to the Gentile Christians; in 2 Thessalonians[2] we can probably see what he had to say

[1] The objection that κοιμηθέντας implies a peaceful death, and therefore not martyrdom, is unsupported either by literary or psychological criticism. The same word is used of the death of St. Stephen (Acts vii. 60), and a martyr's death is, as a rule, pre-eminently peaceful. There is no doubt disturbance and distress, but it is not the martyr who feels them. The real difficulty is rather the curious genitival phrase, διὰ τοῦ Ἰησοῦ—in what sense διά?

[2] The warning on p. 86 must be repeated that this, and all other reference to 2 Thessalonians, is based on the hypothesis that the Epistle is genuine,

as to the persecution of the Jewish Christians. They also were suffering from persecution, and it is possible that the reference in 2 Thess. i. 8, to the persecutors as those who "know not God," ought to be taken as a sign that they were Gentiles. Moreover, St. Paul repeats—perhaps one may say, is careful to repeat—the commendation given to the Gentile Christians for their steadfastness; the Jewish Christians were not their inferiors in this respect.

Thus the news brought by Timothy was consoling, both as to Gentile and Jewish Christians so far as their constancy under the pressure of persecution was concerned; but if we piece together the indications in the Epistles we can see that on some other points his information was less satisfactory.

Timothy reported that there was a line of cleavage between the Gentile and Jewish parts of the community.[1] So much was this the case that it was necessary for St. Paul to insist strongly when writing to the Gentile half (in 1 Thessalonians) that his letter should be read by *all* the brethren, and that his readers should greet *all* the brethren with a holy kiss (1 Thess. v. 26 f.). Possibly also traces of the same anxiety for the unity of the community may be found in the emphatic injunctions "to abound in love to each other and to all" (1 Thess. iii. 12), and "ever to pursue that which is good for each other and for all" (1 Thess. v. 15). Conversely it is possible to see a trace of the same feeling in 2 Thessalonians in the notice drawn

and that Harnack's theory is correct. But this is by no means so certain as the authenticity of 1 Thessalonians; and to this extent the whole of the reconstruction of Timothy's report varies in probability according to the Epistle on which it is based.

[1] This, again, is based on Harnack's theory of 2 Thessalonians, and cannot be regarded as certain.

to the signature guaranteeing the letter, as if the Jewish Christians were suspicious of anything coming from the Gentile community. Possibly we ought even to agree with Harnack that the Epistles imply that the Jewish and Gentile parts of the community rarely or never met together for common intercourse.

To this separateness of the Jewish and Gentile Christians from each other must be ascribed the fact that 2 Thessalonians was ever written. Obviously it was not necessary to instruct Jews, who believed in a Messiah, in the doctrine of a Resurrection, nor is it in the least probable that their conversion had led them to adopt a lax standard of morality, such as would justify St. Paul in urging them to abstain from fornication. Moreover, St. Paul's statement as to the Parousia was, no doubt, defective[1] from the Jewish point of view in that it omitted a statement of the necessary development of evil in the days immediately preceding the coming of Messiah. St. Paul seemed to have felt these objections, and to have perceived that his first letter, in spite of his personal good will, might actually tend to increase the division in the community, and, therefore, he wrote 2 Thessalonians, immediately after the First Epistle, repeating much of what he had already said, but omitting that which might be offensive to Jewish Christians, or was in any case unnecessary, and adding the section about the Antichrist in order to show that he did not intend to give teaching contrary to the general faith of the Jews as to the Parousia.

[1] Bousset's work is here the necessary complement of Harnack's: if we did not know that an expectation of an Antichrist was common among the Jews, we should be unable to understand why St. Paul's teaching as to the Parousia in 1 Thessalonians could be regarded as defective.

Timothy had to report that the main subject of interest in the community at Thessalonica was eschatological; St. Paul's preaching[1] had, no doubt, been that of all the earliest Christians—that the kingdom of God, with its sudden dramatic judgment, and the catastrophic end of society as it was then, was close at hand, and that it was the especial privilege of Christians that their master would be the King in this kingdom. So emphatic had been this preaching of the immediate coming of the kingdom, that it had, no doubt, given colour to the accusation of treason brought against St. Paul, and it had driven the thought of death and its relation to the kingdom out of the minds of the Gentile converts. When, therefore, some of the brethren died—possibly as martyrs—the question arose what their fate would be. Such is clearly the question implied by 1 Thess. iv. 13, "Now we wish you not to be ignorant, brethren, concerning those that sleep, in order that you may not mourn, as do the others that have no hope." But the implications of this fact are not so simply seen.

It is difficult to realize that there was a period in the early history of Christianity when convinced and enthusiastic believers did not necessarily look forward to the resurrection of the "faithful departed," and that this subject was so much at or beyond the circumference rather than the centre of Christian preaching that St. Paul was obliged to supplement his teaching on the point by written instruction. Yet it is intelligible if we consider that the hope of the first Christians was not that they should pass through

[1] Cf. the summary which he gives himself in 1 Thess. i. 9, as to the result —which he regards as satisfactory—of his preaching: "Ye turned to God from idols, to become the servants of a living and real God, and to await His Son from heaven, whom He raised from the dead, Jesus, who saves us from the coming wrath."

death to life, but that they should pass, without dying, from life temporal to life eternal, when the kingdom of God was established, and death, which was the result of sin, not an essential feature of man's nature, was abolished. The hope and belief of the first Christians was that they were proleptic members of that kingdom, and that it was but a short time before its glories would become manifest. It was, moreover, just at this point that there was originally a fundamental difference between Christianity and the "Mystery Religions." The latter also offered men eternal life, and a proleptic participation in its blessings; but they offered its full realization only through the Way of Death, along which the traveller was guarded by the magic formulae communicated to him in Mysteries. The Oriental mysteries offered a "medicine of immortality," but it was an immortality through death, and not over death. Thus the fact that the Gentile Christians in Thessalonica were distressed by the question of the "faithful departed" is a proof that they had accepted Christianity as something different from the Mystery Religions. In this respect they offer a contrast to some of the Corinthian Christians (see pp. 215 ff.). When, therefore, cases of death were found among them, the survivors began to ask whether they ought to add to their eschatological hope a further, or alternative, promise of life through death, similar to that of the Greek Mysteries, or to accept the Jewish doctrine of a resurrection of the dead at the Parousia—a view which was still strange to Gentile minds.

It was therefore necessary for St. Paul to point out to his converts that the latter was the true answer, even though he makes it plain that he regards as the norm survival until the coming of the kingdom, rather than death and resurrection into the kingdom (cf. 1 Thess. vi. 15).

In this case we probably have another side-light on the clash of opinion between three factors. First, the really primitive point of view of the first Christians who expected a triumph of Life over Death, by which they would pass directly into the Kingdom without dying; secondly, the natural expansion of this view along Jewish lines which postulated a physical resurrection[1] for those who died before the coming of the Kingdom; and thirdly, an expansion along Hellenistic or rather Graeco-Oriental lines, which treated the promise of Christianity for those who died as parallel to that of the Mysteries which offered eternal life through death, and so left no room for the idea of a resurrection. It is interesting to note that the development of Christian doctrine united the two last factors. The belief in an ultimate, though remote, day of judgment and of resurrection represents the originally Jewish factor, and the belief in a Paradise of rest and joy for the faithful departed until the Great Day represents the weakened survival of the originally Greek factor which emphasized the idea that eternal life is given by the Sacraments, and that for the initiated Dying is not Death but the passage into a wider and a freer life.

Among the Jewish part of the community, if we may take 2 Thessalonians as a guide, there was—as indeed might have been expected—an equal interest in the eschatological expectation of the coming of the Kingdom, though it is not easy to define it exactly. The passage

[1] The Apocalypse of Baruch shows that the Jewish idea, at least in some circles, was a resurrection of the dead in the form in which they died, followed by a speedy transfiguration into a more glorious condition.

which is important is 2 Thess. ii. 2: "Now I beseech you, brethren, by the coming of our Lord Jesus Christ, and our meeting with Him, that ye be not quickly moved in your mind, or shaken, either by a spirit (of prophecy) or by a 'saying,' or by a letter, as though from me, to the effect that the day of the Lord has set in (ἐνέστηκεν)." The meaning of ἐνέστηκεν is here a difficulty. It cannot be denied that it means "is present" as distinct from "is future" (cf. the usual antithesis between τὰ ἐνεστῶτα and τὰ μέλλοντα, Rom. viii. 38; 1 Cor. iii. 22; Gal. i. 4), but it is impossible to think that any one believed that the Day of the Lord was already come in the sense of the last judgment. The answer to these difficulties is, however, found in the more accurate consideration both of the linguistic and of the dogmatic point. The meaning of ἐνέστηκεν is "is present"—not "is future," or even "is imminent," and also not "is already past"; and the "Day of the Lord" meant not merely the last judgment, but a whole complex of events leading up to the final *dénouement*—it was a "day" in the sense of a "period of time." Thus the meaning of ἐνέστηκεν ἡ ἡμέρα τοῦ Κυρίου may be paraphrased as "we are living in the day of the Lord," and St. Paul's answer is that he rejects this view, and that nothing which he has written must be interpreted as giving it any support, because before the day of the Lord the Man of Lawlessness must be revealed. His position is that the Day of the Lord is imminent—it will, he imagines, come before his own death—but it has not yet come.

What were the reasons which made it necessary for St. Paul to emphasize this point? Two explanations are possible, and it is hard to say which of the two is the more probable. They turn on the interpretation of δι' ἐπιστολῆς ὡς δι' ἡμῶν in 2 Thess. ii. 2.

It is possible that Timothy reported that there were in circulation forged letters, purporting to be from St. Paul, stating that the Day of the Lord had already begun. If so, we must connect with this passage 2 Thess. iii. 17, in which St. Paul draws attention to his handwriting as a guarantee of the genuineness of the letter. "The 'greeting' is in my own—Paul's—hand. This is the sign of genuineness in all my letters—my own handwriting." It must be remembered that letters were, as a rule, dictated (*e.g.* Tertius was the actual scribe of the Epistle to the Romans), so that, unless it was known that some part of the letter was in the actual hand of the sender, identity or difference of script was no proof for or against the genuineness of a communication. It is, however, difficult to see why St. Paul should have written in this way to the Jewish part of the community, rather than to the whole Church, and this view is therefore less acceptable if Harnack's theory be adopted, than on the older (and probably untenable) theory that 2 Thessalonians was written a little later than 1 Thessalonians to the whole community.

The alternative view, which Harnack recommends, is that after St. Paul had written 1 Thessalonians, either before or immediately after sending it, he noticed that his remarks on the Day of the Lord in 1 Thess. v. 1 ff. were open to misconstruction, and that this misconstruction would be especially obnoxious to the Jewish Christians. In this case the reference in δι' ἐπιστολῆς ὡς δι' ἡμῶν is to an erroneous interpretation of 1 Thessalonians, not to the possible existence of forged letters.[1]

[1] The fact that neither of these alternative views is quite satisfactory is in

If this view be adopted Timothy must have reported to St. Paul that there was a tendency among the Thessalonians to regard the "Day of the Lord" as having already begun, and pointed out as a criticism on 1 Thessalonians, after it had been already dictated, that it might seem to encourage this mistake. If so we have here a curious parallel to Hymenaeus and Philetus (in 2 Tim. ii. 18), who said that the Resurrection had already taken place, and it is instructive to compare this point of view with that implied in the reference in 1 Cor. xv. to those who doubted if there would be a resurrection.

It is also possible that in connection with the danger of a misinterpretation of 1 Thessalonians Timothy was obliged to report that among the Gentile Christians there was a tendency to throw doubt on St. Paul's motives. The suggestion is that when St. Paul wrote in 1 Thess. ii. 5 ff., "For neither at any time were we found using words of flattery, as ye know, nor a cloke of covetousness, God is witness. . . . For ye remember, brethren, our labour and travail: working night and day, that we might not burden any of you, we preached unto you the gospel of God," he was hinting that there were some who suggested that he had been animated by the motives which he disclaims and had forgotten the unselfish conduct to which he refers. This is by no means improbable, though we have no means of extracting any further information from the Epistle, and it is possible that St. Paul is not rebutting accusations

itself an argument for Wrede's opinion that 2 Thessalonians is not genuine. Certainly he can explain this particular difficulty better than it is possible to do on the theory of its Pauline authorship. But, then again, he fails, as these views do not, to explain the other features in 2 Thessalonians which seem to be strikingly Pauline. The whole problem is very difficult. No theory is without its weak point, and certainty is unattainable.

against himself, but hinting that his conduct and preaching affords a pleasant contrast to that of other teachers to whom the Gentile Christians were inclined to listen. In either case we have a hint that tendencies were at work at the community of which St. Paul did not approve, and that he endeavoured to find the antidote by reminding his readers of his own example. The question then arises whether we can identify these tendencies.

The first point which attracts attention is the emphatic warnings against immorality in 1 Thess. iv. 3 ff. It is possible that this is merely a general warning against the weakness of human nature; but it is more probable that it is connected with a tendency to regard Christianity as an *opus operatum* after which no material act can affect the spiritual welfare of the believer. Such an attitude would be natural if there were any tendency to regard Christianity solely as a Mystery Religion, and its influence can be traced in several of the Pauline Epistles. In this case we have to consider that in Thessalonica a tendency (more fully described on pp. 176 ff.) was already at work, which pressed in an illegitimate manner the preaching of freedom, and regarded St. Paul as weak and narrow-minded in his attitude towards what was regarded as a merely carnal morality unworthy of attention from the truly spiritual.

Besides this danger of immorality St. Paul warns his readers against neglecting their ordinary work. It is not plain what was the cause of this tendency to idleness: it has often been suggested that it was due to the vivid expectation of the Parousia, which made men regard it as unnecessary to busy themselves with the affairs of a world which would so soon cease to exist. That a vivid expectation of the end has sometimes led to this result is undeniable: Hippolytus [1] narrates the story of a bishop in Pontus who announced that the Parousia would come before the end of the year, with the result that many Christians, who had sold their possessions, were in the end reduced to beggary. But there is no special reason for thinking that this was the case in Thessalonica. In the First Epistle [2] St. Paul says: "But we exhort you, brethren, that ye abound more and more, and that ye study to be quiet and to do your own business and to work with your own hands, even as we charged you, that ye may walk honestly towards them that are without, and may have need of nothing." If this passage followed the eschatological section it might be legitimately supposed that the restlessness described was the result of the expectation of the Parousia, but as a matter of fact it precedes it, and therefore there is no decisive reason for supposing that St. Paul is speaking of "eschatological restlessness and idleness"—if the expression may be used.

A comparison with other passages in early Christian literature suggests a different explanation. It is clear from 1 Corinthians (see p. 223) as well as from 1 Thessalonians and 2 Thessalonians, that St. Paul found it desirable to avoid slander by never being indebted to his converts, and that there were other Christians who by no means followed his example. Moreover, in the later literature, especially in the Didache and the Shepherd of Hermas, there are traces in abundance of an unpleasant type of "professional Christian" who lived on the community. It is not impossible that Timothy's report roused St. Paul's suspicion that this danger was present in Thessalonica,

[1] Commentary on Dan. iv. 19.
[2] 1 Thess. iv. 4 f.

and that this rather than any "eschatological restlessness" was the source of the idleness against which he warns his hearers.

However this may be—and the data are insufficient to allow of a decision—in 2 Thessalonians more emphasis is laid on this question. In 2 Thess. iii. 6–12 he says: "Now we command you, brethren, in the name of our Lord Jesus Christ, that ye withdraw yourselves from every brother that walketh disorderly, and not after the tradition which they received of us. For yourselves know how ye ought to follow us: for we behaved not ourselves disorderly among you; neither did we eat any man's bread for nought; but wrought with labour and travail night and day, that we might not be chargeable to any of you: not because we have not the right, but to make ourselves an ensample unto you to follow us. For even when we were with you, this we commanded you, that if any would not work, neither should he eat. For we hear of some which walk among you disorderly, who work not at all, but are busybodies. Now them that are such we command and exhort by our Lord Jesus Christ, that with quietness they work, and eat their own bread."

This passage cannot be said to add anything to the information given in 1 Thessalonians: nor does it help us to decide whether we have to do with "eschatological unrest," or an undesirable "professionalism," which led men to spend all their time in exciting religious discussions, and to neglect their own affairs. But it puts far more stress on the whole question, and if Harnack's theory be adopted, we are obliged to conclude that this evil was especially present in the Jewish rather than the Gentile part of the community. There is no reason for rejecting this conclusion, even though one would perhaps have rather expected to find restlessness and idleness in Gentile circles. At the same time, it is only fair to notice that this again is one of the strong points against the genuineness of 2 Thessalonians. The natural conclusion from a comparison of the passages in 1 and 2 Thessalonians is that there was a development of the evil in question; but this implies an interval between the two Epistles, and it is generally conceded that if both Epistles are Pauline they must have been written almost at the same time.

Thus Timothy's report may be summed as covering the following points: (1) The persecution of the Christians in the community. (2) The division between the Jewish and Gentile Christians. (3) The anxiety in the community concerning the Parousia, and the fate of those who died before it. (3) The existence of either forged letters, or the probability of doubt as to the meaning of 1 Thessalonians. (4) The evil tendencies in the community to immorality (especially in the Gentile section) and to an idle restlessness especially, but not exclusively, in the Jewish section.

The two Epistles are the comment of St. Paul on this report, and were presumably written soon after Timothy joined St. Paul, according to Acts, in Corinth. The order of events which the foregoing discussion has made appear the most probable may finally be summarized as follows:—

1. St. Paul arrived at Thessalonica in the company of Silas (and possibly Timothy).

2. Three weeks' preaching in Thessalonica with the synagogue as headquarters, some success among the Jews, and much among the God-fearers.

3. The Jews accuse the Christians, before the Politarchs, of treason to the Roman Emperor; security is taken from Jason, and St. Paul and Silas are condemned by default.

4. St. Paul and Silas (and Timothy?) go to Beroea.

5. The Jews from Thessalonica force St. Paul to leave Beroea.

6. The Beroeans take St. Paul to Athens: Silas and Timothy remain.

7. St. Paul sends a message back to Silas and Timothy to join him in Athens.

8. Silas and Timothy come to Athens.

9. Timothy is sent to Thessalonica, Silas probably to Beroea or Philippi.

10. St. Paul leaves Athens and goes to Corinth.

11. Timothy and Silas join St. Paul at Corinth.

12. On hearing Timothy's report, St. Paul sends 1 Thessalonians to the Gentile Christian community in Thessalonica.

13. Almost immediately after sending 1 Thessalonians St. Paul sends 2 Thessalonians to the Jewish Christian community in Thessalonica.

LITERATURE.—The best commentaries are those of E. von Dobschütz, in Meyer's *Kritischexegetisch kommentar über das Neue Testament*, 1909; G. Milligan, 1908; W. Lueken in J. Weiss' *Schriften des N. Ts.*; P. W. Schmiedel, in Holtzmann's *Handkommentar* (1891); and J. B. Lightfoot, in his posthumous *Notes on the Pauline Epistles*. Older and only slightly less valuable works are fully given by E. von Dobschütz (pp. 49–56) in his chapter *Zur Geschichte der Auslegung*. Apart from commentaries, attention may especially be called to Lightfoot, *The Churches of Macedonia*, and *The Church of Thessalonica* in his *Biblical Essays*; W. Lütgert, *Die Enthusiasten in Thessalonich*, in *Beiträge zur Förderung christlicher Theologie*, xiii. 6 (1909); W. Wrede, *Die Echtheit des zweiten Thessalonicherbriefs*, in *Texte und Untersuchungen*, xxiv. 2; A. Harnack, *Das Problem des zweiten Thessalonicherbriefs*, in the *Sitzungsberichte der konigl. preuss. Akademie zu Berlin*, 1910.

CHAPTER IV.

CORINTH.

NONE of the Epistles of St. Paul afford us such ample material for reconstructing the general outlines of Christianity among converts from heathenism as do 1 and 2 Corinthians. There are, of course, many points which will always remain doubtful; but the main difficulty is rather an *embarras de richesse*, and the danger of obscuring the main picture by too close an attention to details. The investigator has two main tasks: first, to trace the course of the current of incident which flows through the Epistles; and secondly, to discover the various points of view which explain the obvious clash of opinions which gave rise to these incidents. Both tasks can only be accomplished by a series of discussions of small problems, followed by the welding together of the results in the form of general conclusions.

The clearest way of proceeding seems to be to divide the discussion into the following divisions:—

I. The foundation of the Church at Corinth.

II. A short preliminary statement of the series of incidents which explain the existence and character of the Epistles.

III. The critical problems connected with these incidents.

IV. The conditions of thought and practice revealed by the Epistles.

I.

The Foundation of the Christian Community at Corinth.

The story of the foundation of the Church in Corinth circles round three points—St. Paul, Apollos, and St. Peter—and can best be told in connection with them.

St. Paul.—In Acts xviii. 1–18 we have an account of the work of St. Paul at Corinth, which it is possible to supplement in a few details from information in 1 Corinthians. The facts are these: after St. Paul left Athens he went to Corinth and joined the family of Aquila, a Jewish tent-maker—St. Paul's own trade—who, though originally belonging to the province of Pontus, had settled in Rome, and only left it in consequence of the decree of Claudius banishing all Jews from Rome. Of this decree we know something more from Suetonius, who connects the riots which led to it with "Chrestus." This must at least mean that a Messianic movement, such as that of the disciples of St. John the Baptist, had reached Rome, and may even mean that Christians had made their way there.[1] It is therefore exceedingly probable either that Aquila and his wife belonged to this type of Messianic Jews, or that they were actually Christians before they met St. Paul. The second alternative is supported by the fact that St. Luke does not state that they were converted by St. Paul's preaching, though it is of course possible that this is merely an accident. In any case, it was with Aquila that St. Paul lodged.

The centre of his preaching was at first, as usual, the

[1] See Chap. VI.; the whole question is naturally more important in connection with the foundation of the Church in Rome, and is discussed under that heading.

synagogue, and he converted Crispus, the "archisynagogue." This title probably means a rank more or less corresponding to the "Elders" of Protestant churches.[1] But the Jews, as a whole, rejected his teaching, and after a stormy scene he abandoned his preaching in the synagogue and took a room for the purpose next door in the house of Titus Justus, a God-fearer. It must be admitted that he chose a position which was not likely to avoid trouble, though it had the advantage of being easily found by the God-fearer who had previously frequented the synagogue.

St. Paul's preaching met with considerable success among the Corinthians, and continued, apparently without any serious hindrance, for two years and six months, during which time, as has been shown (pp. 73 ff.), the Epistles to the Thessalonians were written. But then the Jews brought an accusation against St. Paul that *παρὰ τὸν νόμον ἀναπείθει οὗτος τοὺς ἀνθρώπους σεβέσθαι τὸν Θεόν.* The accusation clearly was that his preaching was illegal, and the illegality seems to be connected with the manner of his

[1] Ἀρχισυνάγωγος is found in Mark v. 22, 35, 36, 38; Luke viii. 49; xiii. 14; Acts xiii. 15; xviii. 17. In Mark v. (and the parallel Luke viii.) and Acts xiii. 15, it is clear that there was more than one ἀρχισυνάγωγος. Luke xiii. 14 seems to point only to one, but it may quite well mean "the ἀρχισ. who was presiding." The position of the ἀρχισυνάγωγος is discussed by Schürer, *Geschichte des jüdischen Volkes*, ed. 3, II. 436 ff. and III. 49 ff. A distinction must be made between the ἄρχοντες, who were the chief members of the synagogue, roughly corresponding to what we should call the "governing body," and the ἀρχισυνάγωγος or ἀρχισυνάγωγοι, who were responsible for the arrangements for the services of worship. Probably in small communities there was one, in larger communities several. The parallel drawn above between the "elders" of a Protestant church and the ἀρχισυνάγωγοι is quite rough, for the functions of the two classes are not precisely the same, and in the Jewish synagogue there was no "minister." The title of ἀρχισυνάγωγος was also used, at all events later, as a purely honorary title, and even given to women and children. Schürer also gives copious references to inscriptions and articles in technical periodicals. Cf. also his *Die Gemeindeverfassung der Juden im Rom in der Kaiserszeit.*

preaching rather than with the form of worship referred to. St. Luke says, "he is persuading men contrary to the Law," not "to worship God contrary to the Law." Moreover, σεβέσθαι τὸν Θεόν has so usually the meaning "to be a 'God-fearer,'" that it is preferable, if possible, to take it in that way here. If so, we ought to say that the accusation was that "he was making an illegal attempt to persuade men to become God-fearers." It is, so far as I can discover, impossible to see any Roman law which could be invoked to support this accusation. Perhaps Blass's[1] suggestion is right, that it is a reference to the privilege conceded by Julius Caesar to Hyrcanus, the son of Alexander, that he and his family should hold all the privileges "according to their own laws."[2] If so, it is intelligible that Gallio, the Proconsul before whom the matter came, dismissed it with contumely, for this decree had no possible bearing on the question at issue. Gallio regarded the whole affair as a squabble between two sets of Jews, in which he had neither interest nor jurisdiction. After his decision there was a curious incident. "They all took Sosthenes, the archisynagogue, and beat him before the bench." Who beat him? and why? The Bezan text thinks that the Greeks did so,[3] in which case the scene must be explained as an act of triumphant violence on the part, if not of St. Paul's Gentile converts, at least of anti-Judaic Greeks, who would scarcely have intervened if they had had no leanings towards St. Paul's teaching. Such an act would be entirely in accordance with human nature, though

[1] See Blass's Commentary, *ad loc.*

[2] Josephus, *Antiquit.*, xiv. 10. 2.

[3] [α]πολαβομενοι δε παντες οι ελληνες μετα (*sic*) σωσθενην τον ἀρχεισυναγωγον. The Latin of Codex Bezae (the Greek is illegible) has an interesting paraphrase of οὐδὲν τούτων τῷ γαλλίωνι ἔμελεν—"tum gallio fingebat eum non uidere."

scarcely with Christian principles. It was no doubt the latter fact which led the scribes of a few late MSS. to read Ἰουδαῖοι instead of Ἕλληνες, as an explanation of πάντες, and gave rise to the usual exegesis of the common text that Sosthenes was the successor of Crispus, and that the Jews beat him for mismanaging the case. This explanation is almost certainly wrong in so far as it assumes that the archisynagogal office was monarchical, and has otherwise not much to recommend it. The fact is that all we know is that Sosthenes was beaten, but whether by Greeks or Jews, and whether because he was an unsuccessful leader of the prosecution or as a convert of St. Paul, it is impossible to determine.[1] It is, however, interesting to note that a Sosthenes is joined with St. Paul in the opening salutations of 1 Corinthians; this may be pure accident, or it is possible that the Sosthenes who was beaten was already a convert, or, as later legend would have it, that he was afterwards converted by St. Paul.

Other converts of whom we hear are Gaius (1 Cor. i. 14), with whom St. Paul stayed on a later visit to Corinth (Rom. xvi. 23), Stephanas, Fortunatus, Achaicus, and perhaps Chloe, all of whom play parts of importance in the period of the history of the Church at Corinth immediately after its foundation. To these must be added Erastus the οἰκονόμος of the city (Rom. xvi. 23), and possibly also Lucius, Jason, Sosipater, Quartus, and Tertius (Rom. xvi. 21 ff.).

It will be seen from the above facts that the Corinthian

[1] So also thought Ammonius: Ἢ διὰ τοῦτο ἔτυπτον τὸν Σωσθένην, ἐπειδὴ καὶ αὐτὸς ἦν μᾶλλον προστιθέμενος τῷ Παύλῳ, ὡς καὶ Κρίσπος ὁ ἀρχισυνάγωγος, ἢ εἰς τοσοῦτον ἐληλακότες μανίας ὅτι ἀποτυχόντες τοῦ σκοποῦ ἑαυτῶν, κ.τ.λ.—exhausting all possibilities without choosing between them (see J. A. Cramer, *Catena Graecorum Patrum*, iii. p. 306).

Church was, like all the Pauline Churches, partly Jewish, partly Gentile, with the latter element predominating, and the question discussed on pp. 37 ff. of the position of the God-fearers is here also of the greatest importance. It is extremely probable that this class of Gentiles, interested in and influenced by Judaism, supplied in Corinth as elsewhere the fruitful soil on which the Christian mission was able to sow its seed successfully.

Apollos.—As the "second founder" of the Corinthian Church, Apollos must be named. According to St. Paul himself (1 Cor. iii. 6), he sowed and Apollos watered, and Acts xviii. 24 ff. gives us the following account of Apollos' conversion and journey to Achaia, which, in the light of the Epistles to the Corinthians, obviously means Corinth:—"And a certain Jew named Apollos, an Alexandrian by race, an eloquent man, and mighty in the Scriptures, came to Ephesus. This man was instructed in the way of the Lord; and being fervent in the Spirit, he spake and taught accurately the things concerning Jesus, knowing only the baptism of John. And he began to speak boldly in the synagogue: but when Aquila and Priscilla had heard him, they took him unto them, and expounded unto him the Way [of God] more perfectly. And when he was disposed to pass into Achaia, the brethren wrote, exhorting the disciples to receive him: who, when he was come, helped them much which had believed through grace: for he powerfully confuted the Jews in public, showing by the Scriptures that the Messiah was Jesus."

The obvious difficulty of this passage is the apparent contradiction between "teaching the things concerning Jesus" and "knowing only the baptism of John." For this reason some critics have given up the whole story as hopelessly corrupt, but there is no need for such drastic measures, and the difficulty lies chiefly in the fact that the background of the incident is a state of things which is so different from anything existing now, or indeed ever existing except among Jewish Christians, that it is hard for us to realize it.

What is the most natural meaning of "knowing only the baptism of John"? Surely it is that Apollos had come into contact with the disciples of St. John the Baptist, and had been baptized with his baptism. We are apt to overlook the fact that not all St. John's disciples became Christians, and that he had a distinct message. His preaching was primarily eschatological: the day of the Lord was at hand, the Messiah was coming, and His kingdom would shortly be established; it was therefore urgently incumbent on every one to repent and to accept the as yet unrevealed Messiah. That was his message: and it would seem from the synoptic Gospels that St. John did not recognize Jesus as the Messiah, whose coming he had foretold, until after his public career was finished, for the Baptism of Jesus is in the synoptic Gospels a sign to Jesus, not to St. John, and it is only in the later form of the tradition in the Fourth Gospel that the baptism becomes a sign to St. John and to his disciples. The point in common between the disciples of St. John and Christians was their belief in the immediate coming of the Messiah, and the gospel which both of them preached was "to serve a living and true God, and to wait for His Son from heaven." The difference between them was that the disciples of St. John did not identify the coming Messiah with any one who had ever yet appeared, while the Christians identified Him with Jesus, who had been raised from the dead, and had been manifested after His resurrection as that heavenly

Being who would carry out the judgment of God, and inaugurate His glorious kingdom. Apollos, then, ought to be regarded as one of the disciples of St. John, who held all the common Christian doctrine of that day, so far as the coming of the Messiah was concerned, but had never heard that there were those who identified this Messiah with the Jesus who had lived and died in Palestine, and had been glorified by God through His resurrection. The common proof both for disciples of St. John and for Christians for their belief in the coming Messiah was the Jewish Scriptures; and to the latter the Messianic passages in these Scriptures were τὰ περὶ Ἰησοῦ, "the things concerning Jesus," just as they are in Luke xxiv. 27. (" And beginning from Moses and from the Prophets, He interpreted to them in all the Scriptures the things concerning Himself (τὰ περὶ ἑαυτοῦ).") It is of course true that the phrase need not mean this: it might mean " the history of Jesus," as it does in Luke xxiv. 19. But when a phrase can be shown by the exhibition of parallel passages to be susceptible of two meanings, it is usually the best exegesis to take that which makes the context intelligible. Now, it is certain that with the exegesis in Acts xviii. 25, that τὰ περὶ Ἰησοῦ means the history of Jesus, the whole story is unintelligible; whereas, it is quite intelligible, if we take the phrase to mean the Messianic passages in the Old Testament, which to the Christian writer of Acts were τὰ περὶ Ἰησοῦ, though, as a matter of fact, Apollos did not, until he met Aquila, know to whom they referred except that he, whoever he was, was the Messiah. With this interpretation[1] the rest of the story presents no difficulties. Apollos came to Ephesus preaching the

[1] Expounded at length by J. H. Hart, in the *Journal of Theological Studies* for October, 1905, in his article on "Apollos."

eschatological gospel of John the Baptist, and Aquila and Priscilla said to him in effect that all that he said was quite true, but that they were able to add to it the important fact that the Messiah was none other than Jesus, who by His resurrection had become a heavenly being, whose glorified nature had been attested by many witnesses. This was an addition to, but in no sense a contradiction of Apollos' previous teaching; all his arguments remained unchanged, but he was able to add to them "that the Messiah was Jesus." It must be noted that a lack of appreciation of the real situation has led both to a change in the text, in the Bezan text, and to a mistranslation even in the Revised Version. The Bezan text is that Apollos taught τὸν Ἰησοῦν εἶναι Χριστόν, and the Revisers wrote "that Jesus was the Christ," but the text is εἶναι τὸν Χριστὸν Ἰησοῦν, which must be "that the Messiah is Jesus." The same mistake, for it really is nothing less, on the part of the Revisers may be seen in Acts xviii. 5, when they render the same formula in the same way: and the reason in both cases is an imperfect appreciation of the part played by the Messianic belief among the Jews. It is of cardinal importance to recognize that the Christology of the first Christians was, in the main, a body of doctrine well known to the Jews and to the God-fearers before the days of Jesus, and that many of them believed in a Christ—a Messiah—before they ever came into contact with a Christian preacher. St. Paul, Apollos, and the other Christian missionaries were to a large extent[1] on ground

[1] The exception to this is probably the Christian teaching in a crucified, suffering, and dead Messiah. There is little or no proof that this was ever a Jewish doctrine, and that is why the Christian exegetes soon made a new set of "Testimonies" to cover this point, introducing a Messianic interpretation of the passages referring to the suffering servant. The Jews have never accepted this exegesis, which indeed can scarcely claim to be *e mente auctoris* (see further, Chap. VI.).

common to them and their audience when they preached a Messiah, and starting from this generally conceded doctrine, they proceeded to identify this Messiah with Jesus. In this respect they differed absolutely from all modern missionaries, for these usually begin at the other end, and starting from the fact of Jesus argue that He and His history can best be explained in the terms of Messianic doctrine—which is often wholly strange to their hearers.

When Apollos had in this way received the completion of his teaching from Aquila, he appears, according to the usual text, to have formed the desire to go and preach in Achaea. According to the Bezan text, he received an invitation to do this from some of the Corinthians who were then in Ephesus. "And certain Corinthians who were staying in Ephesus besought him to come with them and pass into their country, and when he agreed, the Ephesians wrote to the disciples in Corinth to receive him." Both here and in the ordinary text the word translated "pass into" (διελθεῖν) has the almost technical meaning of making a missionary journey.

Apollos must have had much success in Corinth, for in 1 Cor. iii. 6 St. Paul speaks of him as having watered where he had planted. The information given in Acts and just discussed makes it tolerably certain that his preaching was primarily eschatological; but it is also noteworthy that he came from Alexandria, the headquarters of the allegorical and philosophical Judaism represented by Philo. It is not impossible, therefore, that the tendency to seek for philosophy which St. Paul seems to reprove in the Corinthians in 1 Cor. i.–iv., ought to be connected with the party of Apollos to which he also refers.[1] But it must be remembered that this is

[1] The most extreme statement of this possibility will be found in the article

merely guess-work. It does not follow because Apollos was an Alexandrian that he was a disciple of Philo; all that we know is that he was a disciple of St. John the Baptist, and it is a far cry from St. John the Baptist to Philo, even though we must admit that if the desire for philosophy, to which St. Paul alludes, must be connected with one of the parties mentioned in 1 Corinthians, Apollos is the most likely person, of those whom we know, to have consciously or unconsciously started such a movement.

Apollos does not, in spite of his success, appear to have stayed very long in Corinth, for when St. Paul wrote 1 Corinthians, Apollos was with him in Ephesus, and it was doubtful when he would return to Greece, though he intended to do so when a suitable opportunity could be found.

St. Peter.—Dionysius, Bishop of Corinth in the second century, maintained in a letter to Rome that St. Peter also visited Corinth.[1] It is usual to think that this is merely a deduction which he made from the mention of Cephas in 1 Cor. i. 12. It is quite possible that this is the case, but even so it is doubtful whether it is quite so certain that his deduction was wrong. After all, the existence of a party of Cephas in Corinth, alongside of those of Apollos and St. Paul, does suggest very strongly that Cephas, like the others, had actually been in Corinth. It is no doubt possible that the party of Cephas was one which had only heard of St. Peter; but the question is whether we have any reason for supposing that this was the case. Personally, I

quoted above on "Apollos" by J. H. Hart in the *Journal of Theological Studies* for October, 1905; see further on, p. 231.

[1] Ταῦτα καὶ ὑμεῖς διὰ τῆς τοσαύτης νουθεσίας τὴν ἀπὸ Πέτρου καὶ Παύλου φυτείαν γενηθεῖσαν Ῥωμαίων τε καὶ Κορινθίων συνεκεράσατε. Καὶ γὰρ ἄμφω καὶ εἰς τὴν ἡμετέραν Κόρινθον φυτεύσαντες ἡμᾶς ὁμοίως ἐδίδαξάν, κ.τ.λ., quoted by Eusebius, *Hist. Eccl.*, II. 25, 8.

am very doubtful whether we have, and I think that in this respect we are too much under the influence of Tübingen criticism, or criticism which has unconsciously absorbed much of the principles of Tübingen, even when consciously opposing them. The result has been an exaggeration of the Judaism of St. Peter, and this has in turn created a strong prejudice against any tradition which ascribes to St. Peter missionary activity outside the circle of Palestinian Judaistic Christianity. Nevertheless, this prejudice is not supported by facts. What do we know from the Acts about St. Peter? It is not difficult to summarize our knowledge. He appears, first of all, as the leader of "the Twelve" in Jerusalem; at Pentecost he preaches with success to Hellenistic Jews; he comes into conflict with the Jewish authorities, but in the end succeeds in maintaining his position. He next appears as supporting and following up the work of the Hellenist "Seven," outside Jerusalem, in Samaria and elsewhere, and takes the serious step of admitting a Gentile without insisting on his becoming a proselyte and undergoing circumcision. So far from appearing to be the leader of a Judaistic type of Christianity, he is steadily depicted by St. Luke as favouring expansion and liberality. Going on still further, he is represented as supporting the claims of the Antiochene movement at the Apostolic Council. He then disappears from the pages of Acts, but it is noteworthy that later, when St. Paul returns to Jerusalem for the last time, St. Peter is apparently not present. The fact is that for some reason of his own St. Luke did not see fit to tell the further story of any of the Apostles' labours except St. Paul's. The silence of Acts as to St. Peter after the Council does not imply in any sense that he stayed in Palestine, or did not preach either to Hellenistic Jews or to

Gentiles. Did St. Luke intend to return to the story of St. Peter in that third book which he surely proposed writing?

But, it used to be alleged, the Acts is a "mediating" book; we have here not St. Peter as he was, but a Paulinized version of him; the Epistle to the Galatians gives us truth—shows us that St. Paul and St. Peter were opponents, not allies, and that the latter only preached to Jews.

This contention seems to be greatly exaggerated so far as Acts is concerned. No doubt St. Luke saw history in the light of later events; no doubt, also, he was writing with a purpose, and not merely in order to chronicle facts. But the whole tendency of criticism is to show that he was, according to the standards of his day, a competent and honest historian. It is absurd to treat him as infallible, or to find a deep significance in every change of expression, but it is equally absurd to look for apologetic reasons for every statement, and to ignore the probability that the main reason for most of them is that he believed them to be true. Moreover, the conclusion drawn from Galatians cannot stand investigation. All that St. Paul says is that when St. Peter was in Antioch he gave up his usual intercourse with the Gentile Christians under pressure from the emissaries from St. James of Jerusalem, and that St. Paul rebuked him. So far from implying that St. Peter was the consistent antagonist of Paulinism, or of the Antiochene movement, he is represented as friendly to it, and only yielding under pressure to the extremists from Jerusalem. Nor does the statement that it was agreed at Jerusalem that St. Paul should preach to the Gentiles,[1] and the others

[1] Whether the scene at Antioch was before or after the Council, and whether the agreement at Jerusalem was at the Council, or earlier, are points which are here unimportant (see Chap. V.).

to "the circumcision," in the least imply that St. Peter should not travel in the Roman Empire. "The circumcision" covers the Diaspora, as well as Palestinian Jewry, and even if we suppose that St. Peter always wished to keep strictly and literally to this compact, there is nothing to show that he did not travel all over the Roman Empire, as tradition says that he did, preaching to the Jews in the Diaspora, and finally reaching Rome. But if he did this it is practically certain that he would be brought into contact with Gentile God-fearers, just as St. Paul was, and so in the end would be obliged to preach to Gentiles, however much his original plan may have been to confine his teaching to Jews.

In this case we have to repeat the question,—why should we not think that St. Peter really was in Corinth, and that the party of Cephas was composed of those who had been converted by him, just as the other parties were composed of the converts of St. Paul and of Apollos?

The real objection is probably the feeling that if St. Peter had been in Corinth, St. Paul would have said more about him. No doubt he would have done so had he been writing for our benefit, but in writing to the Corinthians the necessity was not so clear; in writing letters no one expatiates on points well known to his correspondent, but on those which are unknown or disputed. We can see this in the precisely parallel case of Apollos; he had been prominent in Corinth, and also had a party of followers, yet we should hear nothing of him in 1 Corinthians, apart from the existence of his party, if it had not been for the accidental fact that he was in Ephesus when St. Paul was writing. Thus, the absence of further references in

1 Corinthians is no proof that St. Peter had not been in Corinth.[1]

Probably, then, St. Peter ought to be regarded, along with St. Paul and Apollos, as one of the founders of the Church at Corinth,[2] and, at least, we must suppose that some of his disciples had visited the city. It is, moreover, not inconceivable that the use of the name Cephas, not Peter, implies that St. Peter was here also preaching to the Jews rather than to the Gentiles, but this is probably too subtle, for, unless the text in Galatians is corrupt, it would seem that St. Paul used "Cephas" and "Peter" indifferently, and on no fixed principle (cf. Gal. i. 18; ii. 7, 8, 11, 14).

More important, however, than any of these points, and much more certain, is the fact that there is no trace in these Epistles that the party of Cephas (or any other party) was Judaistic, or represented the principles of the stiff Jerusalem Church. This is equally important for the understanding of the Epistles to the Corinthians, and as a corroboration of the view expressed above that the figure of a Judaizing St. Peter is a figment of the Tübingen critics with no basis in history.[3]

[1] It is true that St. Paul says, "I planted, Apollos watered, but God gave the increase," and does not mention Cephas. Still this can scarcely be regarded as a very serious point.

[2] It is curious that Silvanus, according to 1 and 2 Thessalonians, was in Corinth with St. Paul; that he then disappears from the Pauline circle; and that he reappears later (if it be the same Silvanus) in the company of St. Peter (1 Pet. v. 12). Is this because the three Apostles, St. Paul, St. Peter, and Silvanus, met in Corinth?

[3] I should be sorry if these remarks seemed to imply disrespect of the Tübingen critics. There is no school to whom we are so much indebted; and Baur's *Paulus* is a work of genius. But they were not infallible, and in some respects their methods had the roughness of pioneers. Largely owing to their efforts we are able in many respects to improve on their results; but those who speak most evil of the Tübingen school have usually never read their books.

In this way the Corinthian Church was founded and built up, first by St. Paul, afterwards by Apollos, and either by St. Peter or some unknown disciple of St. Peter.[1] For our knowledge of the next period in the history of the community we are dependent on the Epistles, and it is now necessary to turn to them and try to extract from them the history which is behind them.

II.

THE INCIDENTS WHICH EXPLAIN THE EXISTENCE AND CHARACTER OF THE EPISTLES.

The general outlines of these incidents can be stated in a very few words—it is the history of a quarrel. To us the principles which lie behind this quarrel are more important than the actual course of its development; but neither the one nor the other is intelligible, unless the fact be grasped that the Epistles were not written by St. Paul to illustrate general principles, or to give an *exposé* of Christian practice, but as definite attempts to deal with extremely concrete questions, which gave rise to a violent quarrel between St. Paul and the Corinthians. Of this quarrel we can see the beginnings in 1 Corinthians, the middle and the end in 2 Corinthians. Who the persons were who opposed St. Paul must be discussed at length later, but it is clear that the difference of opinion was partly doctrinal, partly practical.

[1] There is a curious reference to St. Barnabas in 1 Cor. ix. 6. It is difficult to think that it hints that St. Barnabas had been in Corinth, though there is no reason why he should not have been; perhaps the best suggestion is that it is a reference to the first missionary journey (see J. Weiss, *Der erste Korintherbrief*, p. 235).

What was the general course of the quarrel? To answer this question shortly the results reached in pp. 120–175 must be assumed for the moment, in the hope that the appearance of undue certainty with regard to much-disputed passages may be counteracted by the later paragraphs in which the difficulties are discussed in detail.

The first step which we can distinguish is a letter, no longer extant (it is convenient to call it the "previous letter"), sent by St. Paul to the Corinthians, warning them against associating with immoral persons. No doubt this letter was led up to by information which he had received from Corinth that such a warning was necessary.

After this he was told by members of the household of Chloe, an unknown person who had some relations with Corinth, that the practical question of immorality in the community remained, that it was complicated by a spirit of partizanship and litigiousness, and perhaps also that his letter had not been fully understood. At the same time, or almost immediately afterwards, three Corinthians, Stephanas, Fortunatus, and Achaicus, arrived at Ephesus bearing a letter for St. Paul, asking him a series of questions on practical and doctrinal problems. No doubt they also supplemented their letter in conversation.

In consequence of these communications St. Paul wrote 1 Corinthians, dealing in the first half with the information given by Chloe, in the second with the Corinthians' letter and the information of Stephanas and his comrades. But before sending the Epistle St. Paul instructed Timothy, who was just starting for Macedonia, to go on to Corinth, and to do his best to remedy the scandals in the Church. He also announced his intention—half hopefully, half threateningly—of himself coming before long to Corinth.

Timothy returned, with the unpleasant news that the situation was worse instead of better, and St. Paul himself hurried across to Corinth. Even this failed, and the crisis appeared desperate. As a last resort he wrote a severe letter to the Corinthians, and sent it by Titus, warning the disobedient members of the Church that he proposed to come again, and this time would know how to secure their submission. It is probable that 2 Corinthians x.–xiii. is part of this severe letter.

Soon after this St. Paul left Asia, and made his way overland through Macedonia to Corinth, greatly longing for the report of Titus as to the Corinthian crisis. Titus met him in Macedonia, and was able to report a complete success. The disobedient had been disowned and punished by the majority and had submitted, the crisis was over, and peace restored, though there was a stern minority which still pressed for severer punishment.

St. Paul was overjoyed, and 2 Corinthians i.–ix. is the outpouring of gratitude and relief which he at once wrote, and sent back by Titus to Corinth, commissioning him at the same time to take charge of the arrangements for a contribution for the poor which St. Paul hoped to be able to take to Jerusalem.

Such is the outline of the history of the quarrel which lies behind the Epistles. It will be necessary in the following sections to go through it in detail, to discuss the various points of which it is composed, and to attempt the reconstruction of a picture of the community, or, at all events, of the opposition in it to St. Paul, and the practical questions which were agitating it.

III.

THE CRITICAL AND HISTORICAL PROBLEMS CONNECTED WITH THE EPISTLES.

These problems may best be treated in two subdivisions, according as they belong to 1 or 2 Corinthians, because whereas those belonging to 1 Corinthians are comparatively simple, those belonging to 2 Corinthians form a complex of difficulties which is not surpassed in intricacy by anything in the New Testament.

1 CORINTHIANS.

The points connected with 1 Corinthians are:—

(1) The "Previous Letter" of St. Paul to the Corinthians.

(2) The information given to St. Paul by "those of Chloe."

(3) The mission of Timothy.

(4) The letter of the Corinthians to St. Paul, and the supplementary information given by its bearers.

(5) The time and place of the writing of the Epistle.

(1) *The Previous Letter.*

According to the Acts St. Paul was eighteen months in Corinth, and, when he left it, he went in the company of Aquila and Priscilla as far as Ephesus, and afterwards alone to Antioch and possibly Jerusalem,[1] returning thence to

[1] This is at least a possible interpretation of Acts xviii. 22, *καὶ κατελθὼν εἰς Καισαρίαν, ἀναβὰς καὶ ἀσπασάμενος τὴν ἐκκλησίαν, κατέβη εἰς Ἀντιόχειαν*, in which Ramsay thinks that "going up" means going up to Jerusalem. This seems at first sight far-fetched: the natural meaning is that he went up from the harbour to the town; but the same view seems to have been held by the Bezan scribe, who makes St. Paul gives as his excuse for not staying in Ephesus, "I must at any rate keep the coming feast at Jerusalem." Perhaps it is right.

Ephesus, where he stayed for three years.[1] It is during these three years that the letters to the Corinthians were written, and that the crisis in the Corinthian Church developed.

The first stage probably was that St. Paul was informed by some friend that the Corinthian Christians had a somewhat low standard as to the morality which they expected to find in their associates, and that he wrote them a letter—the "previous letter"—warning them against this failing.

This Epistle is no longer extant, but the fact that it was written and the nature of at least part of its contents is revealed by 1 Cor. v. 9–11, "I wrote to you (ἔγραψα) in my letter not to have company with fornicators,—not that I meant literally (πάντως) with the fornicators of this world, or with the covetous and extortioners, or with idolaters; for then must ye needs go out of the world, but now I write (ἔγραψα) unto you not to keep company with any man that is called a Brother if he be a fornicator," etc. In the translation just given there is, of course, no room for doubt, but the English, unfortunately, does not convey a point of ambiguity which is present in the Greek. A Greek said ἔγραψα, "I wrote," equally of a letter which he had penned ten years previously, and of one which he actually was writing—in referring to which we should say "I am writing"—because he regarded it from the standpoint of the recipient. It is therefore grammatically possible that St. Paul, in 1 Cor. v. 9, is referring to the letter he is actually writing, but this grammatical possibility is excluded in practice by the fact that there is nothing in 1 Corinthians to which he could be referring, and also by

[1] Possibly "in Ephesus" ought not to be taken too strictly. It may include the district of which Ephesus was the centre (see p. 142 f.).

the general drift of the passage. The translation of the first ἔγραψα is therefore certain; as will be seen the second ἔγραψα gives rise to more doubt.

It is therefore universally recognized that the Corinthians must have received a letter from St. Paul, enjoining on them circumspection in their relations to immoral persons.

That this letter is, in its entirety, lost, is of course obvious, but there is nevertheless some degree of probability in the theory, which has often been put forward, that a fragment of it is imbedded in 2 Cor. vi. 14—vii. 1, which runs as follows: "Be ye not unequally yoked together with unbelievers: for what fellowship hath righteousness with iniquity? or what communion hath light with darkness? And what concord hath Christ with Beliar? or what part hath he that believeth with an infidel? And what agreement hath a temple of God with idols? for ye are a temple of the living God; as God hath said, 'I will dwell in them, and walk in them; and I will be their God, and they shall be My people. Wherefore come out from among them, and be ye separate, saith the Lord, and touch not the unclean; and I will receive you. And I will be a Father unto you, and ye shall be My sons and daughters, saith the Lord Almighty.' Having therefore these promises, beloved, let us cleanse ourselves from all defilement of the flesh and spirit, perfecting holiness in the fear of God."

This passage would clearly be exactly the sort of advice which afterwards would necessitate the explanation given in 1 Cor. v. 9; and the theory that it really is a fragment of the lost first letter of St. Paul, is materially supported by the facts that it has no apparent connection with the immediate context before or after in 2 Corinthians, and that if it be removed, 2 Cor. vii. 2 fits on to 2 Cor. vi. 13 in the most natural manner. If the suggested interpolation be removed, we obtain the text: "O ye Corinthians, our mouth is open unto you, our heart is enlarged. Ye are not straitened in us, but ye are straitened in your own affections. Now for a recompence in like kind, (I speak as unto my children,) be ye also enlarged. Open your hearts to us; we wronged no man, we corrupted no man, we defrauded no man. I speak not this to condemn you: for I have said before, that ye are in our hearts to die and live with you." No one who did not know would ever guess that anything had been removed from the middle of this passage.

Although therefore this theory can from its nature never be regarded as more than a probable guess, it must at least be conceded that the guess is attractive; and its probability is enhanced, if the theory be accepted that 2 Corinthians shows signs in other places of not being originally a single letter (see pp. 155–164).

Besides this hypothesis, J. Weiss, in his commentary on the Epistle, has made the suggestion that other fragments of the "previous letter" are embedded in 1 Corinthians. He thinks that there is so great a difference of tone between 1 Cor. x. 1–22 (23) and the remainder of the section as to "things offered to idols," that he attributes it to a different source, probably the "previous letter," and thinks that vi. 12–20, as well as possibly ix. 24–37 and xi. 2–34, belong to the same document. It must be admitted that there is a difference of tone, but an alternative suggestion (and I think a preferable one) is that St. Paul is addressing two different parties in Corinth (see pp. 199–202), partly agreeing with and partly differing from both, and that this explains the change of tone and emphasis in the various sections. However this may be, the fact that a "previous" letter was written seems to be clearly established.[1] But it must remain permanently uncertain at what time it was sent, though, if it be conceded that it was probably written in consequence of information which St. Paul had received from Corinth, it is clearly almost certain that it was written after his return to Ephesus from Syria.

It is not certain how much of the passage in 1 Cor. v. 9 ff. ought to be considered as a quotation of the "previous letter," nor can we be sure of St. Paul's precise motive in referring to it. The context is the case of the incestuous person (see p. 131), and St. Paul emphasized the enormity of the offence by a reference to the "previous letter," but as to the exact meaning of this reference there are two possibilities. In the first place, it is possible that it had been reported to St. Paul, either by "those of Chloe" or by others, that his letter had been misunderstood, and taken to imply a degree of seclusion for Christians which was practically impossible; in the second place, it is possible that it is really only quoted by St. Paul to strengthen his argument, by showing that he is, in the case of the incestuous person, only asking for the particular application of a rule which he had previously stated and the Corinthians had recognized as generally valid. Between these possibilities a decision cannot be made. It would of course be better, if possible, to treat the two ἔγραψα's in the same way, and it is clear that the first one means "I wrote." This supports the view that the whole passage (v. 9–11) is a quotation, or more probably a paraphrase, from the "previous letter," and ought to be translated, "I

[1] This was seen by the writer of the *Acta Pauli*, who invented an apocryphal correspondence between St. Paul and the Corinthians; see Appendix I.

wrote to you in my previous letter not to associate with evil livers—not literally the evil livers of the world, . . . for then I admit (ἄρα) you would needs go out of the world altogether. But I meant under existing circumstances (νῦν δὲ ἔγραψα) not to associate with professing Christians who were evil livers," etc. This translation does justice to the double ἔγραψα, but it strains the meaning of νῦν δέ. Therefore it is possible that we ought to think that St. Paul is correcting a misunderstanding, that only the first few words are quotation, and that the rest is correction. In this case νῦν δὲ ἔγραψα must be taken as an instance of the common epistolary aorist, and translated, "but now I write." This is the view which is more generally adopted; if it be correct, it is probable that part of the information given by "those of Chloe" (though conceivably by some one else) was that the "previous letter" was not fully understood, and perhaps that it had been adversely commented on as practically impossible.

(2) *The Information given by "Those of Chloe."*

Of Chloe herself nothing is known: the most probable hypothesis is that she was a rich lady, either widowed or unmarried, who had a household of slaves or dependents, some of whom were acquainted with St. Paul and probably had been converted by him. But there is nothing to show whether Chloe lived in Corinth or in Ephesus, for the general conditions of the problem are equally well fulfilled by the view that she was an Ephesian connected in some way—perhaps by business of some kind—with Corinth, as by the more usual guess that she was a Corinthian who had relations with Ephesus. The only point certain—and also the only one important—is that "those of Chloe" were in a position to give St. Paul valuable information about the state of things among the Christians in Corinth.

The extent of their information cannot be accurately defined, but it is at least certain that it laid emphasis on the growth of party feeling among the Christians at Corinth. This is shown by 1 Cor. i. 11–12: "It has been told me, brethren, by the [*representatives*] of Chloe that there are divisions among you. I mean that each says 'I am of Paul,' 'and I of Apollos,' 'and I of Cephas,' 'and I of Christ.'" The view which has to be taken of the information implied by these verses depends on the exegesis given to them, and this is unfortunately by no means clear. The most simple view is that "those of Chloe" reported that the community was split up into the parties of Paul, Apollos, Cephas, and Christ, and in some form this view is now generally taken. The difficulties in it are: (1) the curious statement in 1 Cor. iv. 6, "Now these things, brethren, I have transferred in a figure to myself and Apollos for your sakes"; (2) the difficulty of understanding who the Christ party can have been.

The statement in 1 Cor. iv. 6 has sometimes been interpreted as implying that St. Paul had throughout used the names of himself and Apollos as screens for the real party leaders: but this exegesis,[1] though not impossible, is improbable. The natural meaning is that in the previous section (iii. 18—iv. 5), in which St. Paul warns the Corinthians against an excessive estimate of the importance of himself and other leaders, who are after all merely the "ministers of Christ and stewards of the mysteries of God," his intention was really to warn his readers against a similarly excessive

[1] Made popular by Chrysostom and dominant until the time of Beza, who rejected it.

estimate of their spiritual gifts and personal importance. He does not in the least mean that the parties of St. Paul and Apollos did not exist.

The difficulty of identifying the "Christ party" is greater. In no other passage in 1 Corinthians does St. Paul ever refer to any party which regarded itself as especially that of Christ. And in iii. 21,[1] while purposely, as it seems, mentioning the other parties—of Paul, Apollos, and Cephas—he says nothing of a "Christ party," but continues "and ye are Christ's, and Christ is God's." Influenced by this fact Räbiger[2] has suggested that ἐγὼ δὲ Χριστοῦ in 1 Cor. i. 12 is not co-ordinate with the other phrases. In a writer who pays regard to stylistic propriety such a suggestion would be absurd; but St. Paul's style is far from being formally correct, and I am not sure that the least difficult solution to an exceedingly difficult problem is not to translate and punctuate thus: "I mean that each says 'I am of Paul, and I of Apollos, and I of Cephas,'—but *I* am of Christ! Is Christ divided? was Paul crucified for you? or were ye baptized into the name of Paul?" The advantages of it are that it adds to the force of μεμέρισται ὁ Χριστός; and changes it from a most difficult phrase to an intelligible and well-pointed question, and that it brings the whole passage into line with 1 Cor. iii. 4 (cf. iii. 11) and 1 Cor. iii. 21–23, in which the Paul, Apollos, and Cephas parties are mentioned, but Christ appears only as the bond of common unity in which all the parties ought to sink their differences. It is also supported by the fact that Clement in his epistle to Corinth

[1] "For all things are yours; whether Paul, or Apollos, or Cephas, or the world, or life, or death, or things present, or things to come; all are yours, and ye are Christ's, and Christ is God's."

[2] *Kritische Untersuchungen über den Inhalt der beiden Briefen an die korinthische Gemeinde.* Second edition, 1886.

(xlvii. 3) mentions the parties of Paul, Cephas, and Apollos, but not the Christ party. The objections are, first, that it makes the ἐγὼ in ἐγὼ δὲ Χριστοῦ mean something different from what it means in the precisely parallel phrases ἐγὼ δὲ Κηφᾶ and ἐγὼ δὲ 'Απολλώ, and, secondly, that there seems to be a possible reference to the Christ party in 2 Cor. x. 7, "If any man trusteth in himself that he is Christ's, let him consider this again with himself, that, even as he is Christ's, so also are we." This last passage is not absolute proof that the phrase in the First Epistle really refers to a definite party, for, after all, the claim to be Christ's was the ultimate contention of all the parties, and in an inclusive sense was admitted by St. Paul; it is not impossible that St. Paul here means no more than an appeal to the fact that he and his opponent both relied, in the end, on their spiritual experience —the conviction that they were Christ's. Nevertheless, it certainly is the strongest argument that exists, and perhaps turns the scales of probability against the ingenious and otherwise attractive suggestion of Räbiger. A still more radical suggestion, commended among others by J. Weiss, is that ἐγὼ δὲ Χριστοῦ is an interpolation, and due to an original marginal interjection by a pious scribe. This is possible, though personally I prefer Räbiger's hypothesis.

If these views be rejected, and the existence of a Christ party be accepted, we must clearly take as referring to it 2 Cor. x. 7, which practically means that the Christ party was that against which St. Paul fulminates in 2 Cor. x.–xiii. The characteristics of this party will have to be discussed later (see pp. 219 ff.).

There is comparatively little room for profitable discussion as to the parties of Cephas and Apollos. As was said above (p. 116) it has been suggested that the party of

Cephas represents Judaizing propaganda. This is quite improbable, and rests partly on an unnecessary inference from the use of the name Cephas instead of Peter, partly on a largely antiquated theory of Church history, which invented a double stream in early Christianity under the leadership of St. Peter and St. Paul. That there was opposition to St. Paul is unquestionable, but that it was inspired by St. Peter is more than doubtful. Moreover, if there really had been definitely Judaizing propaganda at this time against St. Paul, it is surely more likely to have taken to itself the name of St. James rather than that of St. Peter.

It has also been suggested that the party of Apollos was especially addicted to an exaggeration of Alexandrian philosophy. This theory is partly based on facts, but it is not clear that reference is especially made to Apollos or his party. The point is that immediately after his direct rebuke of partizanship, St. Paul passes, in 1 Cor. i. 17—iv. 21, into a long section in which it may be said that two themes are interlaced,—the relation of his gospel to "wisdom," and a renewed deprecation of partizanship. Certainly it is clear that the partizan spirit in Corinth was in some way connected with an exaltation of "wisdom," and the bearing of this fact will have to be considered when the opposition to St. Paul is discussed (see pp. 231 ff.); but there is no real evidence for thinking that the "exaltation of wisdom" was especially the characteristic of the party of Apollos. It may have been so; and, if so, it may have been due to his Alexandrian associations, but there is nothing to prove it.

Moreover, if we may judge from the obviously friendly relationship between St. Paul and Apollos (cf. 1 Cor. xvi. 12) it is, in any case, improbable that the latter was, any more than St. Paul himself, the conscious cause of partizanship. It was not the leaders—or at least not those whom St. Paul mentions—who were responsible for the parties, but their rash and imperfectly instructed followers. This, no doubt, did give rise among other things to an undue exaltation of "wisdom," and, as will be seen in connection with 2 Corinthians, helped to produce a very critical situation in the Christian community at Corinth.

This information as to the partizanship in the Church at Corinth seems to have been the chief information given to St. Paul by "those of Chloe." It is evident from 1 Corinthians that he regarded it very seriously, and foresaw the possibility that it might give an unpleasant character to the visit to Corinth which he contemplated.[1] "Some," he says,[2] "are puffed up, as though I were not coming to you. But I will come to you shortly, if the Lord will, and I will know, not the word of them which are puffed up, but the power. For the kingdom of God is not in word, but in power. What will ye? Shall I come unto you with a rod, or in love and a spirit of meekness?" To avoid this possibility he sent Timothy[3] to try to bring the Corinthians into a better frame of mind. But before discussing this visit of Timothy, it is desirable to consider certain points which "those of Chloe" may have told St. Paul, and with which Timothy would certainly have had to deal on his arrival.

These points are indicated in 1 Cor. v.–vi., and may be shortly described as (*α*) an instance either of incest or of incestuous marriage; (*β*) a tendency to litigation among

[1] As will be seen (pp. 149 ff.), his forebodings were probably realized.

[2] 1 Cor. iv. 18.

[3] 1 Cor. iv. 17.

Christians in the heathen courts; (γ) a tendency to immorality.

(α) *The Case of Incest.*—What precisely was the question at issue is not clear. St. Paul merely says, "It is actually reported that there is fornication among you, and such fornication as is not even among the Gentiles, that one of you hath his father's wife." Whether this was incest or an incestuous marriage is not stated, nor is it possible to say whether it was "those of Chloe" who brought the report, or some one else. In any case it would seem that the community had not treated the matter seriously enough. "And ye," said St. Paul,[1] "are puffed up, and did not rather mourn, that he that hath done this deed might be taken away from you." He therefore reminds them of the principles laid down in the "previous letter," and adjures them to adopt a firm attitude in this matter, and exclude the offender from their midst.

(β) *The Tendency to Litigation.*—From 1 Cor. vi. 1 ff., it would seem that there was a tendency in Corinth to litigation in the heathen courts between Christians, and St. Paul suggests that these matters ought to be settled by the Christians among themselves. This much is certain; but no hint is given as to the nature of the questions which had led to litigation. It is, of course, plain that the preceding incident—the man who had taken his father's wife—can, whatever it may have exactly been, have easily led to litigation of more than one sort; but there is nothing to prove that this was or was not the case.

The chief importance of the incident is that it is by far the most weighty, if not the only, evidence in the Epistle as to the vexed question whether the Christian Churches

[1] 1 Cor. v. 2.

were organized on a Jewish or Gentile model. There is no evidence in the earlier Epistles of St. Paul which really enables us to sketch, even in outline, the organization of a Christian community at this time, not because there probably was no organization, but because it was not yet a matter which had given rise to polemical discussion. St. Paul says nothing about it, because it was not controversial, and his Epistles are controversial letters, not general statements of universally accepted facts. But here, in the question of litigation, we are given a single valuable hint as to the attitude of the Corinthian Christians. Clearly there was a party which held that disputes ought to be settled by the Church, and another which held that they might be brought before the Roman courts. Apparently the latter was in the majority, though this is not quite plain. Now, this is just one of the points which distinguishes Greek from Jewish ideas. The Jews always claimed that the synagogue was a competent court for all disputes.[1] The Greek *θίασοι*, on the other hand, never seem to have entertained the idea (which would certainly have had a short life at the hands of Roman lawyers) that they had any general jurisdiction over their members. An initiate in the mysteries of Isis went to law with another initiate about ordinary disputes (St. Paul's *βιωτικά*), without any hesitation. The fact that some of the Corinthians were taking the Greek line is therefore important and interesting.[2]

[1] See Josephus, *Antiquit.*, xiv. 10. 2; cf. Schürer, *Geschichte des jüdischen Volkes*, ed. 4, III. 113 ff., and Mommsen in the *Zeitschrift f. d. N. Tliche Wiss.*, 1901, p. 88 ff.

[2] The whole question of the growth of organization belongs rather to the investigation of the background of the later Epistles; but an admirable *résumé*, with references to other literature, will be found in J. Weiss' *Der erste Korintherbrief*, pp. xvi. ff.

(γ) *The General Tendency to Immorality.*—Much the same must be said of the third point. In 1 Cor. vi. 12–20, St. Paul is clearly warning the Corinthians against a laxity of morals, of which he has heard either from "those of Chloe" or from some other source. Obviously it is possible that this is connected with the case of incest, which might not unnaturally have given rise to inquiries by St. Paul from his informant on this subject as to the general level of morality among the Corinthian Christians, while it is, on the other hand, equally possible that there is no connection between the two sections. The view to be taken of the question depends largely on that adopted towards the previous point. If there was a connection between the case of incest dealt with in 1 Cor. v., and the tendency to litigation reproved in the following passage, it is extremely probable that the third section is still connected with the same incident; if, on the other hand, there was no such connection, it is less probable that St. Paul, after dealing with the case of incest and going on to another topic, should turn back once more to his original subject.

Further than this it is impossible to go: we only possess a letter written for the edification of the Corinthians—not to give information to historians,—and it is unreasonable to expect that we can reconstruct out of it all the circumstances to which it refers. Much, no doubt, can be done, but there remains much which can never be entirely cleared up. The question as to the possible relation between this moral difficulty and the doctrinal disputes in Corinth is discussed on pp. 176 ff.

(3) *The Mission of Timothy.*

Closely connected with the information given by "those of Chloe" is the mission of Timothy. In consequence of the reports as to the partizan scandals in Corinth, St. Paul sent Timothy to see if he could reduce the evil, especially as he heard that his own absence was having a bad effect.

"I have sent[1] Timothy," he says, in 1 Cor. iv. 17, "for this very purpose to you, . . . to remind you of my behaviour in Christ," etc. And in 1 Cor. xvi. 10, he returns to the subject, and says, "If Timothy come, see that he be with you without fear; for he worketh the work of the Lord, as I also do: let no man therefore despise him. But set him forward on his journey in peace, that he may come unto me, for I expect him with the brethren." From these two passages it would seem that Timothy was sent off from Ephesus after St. Paul had received the information given him by "those of Chloe," and before the departure of the bearers of 1 Corinthians: but in the second passage St. Paul seems strangely uncertain whether Timothy would really reach Corinth, or, if he did, whether he would not arrive later than the bearers of his letter, in spite of the fact that he had started first.

Further information is not given in 1 Corinthians, nor is the visit of Timothy mentioned in 2 Corinthians, but in Acts xix. 22 it is stated that St. Paul "sent into Macedonia two of them that ministered unto him, Timothy and Erastus," and it is generally supposed that this refers to the mission of Timothy referred to in 1 Corinthians. The obvious

[1] Surely the aorist must be so translated.

advantage of this theory is that it explains why St. Paul thought that Timothy might possibly reach Corinth later than 1 Corinthians. This becomes intelligible if Timothy went round through Macedonia, while the bearers of the letter went by sea. On the other hand, it is true that it is strange to describe a journey from Ephesus through Macedonia and Achaia, merely by a reference to Macedonia. But the possibility of a slight inaccuracy in the Acts ought not to be lost sight of, or it may be that St. Luke wrote Macedonia, because in practice Macedonia was further from Ephesus than was Corinth. On the evidence we can go no further than to say that the visit of Timothy in 1 Corinthians may be identical with that in Acts xix. 21, but that this is not proved, and that the two visits may be separate. As will be seen, the matter is chiefly important in connection with the dating of 1 Corinthians.

(4) *The Letter of the Corinthians to St. Paul, and the Information of its Bearers.*

It would appear from the preceding discussion that 1 Cor. i.—vi. is probably based in the main on the information given to St. Paul by those of Chloe. The rest of the Epistle (vii.—xvi.) seems to rest on a different basis. In 1 Cor. xvi. 17, St. Paul says, "I rejoice at the arrival of Stephanas, Fortunatus, and Achaicus, for that which was lacking on your part they supplied"; and in vii. 1, he refers to a letter which he had received from the Corinthians. It is obvious, putting these two references together, that St. Paul used the verbal communications of Stephanas, Fortunatus, and Achaicus to supplement the Corinthians' information, and it is not unlikely that they were themselves the bearers of the letter.

To distinguish exactly between the information given by the letter and the supplementary matter added by the three Corinthians is neither possible nor really important. But it seems as though the greater part of 1 Cor. vii.—xvi. is directly based on the letter, the various points in which are indicated by a more or less regularly recurring formula. This is to be found as follows :—

περὶ δὲ ὧν ἐγράψατε	...	...	vii. 1
περὶ δὲ τῶν παρθένων	...	...	vii. 25
περὶ δὲ τῶν εἰδωλοθύτων	...	...	viii. 1
περὶ δὲ τῶν πνευματικῶν	...	...	xii. 1
περὶ δὲ τῆς λογίας ...	...	...	xvi. 1
περὶ δὲ Ἀπόλλω ...	...	...	xvi. 12

It will be seen at once that these introductory formulae take with them the greater part of 1 Cor. vii. 1—xvi. 12, that is, the whole of the second half of the Epistle; but there are a few important paragraphs which present difficulties. It is clear that there is no break between vii. 1 and vii. 24, the section concerning marriage, or between vii. 25 and vii. 40, concerning "virgins," or between viii. 1 and viii. 13, concerning things offered to idols, but the next section, ix. 1—x. 13, is not so easy. At first sight it seems to have nothing to do with things offered to idols, but to deal with the question of St. Paul's own behaviour, and it is sometimes regarded as primarily an answer to attacks made upon his authority. It is possible, indeed probable, that there is some reference to these attacks, but if this be taken as the main object of the section it is hard to find any satisfactory explanation for the references to the Jews who were "baptized in the sea and the cloud" in x. 1–13, or for the fact that in x. 14 St. Paul returns to the question of idolatry in such a way as to suggest that he regarded the section ix. 1—x. 13 as contributing to the solution of the question raised by the things offered to idols. It is therefore much more probable that the point which explains the relation between the different parts of the whole answer to the question about "things offered to idols," covering viii. 1—x. 1, is that some of the Corinthians defended the custom of eating such things, partly on the ground that they were free and had authority to eat them—which St. Paul controverts by means of his own example in other matters—and partly on the ground that having been baptized and become Christians they were safe from all evil—which St. Paul controverts by the example of the Israelites who fell in the wilderness in spite of the privileges which they had received.[1]

Thus, from vii. 1 to xi. 1 is entirely given up to questions raised by the Corinthians' letter. The next section is more doubtful. The beginning ("Now I praise you that ye remember me in all things," xi. 2) seems to be a quotation from, or a reference to, an assurance given in their letter, and it is probable that this led up to questions concerning the behaviour of men and women in the Church. Thus, xi. 1–16 is probably directly inspired by the Corinthians' letter, but xi. 17–34, dealing with the question of the celebration of the Eucharist, is introduced by a different formula: St. Paul says, "But in giving this instruction (as to men and women), I do not commend the fact that your meetings are deteriorating instead of

[1] See pp. 178 ff. and 200 ff.

improving; for I hear," etc. That is to say, he is not commenting on their letter, but on information given to him orally, presumably by Stephanas and his companions. This section, therefore, is only indirectly connected with the Corinthians' letter, and was inspired by the verbal communications of Stephanas.

In the next section, xii. 1—xiv. 40, dealing with πνευματικῶν ("spirituals") the introductory formula shows that St. Paul is dealing with the letter, and for the present purpose there are no difficulties to discuss. Chap. xv. is more difficult: it discusses the Resurrection, and begins with the formula "γνωρίζω δὲ ὑμῖν"—"I would have you to know" is perhaps the best translation. Although this is not the same formula as St. Paul elsewhere uses in connection with the letter, it is probable that it is nevertheless a reference, and that we ought to conclude that the Corinthians asked a question concerning the resurrection of the dead. The alternative is to suppose that Stephanas and his friends reported that there were doubts on the subject.

The remaining chapter is less difficult: xvi. 1–11 is concerned with a question in the letter relating to a collection for the poor, and with the projected arrivals of Timothy and St. Paul in connection with it: xvi. 12 is also concerned with a simple question in the letter as to the plans of Apollos, and the remaining verses, xvi. 13–24, are the final greetings and advice of St. Paul, in which he expresses his pleasure at having seen Stephanas, Fortunatus, and Achaicus, and—apparently thinking once more of the parties—advises the Corinthians to follow the guidance of Stephanas.

Thus, the letter of the Corinthians was a series of

questions about practical and doctrinal points as to which the community was in doubt. The fact that there was at that time controversy, or at least uncertainty, on those points is of the greatest importance for the understanding of the general position of Christianity in Corinth, and must be discussed later. It is for the moment sufficient to set out the probable list of questions, together with the references to the places in I Corinthians in which St. Paul deals with them.

Marriage, sexual relations, and divorce	I Cor. vii. 1–24
"Virgins"	I Cor. vii. 25–38
Re-marriage of widows	I Cor. vii. 39–40
Things sacrificed to idols	I Cor. viii. 1—xi. 1
Customs during worship	I Cor. xi. 2—xi. 16
The Eucharist (arising out of supplementary information)	I Cor. xi. 17–34
"Spirituals"	I Cor. xii. 1—xiv. 40
The resurrection of the dead ...	I Cor. xv. 1–58
The collection for the poor	I Cor. xvi. 1–11
The plans of Apollos	I Cor. xvi. 12

(5) *The Time and Place of the Writing of* I *Corinthians.*

It has been seen that I Corinthians is partly comment on information given by those of Chloe, and partly an answer to a letter sent by the Corinthians to St. Paul. The questions are, when and whence did he send it?

By the first question is meant not so much the absolute date of the Epistle, as its relative position in the three years that St. Paul spent in Asia.

The general opinion is that it was early in the year

(according to our reckoning) in which St. Paul left Ephesus and came to Corinth on his way up to Jerusalem for the last time. This view is based on 1 Cor. xvi. 3 ff.: "When I arrive, whomsoever ye approve, them will I send with letters to carry your bounty to Jerusalem; and if it be meet for me to go also, they shall go with me. But I shall come unto you, when I have passed through Macedonia; for I do pass through Macedonia; but with you it may be that I shall abide, or even winter, that ye may set me forward on my journey whithersoever I go, for I do not wish to pay you merely a passing visit. But I shall wait at Ephesus until Pentecost; for a great door and effectual is opened unto me, and there are many adversaries." The suggestion is that these verses show that St. Paul wrote not long before Pentecost, and that the visit which he states that he proposes to pay to Corinth is identical with that which, according to Acts xx. 2, he actually paid after he left Ephesus and had travelled through Macedonia. In this case the letter was written in the spring of the year in the autumn of which St. Paul left Ephesus; and if the intended visit mentioned in 1 Corinthians must be identified with the actual visit described in Acts, no other conclusion can be possible. This identification can be controlled by references to a collection in 2 Cor. viii. 10 and ix. 1 ff., as compared with the First Epistle. In 1 Cor. xvi. 1 ff., St. Paul says, "Now, concerning the collection for the saints, as I gave order to the Churches of Galatia, so also do ye. Upon the first day of the week let each one of you lay by him in store, as he may prosper, that no collections be made when I arrive." It is impossible with any straightforward exegesis to explain this as meaning anything except that the collection was not ready—probably scarcely begun

—at the time when St. Paul wrote. But in 2 Cor. ix. 1 ff. he says, "For as touching the ministering to the saints, it is superfluous for me to write to you, for I know your readiness, of which I glory on your behalf to them of Macedonia, that Achaia has been ready since last year"; and in 2 Cor. viii. 10 he gives the same reference to time: "This is expedient for you, who were the first to make a beginning last year, not only to do, but also to will." In both these places the R.V. translates ἀπὸ πέρυσι, "a year ago," which means, in ordinary English, twelve months, but the more accurate rendering is "last year." Now, for St. Paul, as a Greek Jew, the year must have begun in October, and therefore, if he be writing 2 Corinthians after that date, last year could mean in the previous spring—assuming, that is to say, that 1 Corinthians was written in the spring before Pentecost. If, however, he was writing before October, the date of the Epistle must be put back a full year. The evidence of Acts suggests that the former alternative is the more probable, though it scarcely enables us to form a decisive opinion. According to Acts xx. 6, St. Paul left Philippi on his last journey to Jerusalem in the spring (after the days of unleavened bread). He had reached Philippi from Corinth, where he had stayed three months (Acts xx. 3), so that he must have reached Corinth about the beginning of January. He had come to Corinth from Ephesus through Macedonia, where he must have been in December and probably also in November, as Acts states that he gave them "much exhortation." He was, however, already in Macedonia when he wrote 2 Cor. viii. referring to "last year," and the impression given by 2 Corinthians is that he had already been there some time. Thus the probability certainly seems to be that

2 Corinthians was written during November, early in the Jewish new year; so that 1 Corinthians and the arrangements made in the spring for the collection at Corinth would naturally be described as "last year."

Thus the probability is that 1 Corinthians was written about nine months before St. Paul's visit to Corinth, narrated in Acts xx. 2, to which he was looking forward when he wrote the opening chapters of 2 Corinthians. It will be noted that this implies that he stayed in Ephesus after Pentecost, which he had not originally intended to do. This must be granted on any theory which does not abandon the trustworthiness of Acts.

So far it has been assumed that the Epistle was written from Ephesus. Probably this assumption is correct; but there is one objection which deserves statement. In 1 Cor. xv. 32, St. Paul says: "If after the manner of men (κατ' ἄνθρωπον) I fought with beasts at Ephesus," etc.; and in xvi. 8, he says, "But I shall wait at Ephesus until Pentecost." Would he have spoken in this way, especially in xv. 32, if at the time of writing he was still at Ephesus? J. Weiss[1] thinks this extremely improbable, and is inclined to believe that the Epistle was written in Macedonia. Apparently he interprets 1 Cor. xvi. 5, Μακεδονίαν γὰρ διέρχομαι, to mean, "I am now passing through Macedonia." Curiously enough, however, although he draws this conclusion from xv. 32, he does not accept it for xvi. 8, which he considers to have been really written in Ephesus, and he attributes xvi. 7*b*–9 and 15–20 to the "previous letter." Admitting, however, that there is a superficial difficulty, I cannot see that this partition is here necessary. Διέρχομαι may refer to a future plan: or it may be that 1 Corinthians

[1] J. Weiss, *Der erste Korintherbrief*, pp. xl. ff. and 366.

was really written from Macedonia, but that St. Paul regarded Ephesus as his centre to which he meant to return after his Macedonian journey. In this case, however, the "greetings of the Churches of Asia" are a difficulty. Or again, taking διέρχομαι as a reference to future plans, it is possible that the letter was written from some other town in Asia: we need not suppose that St. Paul actually stayed in Ephesus during the whole of the three years that he made that city his headquarters.[1] The admission that there is a certain difficulty in the usual view that the Epistle was written from Ephesus is therefore the most that can be granted. The difficulty is not, after all, insurmountable: it is *possible* to say, "If I had fought with the beasts at Ephesus,"[2] even in Ephesus, though it would be more natural to say "here" instead of "at Ephesus," and the alternative theories seem to raise more difficulties than they solve. Probably, then, the Epistle was written from Ephesus in the last spring which St. Paul spent in that city.

[1] According to DEFG *al pauc.*, St. Paul stayed at Ephesus with Aquila and Priscilla, for they add to 1 Cor. xvi. 19, after the mention of the Church in their house, παρ' οἷς καὶ ξενίζομαι.

[2] A further problem, which it is not necessary to discuss at length, is quite definitely raised by this verse. When was St. Paul ever in danger of this kind at Ephesus? Either he is alluding to some incident at Ephesus, which can scarcely be that connected with Demetrius the silversmith (Acts xix. 23 ff.), unless St. Luke has greatly understated the situation, or he is stating a wholly imaginary possibility. I think the former is somewhat the more probable, and that St. Paul must have passed through some form of persecution, and presumably imprisonment, of which Acts says nothing. The importance of this is twofold: (1) It corroborates (or is corroborated by) 2 Cor. xi. 23, which, among other trials, wholly unmentioned in Acts, mentions imprisonment. (2) It suggests that critics are perhaps a little rash in thinking that the "Epistles of the captivity," which certainly were written from prison, must necessarily have been written either from Rome or Caesarea. If there be any truth in this view, the θλίψις ἡ γενομένη ἐν Ἀσίᾳ (2 Cor. i. 8) is probably a reference to this, not to the incident of Demetrius; but the further discussion of the point belongs to the history of Ephesus rather than Corinth.

Such are the main critical problems introductory to the study of 1 Corinthians: it will be seen that they prepare the way for a consideration of the far more interesting questions as to the reasons why the Corinthians were divided in their opinions as to things offered to idols, marriage, the resurrection of the dead, and the other points on which they consulted St. Paul.

2 Corinthians.

It is far more difficult to reconstruct the events implied by 2 Corinthians than those underlying the earlier Epistle. In the latter, though there are difficulties as to details, the main point—that it was called out by the information given by "those of Chloe" and by a letter from the Corinthians—has never been in dispute; but in 2 Corinthians more than one point of great importance is likely always to be a matter of controversy.

Starting with the state of affairs which obtained when 1 Corinthians was written and sent off, we know that St. Paul was in Asia, and that Timothy had been sent to Corinth in order to deal with the spirit of partizanship. It was this spirit which had especially distressed St. Paul, especially since it was coupled—in practice, if not in origin—with a low level of morality, and by personal attacks on his own position. The question is how this situation developed in the period, probably only about six months, between the two Epistles. What sort of report did Timothy bring back, and what further circumstances gave rise to 2 Corinthians?

In so controversial a subject the fairest, and in the end probably the clearest, method is to begin by stating the facts, and afterwards to discuss the various interpretations which seem possible.

The indisputable facts, then, may be summarized thus:—

(1) *The Mission of Timothy.*—There is an absolute silence on this subject in 2 Corinthians: it is certain that he had returned, for he is joined with St. Paul in the opening salutation (2 Cor. i. 1), but there is nothing to say whether he had ever reached Corinth, much less any positive evidence as to his reception there.

(2) *A Visit of St. Paul to Corinth.*—Reference is made to a visit of St. Paul to Corinth, unrecorded in the Acts, and unmentioned in 1 Corinthians. This is proved by 2 Cor. xii. 14, "Behold, this is the third time I am ready to come to you," and 2 Cor. xiii. 1, 2, "This is the third time I am coming to you." The former of these passages might possibly be explained as referring merely to an intention, and meaning, "This is the third time that I have formed the plan of coming to you," though this interpretation is not at all natural, but the latter is quite definite and must mean that St. Paul had visited Corinth twice before his final visit, recorded in Acts xx. 2, which he was on his way to make when he wrote the opening section of 2 Corinthians. There is, however, nothing to show unmistakably whether the "second" visit ought to be placed before or after 1 Corinthians.

(3) *A Severe Letter of St. Paul to the Corinthians.*—In 2 Cor. ii. 4, St. Paul says, "Out of much affliction and anguish of heart I wrote unto you with many tears," and in 2 Cor. vii. 8, "Though I made you sorry with my Epistle, I do not now regret it, though I did so once." These descriptions can only apply to a letter which, written under the pressure of circumstances, was so severe that St. Paul was at one time inclined to think that it had been too

harsh. There is no definite proof that it is not identical either with 1 Corinthians or with the "previous Epistle" (see pp. 120–125), but there is a general consensus of opinion that neither of these possibilities is probable, and that the "severe letter" was sent off subsequently to 1 Corinthians.

(4) *The Visits of Titus.*—It is clear that Titus had been sent to Corinth, and that he had rejoined St. Paul in Macedonia. In 2 Cor. ii. 12, St. Paul says, "When I came to Troas . . . I found not Titus, my brother, but taking my leave of them, I went forth into Macedonia," and in 2 Cor. vii. 5, "For even when we were come into Macedonia, our flesh had no relief, but we were afflicted on every side. . . . Nevertheless God comforted us by the coming of Titus," etc. Moreover, from the context of these passages it appears that Titus' mission was successful, for St. Paul expresses both in 2 Cor. ii. and 2 Cor. vii. his satisfaction at the result, and says (in vii. 13) that the spirit of Titus "hath been refreshed by you all," and in vii. 15, that "his (*i.e.* Titus') inward affection is more abundantly toward you, whilst he remembereth the obedience of you all, how with fear and trembling ye received him." It would also appear that Titus, after thus rejoining St. Paul, went back to Corinth. His return and St. Paul's expression of hope for his good reception form the substance of 2 Cor. viii. 1—ix. 15.

Thus we have clear evidence that Titus paid two visits to Corinth, one before and one after 2 Corinthians; that between these two visits he had an interview with St. Paul in Macedonia; and that he then reported his experiences on his first visit.

(5) *The Report of Titus to St. Paul.*—Titus was successful in his first visit to Corinth, but what was the report which he brought from Corinth to Macedonia? Three points are

plain, but each of them gives rise to a further problem which is by no means clear. In the first place, it may be stated with positiveness that the difficulty at Corinth centred in a personal dispute. There were two persons whom St. Paul calls in 2 Cor. vii. 12, "he who did the wrong" (ὁ ἀδικήσας), "he who suffered the wrong" (ὁ ἀδικηθείς). We can even go further and identify him who did the wrong with the person who is described in 2 Cor. ii. 6 ff. as condemned, punished, and penitent.[1] But there is nothing whatever to throw any direct light on the identity of the persons referred to, or on the nature of the offence committed. In the second place, it is clear that the guilty person was condemned to some form of punishment, but there is nothing to show what the nature of this punishment was. Finally, it is in the third place clear that this punishment was inflicted, not by the unanimous vote of the whole community, but by that of a majority. It is described in 2 Cor. ii. 6 as *ἡ ἐπιτιμία αὕτη ἡ ὑπὸ τῶν πλειόνων*, which cannot mean as the R.V. text reads, "this punishment which was inflicted *by the many*," but must be, as it is put in the margin, "by the more," or, as we usually say in modern English, "by the majority." But it is uncertain whether the corresponding minority, which this phrase implies, consisted of those who wished for a severer punishment, or of those who desired greater leniency, or sided with the offender.

These, then, are the facts for which room has to be made in any reconstruction of the events leading up to 2 Corinthians,—a "severe letter" from St. Paul to the Corinthians, and a successful visit by Titus.

[1] "Sufficient to such a one is this punishment which was inflicted by the majority, so that contrariwise ye should rather forgive him and comfort him, lest by any means such a one should be swallowed up with his overmuch sorrow" (2 Cor. ii. 6 ff.).

The problems which must be faced are—

(1) The significance of the silence of 2 Corinthians on the mission of Timothy.

(2) The position of the "second" visit of St. Paul.

(3) The possible identification of the "severe letter" with 2 Cor. x.–xiii.

(4) The visits of Titus to Corinth.

(5) The reconstruction of the report of Titus.

It will also be noticed that, just as the consideration of the critical problems in 1 Corinthians leaves for further discussion the really important question of the point of view of the Corinthian Christians, as implied by their questions to St. Paul, so also the consideration of the critical problems in 2 Corinthians leaves over the question of the character of the party opposed to St. Paul.

(1) The Mission of Timothy.

The silence of 2 Corinthians as to the mission of Timothy has been explained in two ways. Either Timothy never reached Corinth—which explains why St. Luke describes his journey as "to Macedonia"—or he was thoroughly unsuccessful in his object of bringing the Corinthians to a better frame of mind, and when, after all, peace was made between St. Paul and his converts, it was neither necessary nor tactful to refer to his visit. Between these two possibilities final judgment is impossible, but the latter seems much the more probable, and the supposition that Timothy returned to Ephesus, not long after 1 Corinthians was sent, with an extremely unpleasant report, to the effect that the Corinthians would not listen to his counsels, and that the troubles continued, fits in very well with the most probable solutions to the other problems,[1] while as much can scarcely be said for the view that Timothy never reached Corinth at all.

(2) THE VISIT OF ST. PAUL TO CORINTH.

Ought the "second" visit of St. Paul to be placed before 1 Corinthians, or inserted between it and 2 Corinthians? The points which have to be taken into consideration are these: (*a*) 1 Cor. iv. 21, "What will ye? shall I come unto you with a rod, or in love and a spirit of meekness?" supported by 1 Cor. xi. 34, "The rest will I set in order when I come," seems to prove that he not only contemplated a visit, but doubted whether it would be an entirely peaceful one, owing to the parties in the Church. (β) 2 Cor. ii. 1, "But I determined this for myself, that I would not come to you with sorrow again," seems to show that he had, when he wrote, the memory of an unpleasant visit, and it should be noted that in the undoubtedly best text[2] the "again" is closely connected with the "with sorrow." Moreover, in the immediate context of this verse St. Paul's meaning clearly is that some one, who had opposed him originally, had now been punished by the majority. The whole passage 2 Cor. ii. 1–11 must be studied from this point of view.

"But I determined this with myself, that I would not

[1] As a matter of method it should be noted that complicated questions of this kind can only be satisfactorily handled by reducing them to a number of subordinate problems. Each of these problems is capable of alternative solutions, and in choosing between these the critic has to be guided by considering which is consistent with the solutions of other co-ordinate problems. The solutions not consistent with *any* of the alternatives must be struck out.

[2] Ἔκρινα δὲ ἐμαυτῷ τοῦτο, τὸ μὴ πάλιν ἐν λύπῃ πρὸς ὑμᾶς ἐλθεῖν, ℵABCDEFGKLOP al plu., latt.,, syrr. . . . ἐν λύπῃ, *post* ἐλθεῖν min. pauc. . . . *om* πάλιν boh. aeth.

come again to you with sorrow. For if I make you sorry, who is he then that maketh me glad, but he that is made sorry by me? And I wrote this very thing unto you, lest, when I came, I should have sorrow from them of whom I ought to rejoice; having confidence in you all, that my joy is the joy of you all. For out of much affliction and anguish of heart I wrote unto you with many tears; not that ye should be grieved, but that ye might know the love which I have more abundantly unto you. But if any have caused grief, he hath not grieved me, but in part (that I may not press too hardly) you all. Sufficient to such a man is this punishment, which was inflicted by the majority. So that contrariwise ye ought rather to forgive him, and comfort him, lest perhaps such a one should be swallowed up with overmuch sorrow. Wherefore I beseech you that ye would confirm your love toward him. For to this end also did I write, that I might know the proof of you, whether ye be obedient in all things. To whom ye forgive any thing, I forgive also: for if I forgave any thing, what I forgave for your sakes forgave I it in the person of Christ; that no advantage be gained over us by Satan: for we are not ignorant of his devices."

Is it not plain that this passage implies a recent visit which had ended so unpleasantly that St. Paul had determined not to come back if he was likely to undergo similar experiences, and that he was, at the moment of writing, delighted to find that such action had been taken by the community that he was able to return without fear, since the leader of the opposition had been punished by a vote of the majority? It was a party question of some sort which had rendered his previous visit unpleasant, and the removal of this question took away his fear for a repetition of this experience. The natural corollary from these conclusions is that St. Paul's forebodings in 1 Cor. iv. 21, that the party divisions at Corinth would prevent him from having a pleasant visit, had been painfully well fulfilled during a visit between the times of writing 1 and 2 Corinthians.

That this is the natural view is universally conceded; but many interpreters of Corinthians have felt obliged to reject it, because they think that there is no room for a visit of St. Paul to Corinth between 1 and 2 Corinthians. Some of them, therefore, fall back on the very unnatural exegesis of 2 Cor. xii. 14 and xiii. 1, which denies that St. Paul means that he has already been twice to Corinth, and regards him merely as saying that he has three times *intended* to come. Others admit the fact of a second visit, but place it before 1 Corinthians.

The main reason for this view is that on the hypothesis (certainly the most probable) that 1 Corinthians was written in the early spring, and 2 Corinthians in the early winter of (according to our reckoning) the same year, we have to assume more rapid travelling backward and forwards on the part of Timothy, St. Paul, and Titus than is thought to be probable. The objection to it is that there is no trace in 1 Corinthians of this second unpleasant visit, nor is it easy to see that 1 Corinthians supplies one with any material for imagining the cause of this unpleasantness. It cannot have been the partizanship, or the case of incest, or tendency to litigation, or immorality, for on all these points St. Paul seems to be dependent for his knowledge on the recent information of "those of Chloe"; in short, it may be said that, while the topics dealt with in 1 Corinthians supply ample reason for thinking that St. Paul might have (as he says himself in 1 Cor. iv. 21) an unpleasant visit in the immediate future, they give no reason whatever for thinking that he had had one in the past.

Under the influence of these facts Dr. Kennedy has urged that the usual dating of 1 Corinthians is wrong, and that it ought to be placed a year earlier; the main argument for this view is the necessity for finding room for the visit of St. Paul, and, secondly, the belief that ἀπὸ πέρυσι in 2 Cor. ix. 2 implies that 1 Corinthians was written twelve months previously. The reasons for not holding this latter opinion are given on p. 141 ff., and though I quite admit that the evidence seems to be irresistible in favour of a visit of St. Paul to Corinth between 1 and 2 Corinthians, I am not convinced that the time available on the ordinary view of the date of 1 Corinthians is really insufficient. From Corinth to Ephesus was one of the most frequented routes in the whole of the Mediterranean, and owing to the prevalence throughout the summer of north or north-westerly winds (usually more north than west) the journey could be made in either direction with the wind fairly well on the beam; an average passage would scarcely last longer than a week. Thus, all that the supposed difficulty of finding room for St. Paul's visit to Corinth really amounts to, is that we must suppose that between the spring and autumn he was absent from Ephesus perhaps for four weeks,—possibly only a fortnight. Timothy, we know, had already started for Corinth *viâ* Macedonia, before St. Paul wrote 1 Corinthians. Let us suppose that Timothy returned early in May (there is no special reason why it should not have been earlier), with depressing news from Corinth. St. Paul immediately decided to go himself, and returned without any success. He would be back in Ephesus in July, and, as he does not seem to have left there until the autumn, this gives at least two months for him to write the "severe letter" and send it to Corinth with Titus.

In some such reconstruction (which assumes for the moment the results of the discussion as to the mission of Titus, see pp. 164–173) there seems to be nothing impossible. It is surely clear that 2 Corinthians implies a severe crisis in Corinthian affairs of such a nature as to call for energetic action on the part of St. Paul, and it is really harder to imagine that it was long drawn out than that it actually all took place between the early spring and the late autumn of one year.

The objection may of course be made that in 1 Corinthians St. Paul announces his intention of leaving Ephesus at Pentecost, and that the reconstruction given above implies that he stayed on until the summer was over. This objection has, however, little force, for in 2 Cor. i. 15–17 St. Paul shows plainly that he had to some extent changed his plans, even though it may not be easy to see exactly what they were, so that there is no longer any presumption in favour of the view that he left Ephesus at Pentecost in accordance with the intention expressed in 1 Cor. xvi. 8, to be set against the fact that, using the data given in Acts, he seems to have stayed on longer. Moreover, it is not quite accurate to say that St. Paul announced his intention of leaving Ephesus at Pentecost. What he says is, that he will not be able to leave sooner ("I shall stay at Ephesus until Pentecost"); his desire is to see the Corinthians, but until then it is impossible. It is common experience that that sort of plan, when made by a busy man, often has to be emended in the direction of postponement. If in the early spring St. Paul saw no chance of leaving Ephesus before Pentecost, it is not surprising that in the actual event he could not manage to do so before the autumn, especially if, as is suggested, he gave up three weeks or a month to a flying visit to Corinth.

Thus the various events seem to fit into one another, and justify the view that after sending 1 Corinthians, and probably after the return of Timothy with unpleasant news, St. Paul paid a short and unsuccessful visit to Corinth.

(3) The Severe Letter.

Can the "severe letter" be identified either with the "previous letter" or with 1 Corinthians? If not, is it to be found either in whole or in part in 2 Cor. x.–xiii.?

To the former of these two questions a negative answer must certainly be given. It is, in the first place, almost impossible that it should be the lost "previous letter," because St. Paul clearly speaks of himself in 2 Cor. vii. 5, as only learning from Titus what the effect of his letter had been. This excludes the "previous letter" unless we suppose (α) that it had been sent off before either "those of Chloe" or Stephanas, Fortunatus, and Achaicus arrived at Ephesus, but had not yet reached Corinth; (β) that the references to it in 1 Corinthians do not mean that St. Paul had heard that it had been misunderstood, but only that he was afraid that it might be; and (γ) that when St. Paul wrote 1 Corinthians it had not yet struck him that his former letter was so severe that he regretted it. This combination of improbabilities excludes the "previous letter" from serious consideration.

Similarly, 1 Corinthians itself is excluded by the description of the letter given in 2 Cor. ii. 4. Can any one believe that St. Paul wrote 1 Corinthians "out of much affliction and anguish of heart, with many tears"?

It is therefore practically certain that the severe letter referred to in 2 Corinthians is really a Third Epistle, other than 1 Corinthians, or the "previous Epistle." But many critics urge that this hypothetical Third Epistle is not really lost, but may, either in whole or in part, be identified with 2 Cor. x.–xiii.

This view depends on somewhat complicated arguments, and can best be stated in the form of two propositions. (1) There is not only no connection between 2 Cor. i.–ix. and 2 Cor. x.–xiii., but there is an absolute break between them. (2) Internal evidence shows that 2 Cor. x–xiii. was written before 2 Cor. i.–ix., and that it corresponds to the "severe letter" mentioned in 2 Cor. ii. and 2 Cor. viii.

(1) *The break between 2 Cor.* i.–ix. *and* x.–xiii.—The general tone of 2 Cor. i.–ix. is of joy and sudden relief from great anxiety. The typical passage is 2 Cor. vii. 4–7, which describes the whole in a few words. "Great is my boldness of speech toward you, great is my glorying of you: I am filled with comfort, I am exceeding joyful in all our tribulation. For, when we were come into Macedonia, our flesh had no rest, but we were troubled on every side; without were fightings, within were fears. Nevertheless God, that comforteth those that are cast down, comforted us by the coming of Titus; and not by his coming only, but by the consolation wherewith he was comforted in you, when he told us your earnest desire, your mourning, your fervent mind toward me; so that I rejoiced the more." And the same tone may be marked in the concluding words of 2 Cor. ix. 15, "Thanks be to God for His unspeakable gift." Indeed, if 2 Cor. i.–ix. stood alone, we should have no

difficulty in agreeing that the situation which it implies is that St. Paul had sent a letter to Corinth in order to bring the Church there to a better frame of mind, and that he had just heard, to his great relief, that this letter, combined with the presence of Titus, had been entirely successful. "In everything," he writes in 2 Cor. vii. 11, "ye approved yourselves pure in the matter . . . therefore we have been comforted: and in our comfort we joyed the more exceedingly for the joy of Titus, because his spirit was refreshed by you all. For if I have boasted anything to him of you, I was not put to shame; but as we spake all things to you in truth, even so our boasting, which I made before Titus, was found a truth. And his inward affection is more abundant toward you, whilst he remembereth the obedience of you all, how with fear and trembling ye received him."

If we turn to 2 Cor. x.–xiii., we see a wholly different picture. The general tone is one of defending his own position, and threatening severe action against a disobedient Church. The opening words strike this note, which is never completely dropped until the final sentence. "Now I Paul myself beseech you by the meekness and gentleness of Christ, who in presence am lowly among you, but being absent am bold toward you: yea, I beseech you, that I may not be bold when I am present with that confidence, wherewith I think to be bold against some, which think of us as if we walked according to the flesh" is the introduction which leads up to chap. xiii. 2, "I have said, and do say beforehand,—as I did when present the second time, and now when I am at a distance,—to those who have sinned before, and to all the rest, that if I come again, I shall not be lenient."

Thus there can be, and never has been, any dispute but

that the whole tone of the Epistle changes suddenly at chap. x. 1, and that, if 2 Cor. x.–xiii. had existed in a separate form, no one would ever have dreamt of suggesting that it was the continuation of 2 Cor. i.–ix.

(2) *The internal evidence showing that* 2 *Cor.* x.–xiii. *is earlier than* 2 *Cor.* i.–ix., *and that it is the severe letter mentioned in the latter portion.*[1]

This evidence may be described as a series of cross-references from 2 Cor. i.–ix. to 2 Cor. x.–xiii. These references are of two kinds: the first consists of general descriptions in 2 Cor. i.–ix. of the "severe letter" to which 2 Cor. x.–xiii. is seen to answer; the second, of special allusions to the contents of the severe letter, all of which correspond to definite phrases in 2 Cor. x.–xiii.

The general descriptions of the severe letter are the following:—

(*α*) In 2 Cor. ii. 4, St. Paul says that he had written the "severe letter" "out of much affliction and anguish of heart beset with many tears."

(*β*) In 2 Cor. vii. 8, he says, "Though I made you sorry with my letter I do not regret it, though I did regret it,"—that is to say, the letter was so severe that after sending it he was inclined to doubt whether it was not, after all, excessive.

(*γ*) In 2 Cor. iii. 1, he says, "Do we begin again to commend ourselves?"—implying that in the previous letter there had been a marked element of self-commendation.

(*δ*) In 2 Cor. i. 23, he says, "I call God for a witness

[1] This section is almost entirely based on the masterly statement of Dr. J. H. Kennedy in his *The Second and Third Epistles of St. Paul to the Corinthians*, pp. 79–94.

upon my soul, that to spare you I did not come again to Corinth,"[1] and in 2 Cor. ii. 1, "I determined this for myself, that I would not come to you again with sorrow." That is to say, at the time of writing the severe Epistle, the possibility of paying a punitive visit was present to his mind, but was temporarily postponed in order to see what the effect of the letter would be.

Now, if one turn to 2 Cor. x.–xiii., these four general characteristics are all easily discovered. It is impossible to read these chapters without recognizing the intensity of feeling which inspires them, or to fail to agree with Dr. Kennedy that there are "many passages which we can believe to have been blotted with tears." It is similarly obvious that there is (with the possible exception of Galatians) no other passage of the same length in the Pauline Epistles of which it is so easy to believe that its author may have been doubtful as to the propriety of such powerful invective. Still more strikingly is self-commendation the subject of a large part of 2 Cor. x.–xiii. It may indeed be fairly called the central theme of 2 Cor. x. 7—xii. 10. Finally, that St. Paul when he wrote 2 Cor. x.–xiii. was hesitating whether he would come to Corinth, and that this hesitation was due to his fear that if he came he would not be able to spare the Corinthians, is clear from the whole passage, 2 Cor. xii. 20—xiii. 2. "For I fear, lest, when I come, I shall not find you such as I would, and that I shall be found unto you such as ye would not: lest there be

[1] The Greek is *οὐκέτι ἦλθον εἰς Κόρινθον*. This can only mean, "I came not again" (*or* "not any more") to Corinth: though the A.V. and the R.V., apparently under the influence of the exegesis which refused to recognize a "second visit," translate it, "I came not as yet" (A.V.), which is an impossible meaning to get out of *οὐκέτι*, or "I forebare to come" (R.V.), which is scarcely better.

debates, envyings, wraths, strifes, backbitings, whisperings, swellings, tumults: lest, when I come again, my God will humble me among you, and that I shall bewail many which have sinned already, and have not repented of the uncleanness and fornication and lasciviousness which they have committed. This is the third time I am coming to you. At the mouth of two or three witnesses shall every word be established. I have said, and do say beforehand—as I did when I came the second time, and now when I am at a distance—to them which heretofore have sinned, and to all other, that, if I come again, I will not spare." A more accurate description of the frame of mind revealed by this passage could scarcely be given than that which St. Paul gives in 2 Cor. i. 23, of his feelings at the time when he sent off the severe Epistle.

Besides these general descriptions of the severe letter in 2 Cor. i.–ix., to which 2 Cor. x.–xiii. certainly answers in every respect, there are three pairs of passages which seem to amount to definite and verbal cross-references. These can best be shown in parallel columns.

(*a*) "For this cause I write these things from a distance, that I may not when I come deal sharply."—2 Cor. xiii. 10.	"And I wrote this same thing that when I came I might not have sorrow."—2 Cor. ii. 3.

The obvious parallelism between these two passages is increased by the fact that the context shows that "might not have sorrow" in 2 Cor. ii. 3 is an euphemism for "deal sharply." "For if I make you sorry," he says in the preceding verse, "who then is he that maketh me glad, but he that is made sorry by me?"

(β) "If I come again I will not spare."—2 Cor. xiii. 2.	"To spare you I came not again to Corinth."—2 Cor. i. 23.
(γ) "Being in readiness to avenge all disobedience when your obedience shall be fulfilled."—2 Cor. x. 6.	"For to this end also did I write that I might know the proof of you, whether ye are obedient in all things."—2 Cor. ii. 9.

These three pairs of passages are very striking, and gain in force if each be read in its context; it seems difficult to deny that St. Paul, in each case, is referring to the same thing,—in the passage from 2 Cor. x.–xiii. in the present tense, and in that from 2 Cor. i.–ix. in the past.

Moreover, this argument is not only a very strong reason for seeing the "severe letter"—or rather part of it—in 2 Cor. x.–xiii., but it greatly strengthens the case for maintaining that in any case there is no unity between 2 Cor. i.–ix. and x.–xiii. Any theory which maintains that 2 Corinthians is a simple letter, all written at one time, must explain not only why there is a sudden change of tone in the middle (which is generally done by assuming that St. Paul is writing to his friends in one part and to his opponents in the other), but also why there is this remarkable appearance of cross-references from one part to the other, and always of such a nature that the chapters which come at the end of the Epistle, as it is now arranged, refer in the present sense to events which are alluded to in the past tense in the earlier chapters.

This is the case for identifying 2 Cor. x.–xiii. with part of the "severe letter": it can be supported by various subsidiary arguments. For instance, in 2 Cor. x.–xiii. a characteristic feature is the use of the word καυχᾶσθαι ("boast" or "glory") in connection with St. Paul's claims to consideration. "Though I should *glory* somewhat abundantly concerning our authority, I shall not be put to shame" (2 Cor. x. 8); "Let no man think me foolish; but if ye do, yet as foolish receive me, that I also may *glory* a little. That which I speak, I speak not after the Lord, but as in foolishness, in this confidence of *glorying*, seeing that many *glory* after the flesh, I will *glory* also" (2 Cor. xi. 16–18); "If I needs must *glory*, I will *glory* of the things that concern my weakness" (2 Cor. xi. 30); and the list of passages could be extended.

Compare this with 2 Cor. i. 12 ff., "For our *glorying* is this, the testimony of your[1] conscience . . . we are your *glorying*, even as ye are ours," or with 2 Cor. vii. 4, "Great is my *glorying* on your behalf." Do not these passages obtain a heightened significance if we regard them as delicate allusions to the forcible claim to authority in the previous letter, taking the sting out of the "glorying" by giving it a changed application? Similarly, when St. Paul says (vii. 16), "I have *confidence in you*" (Θαῤῥῶ ἐν ὑμῖν), is he not thinking of his earlier statement in 2 Cor. x. 1, "I *have confidence against you*"[2] (Θαῤῥῶ εἰς ὑμᾶς)? Or again, when he says, in i. 15, "And in this *confidence* (πεποιθήσει) I was minded to come to you," is he not deliberately using again, in a pleasant sense, the phrase which he had used

[1] Exegetically the reading ὑμῶν is surely preferable, and it seems to have been the reading of ℵ*B*, though it has been corrected in both MSS. by very early hands. The value of MSS. evidence is at its lowest in distinguishing between ὑμῶν and ἡμῶν. The pronunciation is, and probably was, quite identical.

[2] This is the natural meaning of the words, though they are weakened in the R.V. into "I am of good courage toward you."

unpleasantly in x. 2, "I beseech you that I may not, when present, show courage (θαῤῥῆσαι) with the *confidence* (πεποιθήσει) wherewith I count to be bold against some"?

At the same time, it must be recognized that it is impossible to maintain the older form[1] of this theory which suggested that these four chapters are the whole of the "severe letter." The sufficient proof of this is that it is plain, from 2 Cor. ii. 5–10, that the "severe letter" had been largely directed against some definite person at Corinth, and there is no trace of this in 2 Cor. x.–xiii. This fact was rightly used as a decisive argument against Hausrath, but it has no force against Kennedy's hypothesis that 2 Cor. x.–xiii. is not the whole, but only the concluding part of the "severe letter," and that the earlier chapters which are now lost dealt with the case of St. Paul's opponent.

Thus the result of this complicated argument is to establish the great probability of the view that 2 Corinthians is not a single Epistle, but fragments of at least two Epistles, the last four chapters representing the end of the "severe letter"—which was really St. Paul's Third Epistle to the Corinthians—and the first nine being the letter which he wrote from Macedonia in joy at the success which had attended the "severe letter" and its bearer, Titus. But when one accepts this fact, and couples it with the hypothesis (see p. 122 ff.) that 2 Cor. vi. 14—vii. 1 belongs to neither of these two letters, but to the "previous letter" of St. Paul, it seems necessary to pause. To some extent, of course, the very strongly supported theory which divides 2 Cor. x.–xiii. from 2 Cor. i.–ix. lends strength to the much

[1] Best known through Hausrath's *Der Viercapitelbrief des Paulus an die Korinther*, 1870.

more doubtful hypothesis that 2 Cor. vi. 14—vii. 1 is an interpolation; but the question must be faced whether it be possible to suggest any theory to make plausible the view that 2 Corinthians is composite to a degree which is not probable in any other of the Pauline Epistles.

This theory is presented by Dr. Kennedy. He suggests that whereas 1 Corinthians was from the beginning regarded by the Corinthians as a valuable document, which laid down the law on many important points, the letter written from Macedonia (2 Cor. i.–ix.) was not more than the expression of St. Paul's gratitude for the favourable turn which affairs had taken, and the "severe letter" (2 Cor. x.–xiii.) was of such a nature that they would not be likely to wish to remember it. It was only as St. Paul's letters began to be regarded as "Holy Scripture," and to be valued for their authorship rather than their contents, that either of the two last letters to Corinth became important. By this time they had probably fallen into a bad state of preservation; it was not clear whether the fragments belonged to one or several letters; and the scribes who copied the autographs put together, as best they could, the various pieces of papyrus into one connected whole.

It must be remembered that we have no textual evidence at all for the first stage of the growth of the *Corpus Paulinum*. What we have is a collection of Epistles, from all Churches which had any, in the form in which it came to be generally recognized in the great Church. But there was an earlier period in which the individual Churches were busy in collecting Pauline material from their own archives, and in supplementing this from other communities. The combination of the "severe letter" and the "grateful letter" must have been made in the very beginning, as soon in fact as any copy of them existed at all.[1] Dr. Kennedy suggests that this may have been at the time when Clement wrote to the Corinthians, and drew their attention to their Pauline archives. This is, of course, merely a suggestion of what may have, not what must have happened, but it serves to show that imaginable circumstances may well have arisen which called the attention of the Corinthians to fragments of Pauline letters, which had long lain unheeded in their archives so that no one remembered exactly what they were, and scribes, copying for the first time these new treasures, combined into the form of a single complete letter, what were really the fragments of at least two incomplete ones.[2]

(4) THE VISITS OF TITUS TO CORINTH.

The three passages in which the visits of Titus to Corinth are referred to in 2 Corinthians are the following:—

(*a*) "For even when we were come into Macedonia . . . God comforted us by the coming of Titus, and not by his coming only, but also by the comfort wherewith he was comforted in you, while he told us your longing, your

[1] Dr. A. C. Clark has pointed out to me that there is a somewhat similar instance of combination in Cicero's letters. It appears that there were two drafts of *Ad Fam.* v. 8, and that these have been joined together as a single letter, perhaps by Tiro (see Bardt, in *Hermes*, xxxii. (1897), pp. 267–70).

[2] J. Weiss (see p. 123) goes further, and argues that if we admit the probability that 2 Corinthians is composite, we ought also to recognize the same fact as valid for 1 Corinthians. He would argue that 1 and 2 Corinthians represent the Corinthian edition of St. Paul's correspondence, put together from more or less dilapidated papyri many years after they had been received. There is nothing intrinsically impossible or improbable in this theory; but to my mind Dr. Kennedy's view is preferable. I can see clear evidence for a partition theory in 2 Corinthians, but I am not convinced of the necessity of such a view for 1 Corinthians.

mourning, your zeal for me; so that I rejoiced yet more. . . . Therefore we have been comforted: and in our comfort we joyed the more exceedingly for the joy of Titus, because his spirit hath been refreshed by you all" (2 Cor. vii. 5–13).

From this passage it is plain that Titus joined St. Paul in Macedonia, and brought a good report. Those who take the view advocated above as to the "severe letter" will probably also agree that the most natural interpretation of the facts is afforded by the supposition that Titus was the bearer of the "severe letter," and that the welcome change in the attitude of the Corinthians was effected by the combined influence of the letter and of its bearer.

(β) A further reference to this visit is sometimes found in 2 Cor. xii. 17 ff.: "Did I take advantage of you by any one of them whom I have sent unto you? I asked Titus to go,[1] and I sent the brother with him. Did Titus take any advantage of you? Walked we not by the same Spirit, in the same steps?" That this passage is in some way connected with the visit of Titus from which he returned to Macedonia is not disputed, but the nature of the connection differs according to the view taken of the relation of 2 Cor. x.–xiii. to 2 Cor. i.–ix.

On the assumption that these two sections are both part of the same letter, written after Titus had joined St. Paul in Macedonia, the most probable and generally held hypothesis is that St. Paul is referring to Titus' conduct on the visit from which he had just returned, and perhaps that the chance of "taking advantage" of them, from which he refrained, is in some way connected with the "collection for

[1] This is surely all that the Greek means. "I exhorted Titus" (R.V.) gives a wholly artificial sound to a simple phrase.

the saints" which figured so largely in St. Paul's programme at this period. This latter part is, as will be seen, very doubtful, but for the rest this is the only possible theory for those who reject the partition theory.

If the partition be accepted, and 2 Cor. x.–xiii. be identified with the "severe letter," clearly the reference in this passage cannot be to Titus' conduct during the visit from which he returned to Macedonia, for *ex hypothesi* this visit had not yet been made. In this case, St. Paul is rather seeking to commend Titus as his representative, who will be the bearer of the "severe letter." The meaning, then, of the whole passage from xii. 15 is that he himself never was pecuniarily burdensome to the Corinthians, and that the same was true of his representative, Titus. He says in effect, "You know that from the beginning of my intercourse with the Corinthians, I have never had a penny's profit from them, and the same is true of my representatives. Titus, who is now coming to you, has never made any profit. Can you deny that he always behaved in this respect in exactly the same way as I did myself?"

(γ) In viii. 6 ff.: "We asked Titus that as he had made a beginning before, so he would also complete in you this grace also. . . . But thanks be to God, which putteth the same earnest care for you into the heart of Titus; for indeed he granted our request, yea, being himself very earnest, he went forth unto you of his own accord." From the context it is clear that "this grace," which Titus was to complete, was the "collection for the saints," *i.e.* for the poor Christians in Jerusalem, for this is the subject of the whole of 2 Cor. viii.–ix. Thus it is in any case certain that the return of Titus from Macedonia to Corinth was connected with the "collection for the saints." The question is, however, whether we ought to conclude from St. Paul's language that Titus had been busy with the same question on his previous visit. Purely linguistic exegesis does not give much help on this point. The expression, "this grace also" (*καὶ τὴν χάριν ταύτην*), seems to suggest that Titus is going to do something which has not been done previously, and the repetition of the phrase in the next verse points in the same direction.[1] On the other hand, it may be urged, when Titus was asked to "complete" (*ἐπιτελέσαι*) something, it is implied that he had already made a beginning in the same direction. This is, however, not necessary, and the truth is that the sentence is ambiguous because "this grace also" may be regarded as explaining the addition which Titus had to make to that which he had begun (*προενήρξατο*)—different in kind from his previous work, which needed this addition to complete it (*ἐπιτελέσαι*); or it may be regarded merely as indicating the point at which his work—fully begun already—needed carrying out a little further in the same direction in order to be perfected.

Thus the nicer lexical criticism gives no certain answer to the question, and we are driven back on general considerations, and our knowledge of the "collection for the saints" from other sources. We know from both the Epistles and the Acts that St. Paul was busy with a collection from all his Churches which he proposed to send or take up to

[1] Dr. Kennedy is surely right in his contention that the construction of the Greek in viii. 6 ff. is continuous: *εἰς τὸ παρακαλέσαι ἡμᾶς Τίτον, ἵνα καθὼς προενήρξατο οὕτως καὶ ἐπιτελέσῃ εἰς ὑμᾶς καὶ τὴν χάριν ταύτην, ἀλλ' ὥσπερ ἐν παντὶ περισσεύετε, πίστει καὶ λόγῳ καὶ γνώσει καὶ πάσῃ σπουδῇ καὶ τῇ ἐξ ἡμῶν ἐν ὑμῖν ἀγάπῃ, ἵνα καὶ ἐν ταύτῃ τῇ χάριτι περισσεύητε.* The rendering of the R.V., which puts a stop after *χάριν ταύτην*, and treats *ἵνα περισσεύητε* as the equivalent of an imperative, though it may be paralleled in later Greek, is harsh and quite unnecessary.

Jerusalem. He had already arranged with the Corinthians to take their proper share in his work (1 Cor. xvi. 1 ff.), and was therefore able to boast in 2 Cor. ix. 2 that Achaia had been ready the previous year. At the same time, it is clear that he felt by no means sure that this boast was based on strict fact,—if Achaia had really been ready, there would have been no need to send Titus, or to exhort the Corinthians not to fail him. So far, then, there is no doubt but that the Corinthian collection had already been begun ; but it is exceedingly probable that the period of general disturbance in the Church at Corinth, to which 2 Corinthians testifies, reduced the work of collection to a standstill. Is it conceivable that St. Paul would have sent Titus at this crisis to reduce the Corinthians to subjection, armed with the "severe letter," and at the same time told him to collect subscriptions? It is far more likely that St. Paul left the whole financial question in abeyance until he knew whether the combined effect of Titus' visit and his own severe letter would bring the Corinthians to a better frame of mind.

If we accept the view that the "severe letter" which Titus took with him to Corinth is either lost, or to be identified with 2 Cor. x.–xiii., there is no difficulty in believing that Titus returned to Corinth in connection with the collection, and that he had not previously taken any measures in its direction.

Those, however, who hold the view that the "severe letter" was 1 Corinthians, are bound, in the light of 1 Cor. xvi. 1, to assume that Titus dealt with the matter on his first visit, and they then naturally explain 2 Cor. xii. 18 ("Did Titus take any advantage of you?") as a reference to his conduct in this connection. For such an opinion there is little valid argument; but it is, of course, found in all commentaries or introductions which identify the "severe letter" with 1 Corinthians, as well as in some others which, though they have abandoned this identification, still think that Titus dealt with the matter of the collection on his first visit—not seeing that this view is merely the result of an identification which they do not any longer accept, is in itself contrary to the probabilities of the case, and is not required by the verbal exegesis of the passages in 2 Corinthians germane to the question.

(5) The Report of Titus.

The report of Titus, so far as it is known to us, may be represented thus: "There was a meeting of the community, and under the influence of the 'severe letter' the offender was condemned, and sentenced to a punishment which was approved of by the majority."

The first question is, who was the offender, and what was his offence? The one thing which is here certain is that no confident answer can ever be given. Various lines of probability can be marked out, but the choice between them is almost impossible. It is obviously possible that the partizanship mentioned in 1 Corinthians contains the germ of many of the factors in the situation described in 2 Corinthians. 2 Corinthians—especially chaps. x.–xiii. —seems largely occupied with the defence of St. Paul's authority, and this may have been impugned by any of the parties mentioned in the First Epistle. If the existence of a "Christ party" be accepted, it is possible that a reference to it may be seen in 2 Cor. x. 7, "If any man trusteth that he is in Christ, let him consider this again with himself, that even as he is Christ's, so also are we." If so, we must suppose that the main cause of the dissensions was the development of the Christ party, and possibly that the leader of it was the offender who was punished.

Another line which has often been suggested is that the offender was the man who had taken his father's wife, and the father is sometimes regarded as the offended party. This also is not impossible, but there is no evidence to prove it: it is merely a guess.

Or it might be thought that the root of the evil is to be sought in the tendency to litigation mentioned in 1 Cor. vi. 1 ff., and that the meeting of the community mentioned in 2 Cor. ii. 6 represents the final submission of both parties to St. Paul's opinion that the community ought to judge matters of dispute, and not allow them to be brought before the heathen courts. Once more, the suggestion is not unattractive, but unsupported by evidence.

Still less is it possible to form any clear view as to the nature of the punishment inflicted on the offender: the only thing certain is that it was not exclusion from the community, because St. Paul speaks of the desirability of receiving him with kindliness.

More light can perhaps be thrown on the question of the relationship of the majority who fixed the punishment of the offender to the minority who disapproved of their decision. According to the view, formerly so generally held, that 2 Cor. x.–xiii. was addressed to a rebellious minority, which had not been convinced by Titus, there is no alternative to the interpretation which regards the majority as St. Paul's friends, and the minority as his opponents.

But on the partition theory of 2 Corinthians this exegesis is unnecessary, and a closer consideration of the exact wording of the crucial passage points rather to the view that the minority was the party of St. Paul, or at all events wished for a severer treatment of the offender than the majority had voted. This passage is 2 Cor. ii. 5–7, "If any hath caused sorrow, he hath caused sorrow, not to me, but in part (that I press not too heavily) to you all. Sufficient to such a one is this punishment which was inflicted by the majority, so that ye should contrariwise rather forgive him and comfort him, lest by any means such a one should be swallowed up with his overmuch sorrow. Wherefore I beseech you to confirm your love toward him." The most natural exegesis, and that which gives the most force to the separate phrases of this passage, is that the offender had been unanimously condemned,—he had caused sorrow to them all,—that the majority had fixed an appropriate penalty, and that St. Paul is addressing the minority,—he distinguishes "the majority" from "you,"—who still cherished angry feelings towards the offender, in order to persuade them to acquiesce in the sentence of the majority, and not to press for heavier punishment. It is also fairly plain that the reason why this minority was still unsatisfied was a feeling of loyalty to St. Paul, who therefore emphasizes his own satisfaction with the action of the majority,—in other words, the "minority" of 2 Corinthians is most probably to be identified with the "party of Paul" of 1 Corinthians. This conclusion is supported by the fact that St. Paul says nothing at all about the justice of the sentence, but only defends its adequacy (ἱκανὸν τῷ τοιούτῳ, κ.τ.λ.). No one, then, denied that it was just, but there were those who doubted that it was adequate. Finally, the τοὐναντίον (contrariwise) is only intelligible if we suppose that those of whom St. Paul is speaking did not propose to adopt a forgiving attitude.

Thus the most straightforward exegesis of this passage is that the minority were the Pauline party, who thought that their master's position demanded a severer sentence than that which the majority had inflicted. On the supposition that 2 Cor. x.–xiii. does not belong to 2 Cor. i.–ix., but is really part of the severe letter, which helped to bring about that state of feeling in the community which led up to the general condemnation of the offender and his punishment by the vote of the majority, there is no difficulty in accepting this exegesis. On the other hand, it is almost impossible of acceptance by those who reject the partition theory, and regard 2 Cor. x.–xiii. as addressed to a still rebellious minority. They are forced to adopt the view that the majority, not the minority, were the party of St. Paul, that the "you" spoken of directly after "the majority" (. . . ἡ ἐπιτιμία ἡ ὑπὸ τῶν πλειόνων, ὥστε ὑμᾶς, κ.τ.λ., 2 Cor. ii. 6 f.) is to be identified with, not distinguished from the majority, and that when St. Paul said that the sentence was sufficient, he meant that the majority (thus identified with the "you") might now be content to forgive the offender, as the minority wished them to do.

This exegesis seems in several points unnatural and forced: it is, however, perhaps not absolutely inadmissable, and is probably the only possible view if 2 Cor. x.–xiii. be regarded as directed against a rebellious minority.

It is perhaps not unfair to point out that it is an indirect argument of considerable value in favour of the "partition theory" that it enables a natural and easy exegesis to be given in so many places which are obscure and difficult on any other hypothesis.

It is now possible to piece together the results of this examination of single problems, and by using the results which seem most probable, either in themselves or in relation to other points, to give a connected description of the course of events from the sending of 1 Corinthians to the second mission of Titus with 2 Cor. i.–ix.

Soon after 1 Corinthians had been sent, Timothy rejoined St. Paul, and reported the result of his mission and the general condition of the community at Corinth. It was not a pleasing story which he had to tell: the partizanship, which "those of Chloe" had mentioned, instead of disappearing had increased; there was an open hostility to St. Paul's personal authority; possibly the case of incestuous marriage continued to be a scandal, and the disagreements which had led to litigation continued. It was plain that energetic measures were called for, and St. Paul went over to Corinth as soon as he could find an opportunity—that is to say, probably within two or three days. Even this failed: the Corinthians would not listen, and St. Paul, seeing that he was doing no good, and probably also knowing that he was needed in Ephesus, went back, declaring that if he came again he would not spare, but would adopt strong measures. At Ephesus he penned a severe letter, of which 2 Cor. x.–xiii. is the latter portion, and asked Titus to take it, and at the same time to try to bring the Corinthians to a better state of mind. Titus went, and the combination of his words with St. Paul's letter was successful. A general meeting of the community was held, and St. Paul's authority was recognized. It was agreed that the offending member, who was the cause of the trouble, was to be condemned, but there was a difference of opinion as to the punishment which should be meted out to him. In the end, however, the majority inclined to mildness, leaving a minority still demanding severer measures, or at all events not prepared to treat the offender with friendliness. This was no doubt lamentable, but there can be no doubt but that in the main the situation had been enormously improved, and that Titus' mission and the "severe letter" had been completely justified by their results. Titus, therefore, left Corinth to return to St. Paul.

In the meantime St. Paul had left Asia—possibly we ought to put, at this point, the uproar in connection with Demetrius and the worshippers of Artemis—and made his way first to Troas, and afterwards to Macedonia. Here Titus found him, and relieved his fears by his favourable report. Immediately he wrote 2 Cor. i.–ix., and sent Titus once more back to Corinth with it, to urge his over-zealous friends to forgive the offender, and also to pick up the threads of the organization for the "collection for the saints," which the troubles in the Church had broken off. St. Paul himself was busy in the work for this collection in Macedonia, and he hoped that Titus would act as his representative in Achaia, to work up the methods which he had suggested in 1 Cor. xvi. 1 ff., so that when he reached Corinth himself there would be no further delay.

To complete the story we must turn to Acts xx. 3. From this we learn that St. Paul reached Corinth in the winter, and that he stayed there three months. He intended to sail thence to Syria, but at the last moment a plot was laid against him by the Jews, and he returned through Macedonia. What was this plot? Was it entirely apart from the previous troubles in the Church? We are absolutely ignorant, and with this sinister episode the curtain falls on the Christian community at Corinth, not to rise again until forty years later, when fresh quarrels drew forth remonstrances from the Church at Rome in what we usually call the First Epistle of Clement.

Here, then, we have the skeleton of the story of St. Paul and the Corinthians: to clothe it with flesh it is now necessary to consider the real nature of the problems raised by the Corinthians in 1 Corinthians, and the character of the opposition to St. Paul which is revealed in 2 Corinthians.

IV.

The Problems of Thought and Practice revealed by the Epistles.

These problems may in general be described as being concerned with the questions put before St. Paul by the Corinthians. We have to ask in each case, why such questions were raised, and to deal with the much-disputed question of the nature of the opposition to St. Paul.

The points at issue may conveniently be divided into the following classes:—

(1) Sexual questions.

(2) Questions relating to Inspiration by the Holy Spirit.

(3) The Resurrection of the Dead.

(4) The opposition to St. Paul.

The second of these headings covers three of the questions put to St. Paul—as to things offered to idols, as to spiritual gifts, and as to the arrangement of worship, including the Eucharist—but they are all so closely connected by the idea of inspiration, that they are best treated together.

(1) Sexual Questions.

Nothing is more natural than that questions of sexual morality should be important in Corinth,[1] for it was famous both for the opportunities which it afforded for every sort of immorality, and for the manner in which these were brought into connection with cultus (especially in the worship of Aphrodite) of an originally Oriental and frequently obscene nature. Thus it is not strange that we find the Epistles revealing a series of practical problems connected with sex, and pointing to the existence of two divergent lines of thought, one ascetic and the other libertine.

These practical problems may be divided into two classes, relating to fornication and to marriage; and the latter subdivided into the questions of (α) Marriage in general. (β) Divorce; (γ) Re-marriage; (δ) Virgins.

Fornication.—In three places in 1 Corinthians St. Paul deals with the question of fornication: 1 Cor. v. 1–13; vi. 12–20; x. 8. In the first of these three he is dealing with a special case, which would apparently be more correctly described as incest. What exactly it was is a problem which belongs

[1] It is perhaps scarcely necessary to point out that the Corinth of the first century is not the original Greek city. This was destroyed by Mummius in 146 B.C., and it remained for a long time in ruins and deserted. It was rebuilt about a century later by Julius Caesar, under the name of Laus Julia Corinthus, as a Roman colony, and in 27 B.C. became the capital of the province of Achaia under a Proconsul. See further, W. M. Ramsay on "Corinth" in Hastings' *Dictionary of the Bible*, and J. Weiss on *Griechenland in der Apostolische Zeit* in Herzog's *Realencyclopædie*, ed. 3, vol. vii., pp. 160–168. The latter gives a valuable series of references to other books and authorities.

rather to the exegesis of the Epistle; it is not for our purpose very important. In the second and third, however, he speaks generally, and it is clear that fornication was really a serious evil in the Christian community. The problem for us is to understand how this can have been the case. It is obviously not simply an instance of human weakness; but that the Corinthians really had a low standard of morality on the subject, and defended their practices as not incompatible with Christianity.

The solution is to be found in 1 Cor. vi. 12 and x. 8. On the one hand, some of the Corinthians had argued that "all things were lawful," and that fornication is as much a purely physical, morally indifferent action as eating and drinking are. This is clearly the background of the argument, "Meats for the belly, and the belly for meats," which is probably a reference to, if not a quotation from, the statements of the Corinthians. St. Paul combats this argument, and maintains the permanence of the "body," as against the impermanence of the "belly" (1 Cor. vi. 13 ff.). The whole contention of St. Paul is only intelligible if we grasp the fact that he is reasoning with people who say, "The body does not matter: what we eat and drink does not affect the soul: and the same thing is true of all physical functions."[1]

A slightly different, but cognate point of view is revealed by 1 Cor. x. 8. Here St. Paul is speaking primarily of things offered to idols, and chapter x. is explicable only if we see that it is a warning against the view that Christians

[1] It is worth noting in this connection that this sort of argument, or rather the necessity for meeting it, was one of the reasons why early Christianity was so anxious to hold the doctrine of a resurrection of the flesh. The opposite view was frequently connected with a low standard of morality. A study of Athenagoras is instructive on this subject.

are safe because they have been initiated into the Christian mysteries. St. Paul combats this view by showing that safety was not obtained by the Israelites, who were the types of Christians, although they also had, typically, enjoyed the mysteries of Baptism and the Eucharist. Therefore, he argues, we must avoid the things which, as the history of the "types" shows, can be fatal to us as they were to them.

The importance of these facts, simple and short though their description may be, is considerable. They are the proof that over against a scrupulous and ascetic party there was another which went to the other extreme, regarding the Christian as a "spiritual" person, who by initiation into the mysteries was raised above carnal considerations, and could not be affected by anything which he did with his body. To modern minds there is something extraordinary in the suggestion that the spiritual freedom of the Christian could be so extended. But it must be remembered that the Graeco-Roman point of view was quite different. Not only was fornication—for men—considered a matter of small or no importance, but it actually was regarded in some cases as possessing a religious value. The prostitutes in the temple of Aphrodite at Corinth were not, in their own opinion, immoral; nor were they influenced by immoral motives, but by a religious impulse.

Corruptio optimi pessima; and it is in the twentieth century, in the West of Europe, difficult to realize the possibility of a religious impulse expressing itself in immoral acts, but the fact is nevertheless indisputable that it has formerly done so. The point is that cultus—the ritual expression of religious impulse—is not a measure of religion only, but also of other elements in the nature of the person who is trying to express this impulse. Go back two thousand years and you will find that the nature of many men was such that they attempted to express, and to stimulate,[1] their religious life by sexual excesses: or, if you will travel in space instead of in time, the same thing can be found to-day in Africa, or even in some of the lower Indian cults. Go back still further in time, or penetrate to still lower depths of primitive human nature, as it still survives in Africa, and you will find men arousing and satisfying their religious instincts by human sacrifice; and if you reach to the last depths, you will find that there is a religious basis even to the horrid rites of cannibalism. Primitive man is not only religious, but he is also obscene, cruel, and superstitious, and these evil characteristics always show themselves in combination with his religious rites.

Nothing comes out more clearly in the history of religions, than that religion, in the attempt to work out forms of worship, has had to deal with three enemies—cruelty, obscenity, and superstition. The first of these had been practically conquered, for civilized nations, before our era; the conquest of the second was the especial task of primitive Christianity. It was necessary for the Church, which inherited the high moral standard of Jewish cultus, to fight over again in the West the battle for a pure worship, which the prophets of Israel had won for the Jews six hundred years before. The struggle is so remote from our generation, that it is hard to realize that our forefathers had to fight hard to prevent Christian culture from becoming corrupted, but clear traces of the struggle can be found in the Apocalypse,

[1] The two things always go together: cultus was defined above as "the ritual expression of religious impulse." It might equally well be called the "ritual stimulation of the religious impulse."

in Jude, in 2 Peter, in Irenaeus, Hippolytus, Clement of Alexandria, Epiphanius, the *Pistis Sophia*, and minor authorities. In all of them we can see the struggle against various forms of obscene heresies,[1] and only when we realize how widespread these heresies were, can we understand how it is that Justin Martyr, while repudiating the charges of immoral feasts, admits that they may be based on the deeds of heretical Christians who bring discredit on a name which they have no right to use, just as false philosophers bring discredit on philosophy.[2] How well Christianity succeeded[3] can be seen by the difficulty which we experience in realizing that the task ever existed, and part of the importance of 1 Corinthians is that it gives us a glimpse of the beginning of the struggle.

Marriage.—(*a.*) *Marriage in General.*—As to marriage itself, it is not difficult to see the background from which the questions, which St. Paul answers, must have arisen. Some of the Corinthians were opposed altogether to marriage (cf. 1 Cor. vii. 1, 2); and some were anxious to deprive it of any sexual significance (cf. 1 Cor. vii. 3–7). Yet there was no unanimity on the question, and therefore it was necessary to consult St. Paul, who adopted the intermediate position of recognizing the propriety of marriage, and that in the fullest sense, though he recommended the

[1] Few people are aware of the horrible nature of the ritual practices of some of the Gnostics. The description, for instance, of the Carpocratians in Clement of Alexandria, or some of the allusions in the *Pistis Sophia*, would be wholly untranslatable.

[2] Justin, I. *Apol.* 26.

[3] It would of course be unfair to say that it was only the Church which made the attempt. Many of the Cynic-Stoic philosophers preached an ethical gospel of the highest kind, and no doubt their efforts did much good. Still, in the end, they ceased to exist, and the Church survived. In this sense the triumph of higher morality was the triumph of Christianity.

ascetic life to those who could endure it, whether married or unmarried.

To reconstruct with precision the arguments of the ascetic party is impossible, but we shall probably not be wrong in holding that two considerations played the main part. In the first place, there was the feeling that the "time was short," and that the Kingdom of God would belong to those who "neither marry nor are given in marriage, but are as the angels."[1] This view was very strong in early Christianity, and in some circles was carried so far as to exclude the permanence of sex in the kingdom. It is possible that some of St. Paul's own teaching may have been interpreted in this way. When, for instance, he said that in "Christ Jesus there was neither male nor female,"[2] the conclusion might be drawn that he meant that sex would not exist in the Kingdom.[3] This is also the view which probably lies behind the apocryphal saying of Christ in II. Clement 12, "For the Lord Himself being asked by some one, when His kingdom should come, said, When the

[1] Matt. xxii. 30 = Mark xii. 25 = Luke xx. 34 ff. It is true that this phrase is actually connected in St. Mark with the resurrection, not with the Kingdom, but only because the resurrection is, for the dead, the means of entry into the Kingdom. It is instructive to note how St. Luke's version of the section is really intended to bring out this fact: "*The sons of this world* (αἰῶνος) *marry and are given in marriage, but they who are permitted to attain to that world*, and the resurrection from the dead, neither marry nor are given in marriage, *for neither can they die any more*, for they are as if angels (ἰσάγγελοι), *and are 'sons of God,' because they are sons of the resurrection.*" The words in italics are St. Luke's additions. It is unimportant for the present purpose, but it is noteworthy that this passage in Luke is singularly full of interesting and very early variants.

[2] Gal. iii. 28; cf. also p. 209 for another use to which a strained exegesis of this view may possibly have been put.

[3] Cf. Clem. Alex., *Paed.*, i. 4, "ἐν γὰρ τῷ αἰῶνι τούτῳ," φησίν, "γαμοῦσι καὶ γαμίσκονται," ἐν ᾧ δὴ μόνῳ τὸ θῆλυ τοῦ ἄρρενος διακρίνεται, "ἐν ἐκείνῳ δὲ οὐκέτι," and according to Hippolytus the Naassenes regarded Adamas, the "ἄνθρωπος," as a sexless person, or rather as ἀρσενόθηλυς, cf. *Refut.*, v. 7.

Two shall be One, and the Outside as the Inside, and the Male with the Female, neither Male nor Female," though the writer of II. Clement himself gives a different explanation.[1] In the second place, there was undoubtedly a strong ascetic feeling, at all events partly—and, perhaps, chiefly—due to reaction against the general immorality of the Greek world, and of Corinth in particular. This feeling was not specifically Christian; it was found among the Essenes, who were absolutely celibate, and also among the Therapeutae, whose headquarters were in Alexandria. Especially important, however, are the Stoics, whose doctrine on the question of marriage was that it was an association for the mutual comfort of husband and wife, who stood on an equality of rights. Against the low level of morality in the Empire the Cynics and Stoics protested and preached as strongly as Jews or Christians.[2] It is doubtful whether they can be said to have encouraged celibacy, but certainly they enjoined continence. It is, therefore, quite natural that there was a celibate party in Corinth.

In the same way, it is easy to understand the existence of the party, to which St. Paul refers in 1 Cor. vii. 3–7, holding that marriage in the full sense was undesirable, and recommending that those who were already married should wholly abstain from marital relations.[3] This feeling was,

[1] He says that it means *ἵνα ἀδελφὸς ἰδὼν ἀδελφὴν οὐδὲν φρονῇ περὶ αὐτῆς θηλυκόν, μηδὲ φρονῇ τι περὶ αὐτοῦ ἀρσενικόν*,—a fine example, it seems to me, of the way in which eschatological expectation was transformed into ethical precepts. It does not seem necessary here to discuss the relation of this "saying" to the Gospel of the Egyptians. See Preuschen, *Antilegomena*, p. 2, for the text of the latter.

[2] See especially Musonius *ἐκ τοῦ τί κεφάλαιον γάμου*, ed. Hense, p. 67, quoted in Lietzmann's Commentary on 1 Corinthians, p. 160. Cf. Wendland, *Die Hellenistische-Romische Kultus*, pp. 18 and 39–53.

[3] There is a large literature on this subject in early Christian and Jewish

no doubt, the natural outcome of the general belief,[1] both among Jews and Greeks, that all sexual relations were in themselves, if not sinful, at least "not holy," so that they demanded ritual purification before a state of "holiness" could be regained. It was part of the general Christian position that Christians are, and must remain "holy" (ἅγιοι is almost a technical name for Christians), so that those who still retained the semi-physical conception of holiness naturally were inclined to regard all sexual intercourse as forbidden to Christians.

(β) *Divorce.*—This question arose, so far as we can see, from two reasons. In the first place, there was the ascetic tendency mentioned above, which led some Christians to regard marriage as immoral, and, therefore, to regard divorce as desirable for Christians. Against this St. Paul quotes the absolute prohibition of the Lord for husbands and wives to leave each other.[2] In the second place, there was the question of mixed marriages, or, rather, of married couples of which only one was converted to Christianity. Some of the Corinthians were inclined to think that it was the duty of Christians, under such circumstances, to separate from all association with the heathen, and it is easy to imagine that St. Paul's "previous letter" (see pp. 120 ff.) had seemed to support this opinion. St. Paul's advice is that, unless the

writings. Cf. the note in J. Weiss' *Commentary*, p. 174, and there is much more in the later documents of the Byzantine Church.

[1] Cf. Exod. xix. 15; Lev. xv. 18; 1 Sam. xxi. 5, etc. Further references are given by Wetstein. Also cf. Dittenberger, *Syll.*, ii. 566 (p. 264 ff.) and 567 (p. 267), and Leitzmann's *Commentary*, p. 105.

[2] It is interesting to notice that he shows no trace of any knowledge of an exception to this prohibition. See further *Expositor*, November, 1910, on "Early Christian Teaching as to Divorce," in which I have explained my reasons for thinking that primitive Christianity only recognized divorce in the sense of a separation, and did not regard the "exception" in Matt. v. 32 as giving any sanction to re-marriage.

heathen husband or wife desires separation, the marriage tie holds good. It should, however, be noted that neither he nor the Corinthians appear to contemplate re-marriage for the Christian separated from his wife, or the possibility of any one who is already a Christian desiring to marry a heathen.

(γ) *Re-marriage.*—From 1 Cor. vii. 39 ff., it is plain that the question of a second marriage for widows had been raised. But it does not appear that it was a point on which there was any very lively controversy.

(δ) *Virgins.*—In 1 Cor. vii. 25–38, St. Paul discusses the question of "Virgins." There are many difficulties in reconstructing from his language exactly what or who these virgins were, and the question will probably always be obscure. The best way of approaching the subject is to take the crucial passages from St. Paul, and note the exegetical difficulties. A translation is here insufficient by itself, as it has a tendency to obscure the points at issue. I therefore give Greek and English in parallel columns:—

Περὶ δὲ τῶν παρθένων ἐπιταγὴν Κυρίου οὐκ ἔχω, γνώμην δὲ δίδωμι ὡς ἐλεημένος ὑπὸ Κυρίου πιστὸς εἶναι. Νομίζω οὖν τοῦτο καλὸν ὑπάρχειν διὰ τὴν ἐνεστῶσαν ἀνάγκην, ὅτι καλὸν ἀνθρώπῳ τὸ οὕτως εἶναι. δέδεσαι γυναικί; μὴ ζήτει λύσιν· λέλυσαι ἀπὸ γυναικός; μὴ ζήτει γυναῖκα. ἐὰν δὲ καὶ γαμήσῃς, οὐχ ἥμαρτες, καὶ ἐαν γήμῃ ἡ παρθένος, οὐχ ἥμαρτεν . . . εἰ δὲ τις ἀσχημονεῖν ἐπὶ

"Now concerning the virgins, I have no commandment of the Lord, but I give my judgment as one that hath obtained mercy of the Lord to be faithful. I think, therefore, that this is good, by reason of the present necessity, that it is good for a man to be as he is. Art thou bound unto a wife? Seek not release. Art thou released from a wife? Seek

τὴν παρθένον αὐτοῦ νομίζει, ἐὰν ᾖ ὑπέρακμος, καὶ οὕτως ὀφείλει γίνεσθαι, ὃ θέλει ποιείτω· οὐχ ἁμαρτάνει· γαμείτωσαν. ὃς δὲ ἕστηκεν ἐν τῇ καρδίᾳ αὐτοῦ ἑδραῖος, μὴ ἔχων ἀνάγκην, ἐξουσίαν δὲ ἔχει περὶ τοῦ ἰδίου θελήματος, καὶ τοῦτο κέκρικεν ἐν τῇ ἰδίᾳ καρδίᾳ, τηρεῖν τὴν ἑαυτοῦ παρθένον, καλῶς ποιήσει. ὥστε καὶ ὁ γαμίζων τὴν ἑαυτοῦ παρθένον καλῶς ποιεῖ, καὶ ὁ μὴ γαμίζων κρεῖσσον ποιήσει.

not a wife. But even if thou married, thou didst not sin; and if the virgin married, she did not sin. . . . But if any man think that he is unseemly towards his virgin, if he be passionate, and 'it must be so,' let him do what he wishes: he doth not sin: let them marry. But he that standeth stedfast in his heart, having no necessity, but hath power over his own will, and hath determined in his own heart to keep his virgin, shall do well. So that also he that giveth his virgin in marriage, doeth well, and he that giveth her not shall do better."[1]

It will be noted that the translation here given departs in three important points from that of the usual English version. (1) The word "daughters" after "virgins," is omitted in vers. 36 ff. (2) *ὑπέρακμος* is translated "passionate" instead of "pass the flower of her age," and is made to apply to the man, not to the virgin. (3) In ver. 38 *ὥστε καὶ ὁ γαμίζων* is translated "so also he that giveth in marriage," instead of "so both he that giveth in marriage," and it is further suggested in the footnote that *γαμίζων* perhaps means "marries," not "gives in marriage."

[1] Or, "so that both he that marrieth his virgin doeth well, and he that marrieth her not, shall do better."

These differences may fairly be said to sum up the problem. The English version, following a tradition, which is at least as old as Chrysostom, conceives that the situation of which St. Paul is speaking is merely that of a father with unmarried daughters, whom he may or may not give in marriage. The suggestion is that the Corinthians were divided in opinion as to whether it was ever desirable to allow daughters to marry, and that St. Paul expressed the opinion that the matter was one for the individual conscience of the father in question, but that the better course, when no scruple was felt, was to prevent marriage.

The difficulty of this interpretation is in ver. 36. Here γαμείτωσαν must mean "let them marry." Who? The virgin is one of the parties to the marriage, and the natural view is that the man in question is the man who "thinks that he is unseemly[1] towards his virgin," and that it is he who is ὑπέρακμος. In this case, ὑπέρακμος means "over-passionate," taking ἀκμὴ in the sense, which it has in *Constitutiones Apostolicae*, iii. 2,[2] of passion, not that of youth. Furthermore, the view that ὑπέρακμος refers to the man is supported by the parallelism of the sentences.

εἰ δέ τις ἀσχημονεῖν ἐπὶ τὴν παρθένον αὐτοῦ νομίζει,	ὃς δὲ ἕστηκεν ἐν τῇ καρδίᾳ αὐτου ἑδραῖος,
ἐὰν ᾖ ὑπέρακμος,	μὴ ἔχων ἀνάγκην,
καὶ οὕτως ὀφείλει γινέσθαι,	ἐξουσίαν δὲ ἔχει περὶ τοῦ ἰδίου θελήματος, etc.

It is clear here that there is a correspondence between the two cases, and that the antithesis is between the man "who can" and the "man who cannot." St. Paul is not always

[1] ἀσχημονεῖν is frequently used with a sexual reference. Cf. Rom. i. 27.

[2] προφάσει τοῦ μὴ δύνασθαι κρατεῖν τῆς ἀκμῆς ἐπὶ δευτερογαμίαν ἐλθεῖν. It is remarkable that ὑπέρακμος is apparently an absolute unique word.

attentive to details of style, but the point is certainly not without importance. It is not, however, essential to the argument; we do not really know what ὑπέρακμος means, and its translation cannot be the real basis of the argument. The main point is that St. Paul says, that under certain circumstances the virgin and some one else may marry; as the circumstance which he puts in the foreground is the frame of mind of the man whose virgin she is, presumably he is the "some one else."

But if it be conceded that γαμείτωσαν must mean "let the virgin and 'the man who cannot,' marry," it is plain that the man in question is not the father of the virgin, and that the translation "virgin daughter" must be abandoned. It will presently be shown what the relation between the man and the virgin probably was; but it is first desirable to consider the question of γαμίζω. The difficulty is that the word is not found outside the New Testament. Strictly speaking, it ought to mean, as the old grammarians[1] recognized, "give in marriage," according to the rule by which verbs in -ίζω are causative. But there are many exceptions; γνωρίζω, for instance, means "I know," ἐλπίζω means "I hope," χρονίζω, "I tarry," ὑβρίζω, "I insult," etc. Some of these words are, indeed, possibly not degenerated causatives, but doublets formed by a false analogy from aorists in -ισα; so, ἐγάμησα (in pronunciation indistinguishable from ἐγάμισα) might give rise to a false present, γαμίζω.[2] If it means

[1] Apollonius, *De Syntaxi*, iii. 31, quoted by Lietzmann, p. 111, says, τὸ δὲ "γαμίζω" "γάμου τινὶ μεταδίδωμι."

[2] Modern Greek seems here to be no help, except in so far as it is perhaps noteworthy that γαμεῖν has lost its meaning, and is now an almost or quite disreputable word. Lietzmann (p. 111) also suggests that γαμίζω may mean to "celebrate a marriage." Many verbs meaning "to celebrate" end in -ίζω. It is of course plain that Mark xii. 25 and Luke xvii. 27 throw no light on the difficulty. The verb can there be equally well translated in either way.

"marry," then the meaning in this passage is clear, and the reference is still to the question, whether a man shall marry a "virgin" or not. If it means "give in marriage," it implies that the man is in a position to give his "virgin" in marriage to whom he will. Obviously, this agrees better with the traditional exegesis that παρθένος is a "virgin daughter." It does not, however, absolutely require it, for it is not impossible St. Paul is considering here the further case of a man who does not wish to marry his "virgin" himself, but to give her to some one else. If so, the first καὶ is not to be translated "both," but "also," for it is not parallel to the second καὶ, but introduces a new problem. It must, however, be admitted that this seems less natural, and therefore if the "daughter" hypothesis be abandoned, probably we ought to take γαμίζω as meaning "marry," not "give in marriage."

The question has then to be faced, in what other relation could the man in question stand to his "virgin," so that he had not married her, but could do so if he wished. The answer is probably to be found in the institution of "spiritual marriage," which existed among the Therapeutae and among Christians for at least 300 years, but was gradually driven out, in consequence of the scandals to which it had given rise. The best statement of the whole of the literary evidence on the subject can be found in the *Virgines Subintroductae* of Prof. H. Achelis. The main points are these:—Among the Therapeutae,[1] men and women lived

[1] Described in Philo's *De Vita Contemplativa*. Doubts have been thrown on the genuineness of this by Lucius, *Die Therapeuten und ihre Stellung in der Geschichte der Askese*; his view is also supported by Schürer, *Geschichte d. Jud. Volkes*, ed. 4, iii. p. 687 ff.), where a full bibliography is given. But Bousset, Cohn, Drummond, Friedländer, Dieterich, and Conybeare regard the book as genuine. The best statement of the case for the genuineness is F. C. Conybeare's *Philo about the Contemplative Life*, 1895.

together in a colony arranged on the same lines as the later "lauras" of Christian monasticism, so that each lived apart as a hermit, or something similar, but all came together at intervals for worship. The details of the arrangement of this colony are obscure, but the fact that men and women lived together, and that marriage was excluded is apparently indisputable. In the desert country, in which the original Therapeutae colony was placed, this "living together" did not imply any very close association, but one can easily imagine what it may have led to, if the attempt was made to adapt it to the circumstances of life in the great cities. If, however, we pass over 1 Corinthians, we find no evidence that this step was taken until the second century. But in the second and succeeding centuries, we find abundant proof that the custom had already been adopted by Christians. It is not necessary here to rewrite a well-known chapter of Church history; it is sufficient to note that the evidence of Irenaeus, Tertullian, Cyprian, and perhaps Hermas,[1] shows that the custom of "spiritual marriage" with "virgins" was common in the Christianity of the second and third centuries, though it was possibly always regarded with dislike by the leaders of the great Church. After the fourth century it is still widely found, but is treated as a definite evil, and was gradually stamped out.[2]

It is extremely probable that this curious side-track of

[1] Hermas is always quoted; I do not feel personally quite so certain that the famous passage in *Sim.* ix. 11, is really a direct reference to *virgines subintroductae*—to use the later name for them—but it is at least an indirect reference.

[2] See especially the Councils of Elvira, Ancyra, and Carthage, and, in addition to the work of Achelis, H. Koch's *Virgines Christi*, in *Texte und Untersuchungen*, xxxi. 2, pp. 59–112. It is also interesting to note the foreshadowing of modern results in a forgotten treatise of Muratori *De Synisactis et Agapetis* (written about 1709), recently pointed out by F. C. Conybeare, in *Myth, Magic, and Morality*, where the whole question is discussed (pp. 210 ff.).

history leads us to the true explanation of 1 Cor. vii. The suggestion is that men and women had made a practice of living together under a vow of virginity, and that, in some cases, the situation was proving too great a strain for human nature. Under these circumstances, St. Paul's advice was sought. His answer is, "Let them marry." At the same time, he does not agree with those who apparently had doubted—as the later Church also doubted—the desirability of the custom altogether; for those who can keep to their purpose he regards it as good. But the question is, How many cases does he distinguish? Clearly, in ver. 36, ending with "let them marry," he deals with the case of a man and a "virgin" who are neither of them contented with a spiritual marriage, and desire to join in wedlock with each other. In the earlier verses, however, he seems to be dealing with the case of possible marriage, for the man or the virgin, with some third party; possibly we can also conclude from this passage that this "spiritual marriage" was regarded, at least by some of the Corinthians, as not incompatible with a real marriage. Here, also, St. Paul clearly sides with those who admitted marriage both for the man and for the "virgin." The final case is, perhaps, contained in v. 38, and alludes to the possibility of giving the "virgin" in marriage to some one else.

That the details of any solution to the problem presented by 1 Cor. vii. 25–38 are uncertain, will be admitted by all who have really considered it at all closely; but the view that has been presented by Achelis seems to present fewer difficulties than any other, and recent commentaries all show a tendency to accept it. If so, we have to consider that the background of the chapter is the existence of a class of men and women who vowed themselves to live together not in wedlock, but in virginity. Such an institution was clearly the result of the ascetic tendency mentioned on p. 182, and the problem arose from the conflict between this institution and human nature.

The controversy as to the relation of Christianity to sexual questions lasted for many generations, and it would be far from the truth to suppose no false steps were made by the Church on this extremely difficult question. The institution of "spiritual marriage" was clearly a false step, and was comparatively soon retracted. It would be out of place here to discuss the later course of development on other points, but it is worth noting that the ascetic element in early Christian teaching is being shown more and more clearly by modern research to have been far more widespread and to be far more primitive than comparatively recent writers have allowed. The view that marriage is a concession to human weakness, and incompatible with the highest Christian ideal, is probably primitive. It was clearly the view of St. Paul when he wrote to Corinth (even though a somewhat more liberal opinion is perhaps expressed in the Epistle to the Ephesians, of which, however, the authenticity is doubted by many quite cautious critics), and there was clearly a party in Corinth who thought that he conceded too much. If we go on to the succeeding centuries we find the extremest asceticism consistently preached as the counsel of perfection. I cannot see how it is possible to deny that the general teaching of the Christian Church from St. Paul to the Reformation is that the life of the celibate is higher *qua talis* than that of the married Christian.

(2) Questions relating to Inspiration by the Holy Spirit.

The questions of the Corinthians concerning things offered to idols, spiritual gifts, and the regulation of worship, including the Eucharist, all depend on the general belief as to the spirit-world which obtained in the first century.

According to popular opinion, the world was full of spirits (*πνεύματα* or *δαιμόνες*) good and bad, which were able to take possession of, or to obsess, not only human beings, but even inanimate objects. One of the main reasons for which the ordinary man took part in religious ceremonies was to avoid obsession by evil daemons and to secure obsession or inspiration by good spirits. The various Mysteries were largely regarded from this point of view. Moreover, when this inspiration had once been obtained the religious services remained valuable, because they afforded the means by which the inspired person allowed the spirit which was in him to speak to others, and communicate the will of the gods.

These spirits or daemons were beings intermediate between gods and men. Some of the gods even had originally been daemons, and some of the daemons were the spirits of the dead men who had gained promotion by the distinction of their careers on earth.[1] The spirits were especially the intermediaries between the higher gods and men, and thus corresponded almost exactly to the angels of Jewish

[1] The best statements as to the daemons may be found in Plutarch in many passages; an excellent *résumé* of them is given in Glover's *The Conflict of Religions in the Early Roman Empire*, p. 94 ff. It must, however, be remembered that Plutarch represents the opinion of an educated theologian; the importance of the daemons for the general mass of people is indicated by the magical papyri.

theology. But, just as in Jewish theology, there was not a sharp line of definition between the angels of God and the Spirit (Ruach) of God, so also in the Greek world the idea of the daemon sent by the god passed imperceptibly over into that of the spirit of the god, which was, in one sense, the god himself. Hence the confusion in practical affairs between the daemon of the emperor, and the emperor himself. Probably the average Roman citizen was quite vague as to whether the divinity of the emperor was due to a daemon or spirit who inspired him, or to some special property of the man who was emperor. In the same way he would probably have found a difficulty in distinguishing between the daemon who had helped Augustus, and the Divus Augustus who had been deified. Was it the daemon or the man, or both?[1]

So also in the Mysteries, what did the initiate receive? A daemon ancillary to the god, or an "effluence" from the god, his spirit, which was in some sense the god himself? Probably there was a general vagueness on these points.

In any case, the view that the world was full of these daemons or spirits was undoubted. Moreover, the difference between Greek and Jewish doctrine was really small. The Jew in the Diaspora, at all events, may be said to have distinguished three factors: (1) The angels, the ministers of Jahveh on earth, who looked after all the details of human life. (2) The Spirit of Jahveh, which inspired the prophets, and was believed by the Christians to have been especially given to them. (3) The δαιμόνια, or devils. These were the

[1] Ultimately, of course, the Roman empire settled down to a belief in the actual divinity of the reigning emperor, as such. But this was the end of a development of thought which deserves more detailed treatment than it has at present received.

ghosts of the "giants" who had perished in the Noachian deluge, and the "giants" were the progeny of the disobedient angels who had neglected their duty, and entered into wedlock with women.[1] Part of the work of the Messiah was to be their destruction, but until the "Kingdom" came they wandered through the world, seeking re-incarnation, and causing sickness, but yielding to the power of exorcism.[2]

Of these three points the first affords an exact parallel between the angels and the beneficent daemons. The second affords a parallel in so far as the "Spirit of Jahveh" is parallel to the "spirit" of the god imparted in the Mysteries, or speaking through the oracles and prophets. It is also remarkable that just as the distinction in Jewish theology between Jahveh and the Spirit of Jahveh is not consistently sharply drawn, so too, in the magical papyri, the distinction between the god and his spirit is sometimes made and sometimes ignored.[3] Moreover, just as the Greek was vague as to the distinction between a daemon ancillary to the god, and the spirit effluent from the god himself, so among the Jews there was probably a tendency to confuse the Spirit of Jahveh with the Angel of Jahveh, and the Angel of Jahveh with the angels in general. Thus in Jewish and Christian circles, there was at first a tendency

[1] Full descriptions of their misdeeds and fate are given in Enoch vi.–xix., and in Jubilees iv.–v. References to the same belief are found in Matt. viii. 29; xii. 24–28; Luke xi. 24–26; Jude 6; 2 Peter ii. 4.

[2] Hence the point in Matt. viii. 24: the devils ask, "Art Thou come to torture us *before the time?*" They do not question the Messianic personality of Jesus, but only protest that He has not yet received the active functions of the Messiah.

[3] Cf. Reitzenstein, *Hellenistiche Mysterien Religionen*, p. 137. It is very important to notice how complete Reitzenstein succeeds in showing the error of the view formerly adopted by some theologians, that the concepts πνεῦμα, πνεῦμα Θεοῦ, are exclusively Biblical.

to hesitate whether to speak of "The Spirit" or the "Spirits." So far there is a very close resemblance between Jewish and Greek thought. The difference is really only to be found in connection with the doctrine of God. For the Jahveh of the Jews was not parallel with the gods of the Greeks, as, for instance, Plutarch conceived them, but with the Absolute, or with the Logos, who was above them all, and from whom all being, divine, daemonic, or human, derived its origin.

According, then, to the ancient view of the universe the world was full of spirits, good and bad. How was man to avoid the bad and gain the good? The universal answer was that there were various acts or ceremonies by means of which intercourse with the spirits was rendered possible. These acts belonged in the main to every kind of human function. Eating and drinking were especially regarded from this point of view. There was always a danger that an evil spirit would be attracted by food and drink, and endeavour to enjoy it by obsessing the person who ate it. Hence, according to Porphyry, the symptoms of indigestion. "Every house," says he, "is full of them, and on this account when they are going to call down the gods, they purify the house first and cast those daemons out. Our bodies also are full of them, for they especially delight in certain kinds of food. So when we are eating they approach and sit close to our body; and this is the reason of the purifications, not chiefly on account of the Gods, but in order that these evil daemons may depart. But most of all they delight in blood and impure meats, and enjoy these by entering into those who use them. For universally the vehemence of the desire towards anything, and the impulse of the lust of the spirit, is intensified from no cause than their presence, and they also force men to fall into inarticulate noises and flatulence by sharing the same enjoyment with them."[1] For this reason food had to be protected by being given up to the power of some more powerful and beneficent being; it was consecrated—sacrificed—to some god, and then it was safe: no evil spirit would dare to touch it. Or, in the alternative, it was possible to consecrate and protect the eater; for in the same way, if he were already in the power of some god, no evil spirit would be able to approach him. Those who had been initiated in the Mysteries were safe from evil spirits. In this way evil spirits could be avoided.

How could good spirits be gained? This was especially the object of the Mysteries, and just as evil spirits entered by means of food, so also did the good ones. The sacrificial meals of the Mystery Religions were, at least from one point of view, means of gaining obsession by a good spirit connected with or even identified with the god of the Mystery in question. Men and women ate with the god in order to be taken possession of; or they went to the temple and lived there for the same purpose. Nor was this all: not only could they eat with the god, but they could actually eat food in which the god was, and so eat the god himself. Probably there was much vagueness of thought as to whether the god was in the food, or was joining in the eating of it: but there is ample evidence for both points of view in the Greek world. The former theory is especially

[1] Porphyry, quoted by Eusebius, *Praeparatio Evangelica*, iv. 23. It is noteworthy how very nearly daemonic possession played the same part in ancient pathology as bacterial infection does in modern; disease was regarded as due to a daemon; if you could drive him out you could cure the disease. The same sort of thing is now said of bacilli, which, however, have the advantage that they can be seen under the microscope.

common, and hence it was customary to speak of the "table" (τραπέζα) of the god, and of "laying a place for him" (κλίνην στρῶσαι τῷ θεῷ). Moreover, from the story of Paulina [1] it would seem that invitations to dinner in the temple of Isis sometimes included passing the night there. The still cruder theory that the god is present in the sacrificial food, and thus passes into the being of the worshipper is less widely, but quite sufficiently, attested. For this custom it is not easy to quote single passages, but the collected evidence from all sources provides overwhelming testimony for the view that one period in the development of cultus comprised two central beliefs: first, that the god was incarnate in various persons, especially royal persons; secondly, that the divine nature in them could be assimilated by eating them. Thus far back in the history of mankind it is probable that every race has passed through a period of the religious cannibalism which still survives in some parts of Central Africa. But many centuries ago among the Greek and Roman races, this savage rite was superseded by the custom of eating the representative of the god, either in the form of an animal, or of some other form of food in which he was regarded as incarnate. As civilization advanced the details became less and less crude, but the rite of "eating the god" still remained, and was, no doubt, inextricably mixed up with the cognate idea mentioned above of eating with the god.[2] The exact point of view of

[1] Josephus, *Antiquitt.*, xviii. 3, 4. Paulina was, under these circumstances, seduced by her lover, who had bribed the priests to allow him to appear as the God Anubis. There appears to be no reason to doubt Paulina's *bona fides*.

[2] The subject may be studied in Frazer, *Golden Bough*, 2nd edition, vol. ii. pp. 318–366. Farnell, *Cults of the Greek States*, vol. v. cap. v., on Dionysiac ritual, especially pp. 164 ff.; and Harrison, *Prolegomena to the Study of Greek Religion*, cap. x., on the *Orphic Mysteries*, especially the section on the

individuals was no doubt as "foggy" and confused as it always was on subjects of this nature which are concerned partly with a real spiritual experience and partly with an artificial intellectual explanation.

The signs of possession by a good spirit were various: no doubt they were usually unobtrusive, the worshipper merely felt convinced that he had received benefit. But sometimes plainer symptoms could be observed in the form of ecstasy, prophecy, glossolalia, *i.e.* unintelligible speech, and visions. All of them differed very little from the signs of possession by an evil spirit, and it was often a matter on which opinion differed sharply whether the obsessed should be congratulated on his spiritual endowment, or exorcised to save him from the clutches of a daemon.

The Things offered to Idols.—It is not difficult to see how completely the belief in spirits or daemons is the background of this section. To reconstruct the precise opinions of St. Paul is indeed more difficult than to understand what he is discussing.

"Things offered to idols" (εἰδωλόθυτα)[1] might be taken in at least two senses. From one point of view the greater part of the meat sold in the shops was "offered to idols," as the animal from which it was taken had usually been consecrated to some god, even if it were only by the

Omophagia, pp. 478–500. In all these a long series of references will be found to passages in original documents and to modern treatises on special points. Other references to German books will be found in Lietzmann's Commentary on 1 Corinthians, pp. 124 ff.

[1] This is apparently the Christian and possibly Jewish term. The usual expression was ἱερόθυτον or θεόθυτον. See J. Weiss on 1 Cor. viii. 1 (p. 214). He gives references, among others, to Plutarch, *Moralia*, p. 729 C.; Pollux, *Onomast.*, i. 29. According to Phrynichus, *Ecloga*, p. 159 (Lobeck's edition), θεόθυτον is the older term, which he recommends to the exclusion of ἱερόθυτον.

ceremonial burning of a few hairs. Thus, in this strict sense, to avoid eating things offered to idols was difficult, if not impossible. It would, however, appear that it was not quite impossible, for St. Paul implies that by making inquiry the Corinthians might be able to avoid such meat.

But besides this, it was possible to use *εἰδωλόθυτα* with a restricted reference to actual participation in the sacrificial meals. As to these meals a misconception is easy. We are inclined to look on them as solemn religious services. Some of them no doubt were: but others probably resembled a dinner-party more closely than a church-service. It was the custom to issue invitations to dinner in the temple, and the fiction was that the god was himself the host.[1] Thus "things offered to idols" had a social as well as a religious importance, and an attempt was made to combine physical satisfaction with "spiritual" edification. To avoid them altogether was difficult, and certainly would hinder social intercourse to an enormous extent.

Apparently, there were two opinions on the matter in Corinth: one party maintained that an idol was nothing, and that therefore things offered to idols had no importance: they thought that the whole matter was indifferent, and that Christian freedom justified them in doing as they wished. Another party held the opposite opinion and thought that, cost what it might, Christians ought to abstain absolutely from the contamination of things offered

[1] Cf. *Pap. Oxy.*, i. 110: *ἐρωτᾷ σε Χαιρήμων δειπνῆσαι εἰς κλείνην (κλίνην) τοῦ κυρίου Σαράπιδος ἐν τῷ Σαραπείῳ αὔριον ἥτις ἐστὶν ιε, ὥρας θʹ*. See also *Pap. Oxy.*, iii. 523: *ἐρωτᾷ σε Ἀντώνιος Πτολεμαίου διπνῆσαι παρʼ αὐτῷ εἰς κλείνην τοῦ κυρίου Σαράπιδος ἐν τοῖς Κλαυδίου Σαραπίωνος τῇ ις ἀπὸ ὥρας θʹ*. Cf. Aristides, *In Serapidem* (*Or.*, viii. p. 93 f., Dind.): *καὶ τοίνυν καὶ θυσιῶν μόνῳ τούτῳ θεῷ διαφερόντως κοινωνοῦσιν ἄνθρωποι τὴν ἀκριβῆ κοινωνίαν, καλοῦντες τὲ ἐφʼ ἑστίαν καὶ προιστάμενοι δαίμονα αὐτὸν καὶ ἑστιάτορα.* The fullest note on the subject will be found in Lietzmann's Commentary on 1 Corinthians, p. 124.

to idols.[1] The strict school argued that to eat things offered to idols was a form of idolatry, and dangerous because of the daemons.[2] The "enlightened" school argued that idols had no real existence, that the food was not really affected by being consecrated to the non-existent, and therefore that it really did not matter if Christians bought it in the market, or took part in meals at which it was eaten. But besides this the "enlightened" school also argued that, even admitting the possible influence of consecrated food on others, they were themselves safe because through the Christian Mysteries they had gained the protection of a higher power. This argument is implied by 1 Cor. x., where St. Paul retorts that they are no more safe than were the Israelites, the type of the Christians. The Israelites had all received the types of Baptism and Eucharist, in the crossing of the Red Sea, in the feeding

[1] This much is clear from 1 Corinthians on any hypothesis. The difficulties in the section 1 Cor. viii. 1—x. 33, are not in seeing what were the different points of view among the Corinthians, but in answering the questions (1) Did St. Paul deal with both of them at the same time? or did he, as J. Weiss thinks (see p. 123), deal with one in the "previous letter," and the other later on in consequence of a misunderstanding of his advice? (2) Can the point of view of St. Paul in viii. 1–13 be regarded as really consistent with that in x. 20? Personally, I doubt if it can; but complete consistency is never reached by any one. The solution to the difficulty is psychological, not literary.

[2] There is a constant confusion of thought in early Christian thought as to idols. On the one hand, there was the argument, derived from the Jewish prophets, that an idol was only an image made by man, and wholly powerless, and that the gods of the Greeks were not gods at all, and had no existence in fact. On the other hand, was the identification of the gods with daemons and fallen angels, and the belief that in some way these daemons were connected with the images of the gods and with the temples. A very instructive passage is Ps. Apuleius, *Asclepius*, xxxvii.: "Quoniam ergo proavi nostri multum errabant . . . invenerunt artem qua efficerent deos, cui inventae adjunxerunt virtutem de mundi natura convenientem eamque miscentes, quoniam animas facere non poterant, evocantes animas daemonum vel angelorum, eas indiderunt imaginibus sanctis divinisque mysteriis, per quas idola et benefaciendi et male vires habere potuissent."

on manna in the wilderness, and in drinking from the rock. Nevertheless, they fell, and the fall should be an example to Christians not to commit the same mistakes. The whole of this section in its context is only intelligible as directed against the argument that those who have been initiated into the Christian Mysteries may safely do anything they like,—they have attained safety (σωτηρία), which was the object of all the Mysteries.

This difference of opinion between two parties in Corinth is clearly reflected in St. Paul's advice, and explains its strange turns and apparent inconsistencies. This is especially marked in 1 Cor. x. 14 ff. Here St. Paul is conceding to the scrupulous party the correctness of their objection to idolatry; but he is thinking all the time of the effect his words will have on the party of freedom, and therefore he turns to them and invites them to consider accurately the exact force of his admission.[1] He quite accepts the propositions of the party of freedom that an idol is nothing, and that food sacrificed to idols has no especial value, but he does admit, as a concession to the scrupulous, that the sacrificial meals do contain the possibility of "infection" from daemons. The position is not wholly logical, for the Christian word εἰδωλόθυτον, as compared with the true Greek phrase ἱερόθυτον or θεόθυτον, implies the view that the heathen gods are illusions—without any real existence. But this sort of inconsistency is common to humanity. All of us must be aware that on many points our position is a wholly illogical combination

[1] J. Weiss sees no difference between φημὶ and λέγω. Surely this is inaccurate; of course, φησὶ and φασὶ are neutral expressions, but I suggest that φημὶ always implies some degree of assent to a proposition, explicit or implicit, and so often comes to mean "I admit."

of half-belief, half-scepticism, which we cover but do not justify by calling it an "open mind."

Do the Apostolic Decrees also lie behind this difference of opinion in Corinth? Certainly they are not quoted; but I see no reason to state definitely that they cannot have been known in Corinth. On the contrary, I think it is quite possible that they had been appealed to by the stricter party, and that St. Paul's answer is intended as giving his view of the justification and meaning of the decree so far as things offered to idols are concerned. Still, this cannot be proved, and all that can be said as to the existence or non-existence of the decrees in Corinth is that neither can be established.

"*Spiritual persons*" (or "*gifts*"?).—When St. Paul begins 1 Cor. xii., περὶ δὲ τῶν πνευματικῶν, does he speak of persons or gifts?[1] Obviously πνευματικῶν may have either meaning, but since in the immediate context St. Paul is discussing persons, not gifts, and the way to distinguish the true from the false πνευματικός, it is probably better to treat it as masculine[2]—"spiritual persons," or what the Germans more conveniently term *pneumatiker*. But at all properly to appreciate the meaning of the word in the ancient world of thought, we must grasp the fact firmly that the Spirit was a concrete "something" or "some one." Judged by modern standards, one might almost say it was material, and in popular thought it was probably regarded as belonging to the same category of substance as air, or sometimes as light.[3] The point is that we are apt to use

[1] In 1 Cor. ii. 15; iii. 1; xiv. 37, πνευματικὸς is used of persons, almost as the equivalent of a substantive; in ix. 11; xiv. 1; xv. 46, the neuter is used, but in each case with a distinct reference to a substantive in the context.

[2] So thinks J. Weiss, p. 294.

[3] The German word gives the meaning far better—*Lichtstoff*.

"spiritual" and "spirit" in the sense of a "frame of mind" (*stimmung*) which pays no special attention to carnal or material objects, and is busy with ideals. That is not what πνευματικὸς meant in the first century; it meant a man who was obsessed by a πνεῦμα which was not his own, but had come into him from without.

The signs of this spiritual obsession were various, but they were chiefly ecstatic. That is to say, the proof of the existence of the spirit within was that the man did things which he otherwise could not do. This supernatural power might manifest itself in act or in word. The inspired person might develop powers of healing or do other miraculous deeds; the magical papyri show that this was as common in heathen circles as it was among Christians,[1] and even extended to the resuscitation of the dead.[2] But more important than these were the gifts of prophecy and glossolalia. The "prophet" was a familiar figure in the ancient world, and the explanation given of his utterances was the same in all nations. The Spirit was speaking through him. He was only an instrument by means of which God revealed His will to the world. The prophets of the Old Testament were regarded by the first Christians as verbally and literally inspired, and the Christian prophets belonged to the same class. "For among us," says Justin to the Jew Trypho, "prophetic gifts (χαρίσματα) still exist, which shows that the privileges formerly belonging to your nation have been transferred to us,"[3] and in the first

[1] Cf. 1 Cor. xii. 29 ff.

[2] Cf. Reitzenstein, p. 137: ὁρκίζω σε, πνεῦμα ἐν ἀέρι φοιτώμενον, εἴσελθε, ἐνπνευμάτωσον, δυνάμωσον, διαέγειρον τῇ δυνάμει τοῦ αἰωνίου θεοῦ τόδε σῶμα. The πνευματικός, himself inspired, is here appealing to the Spirit to restore a corpse. The train of thought is not perfectly logical, but there is not much doubt as to what it was.

[3] *Dial. c. Tryph.*, 82.

Apology he explains that prophets are those "through whom the prophetic Spirit has foretold the future."[1] In the same way the prophetic speaker in the Odes of Solomon says, "As the hand plays on the harp, and the strings sound, so speaks the Spirit of the Lord in my members."[2] In the same way Epiphanius tells us that Montanus[3] claimed that he was used by the spirit as a man plays on the lyre, and the same image is found in Ps. Justin's *Cohortatio ad Gentes*, "The divine 'plectrum' comes down from heaven, using righteous men as a harp or lyre in order to reveal to us the knowledge of divine and heavenly things."[4]

But this belief that divine spirits spoke through men was not specifically Jewish or Christian: men like Apollonius of Tyana or Alexander of Abonoteichos were regarded not as exceptionally gifted men, but as men through whom the god spoke. The prophet was the instrument by which God revealed Himself. It was naturally only a step further to confuse the inspired person with the divine spirit, and so reach the Greek concept of the θεῖος ἄνθρωπος.

Thus the language of these inspired persons was not ordinary language. Sometimes it was intelligible, and sometimes it was unintelligible; in the former case it was prophecy, in the latter glossolalia. The difference between glossolalia and prophecy was only that glossolalia was unintelligible; it was a language which could only be understood by those to whom the Spirit gave the power of interpreting it. The picture of glossolalia given by St.

[1] *Apol.* I. 31. [2] Odes of Solomon, 6.

[3] Epiph., *Haer.* 48, 4: ὁ ἄνθρωπος ὡσεὶ λύρα, κἀγὼ ἐφίπταμαι ὡσεὶ πλῆκτρον. ὁ ἄνθρωπος κοιμᾶται, κἀγὼ γρηγορῶ· ἰδοὺ κύριός ἐστιν ὁ ἐξιστάνων καρδίας ἀνθρώπων, κ.τ.λ.

[4] *Cohortatio ad Graecos*, 8; cf. also Athenagoras, *Pro Christianis*, 9: συγχρησαμένου τοῦ πνεύματος ὡς εἰ καὶ αὐλητὴς αὐλὸν ἐμπνεῦσαι.

Paul in 1 Cor. xiv. can be compared with hostile pictures drawn by Celsus of Palestinian Christian prophets, and by Irenaeus of Marcosian prophetesses.[1] In the strange words in the magical papyri we probably have references to glossolalia in heathen circles.[2]

Besides these manifestations of the spirit through the acts and speech of the obsessed, there were also visual manifestations in which the πνευματικὸς saw visions—revelations or ἀποκαλύψεις—in which he was taken in the spirit to the hidden world. Here, again, there is no difference between the Christian and the heathen belief. St. Paul knew a man who was taken up into the third heaven, and Apuleius describes the experiences of Luciusi n the Mysteries of Isis. "I drew near," says Lucius, "to the confines of death; I trod the threshold of Proserpine; I was borne through all the elements and returned. At midnight I saw the sun flashing with bright light; gods of the world above, gods of the world below, into their presence I came." Whether Apuleius and St. Paul are either or both giving their own experience is questionable, but undoubtedly both believed in the genuineness of what they described.[3] Nor did the Christians ever suggest that the heathen experience was different from their own;[4] they only urged that it was due to an evil spirit instead of to a good spirit.

[1] Cf. Origen, *Contra Celsum*, vii. 8, 9; and Irenaeus, *Adv. Haer.* i. 13, 2 (ed. Massuet).

[2] See Weinel, *Die Wirkungen des Geistes*, p. 77, and see Appendix on p. 241.

[3] 2 Cor. xii. 1 ff.

[4] This seems to be the meaning of the difficult passage (1 Cor. xii. 2). The text (οἴδατε ὅτι ὅτε ἔθνη ἦτε πρὸς τὰ εἴδωλα τὰ ἄφωνα ὡς ἂν ἤγεσθε ἀπαγόμενοι) is certainly corrupt, and probably cannot be emended; but, as Chrysostom saw (cf. Cramer's *Catena*, *ad loc.*), it is a reference to the experiences of obsession among the Corinthians before their conversion, and is intended as the basis of the following argument.

This last point explains the importance of the first question which the Corinthians propounded. How were they to distinguish the πνευματικὸς who was inspired by a holy spirit, from the πνευματικὸς who was inspired by an evil spirit? Both did much the same things, but whereas he who was inspired by a holy spirit deserved the implicit obedience due to the infallible voice of God, or a good daemon, the other must be avoided, and attempts made to rid him of his obsession. It is also easy to see how fruitful a soil this general belief supplied for the later development of Christological doctrine. The Christian, especially the Christian prophet, was inspired and possessed by a holy spirit. This holy spirit came from his Lord and Saviour,[1] Jesus. That seemed wholly natural: if Jesus was a Redeemer-God, of course His Spirit was given to those who shared in His mysteries. But was this Spirit a spirit which had inspired Jesus? or had Jesus become a spirit or daemon? or had He from the beginning been a spirit? and similar questions were at first not asked,[2] though the development of Christian doctrine showed that they were raised later.

Thus the practical question arose how the πνευματικὸς who was inspired by the "Spirit of Jesus" could be distinguished from the πνευματικός who was inspired by an evil spirit. That is the problem which St. Paul had to face, and he solved it by saying that if the πνευματικὸς

[1] Just as the initiate in the Osiris Mysteries spoke of Osiris as *Lord and Saviour*: it does not, of course, follow that the words meant quite the same, but it explains why there was no difficulty in persuading the Graeco-Roman world of the propriety of these expressions. They are not specifically Christian, but are common to the Mystery Religions.

[2] Each of these questions might have been asked about Osiris or any of the other "redeemer-gods," but, so far as I am aware, there is no evidence that they were raised.

recognized Jesus as Lord, he was inspired by a holy spirit;[1] but that if he said "Jesus is accursed," he was not inspired by a spirit of God. There he leaves the question; but it is obvious that this simple test was likely to prove insufficient, and it is not surprising that the next century reveals other solutions. The same problem, for instance, is faced in the Johannine Epistles. "Try the spirits," says the writer, "because many false prophets have gone out into the world" (1 John iv. 1); and he gives a doctrinal test which goes a little further than St. Paul's. "Every spirit," he says, "which confesses Jesus as a Messiah come in flesh is of God." Parallel with this doctrinal test is another, found in the *Didache* and the *Shepherd* of Hermas, which suggests that conduct is the test of inspiration; and Ignatius[2] proposed to leave the decision of the question to the Bishop, and this method ultimately became general.

The other question which the Corinthians propounded was concerned with the relative value of the gifts (*χαρίσματα*) by which the Spirit manifested itself. It is not necessary now—indeed, it is outside the scope of this book—to consider the details of St. Paul's answer. The question is, What light can be thrown on the situation at Corinth? It is important to notice that practically all distinction in the community is regarded as a gift of the Spirit. To this are ascribed healings, miracles, prophecy, the power of distinguishing spirits, glossolalia, and the interpretation of glossolalia. The question which agitated the Corinthians was the relative value of these gifts, and St. Paul's answer, though given at some length, and rising to the most

[1] It is worth noting that St. Paul says *πνεύματι ἁγίῳ*, not *τῷ πνεύματι ἁγίῳ*, but I am not sure whether the point will ultimately prove to be really important.

[2] Chronologically earlier than Hermas, or (probably) the *Didache*.

eloquent heights, is comparatively simple,—he states that social not individual value is the standard by which the gifts must be measured, and that none of them are useful without sympathy (ἀγάπη). But it is also quite plain that this is not exactly the point which the Corinthians had proposed. Their question was inspired by a divergence of opinion as to the more ecstatic gifts, prophecy and glossolalia; some thought that they were of supreme importance; others regarded them as undesirable. The former type is more fully dealt with by St. Paul, but the existence of the latter is vouched for by the advice, "Forbid not to speak with tongues." The importance of this will become plain in the next paragraph.

The Regulation of Worship.—It is clear from St. Paul's statement that the great respect claimed for the gifts of the Spirit was the main reason for difficulties connected with religious services. St. Paul says in 1 Cor. xiv. 23–35: "If therefore the whole Church be come together into one place, and all speak with tongues, and there come in those that are unlearned, or unbelievers, will they not say that ye are mad? But if all prophesy, and there come in one that believeth not, or one unlearned, he is convinced of all, he is judged of all: and thus are the secrets of his heart made manifest; and so falling down on his face he will worship God, and report that God is in you of a truth. How is it then, brethren? when ye come together, every one of you hath a psalm, hath a doctrine, hath a revelation, hath a tongue hath an interpretation. Let all things be done unto edifying. If any man speak in a tongue, let it be by two, or at the most by three, and that in turn; and let one be an interpreter. But if there be no interpreter, let him keep silence in the church; and let him speak to himself, and to God. Let the prophets speak two or three, and let the others judge. If any thing be revealed to another that sitteth by, let the first hold his peace. For ye may all prophesy one by one, that all may learn, and all may be exhorted. And the spirits of the prophets are subject to the prophets; for God is not the author of confusion, but of peace, as in all churches of the saints. Let your women keep silence in the churches: for it is not permitted unto them to speak; but let them be in subjection, as also saith the Law. And if they will learn any thing, let them ask their own husbands at home: for it is shameful for a woman to speak in the church."

The picture drawn of the state of things in Corinth is plain enough: everything was being sacrificed to the "gifts" of prophesy and glossolalia. The prophets all spoke at once, and even women claimed to be heard. It is not unnatural that, under these circumstances, there was a party which was ready to "quench the Spirit," and "forbid prophecies"; and that there was considerable friction between the ecstatic and the more sober members of the community.

The question of the women is a little more complicated. It appears that there was a party, no doubt composed largely of women, who thought that women were in no respect inferior to men. It must be admitted that they could appeal with some force to St. Paul's own teaching that in Christ Jesus there is neither male nor female. Therefore they insisted that women should be allowed the same freedom of prophecy in the community as men enjoyed. Against this party we can imagine that it was argued that, although it might be true that in Christ Jesus there is no difference between male and female, this does not apply in practice to life in this world, and a protest was raised against behaving as though the kingdom of God were already come. A further point was concerned with dress. From 1 Cor. xi. 3 ff., it appears that the general custom was then—as now—for women to have their heads covered in church, and for men to be bareheaded. It is the task of the interpreter of St. Paul to explain the justification which St. Paul gives of this custom: it is by no means plain, and ver. 10 in particular, "For this cause ought the woman to have power on her head because of the angels," provides a problem which is likely to remain insoluble. But it is quite simple to see the situation which called forth his remarks. The point which is remarkable is that the custom to which the Corinthian women objected, and St. Paul adhered, was the Greek, not the Jewish practice.[1]

The Eucharist.—The Eucharist is so closely connected with controversies of every kind that it is desirable to define somewhat closely precisely what points belong to the present discussion. Regarded as an historical problem, it may be said to confront the student of Christian origins with the following questions: (1) What is the value of the account in the Synoptic Gospels of the institution of the Eucharist, and what was (supposing the historical nature of the story to be accepted) the real meaning of Jesus? (2) What was the view held by the Corinthian Christian as to the meaning of the Eucharist, and in what form was it

[1] Cf. Plutarch, *Quaest. Rom.*, 84, p. 267*a*: συνηθέστερον δὲ ταῖς μεν γυναιξὶν ἐγκεκαλυμμέναις, τοῖς δὲ ἀνδράσιν ἀκαλύπτοις εἰς τὸ δημόσιον προιέναι. Cf. also Dio Chrysostom, who (*Or.*, 33, 48 ff.) rebukes the degeneracy which in Tarsus began to allow women to walk in the streets without a veil covering the face, and points out the dangers of daemons entering by the ears or nose. See also Lietzmann's note, p. 128.

celebrated? (3) In what direction did St. Paul think it desirable to amend the Corinthian practice or doctrine? (4) How far did the Christian custom of the next generation agree with or differ from the lines laid down or sanctioned by St. Paul? Of these four problems the second is that which is necessary for the present purpose; the first and fourth are scarcely germane to it at all; and the third only quite partially.

We have, then, to ask what was the form in which the Corinthians celebrated the Eucharist, and what doctrine they attached to it. This can best be discussed under the two heads of form and doctrine.

The form of celebration is indicated by St. Paul's comments in I Cor. xi. 20–21, and his advice in I Cor. xi. 33. In the former passage he says, "Now when you assemble together it is not possible to eat a Lord's supper, for each takes his own supper at the meal, and one is hungry and another is drunken."[1] In the latter he says, "therefore, when ye assemble, wait for each other at the meal."

From this material two points are clear. First, the "Lord's supper" was a true meal, not merely a ceremonial or symbolical eating, that the custom was for individuals to bring food for this meal, and secondly, that owing to the bad habit, which St. Paul rebukes, of each eating what he brought himself, there was an undesirably unequal distribution of the provisions, and an unseemly tendency not to

[1] Two points are doubtful in this translation. (α) Does ἐπὶ τὸ αὐτὸ really go with συνερχομένων, or with οὐκ ἔστιν? Commentators are almost unanimous in favour of the former view, but I am not sure that the point is quite certain. (β) What is the meaning of προλαμβάνει? Most commentators say, "takes in advance," but the evidence of the papyri (see the *Expositor* for March, 1911) goes to show that it probably only means "take."

wait until the whole community was present. It also seems, from the way in which St. Paul introduces the whole question by a reference to the divisions in the Church,[1] that the secret cause for this behaviour was the partizanship of the Corinthians: instead of there being one meal for the whole community, there was a tendency to divide into groups and cliques which did not share their food with each other.

It is sometimes thought that this meal ought to be separated from the Eucharist, and be identified with the Agape. This view is untenable for two reasons. In the first, it is clear that St. Paul is speaking of the Eucharist in I Cor. xi. 23 ff., and there is no trace of any break in his argument between this passage and the preceding section, in which an actual meal is clearly being discussed. In the second place, it is extremely doubtful whether there was a distinction between Agape and Eucharist. In the letters of Ignatius the words are clearly synonyms, and Batiffol has gone far towards proving that the supposed difference between the two elsewhere is based on no solid foundation.[2]

The doctrine of the Eucharist,[3] as it was held by the Corinthians, is primarily illustrated by I Cor. x. 16–20. In this passage St. Paul says, "The cup of blessing which we bless, is it not a sharing in the blood of Christ? The bread which we break, is it not a sharing of the body of Christ? . . . but what they (*i.e.* the heathen) sacrifice, they sacrifice not to God, but to daemons: I would not have

[1] I Cor. xi. 18 ff.

[2] Batiffol, *Études d'histoire et de Théologie positive*, pp. 277–311.

[3] See especially Heitmuller's *Taufe und Abendmahl bei Paulus.* This book is so clear and so thorough that it has an importance out of all proportion to its size.

you share in daemons. You cannot drink the cup of the Lord and the cup of daemons; you cannot share the table of the Lord and the table of daemons." The importance of this passage is that St. Paul is here not discussing doubtful points in the Eucharist, or giving instruction concerning it, as he is in 1 Cor. xi. 17–34, but is using the general and undisputed belief of Christians as to the Eucharist in order to establish his position with regard to things offered to idols. He clearly means that the Corinthians know quite well that the Eucharist is a rite which really conveys that which the heathen erroneously thought to obtain in their sacrificial meals—that is, the participation in the Divine nature.

A further light on the doctrine of the Eucharist is thrown by 1 Cor. x. 3 ff. Here St. Paul speaks of the manna which the Israelites ate in the wilderness as "spiritual food," and the water from the rock as "spiritual drink." His argument is, "the Israelites—like you—had spiritual food and drink, yet they fell." He can scarcely be referring to anything except the Eucharist; and if so, he implies clearly that in the Eucharist Christians received the "Spirit" in the form of food and drink. When we remember that to St Paul "the Lord is the Spirit," and that His body was "spiritual," it is plain that the only conclusion we can draw is that the Corinthians regarded the Eucharist as food and drink, by eating which they enjoyed communion, or participation, in the life of Jesus, as a Spirit;[1] or, to express it

[1] We have to guard against an obscurity of thought due to a change in the meaning of words. "Spirit" is not always a translation of πνεῦμα. One can see this by considering how the ordinary phrase "he has the spirit of St. Paul" would be translated into New Testament Greek. Probably one would write τὰ τοῦ Παύλου φρονεῖ: the obvious ἔχει τὸ πνεῦμα Παύλου would mean something different—"he is inspired by the same supernatural being which was in Paul," or perhaps, "which Paul has now become."

differently, by it they became ἔνθεοι—ἐν Χριστῷ—just as the participants in the Eleusinian Mysteries believed that they became ἔνθεοι, by means of a meal, in which they partook, in some mysterious manner, of the body of Dionysus.

Whether there was any special service of consecration for the elements is not clear, but the expressions "the cup of blessing which we bless," and "the bread which we break,"[1] in 1 Cor. x. 16, probably point to some liturgical formula, which was regarded as endowing the bread and wine with its miraculous properties.

The question remains whether the Eucharist was generally regarded as a commemoration of the death of Jesus. That St. Paul so regarded it is, of course, proved by 1 Cor. xi. 26: "For so often as ye eat this bread and drink the cup, ye show forth the Lord's death." It is, however, just possible, though not, I think, probable, that this was not part of the general Corinthian faith, but that St. Paul was reminding them of a point which they had overlooked. It would, in any case, be an idea which would seem to Gentile minds quite natural, and precisely similar to one of the most frequent forms of sacrificial meal. This was the sacrificial meal instituted by the testament (διαθήκη; cf. Mark xiv. 24) of some rich and pious person who left instructions that a meal should be held in his memory in the temple of one of the gods. These meals were thus commemorative of a dead person; but they were also sacraments, by means of which a union with Divine life was accomplished.[2]

[1] The question is raised by this expression whether the common phrase in Acts, ἡ κλᾶσις τοῦ ἄρτου, refers to the Eucharist. Personally, I incline to think that it does, but the question is scarcely within the limits of the present work.

[2] Cf. the long list of quotations in Leitzmann's *Commentary*, pp. 160–164, of which the most important are CIG. ii. 2448; CIL. xiii. 5708; CIL. vi. 10,234; CIL. xiv. 2112.

The importance of these points is considerable. It is impossible to pretend to ignore the fact that much of the controversy between Catholic and Protestant theologians has found its centre in the doctrine of the Eucharist, and the latter have appealed to primitive Christianity to support their views. From their point of view the appeal fails: the Catholic doctrine is much more nearly primitive than the Protestant. But the Catholic advocate in winning his case has proved still more: the type of doctrine which he defends is not only primitive, but pre-Christian. Or, to put the matter in the terms of another controversy, Christianity has not borrowed from the Mystery Religions, because it was always, at least in Europe, a Mystery Religion itself.

(3) THE RESURRECTION OF THE DEAD.

It is clear from 1 Cor. xv. that there was a party at Corinth which denied that there would ever be a resurrection of the dead. It is also plain that there was nevertheless no dispute as to the resurrection of Christ, for the whole argument of St. Paul is based on the fact that there was a general consent on that subject. It has sometimes been thought that this implies that the Corinthians had no hope of any future life beyond death. But this view is an unjustifiable conclusion from 1 Cor. xv. 17–19. St. Paul is here arguing that there must be a resurrection, because a future life is impossible without one, and that the hope of the Christian to share in the life of Christ necessitates that he should rise from the dead just as Christ did. Moreover, the idea that there was no future life is as wholly foreign to the point of view of the "Mystery Religions" of the Corinthian world, as it was to that of Jewish theology.

The question was not whether there would be a future life, but whether a future life must be attained by means of a resurrection, and St. Paul's argument is that in the first place the past resurrection of Christ is positive evidence for the future resurrection of Christians, and in the second place that the conception of a resurrection is central and essential in Christianity, which offers no hope of a future life for the dead apart from a resurrection.

As was said in connection with the similar question in Thessalonica, the situation is only intelligible if we take into consideration the general views associated with the Mystery Religions. These religions all made the same offer —life through death, given by mysteries which secured association with a divine saviour, who had himself also passed through death. But even though some of these mysteries—notably those connected with Attis and Osiris —spoke of an actual resurrection of the dead god, they rarely seem to have conceived the idea of a general resurrection of the dead on the lines of Jewish belief.[1] The point of difference is this: the Greek expected that after death the spirit, which was divine, at all events after initiation into

[1] The only Mystery Religion which had quite certainly anything of this nature was Mithraism. In this there was, alongside of the more typical teaching of the journey of the soul through the heavens, the doctrine of a resurrection of the dead, at the return of Mithra. "Mithra," says M. Cumont (*Les Mystères de Mithra*, p. 121), "will redescend and raise up mankind. They will all come forth from their tombs, resume their former appearance, and recognize each other. The entire race will be reunited in a great assembly, and the god of truth will separate the good from the bad. Then, as a last sacrifice, he will slay the divine bull, will mix its flesh with the consecrated wine, and offer to the just this miraculous beverage, which will give them immortality." But it is not probable that Mithraism was widely spread in Corinth in the first century. The rise of Mithraism was contemporaneous with that of Christianity, and both owed their success greatly to the fact that they stood out from the other Mystery Religions by their ethical character.

the mysteries, was set free from the trammels of the flesh, which it left behind. The flesh remained in the grave, and was gradually dissolved into the elements of which it had been composed: the spirit went through the heavens armed with the secret knowledge (γνῶσις) which enabled it to pass the various doors and their guardians, and as it went it left behind at each stage something more of the things which limit or defile. For it is not only the flesh which is bondage: the intellect, the emotions, the desires, all belong to the lower spheres of being, and each is cast aside as the realm to which it belongs is passed through.[1]

The Jewish doctrine, on the other hand, found its centre in the idea of a resurrection. It did not always postulate a permanent resurrection of the flesh as such, but a resurrection which was preliminary to a change from flesh into spirit.[2] On the other hand, there were some Jewish schools which looked for a resurrection of the flesh, and its immortality as such in the kingdom of God. So, for instance, the writer of the fourth book of the Sibyllines says—

> ἀλλ᾽ ὅταν ἤδη πάντα τέφρη σποδόεσσα γένηται
> καὶ πῦρ κοιμήσῃ θεὸς ἄσπετον ὥσπερ ἀνῆψεν,
> ὀστέα καὶ σποδιὴν αὐτὸς θεὸς ἔμπαλιν ἄνδρων
> μορφώσει, στήσει δὲ βροτοὺς πάλιν, ὡς πάρος ἦσαν.
> καὶ τότε δὴ κρίσις ἔσσετ᾽, ἐφ᾽ ᾗ δικάσει θεὸς αὐτός
> κρίνων ἔμπαλι κόσμον . . .
> ὅσσοι δ᾽ εὐσεβέουσι, πάλιν ζήσονται ἐπὶ γαῖαν

[1] Cf. Bousset, "Die Himmelsreise der Seele," in the *Archiv fur Religionswissenschaft*, iv. (1901), pp. 136–169 and 229–273. This is a most learned article, and its study is essential to any thorough appreciation of this question.

[2] Cf. the *Apocalypse of Baruch*, chaps. xlix.–li. Baruch does not actually say that the dead will become spirits, but he says that they will be transformed into the splendour of the angels; and the angels were certainly not flesh.

πνεῦμα θεοῦ δόντος[1] ζωήν θ' ἅμα καὶ χάριν αὐτοῖς εὐσεβέσιν, κ.τ.λ.[2]

Thus it is natural that at Corinth there was a division of opinion among the Christians as to a resurrection of the dead. It was not that any one questioned the immortality of the soul, or doubted that Jesus had conquered death. But there were some who did not think that this implied a resurrection of the flesh, and did not believe that the flesh could become incorruptible or immortal; on the other hand, those who had been more closely in contact with Jewish Apocalyptic teaching regarded a resurrection as a necessary part of the coming of the Kingdom.

It is easy to see St. Paul thinking first of one party and then of the other as he writes I Cor. xv. On the main issue he agrees with the Jewish point, insists on the parallelism between Christ and the Christian, and combats the objection as to a resurrection of the flesh by arguing that a "body" may be of "spirit." Then he turns round and recognizes the element of truth in the Greek position. "I admit," he says (φημί), "that flesh and blood cannot inherit the kingdom of God," and proceeds to adopt the doctrine of a change of substance at the moment of resurrection. If we may freely paraphrase his words, what he says is: "The Jewish party is right in thinking that those who die before the coming of the kingdom do not pass individually and separately into heaven. They will sleep until the resurrection, and then—this is the Christian mystery—they will be raised up as spiritual bodies. On the other hand, the Greek party is right in thinking that

[1] I think that this means breath, or spirit, but is hardly equal to a change into a spiritual nature.

[2] *Or. Sib.*, iv. 179–190.

there is no resurrection of the body as flesh: flesh and blood have no part in the kingdom of God; it is right in thinking that our flesh belongs to the corruptible world, and cannot pass into the world of eternity and incorruptibility. Nevertheless, the Greeks do not understand the true nature of the Christian mystery; it is not, like the heathen mysteries, a promise of a passage into an eternal but incorporeal life; it is the promise of a change of substance which will affect both living and dead, when the Parousia comes, so that our bodies, instead of consisting of corruptible flesh and blood, will become spiritual, and consist of the same substance as do God and His attendants." It will be noted that the question of the period after death and before resurrection does not seem to have been discussed. This was, no doubt, due to the immediate expectation of the Parousia.

(4) THE OPPOSITION TO ST. PAUL.

Since the modern investigations of early Christian history were taken in hand, there have been two main lines of opinion as to the nature of the opposition to St. Paul in Corinth. According to one view it was a new manifestation of the Judaizing propaganda, which had its centre in Jerusalem and was controverted in the Epistles to the Galatians and to the Romans. According to the other it was inspired by a desire to go still further than St. Paul in the direction of freedom from the Law, and to lay even greater stress on the spiritual nature of Christianity. Each of these opinions rests on the *prima facie* obvious meaning of one or two passages, and the real difficulty is that, whichever view be taken, either an exegesis has to be adopted for some passages which is not the most natural, or a position of affairs has to be supposed to exist for which no direct evidence can otherwise be adduced.

In favour of the view that St. Paul's opponents were Judaizers, are, in the main, two references in 2 Corinthians, with each of which various less important references may be grouped.

(α) In 2 Cor. xi. 5, and again in 2 Cor. xii. 11, St. Paul refers to his opponents as the "ultra apostles" (οἱ ὑπερλίαν ἀπόστολοι). The most natural interpretation is that this refers to the leaders of the Church at Jerusalem, to the "Twelve" in particular, and that it ought to be especially connected with the mention of a Cephas party in 1 Cor. i. 12. With these may be grouped the reference in 1 Cor. ix. 4 ff. to Cephas and to the "brothers of the Lord." "Have we not a right to eat and to drink? Have we not a right to take about a Christian wife, as do the other Apostles and the brothers of the Lord and Cephas?" The exegesis of this passage is doubtful, but it is at least certain that the general meaning is that St. Paul did not do the same as the other Apostles, and that from this fact the conclusion had been drawn that he had not the same rights as they had. It cannot be denied that the mention of Cephas and still more of the brothers of the Lord is *prima facie* evidence for a Judaizing movement of the Jerusalem type.

(β) In 2 Cor. xi. 22, St. Paul says, "Are they Hebrews? So am I. Are they Israelites? So am I. Are they the seed of Abraham? So am I." This undoubtedly proves that at least some of his opponents were Jews, and there is a *prima facie* probability that Jews may have belonged to the Judaizing school of Jerusalem. With this passage may be grouped 2 Cor. xi. 14 ff., "Even Satan fashioneth himself into an angel of light. It is no great thing, therefore, if his ministers also fashion themselves as ministers of righteousness." It is considered that διάκονος δικαιοσύνης is the claim made by Judaizers, and is, as it were, the other side of the accusation which they brought against St. Paul, that he reduced Christ to the position of a διάκονος ἁμαρτίας (Gal. ii. 17). But this is not really a very strong argument, for St. Paul would certainly have claimed that he was in actual fact a minister of righteousness. His point is that the appearance of being ministers of righteousness, which his opponents, in common with all other Christians, presented to their hearers, was delusive and due to the deceits of Satan, rather than to the grace of God.[1] His statement is probably no guide as to the nature of the opposition to his teaching. Much the same can be said of 2 Cor. xi. 4, in which St. Paul refers to "another Jesus," "another spirit," and "another gospel" in connection with his opponents. It is of course natural to compare this with Gal. i. 6, in which he says, "I marvel that you are so quickly perverted . . . to another gospel"; but, entirely apart from the extreme difficulty of the exegesis[2] of both passages, the most

[1] It is interesting to note that this opinion is characteristic of Early Christianity, and is found in many forms. For instance, the explanation given in 1 John of false prophets, is not that they are swindlers or charlatans, but that they are inspired by the wrong sort of spirit. So also says Hermas. Similarly, the Apologists explain the resemblances between Christian and heathen cultus and theology to the imitations of the daemons (who are identical with the gods of the heathens), intending to present misleading and false fulfilments of the prophecies of the Old Testament. (Cf. especially Justin Martyr's *Apology*, and Tatian's *Oratio ad Graceos*.) The doctrine that the daemons were the source of many mythological stories is not in itself specifically Christian; it is, for instance, found in Plutarch (*De Iside et Osiride*, p. 360 *d*). But in Justin Martyr, Tatian, Tertullian, and other Christian writers the view taken was in so far somewhat different in that all the gods of the Gentiles were identified with daemons, and these again with fallen angels.

[2] A full discussion of these passages is here impossible; but I incline to

that really follows is that both in Corinth and in Galatia, St. Paul regarded the teaching of his opponents as different from his own; it is wholly uncertain whether the difference was in each case in the same direction.

Such is the main case for the view that St. Paul's opponents were Judaizers: it may be—and often has been—expanded at great length,[1] but it has not gained in strength in the process. Similarly, the great objection to it can be stated in one sentence,—there is from the beginning to the end of the Epistles to the Corinthians not the faintest trace of any controversy as to that insistence on circumcision and on the Law, which we recognize as cardinal in those to the Galatians and Romans. One asks whether, in face of this silence, there is no other preferable exegesis of the passages which seem to point to Judaizing, and there is every reason for giving consideration to the other view, which does not identify St. Paul's opponents with Judaizers.

According to this view, the opponents of St. Paul were an antinomian and libertine type, who laid great emphasis on the "Spirit" which they had received, and regarded themselves as πνευματικοί, raised in consequence of their gift

the view that, as a matter of fact, there is a real difference between 2 Cor. xi. 4 and Gal. i. 6. In the latter St. Paul seems to say that there really is a difference between his gospel and that of his opponents. In the former he seems to be arguing that his opponents can make no real claim to superiority, because, as a matter of fact, they do *not* preach a different Jesus, or spirit, or gospel. But I should be sorry to build anything on this view,—or indeed on any other interpretation of these passages.

[1] The classical statements are F. C. Baur, "Die Christuspartei in der Korinthischen Gemeinde," in the *Tübingen Zeitschrift*, 1831, part 4, pp. 61 ff. Also in his *Paulus*, 1845, pp. 260 ff.; C. Holsten, *Evangelium des Paulus*, 1880, pp. 196 ff.; and C. Weizsacher, *Apostolisches Zeitalter* (2nd edition), pp. 299-311. It is also adopted in the main in the commentaries of A. Klöpper and G. Heinrici. I do not know of any outstanding work in English which defends this position at length, though it is adopted without much discussion by several writers.

above the weakness of other men. The main evidence for this view is to be found in the references contained in 2 Cor. x.–xiii.[1] The most important of these is at the very beginning (2 Cor. x. 2), where St. Paul speaks of those who "regard us as walking according to the flesh." The implication is clear that his opponents regarded themselves as walking according to the Spirit, as πνευματικοί. In complete agreement with this are traces which we can recover of the reasons for which they impugned St. Paul's apostolate and maintained their own superiority. These reasons seem to have been four. (α) He did not work sufficient miracles: this is implied in 2 Cor. xii. 11 ff., "For in nothing was I inferior to the ultra-apostles, even if I am of no importance. The signs of an Apostle were wrought among you in all patience, by signs, and marvels, and miracles." (β) He did not enjoy the same visions and revelations: this is implied by the whole section on visions (2 Cor. xii. 1–10). It is here not plain whether St. Paul means himself or some one else, by the man who was "taken up into the third heaven," but it is certain that he is defending himself against those who lay great stress on visions, and claim a superiority to him on this point. (γ) He did not take the proper position of an Apostle, and live at the expense of the community: this accusation is clearly the background of the section 2 Cor. xi. 7–11, in which St. Paul defends his practice of taking nothing from the Corinthians. (δ) From 2 Cor. x. 3–18[2] we have to conclude that contempt was

[1] The value of this evidence is of course increased if, as has been argued above (p. 157), 2 Cor. x.–xiii. is part of the "severe letter"; but it remains of only slightly less importance if it is St. Paul's attack on a still rebellious minority.

[2] The text of x. 10 is rather important: should we read φησί or φασί? If the former, there is a clear reference to some individual opponent. The

cast on St. Paul's personal appearance. It must not be thought that this was merely vulgar abuse: the point was that it was argued that St. Paul had not got the impressive powers which resulted from the gift of the Spirit.[1]

The view that St. Paul's opponents were πνευματικοί, who regarded him as walking according to the flesh, may probably be supported by the difficult passage 2 Cor. v. 16. St. Paul says, "Even if we have known Christ according to the flesh, yet now know we Him so no more." In this part of 2 Corinthians he is, it is true, not attacking his opponents, but rather acknowledging the correctness of the action of the community, and urging his own friends not to ask for more; but the influence of the controversy can still be traced, and the most natural exegesis is that St. Paul is referring to some accusation of having only a knowledge of Christ according the flesh. He admits that there was a time when this was true, but says that that time is now past: he is, in the best and truest sense of the word, a πνευματικός quite as much as his late opponents. If this exegesis be right, it supports the view that St. Paul's opponents were πνευματικοί, and it certainly seems to be the most simple and natural interpretation.[2]

evidence is not decisive: φησί is found in ℵDEFGLKP d e boh. aeth.[pp]; φασί in B f g, Vulg. Syrr. Personally, I am more impressed by the combination ℵD boh.

[1] In this connection the meaning of "delivering to Satan" (1 Cor. v. 5) is interesting. A full discussion of the point is outside the scope of the present book, but it certainly means something concrete and realistic, and by no means merely the reading of a sentence of excommunication.

[2] On the theory that the opponents were Judaizers, it is suggested that the passage means that they had urged that St. Paul had once held the same opinions as themselves. I cannot regard this as at all probable. St. Paul clearly admits that the accusation—which he defines as knowing Christ according to the flesh—was once true. Now, he had once been an anti-Christian Jew, but when had he ever been a Judaizing Christian? The passage seems to me quite

The general result of a consideration of these passages, if they stood alone, would be sufficient to show that St. Paul's opponents were πνευματικοὶ rather than Judaizers.[1] But unfortunately they do not stand alone, and they have to be considered in connection with the passages previously discussed, which seem to point to Judaizers.

Certainty is probably not to be reached, but various lines which the discussion must always follow can be indicated. It is quite clear, for instance, that the passages pointing to Judaizing derive their force not from direct statements, but from the conclusions drawn (1) from the fact that St. Paul's opponents were Jews, (2) from the fact that they claimed a superior apostolate. Neither of these facts is the equivalent of a statement that they were Judaizers, and on the other hand have to be set what amount to direct statements that they were πνευματικοί. The problem is, Can there have been Jews who claimed to be πνευματικοί, and to be, as apostles, superior to St. Paul, who were nevertheless not Judaizers? or, in the alternative, Can there have been Judaizers who were πνευματικοί, but did not preach either the circumcision or the Law?

To some extent the matter depends on the definition of terms. What, in the first place, do we mean by a Judaizer?

unintelligible, except on the hypothesis that St. Paul is dealing with an accusation that he lacked something which his opponents possessed. This is easy to understand if these opponents were πνευματικοί, not if they are Judaizers. The question as to when St. Paul knew Christ according to the flesh remains. Personally, I think he means before the Conversion, but the point is not of crucial importance for the present purpose. See J. Weis, *Paulus und Jesus*, pp. 24–26.

[1] Long and more or less partizan treatments of the problem from this point of view may be found in Schenkel, *De ecclesia Corinthia primaeva factionibus turbata*, Bâle, 1838, in Godet's *Commentary*, and—far the best statement—in W. Lutgert's *Freiheitspredigt und Schwarmgeister in Korinth*, though the identification of the πνευματικοὶ with the Christ party is very doubtful.

The classical definition is given us by St. Luke in Acts xv. 1: "And some who came down from Judaea began to teach the brethren 'that unless you are circumcized according to the custom of Moses you cannot be saved.'"[1] Galatians and Romans are clearly an answer to such a propaganda.[2] But do we find that type of Judaizing elsewhere? I see no evidence for it.[3] If therefore we use "Judaizing" to mean the same tendency as that combated in Galatians and Romans, we have to admit that it is not an appropriate name for the opponents of St. Paul in Corinth, and are driven to seek some other explanation for the facts that these opponents were Jews, and that they claimed a superior apostolate.

With regard to the fact that they were Jews, it is necessary to disabuse ourselves of the idea that all Jews in the time of St. Paul—quite apart from Christianity—were in agreement with the strictly legalistic point of view of Jerusalem. There is a far too general tendency to forget that the Talmudic literature is in some respects not only no help, but positively a hindrance to the correct understanding of Judaism in the first century, because it represents the one-sided survival of a single element in that Judaism to the exclusion of others. In this respect the New Testament is a superior authority to the Talmud, though its evidence is no doubt often warped by partizan feelings. Philo is in some ways the best source which we

[1] Cf. also Acts xv. 5.

[2] As is shown later (see pp. 300 ff. and 361 ff.), it is possible that both these Epistles may originally belong to the period before the Council; but in any case the longer recension of Romans does not do so, and shows that a truly Judaizing spirit existed in Rome, contemporaneously, or almost so, with 2 Corinthians.

[3] Probably the κατατομή in Philippians refers to Jews, not to Judaizing Christians.

possess, and is certainly so for the Diaspora with which we are at present concerned. Now, as was said on pp. 24 f., the evidence of Philo is explicit that there were Jews who had entirely abandoned the practical observance of the Law, and gave it a wholly symbolical meaning. They were to an even greater extent than Philo himself imbued with a Greek spirit, and consciously or unconsciously they were syncretistic. We have, so far as I am aware, no evidence that there were Jews of this type in Corinth; but since they existed in Alexandria, it is more probable than not that they were also found in Greece. If so, we have an easy solution to the problem afforded by the existence of opponents of St. Paul, who were Jews, but *πνευματικοί*, not Judaizers. We have to deal, in fact, in Corinthians and Galatians, with two streams of development in Judaism, both of which were attracted by Christianity, but both preserved after their conversion their own peculiarities. In Galatians we have the stream of strict legalism, which had its centre in Jerusalem: it regarded St. Paul as a dangerous innovator, who was introducing into Christianity one of the unhappy heresies from which the Diaspora suffered. In Corinthians we have the stream of antinomism, which possibly had its centre in Alexandria, and certainly was a peculiarity of the Diaspora; it regarded St. Paul as an inconsistent weakling, imperfectly influenced by the Spirit, and not yet completely loose from the legal bondage of Jerusalem. That this hypothesis is probable can be seen most clearly if we compare Corinthians and Galatians with regard to the mutual attitude of St. Paul and his opponents. In Galatians he appeals to his converts "after beginning in the Spirit not to end in the flesh." Thus he makes by implication the accusation that his Judaizing opponents were "walking according to the flesh"; but in 2 Corinthians it is his opponents who make this accusation against him—the situation is reversed. In Galatians he defends the right of teachers to be supported by the community; but in Corinthians he was apparently himself attacked for not exercising this right.[1] In Galatians the contrasts are the Law and Christ, Works and Faith, Merit and Grace; in Corinthians they are Power and Weakness, Self-confidence and Modesty, Pride and Humility, Wisdom and Ignorance, Spirit and Flesh. Nothing could be plainer than that the situations in the two Epistles are quite different.

So far, however, nothing has been said of the question of the apostolate. If the "ultra-apostles" were not the leaders of the Jerusalem Churches, who were they? At first sight this seems an insurmountable difficulty, but I believe that it is largely unreal, and due partly to the influence of comparatively early changes in the meaning of the word "apostle," such as only recent discoveries enable us to appreciate, partly to the influence of the incorrect views of early history, which were brought into currency in the nineteenth century.

What was an "apostle" in the early Church? He was a missionary. The Twelve were Apostles because they had been given a mission among the villages of Galilee by Jesus; they were the Apostles *par excellence*. But they were not the only Apostles: St. Paul was an Apostle, St. Barnabas was an Apostle, and the evidence of the *Didache* is conclusive that at the beginning of the second century "apostle" was not the name of a small and select body of

[1] The contrast between Galatians and Corinthians is admirably worked out, at considerable length, by Lütgert, *Freiheitspredigt und Schwarmgeister in Korinth*, pp. 70, 73. He also gives a long discussion of all the various attempts which have been made to explain the contrast.

men, but of all those who were fulfilling certain definite functions. A probably mistaken exegesis of 1 Cor. ix. 1 has done something to obscure this question. In the context of this passage St. Paul has been discussing the question of things offered to idols, and has said that he would rather never eat meat again than give offence to weaker brethren; he then goes on, "Am I not free? am I not an Apostle? have I not seen Jesus our Lord? are not ye my work in the Lord? If I am no Apostle for others, at least I am to you, for ye are in the Lord my seal of fellowship." It is customary to regard this passage as the answer to an attack on St. Paul's apostolate: indirectly it may be so, for the troubles in Corinth broke out soon afterwards; but directly and principally it has to do with the question of things offered to idols. It is a mistake to think that all the qualifications mentioned in ix. 1 ff. are intended to prove that he was an Apostle. The main point is the argument that he, in spite of his privileges, prefers not to use them lest he should give offence, and that the Corinthians ought in the same way to consider the feelings of others in relation to things offered to idols. It is only incidentally that he puts in a parenthesis defending his apostolate. If this be so, the three clauses, "Am I not free? am I not an Apostle? have I not seen Jesus our Lord?" are three separate claims to distinction, and it is an exaggeration to say that St. Paul only regarded as "apostles" those who had seen Jesus. If this had been the meaning of "apostle," there could have been no apostles in the second century, and very few at the end of the first.[1] Yet, as a

[1] One can form some idea of the real nature of the facts if we ask how many of those who took part in the passing of the Reform Bill of 1832 survived to 1890–1900.

matter of fact, apostles were sufficiently numerous for it to be necessary for the *Didache* to make rules for their reception, and for distinguishing between true and false.[1]

A consideration of this fact shows that the existence of "apostles" among St. Paul's opponents, is not the proof that they were Judaizers. Of course the expression, "ultra-apostles" (*οἱ ὑπερλίαν ἀπόστολοι*), undoubtedly suggests to our minds the original Apostles, whose followers might have been supposed to emphasize their superior claims. Yet it need not be so; there is nothing in the Epistles to the Corinthians to show that the question of "originality" was discussed, and therefore I do not believe that, in the face of the other facts, we have any right to assume that the "ultra-apostles" were the Jerusalem Apostles, or that the party which appealed to them was that of Cephas. They were probably merely those who advanced arrogant claims on the ground of their apostleship.

A final and decisively certain result is probably unattainable. I have tried to show why it seems to me probable that St. Paul's opponents were *πνευματικοί*, and not Judaizers. I hope I have also adequately drawn attention to the points in favour of the view which I reject, though it is notoriously impossible to be really quite sympathetically fair to opinions which one does not hold. So far, however, I have chiefly discussed the evidence of 2 Corinthians, which in any case belongs to the time when the differences between St. Paul and his opponents had developed and been made plain, and is therefore the proper basis of any

[1] Πᾶς δὲ ἀπόστολος ἐρχόμενος πρὸς ὑμᾶς δεχθήτω ὡς Κύριος· οὐ μενεῖ δὲ εἰ μὴ ἡμέραν μίαν· ἐὰν δὲ ᾖ χρεία καὶ τὴν ἄλλην· τρεῖς δὲ ἐὰν μείνῃ ψευδοπροφήτης ἐστίν· ἐξερχόμενος δὲ ὁ ἀπόστολος μηδὲν λαμβανέτω εἰ μὴ ἄρτον, ἕως οὗ αὐλισθῇ· ἐὰν δὲ ἀργύριον αἰτῇ ψευδοπροφήτης ἐστί. *Did.*, xi. 4–6.

investigation. It now remains to ask how far the undeveloped form of this opposition can be traced in 1 Corinthians.

The main point is the relation of the opponents of St. Paul to the persons aimed at in 1 Cor. i.–iv. It would be outside the present purpose to discuss the light which these extraordinarily important chapters throw on St. Paul's own teaching[1]; but it is clear that he is protesting against an undue desire for "wisdom," that he maintains that his converts are showing by their quarrels that they are not truly spiritual (πνευματικοί), and that it is for this reason that he has been unable to give them the "wisdom" which they desire, or to regard them—as they do themselves—as "spiritual." If it be conceded that the opponents of St. Paul were πνευματικοί, it is impossible not to think that they were identical with the persons to whom he refers in the opening chapters of 1 Corinthians. But, if one goes further, and asks if this enables us to identify these persons with the parties of Apollos, or Cephas, or Christ (if there was such a party), the answer must be indeterminate. Everything is possible. Apollos may have been incautiously inclined to philosophize, or he may have belonged to the extreme allegorizing sect of Alexandrian Jews, or the Christ party may have consisted of those who claimed that they were inspired by the Spirit of Christ, and that nothing else mattered. But there is no proof, and there can never be anything, because there is no evidence. More or less imaginative sketches can be found in almost all the books cited on pp. 222 and 225. Personally, I do not see how it can ever be possible to say more than that the general tone of 1 Cor. i.–iv., coupled with the Alexandrian history of Apollos, makes the party of

[1] Let me, however, draw attention to the very valuable contribution of Prof. Reitzenstein, in his *Die hellenistischen Mysterienreligionen*.

Apollos not improbable as a "spiritual" party, but that, if 2 Cor. x. 7 be regarded as a reference to a "Christ party," then it is more probable that it was this party which was dealt with in 1 Cor. i.–iv., and that from it the hostility to St. Paul was chiefly developed.

Much the same can be said of the parties revealed by the considerations of the questions discussed in the later chapters of 1 Corinthians, and especially by the points dealt with on pp. 175 ff. Clearly there was a party in Corinth which pressed the importance of the Spirit in connection with sacrificial meals, the Eucharist, and the regulation of worship; and St. Paul, in dealing with these questions, had leaned decidedly more to the side of their opponents. This would be an adequate explanation of the rise of really serious opposition to his authority, such as is indicated in 2 Corinthians.

On the whole, therefore, 1 Corinthians not only does nothing to impugn the conclusion reached from 2 Corinthians, that St. Paul's opponents were πνευματικοί, but it definitely supports it, by the proof which it gives that there were πνευματικοὶ in Corinth, and that St. Paul had treated the differences of opinion between them and the rest of the community in a manner which was extremely likely to rouse opposition.

* * * * * *

The consideration of the Epistles to the Corinthians has led us to a mass of small but mutually related problems, many of them excessively dull to all except those who find that literary criticism offers the same kind of interest as a game of chess. But, if we view the mass of details from a little distance, we can trace the general appearance of the Christian community at Corinth, and the picture thus presented is of the greatest importance, for there is in the first century no presentment of any other Church on the same scale.

The majority of the Church was no doubt drawn from the God-fearers, though there were some Jews, probably belonging to the "liberal" type, which then existed in the Diaspora. But the main feature was that they all accepted Christianity as a Mystery Religion, which really could do what the other Mystery Religions pretended to do. Jesus was to the Corinthians the Redeemer-God, who had passed through death to life, and offered participation in this new life to those who shared in the mysteries which He offered. These mysteries were Baptism and the Eucharist, and there was unanimity in Corinth as to their central importance.[1]

But differences began to be manifested so soon as practical conclusions were drawn from this belief. The mysteries gave eternal life because in them the Spirit was received: but were those who manifested the more striking gifts of the Spirit necessarily better than other Christians? Here there was a difference of opinion. Or again, did this inspiration abolish the distinction, and put women on an equality with men in the Church? Here, again, was difference. Or once more, was the Christian bound to a strict abstinence from all that is carnal, because he had become

[1] Otherwise St. Paul would not have been able to use them as the foundation of his arguments as he does in I Cor. x. (cf. Rom. vi.). It is impossible to over-estimate the importance of realizing that, if we want to discover the central points of early Christian doctrine, we must look not at those to which St. Paul devotes pages of argument, but at those which he treats as the premises accepted equally by all Christians. It is from neglecting this principle and constructing a "Paulinismus" exclusively on the basis of the long controversial passages in the Epistles, that critics have found themselves faced by the fact that they can find no other traces of this "Pauline Christianity" in the early Church. The fact that they cannot do so is really the *reductio ad absurdum* of their reconstructive arguments.

spiritual? or was he set free to do as he liked with his body? Asceticism or Libertinism: which was it to be? And from this Maëlstrom of cross-currents of opinion arose the quarrel between St. Paul and those πνευματικοί who pushed their arguments to an extreme, and drew wrong conclusions from the gift of the Spirit.

So much we can see: those are the main features of the picture. If we look again we can note the absence of other things which we should have expected. There is no trace of any Judiastic controversy as to Circumcision or the Law, no trace of any question as to "Israel after the flesh," and no trace of any controversy as to the meaning of the death of the Messiah. The last point seems the strangest; but it is really natural enough. The death of the Redeemer was as common an idea among the Greeks as the death of the Messiah was strange among the Jews. That St. Paul preached "Christ crucified" is certain. No doubt many Greeks regarded it as foolishness, because they did not believe that Jesus was a Redeemer-God, or because they allegorized all similar stories, and found no reason to believe in an historical Redeemer. But for those Greeks who did accept Christianity the redeeming death of the Divine Being seemed natural, and, so far as these Epistles show, there was as yet no discussion in Corinth as to the reason why this death had been necessary, or how it came to be efficient.

LITERATURE.—Much information will be found in commentaries on the Epistles to the Corinthians. Of these there is nothing in English to be compared with the commentaries of Lietzmann in the third volume of Lietzmann's *Handbuch zum neuen Testament*; J. Weiss's *Der erste Korintherbrief* in Meyer's *Kritisch-exegetischer Kommentar über das Neue Testament*, 9th edition; P. W. Schmiedel in Holtzmann's *Hand-commentar zum neuen Testament*; G. Heinrici (on the Second Epistle) in Meyer's 8th edition; and W. Bousset in J. Weiss's *Die Schriften des Neuen Testaments*. Besides these there are important articles in the *Encyclopædia Biblica* by W. Sanday, and in Hastings'

Dictionary of the Bible by A. Robertson. Both these articles ought to be studied as representing the strongest presentment of the case against the division of 2 Corinthians into two letters. But on this question the most thorough book in any language is J. H. Kennedy's *The Second and Third Epistles to the Corinthians*. On special points the following books are important:—H. Gunkel, *Die Wirkungen des heiligen Geistes nach der populären Anschauung der apostolischen Zeit, und der Lehre des Apostels Paulus*; W. Heitmuller, *Taufe und Abendmahl bei Paulus*; M. Goguel, *L'Eucharistie* (gives a valuable account of recent work, as well as new suggestions); R. Reitzenstein, *Die hellenistischen Mysterienreligionen*; W. Lutgert, *Freiheitspredigt und Schwarmgeister in Korinth*.

APPENDIX I

THE APOCRYPHAL CORRESPONDENCE OF ST. PAUL WITH THE CORINTHIANS

IN the Armenian canon there was a correspondence between St. Paul and the Corinthians, of which many MSS. are extant, and the quotations of Aphraates and Ephraim show that this was derived from the Old Syriac, which was the basis of the Armenian text. The same correspondence was found by Bergen in Milan (1891) and Bratke in Laon (1892) in two Vulgate Latin MSS. Finally, C. Schmidt discovered the same correspondence in the Coptic version of the *Acta Pauli*, and showed that an acute suggestion of Zahn was correct, that the correspondence was originally an extract from this ancient apocryph, which probably was written in Asia late in the second century (see Tertullian, *De Baptismo*, 17).

It would be beyond the province of the present book to discuss the importance of this document. It is plain that its presence in the Syriac canon (from which the Armenian cannot be separated), and in two local texts in Latin, points to the time when the *Corpus Paulinum* was not yet completely closed. Moreover, the bearing of the correspondence on the controversy with second century Gnosticism is very clear: it is in this respect an excellent example of the way in which in apocryphal books there was no half-hearted tendency to make Apostles contribute to contemporary polemics.

The translation below is based on Harnack's reconstruction of the text in H. Lietzmann's *Kleine Texte*, 12, in which is given a critical apparatus of the Coptic, Syriac, Armenian, and Latin, together with the text of Bergen's Latin MS. Recent literature of importance is C. Schmidt, *Acta Pauli* (1905), and Harnack, *Untersuchungen über den apokryphen Briefwechsel der Korinther mit dem Apostel Paulus*. A full account of earlier books is given by Zahn, *Geschichte des Neutest. Kanons*, ii. 2, pp. 592 ff.

The Epistle of the Corinthians to Paul.

Stephanus and the elders who are with him, Daphnus and Euboulos and Theophilos and Xenon to Paul, greeting in the Lord.

There have come to Corinth two men, Simon and Cleobios, who are turning aside the faith of some by harmful words, which do thou test, for we have never heard such things either from thee or from the other Apostles, but we hold fast to that which we received from thee and the rest. As then the Lord had mercy on us, come to us, that while thou art still in the flesh we may again hear these things from thee; for we believe, as it was revealed to Theonoes, that the Lord has saved thee from the hand of the lawless. Now what they say and teach is this: it is not, they say, necessary to use the prophets, that God is not Almighty, that there is no resurrection of the flesh, that man is not the creation of God, that Christ has not come in the flesh, and was not born of Mary, and that the world belongs not to God but to angels. Therefore, brother, make all haste to come to us, that the Church of the Corinthians be not made to stumble, and that the folly of those men be brought to nought. Farewell in the Lord.

THE EPISTLE OF PAUL TO THE CORINTHIANS.

Paul the prisoner of Jesus Christ to the brethren, who are in Corinth, greeting. In my many troubles I do not wonder that the teachings of the Evil One make such progress; but my Lord, Jesus Christ, will hasten His coming, bringing to nothing those who corrupt His word. For I delivered to you in the beginning that which I received from those who were Apostles before me, who had been all the time in the company of Jesus Christ, that our Lord Jesus Christ was born of Mary, of the seed of David, when the Spirit had been sent from heaven from the Father to her, that He should come into this world, and set free all flesh through His flesh, and raise us up in the flesh from the dead, as He had shown Himself an example for us; and that man was created by the Father, for this cause also he was sought when lost, that he might be made alive by the adoption as a son. For God Almighty, the Creator of heaven and earth, first sent the prophets to the Jews that they might be torn away from their sins; for His plan was to save the house of Israel, for this cause he sent a portion of the Spirit of Christ into the prophets who announced the true worship at many times. But the Prince of the world (ὁ δὲ ἄρχων[1]) being unrighteous, because he wished to be God, laid hands on them, and slew them, and thus bound all flesh of men to his will. But God Almighty, being righteous, did not wish to reject His creation, but had pity on it, and sent His Spirit into Mary,

[1] The actual Greek is here given in the Coptic.

in order that the evil one might be shown to be conquered through the flesh, in which he had boasted. For through His own body did Jesus Christ save all flesh, making manifest the temple of righteousness in His own body, by which we were saved.

For be well assured that those men are not the sons of righteousness, but of wrath, who reject the plan of God, saying that heaven and earth, and that which is in them, are not the work of God, for they hold the faith of the accursed serpent. Therefore put them from you and fly from their teaching. But for those who say there is no resurrection of the flesh there shall indeed be no resurrection, for they do not believe that the dead (*i.e.* the Lord) thus rose. For they ignore, O Corinthians, the grains of wheat, or of other food, which are cast bare into the ground and after they have decayed spring up, having obtained a body according to the will of God. And He raises up not only that which was sown but, by His blessing, many times as much. But if we ought not to make a parable from the seeds, understand how Jonah the son of Amathai, when he would not preach to the Ninevites, was swallowed by the whale; and after three days and three nights God heard the prayer of Jonah from the depths of Hades, and nothing of him was hurt, neither hair nor eyebrows. How much more will He raise up us who believe on Christ Jesus, as He also rose? and if the dead man let down by the children of Israel on to the bones of the prophet Elisha rose from the dead in his body, how much more shall you, who are let down on the body and bones and spirit of Christ, be raised up in that day, and keep your flesh?

If then ye receive anything else, let no man trouble me, for I bear these bonds, that I may gain Christ, and I carry in my body His marks, that I may attain to the Resurrection of the dead, and whosoever shall walk in the rule, which he received from the blessed prophets and the holy Gospel, shall receive a reward: but he who trangresses these, the fire is for him and for those who thus run, who are generations of vipers, whom do ye reject in the power of the Lord, and peace shall be with you.

APPENDIX II

GLOSSOLALIA AND PSYCHOLOGY

ON page 204 it is stated that glossolalia is unintelligible speech. The statement is sufficiently correct, and to discuss it in the text would have been a needless discursiveness, but the point deserves some further explanation.

That glossolalia was in the main unintelligible is clear from St. Paul's words in I Cor. xiv.: "He that speaketh in a tongue edifieth himself, but he that prophesieth edifieth the congregation" (xiv. 4). "He that prophesieth is greater than he that speaketh with tongues, except he interpret" (xiv. 5). "If I pray in a tongue my spirit prayeth, but my understanding is unfruitful" (xiv. 14). "If all speak with tongues and there come in men unlearned or unbelieving, will they not say that ye are mad?" (xiv. 23). "If any man speaketh in a tongue . . . let one interpret" (xiv. 27). These passages are meaningless if glossolalia was not a form of generally unintelligible speech. At the same time, certain other facts have to be considered which tend to show that in some cases glossolalia took a different form.

In the first place, the evidence of St. Paul throws a little further light on the question. It is significant that in I Cor. xiii. I he further defines "tongues" as "tongues of men and angels." It is therefore probable that some forms of glossolalia were regarded as the speech of a spirit, speaking through a human being, but using angelic, not human, speech. Moreover, the mention of interpreters in 1 Cor. xiv. suggests that some people were able to understand the otherwise unintelligible speech of those who used glossolalia.

Secondly, the narrative of the day of Pentecost in Acts ii. shows, at the least, that St. Luke was acquainted with some form of glossolalia which was intelligible, though not the usual language of the speaker. This narrative presents several difficulties, but for the present purpose the points of importance can be shortly presented. Taking the narrative as it stands, it presents the difficulty that some of those who heard the Christians speak with tongues thought that they were drunk, and St. Peter's speech is directed against this accusation. Others, however, were annoyed to hear them speaking foreign languages. Now, it is quite certain that intelligible speech in a foreign language showing forth the wonderful work of God has never been regarded as the effect of strong drink. Two explanations are possible: either St. Luke has misunderstood the situation, and has converted what was originally an ordinary instance of glossolalia, into speech in a foreign language, or the Apostles really did use language which, to those who knew it, was intelligible, but to others appeared to be gibberish—the sort of verdict which St. Paul actually warned the Corinthians that an outsider would pass on their glossolalia. It is unnecessary to discuss these possibilities, for even if we take the view that St. Luke misunderstood the situation, this implies that he was acquainted with glossolalia which took the form of speaking a foreign language, otherwise why should he have misunderstood the original narrative? Thus, whatever critical view we take of the narrative in Acts it has to be admitted that it points to glossolalia in foreign languages.

The questions now arise: (1) Can we trace anything similar to this glossolalia in other times? (2) Can we at all explain what it is?

Traces of glossolalia in other circles than that of Apostolic Christianity, though not common, are sufficient to show that it existed at other times, and to throw some light on its nature.

A very remarkable light on "the tongues of angels" is thrown by the Testament of Job.[1] In this (chap. xlvii.) Job is represented as showing his three daughters a wonderful girdle which had been divinely given him. This, he says, will bring them into "the greater world" (τὸν μείζονα αἰῶνα), to live in the heavens. When his daughters put it on they each received a new heart, and began to speak in superhuman language. According to Dr. James' text, the first, called Hemera, spoke the angelic tongue (ἀγγέλικῃ διαλέκτῳ), the second, called Kasia, spoke in the tongue of "principalities" (ἀρχῶν), and the third, Amalthia, spoke in the tongue of "those on high" (τῶν ἐν ὕψει), or, as it is also called, the tongue of the cherubim.

The magical papyri also go far towards clearing up the problem. Part of the magic consisted of the use of strange words which might be equally regarded as magical charms to affect a spirit who would understand and be compelled by their hidden meaning, and as the language which was used by the spirit who was in possession of an inspired person. Some of these words appear to be taken from Semitic languages, some to be merely gibberish. For

[1] *Texts and Studies*, v. 1, *Apocrypha Anecdota II.* by M. R. James, pp. 104 ff.

instance, in the often-quoted Leiden papyrus Hermes is invoked,[1] *πάσῃ φωνῃ καὶ πάσῃ διαλέκτῳ . . . ἀχεβουκρωμυ, ὃ μηνύει τοῦ δίσκου τὸν φλόγα καὶ τὴν ἀκτῖνα οὗ ἡ δόξα ααυ ηηη ωωω . . . κτίζων τὸν κόσμον ιιι ααα ωωω, ἐν ᾧ δὲ ἔστησας τὰ πάντα σαβαωθ αρβαδ Ἰάω Ζαγουρη, κ.τ.λ.*, and in cod. Paris. 2316 a hymn of Moses begins *βελὼν θαβὼρ ἀκανθὰ ναμελὰ λαμβαλὰ ἀριμισαὶ βισαασμά, κ.τ.λ.*

That glossolalia continued for a long time among Christians can be seen from Irenaeus and Tertullian.

Irenaeus says, "Propter quod et Apostolus ait: Sapientiam loquimur inter perfectos; perfectos dicens eos qui perceperunt Spiritum Dei quemadmodum et ipse loquebatur. Quemadmodum et multos audivimus fratres in ecclesia, prophetica habentes charismata, et per spiritum universis linguis loquentes (*καὶ παντοδαπαῖς λαλούντων διὰ του πνεύματος γλώσσαις*,—the Greek is quoted by Eusebius, *Hist. Eccl.*, v. 7, 6)." Tertullian challenges Marcion to equal the deeds of the Church, and says, "Edat aliquem psalmum, aliquam visionem, dumtaxat spiritalem, in ecstasi, id est amentia, si qua linguae interpretatio accessit; haec omnia a me facilius proferuntur."[2]

[1] See J. Weiss, *Der erste Korintherbrief*, p. 338 ff.

[2] Iren., *Adv. Haer.*, v. 6, 1. Tert., *Contra Marc.*, v. 8. Cf. also Justin Martyr, *Apol.* II. 6, and other passages mentioned by Harvey in his note on the passage from Irenaeus; but they do not exactly cover glossolalia so much as prophecy and other miraculous *χαρίσματα πνευματικά*. Attention may also be drawn to the hostile account of Palestinian prophets given by Celsus (Origen, *Contra Celsum*, vii. 9): *οἱ δὲ . . . ἐπιφοιτῶντες πόλεσιν ἢ στρατοπέδοις, κινοῦνται δῆθεν ὡς θεσπίζοντες· πρόχειρον δ' ἑκάστῳ καὶ σύνηθες εἰπεῖν, ἐγὼ ὁ Θεός εἰμι, ἢ Θεοῦ παῖς, ἢ πνεῦμα Θεῖον . . . ταῦτα ἐπανατεινάμενοι προστιθέασι ἐφεξῆς ἄγνωστα, καὶ πάροιστρα, καὶ πάντῃ ἄδηλα, ὧν τὸ μὲν γνῶμα οὐδεὶς ἂν ἔχων νοῦν εὑρεῖν δύναιτο, κ.τ.λ.*, and the equally hostile account of Gnostic glossolalia given by Irenaeus (*Adv. Haer.*, I. xiii. 3 (Massuet)) ". . . concalefaciens animam a suspicione quod incipiat prophetare, cum cor ejus multo plus quam oporteat palpitet, audet, et loquitur deliriosa, et quaecunque evenerint omnia, vacue et audacter," etc.

By the time of Chrysostom, however, glossolalia and prophecy were apparently unknown in the Church, and he expresses his difficulty in explaining what it was.[1]

In later generations glossolalia has appeared spasmodically at times of great religious excitement. Probably research would show that no "revival" has been without something like glossolalia, but the two clearest and most famous examples have been supplied by the history of the Camisards in France and the Irvingites in England.

The most remarkable instances of glossolalia in recent times are supplied by the Camisards and the Irvingites, and, curiously enough, while the one illustrates glossolalia of the kind which resulted in unusually clear speech, the other illustrates the purely unintelligible form.

The Camisards were a sect of French Protestants among the peasantry of the Cévennes, who, in the beginning of the eighteenth century, carried on a fierce resistance to the persecution which ensued on the Revocation of the Edict of Nantes. A full account of their remarkable psychological characteristics will be found in D. A. Bruey's *Histoire du fanatisme*, 1737, vol. i., especially pp. 148 ff. The main points are that various persons, sometimes children, were seized with slightly convulsive attacks, ending in unconsciousness, during which they uttered exhortations in good French, although, in their ordinary state of consciousness, they were incapable of speaking anything but the Romance patois of the Cévennes. It should be noted that they were acquainted with French through their devotional use of the Huguenot Bible.

[1] Τοῦτο ἅπαν τὸ χωρίον σφόδρα ἐστὶν ἀσαφές. τὴν δὲ ασάφειαν ἡ τῶν πραγμάτων ἄγνοιά τε καὶ ἔλλειψις ποιεῖ τῶν τότε μὲν συμβαινόντων, νῦν δὲ οὐ γινομένων. Cramer's *Catena*, v. p. 223.

The Irvingites are a still better known instance. In the early years of the nineteenth century the glossolalia in Edward Irving's chapel was notorious, and attracted the curiosity of, among others, George Greville.[1] His account is that the voice of the speaker, "after ejaculating three 'Ohs,' one rising above the other in tones very musical, burst into a flow of unintelligible jargon, which whether it was in English or gibberish I could not discover. This lasted five or six minutes, and, as the voice was silenced, another woman, in more passionate and louder tones, took it up. This last spoke in English, and words, though not sentences, were distinguishable. . . . She spoke sitting under great apparent excitement, and screamed on till, from exhaustion as it seemed, her voice gradually died away, and all was still."

The parallel to the account of glossolalia at Corinth could scarcely be closer, and Greville adequately represents the ἄπιστος ἢ ἰδιώτης, against whose unfavourable judgment St. Paul warned the Corinthians.

Turning to the question of the immediate cause of glossolalia as a psychological phenomenon, it is important to notice that two main types can be recognized: (1) Intelligible speech in a foreign language; (2) Unintelligible speech in a known or unknown language. The connecting link between these two classes is that in neither case is the speech under the complete control of the speaker, though sometimes the lack of control is partial, sometimes absolute. It is this lack of control which is the further connecting link with prophecy in which intelligible speech is used in a known language, but the speaker says, not what he wishes, but

[1] *Memoirs*, III. chap. xxii. I am indebted to Mr. Conybeare for showing me this passage. Cf. *Myth, Magic, and Morals*, p. 93.

what he feels that he must. Thus the psychologist, just as the early Christian did, regards prophecy and glossolalia as cognate phenomena; the difference is in the explanation which he offers.

So far as the consideration of the immediate cause of the phenomena is concerned, these cases do not present much difficulty to those who are in any degree acquainted with modern pathological psychology. They are merely three instances of the disturbance of the speech centres of the brain under stress of emotion, and of the influence of the subliminal consciousness as soon as the normal working of the mind has been temporarily impeded. One of the real advances of knowledge in pathology has been the certain establishment of the fact that the intelligent exercise of human functions, such as movement, sight, and speech, is under the control of definite parts of the brain. If you impede the part of the brain, known as the speech centre, which controls language, you produce either dumbness or, if the centre be not wholly destroyed, aphasia, that is, an inability to use certain words, or paraphasia, that is, a tendency to confuse words. These are common phenomena in some of the most ordinary types of paralysis, in which the immediate cause of the disease is a lesion of some sort affecting the speech centre. For instance, if a man has an apoplectic fit caused by the breaking of a small blood-vessel in the brain, if the blood be effused at the speech centre, his speech will be destroyed or impaired, until the blood be absorbed. If the absorption be complete, his speech will recover completely; if not, he will speak badly for the rest of life, unless, which is believed sometimes to happen, another "centre" takes over the work of the injured part of the brain.

In the same way anything which, generally speaking, increases the activity of the speech centre[1] will increase the power of speech. This is what is actually accomplished by some forms of education, and still more by some professions. Forms of teaching which constantly demand quick and ready answers *vivâ voce* develop the speech centre, and so do the professions of barristers, or of clergymen.

The most important point, however, for the present purpose, is that the speech is readily though temporarily affected, in a precisely similar manner, by the stress of emotion, of whatever kind. The exact form of the affection depends on two variables, the degree of the emotion, and the nature of the person. In some cases it works favourably: emotion seems to stimulate the speech and cognate centres, and the result is that the speaker is conscious that he is speaking well. He enjoys the comfortable assurance that, whereas under normal conditions he has scarcely enough words to say what he wishes, under the stimulus of slight emotion he is temporarily blessed with the power of seeing synonyms at once, and of being able to pick and choose his expressions without either haste or hesitation. In other

[1] By increasing the activity of the speech centre I include, of course, both the quickening of the connections with other centres, and also the removal of the normal inhibition. The latter point is rather interesting. One of the factors in controlling, and sometimes hindering speech, is the normal inhibitory influence of such things as instinctive caution, perception of the possibility of misunderstanding, etc. If this be removed an unusual freedom of speech ensues. One of the first symptoms of alcoholic intoxication is this removal of inhibition. Hence *in vino veritas*, and hence the fact that a glass of champagne produces fluency (in some persons), while a bottle produces incoherence. Psychologically, what happens is that a small quantity of alcohol tends to remove the normal inhibition, while a large dose disturbs and ultimately paralyzes the working of the speech centre.

cases (and almost always if it be carried too far), emotion works unfavourably. It disturbs the speech centre by an excess of stimulus, and the result is confused expression, obscure utterance, and in the end temporary paraphasia.

These effects are produced by any emotion : they prove the presence of emotional disturbance, but not its character. Love or hate, pathos or humour, the highest spiritual religion or the lowest immorality, all have their emotional side; and the emotions which they arouse produce in the end the same symptoms.

It is plain that this is the explanation of that type of glossolalia which consists of unintelligible language. It was, in more or less technical language, temporary paraphasia induced by religious emotion. In the same way, some forms of prophecy are to be explained as a temporary and favourable excitement of the speech and cognate centres, induced by religious emotion.

But this does not explain the other features of some cases. It does not explain the belief that the prophet utters things which he did not previously know; nor does it explain the rare cases of speech in a foreign language.

It is here that the much discussed and often exaggerated "subliminal consciousness" helps us to the outlines of an explanation. The point is this: besides our ordinary waking consciousness there is a wider sphere, which only occasionally comes into the field of our observation. Roughly speaking, one may say that reason, memory, and effort, work in the sphere of the ordinary, or supraliminal, consciousness, while instinct and habit work in the sphere of the subliminal consciousness. Usually speech, and most of the actions of daily life, are under the control of the supraliminal consciousness. But when we act instinctively our actions are controlled by the subliminal consciousness. For instance, an Englishman riding a bicycle on the Continent for the first time knows that he ought, contrary to his usual practice, to keep to the right; but if a sudden emergency arises, and he acts instinctively, he will certainly swerve to the left, in spite of his consciousness that this is wrong. Some actions, again, especially in the world of sport, are an extremely complicated mixture of instinct and reason, or of the supraliminal and subliminal consciousness; very interesting, for instance, is the psychological analysis of the act of bowling at cricket.

What the precise relations are between the supraliminal and subliminal consciousness, psychologists have apparently not yet determined. It is, however, an established fact that, by the exertion of strain on any given centre of the brain, the supraliminal consciousness can be partially or completely "thrown out of gear," and that in such cases people do and say exceptional things of which neither they themselves nor any one else ever thought them capable.

The importance of this for the present purpose is that it sometimes happens in such cases that when the supraliminal consciousness has been "thrown out of gear," the person affected suddenly develops a power of expressing new thoughts, and shows a knowledge of facts which no one, even himself, thought that he possessed. It is obvious that this covers tolerably well the facts of prophecy; especially does it illuminate the difference between prophecy and preaching. The preacher announces to the best of his ability the truths which he has learnt: he knows beforehand what he is going to say, and the limits of his message are those of his own ordinary supraliminal consciousness. The prophet does not always know beforehand what he is going to say: his words are only partly under his own control: sometimes he is as much surprised as any one else at what he says: for the limits of his message are those of his subliminal consciousness, which in ordinary circumstances is in abeyance, and as little known to his own ordinary intelligence as to that of other persons.

Quite rare, but still quite sufficiently attested, are exceptional cases in which, under the influence of strain bringing the subliminal consciousness into active working, persons have suddenly began to speak and understand foreign languages; usually it has been possible to show that they had either in childhood or in some other way had opportunities of learning them. This covers the indications that among the early Christians glossolalia sometimes took the form of speaking foreign languages.

The importance of these results is that they tend to show that prophecy and glossolalia, which the early Christians connected so closely with each other, are really cognate psychological phenomena due to stress caused by religious emotion. In this way psychology really does explain the symptoms, and explains them better than did the ancient hypothesis of obsession by spirits. At the same time, it must be remembered that the question remains, what is the cause of the religious emotion which gives rise to these symptoms? Psychology explains the immediate cause of the phenomena; but what is the ultimate cause? that is to say, what is religion? To discuss this problem would be outside the limits of the present book, which have perhaps been already passed, but I cannot refrain from saying that if I do not mistake the signs of the times the really serious controversy of the future will be concerned with this point, even among those who are agreed in assigning the highest value to religion, and that the opposing propositions will be: (1) that religion is the communion of man, in the sphere of the subliminal consciousness, with some other being higher than himself; (2) that it is communion of man with his own subliminal consciousness, which he does not recognize as his own, but hypostasizes as some one exterior to himself. Those who wish to prepare for this controversy will do well to study on the one hand the facts of religion—not of theology—and on the other the principles of psychology.

LITERATURE.—The best treatment will be found in J. Weiss, *Der erste Korintherbrief*, pp. 335-339, but according to him a book will shortly be published on *Das Zungenreden* by Edison Mosiman, giving a full history of the phenomena in all ages. Important also are Feine's article on *Zungenrede* in the *Realencyclopædie für prot. Theologie*, ed. 3, and Reitzenstein's Poimandres (esp. p. 55). The psychological facts are clearly stated in James' little *Textbook of Psychology* or in his larger *Principles of Psychology*, as well as in more technical books written from a more exclusively medical standpoint.

CHAPTER V

THE EPISTLE TO THE GALATIANS

THE problems connected with the background of the Epistle to the Galatians are almost the exact opposite of those in the Epistles to the Corinthians. In the latter, the questions of place and date are tolerably certain, and of quite subordinate importance, but it is both difficult and important to determine the nature of the controversy which called forth the Epistles. In the former, on the other hand, the nature of the controversy is quite plain, but it is extremely hard to fix the places from which and to which St. Paul wrote, or the time at which he sent the letter.

The nature of the controversy is clearly fixed by the whole trend of the Epistle. From beginning to end, it is engaged in controverting the proposition that Gentile Christians ought to be circumcised and observe the Jewish Law; it is also obvious that this proposition had been set up by Christian teachers who had come to Galatia after St. Paul had left his converts, and we can scarcely be wrong in identifying these teachers with those of the Jerusalem propaganda described on pp. 29 ff. So much is plain, and it is only subordinate points which will later require further discussion. But the difficulties begin when one asks (what is, after all, in reality the previous question) where did the Galatians live, and when did St. Paul write to them? It is, therefore, necessary to discuss these questions at some length.

I. Where was Galatia?

There are two meanings which can conceivably be given to the word "Galatia." It may mean the comparatively small district which was once the Kingdom of the Galatae, a Celtic people, generally supposed to be identical with the Galli of Western Europe,[1] who are also called Γαλάται by Greek writers; or it may be the much larger district which the Romans made into the Province of Galatia.

The Galatians invaded Asia in the third century before Christ, and ultimately occupied a district towards the north of the ancient kingdom of Phrygia. Later on they came more or less under the domination of Pontus, and played an important part in the wars between the Romans and Mithridates. Ultimately, in the first century before Christ, the kingdom of Galatia passed into the possession of Amyntas, King of Pisidia, together with other territory. Amyntas was the tributary of the Romans, and on his death in 25 B.C. the Romans took over all his possessions as a new Province of the Empire, and gave it the name of Galatia, because the ancient kingdom of Galatia was the most important part, and contained Ancyra, the capital of the whole. Thus, politically, all the inhabitants of the Province, which included Derbe, Lystra, Iconium, and Pisidian Antioch, the cities visited by St. Paul on his first journey, were Galatians, while ethnographically only the inhabitants of a comparatively small

[1] It is amusing to note that various writers, whom it is kinder not to mention, have waxed eloquent on the permanence of national characteristics, as illustrated by the fickle Galatians in the first century and the French in the nineteenth.

district to the north could be so called.[1] The question is whether St. Paul means "political Galatians," or "ethnographical Galatians."

To form a choice between these two possibilities a very important preliminary question is whether the Acts represents St. Paul as founding Christian communities in the Kingdom or in the Province of Galatia. For this purpose two passages in the Acts have to be considered, in which there is a reference to "Galatia."

(1) Acts xvi. 6: *Διῆλθον δὲ τὴν Φρυγίαν καὶ Γαλατικὴν χώραν κωλυθέντες ὑπὸ τοῦ ἁγίου πνεύματος λαλῆσαι τὸν λόγον ἐν τῇ Ἀσίᾳ ἐλθόντες δὲ κατὰ τὴν Μυσίαν ἐπείραζον εἰς τὴν Βιθυνίαν πορευθῆναι, καὶ οὐκ εἴασεν αὐτοὺς τὸ πνεῦμα Ἰησοῦ, παρελθόντες δὲ τὴν Μυσίαν κατέβησαν εἰς Τρῳάδα.*

The question here is, What is the district described as Galatian? The answer is not simple, and such authorities as Lightfoot and Ramsay[2] are found to give different answers.

There is, unfortunately, a small but important variant in the text concerning the first word—*διῆλθον*. The text given is that found in ℵBCDE d e, and some others against the mass of late MSS., which read *διελθόντες*. There can be no doubt but that on purely manuscriptal grounds *διῆλθον* deserves the preference; but Lightfoot, Ramsay, and Askwith[3] all show a certain preference for *διελθόντες*, mainly on the ground that *διῆλθον* is the easier reading

[1] See further Appendix I. and the map accompanying it.

[2] See Ramsay's *Church in the Roman Empire*, pp. 77 ff., and Lightfoot's *Epistle to the Galatians*, p. 22.

[3] E. H. Askwith, *The Epistle to the Galatians: an Essay on its Destination and Date* (Macmillan and Co., 1902). This is by far the most thorough statement of the questions concerned, which has as yet been made, either in English or German. It does not, however, seem to be sufficiently well known, perhaps because it is too thorough and too scientific to attract superficial attention.

grammatically, and may have been introduced in order to simplify the long and awkward string of participles which διελθόντες introduces. It is hard to think that there is much real weight in this argument; but in view of the fact that the opinion exists, it is desirable to follow Askwith's example and consider both forms.

If διελθόντες be read, we have a series of participles (διελθόντες . . . κωλυθέντες . . . ἐλθόντες) qualifying ἐπείραζον. The only natural interpretation is that these three participles represent three stages which led up to the attempt to enter Bithynia. In other words, the writer means to say, "First they went through τὴν Φρυγίαν καὶ Γαλατικὴν χώραν, secondly they were prevented from preaching in Asia, finally they came opposite Mysia and tried to enter Bithynia." The important point is that it implies that the Φρυγία καὶ Γαλατικὴ χώρα was traversed before Asia was reached.

If διῆλθον be read, the matter is not so plain: κωλυθέντες may be retrospective, and in that case the sentence means "they passed through the Phrygian and Galatian region, because they had already been prevented from preaching in Asia." In that case the region in question was reached after Asia had been found to be shut against their preaching. But this meaning is not necessary. It is a grammatical heresy to suppose that the Greek aorist participle must imply a temporal relation: it is strictly timeless, and the context determines whether the relation between the acts implied in the main verb precedes, follows, or is simultaneous with those implied in the participle. So here διῆλθον κωλυθέντες means "they passed through, in a state of inability to," etc., and nothing is said as to whether this state of inability was reached before, after, or during the passing through. Moreover, it is a general rule of Greek grammar that the participle rather than the main verb is emphatic; the stress is not on the "passing through" (which probably implies preaching, as διέρχεσθαι has almost the technical sense of "to make a missionary journey"), but on the fact that they were hindered from preaching in Asia. Thus, though κωλυθέντες may be retrospective, it need not be taken in this sense.

It is, therefore, necessary to ask whether the phrase, τὴν Φρυγίαν καὶ Γαλατικὴν χώραν, is more easily interpreted as a place reached after the frontier of Asia, or as one which had already been passed through.

It is first desirable to notice the exact meaning of the Greek phrase. It cannot mean "Phrygia and the Galatian district," which would be τὴν Φρυγίαν καὶ τὴν Γαλατικὴν χώραν—a reading which is actually found in later MSS., and was certainly introduced in the interest of the belief that two districts were indicated. Nor can it mean "the Phrygian and Galatian districts," which would require τὰς Φρυγίας καὶ Γαλατικὰς χώρας. In fact, it can only mean one thing—the χώρα which is Phrygian and Galatian, or more shortly the Phrygo-Galatic χώρα.[1] This much is common ground to Lightfoot and Ramsay. But at this point they differ: Lightfoot thinks that the phrase means "the country which was once Phrygia and Galatia," or alternatively the parts of Phrygia bordering on Galatia. Ramsay thinks that it means the district in the Province of Galatia which had originally been Phrygian, and was probably known in Latin as *Regio Phrygia Galatica.*

To appreciate this question it is necessary to take into

[1] Zahn's explanation (*Kommentar zum N.T.*, bd. ix. p. 16), that St. Luke means "Phrygia, and a part of Galatia," seems to me to be linguistically impossible. Φρυγίαν must be an adjective and co-ordinate with Γαλατικήν.

consideration the really great change in our knowledge of the political geography of Asia, and of the nomenclature applied to it, made by the recent researches of archaeologists, especially Ramsay. The main point is that by the time of St. Paul an enormous province had been created in the middle of Asia Minor, with the old Kingdom of Galatia as its centre.[1] Among the parts of other kingdoms which had been attached to it were ethnologically Phrygian districts, including Antioch and Iconium, and Lycaonian districts, including Lystra and Derbe. Other parts of Phrygia belonged to the Province of Asia, and other parts of Lycaonia to the Regnum Antiochi, which was not yet incorporated into any province. Thus it would be natural to describe the part of Phrygia which was in Galatia as Phrygia Galatica, in contrast to Phrygia Asiana, and the part of Lycaonia as Lycaonia Galatica in contrast to Lycaonia Antiochiana.

In the light of these facts it is clear that the most probable explanation is that *ἡ Φρυγία καὶ Γαλατικὴ χώρα* means the district of Phrygia recently added to the Province of Galatia,—Phrygia Galatica. It is indeed hard to see what other district could be meant, for the fact that Galatia proper had two hundred years previously been Phrygian would hardly justify us in applying to it the phrase "Phrygo-Galatic district."

Moreover, consideration of the map shows that a nice discrimination between "retrospective" and other exegesis of *κωλυθέντες* is unnecessary. The hindrance to St. Paul's preaching was probably just before or just after he entered the Phrygo-Galatic region, and in consequence of this hindrance he continued his journey across it, instead of

[1] See further Appendix I. and map facing p. 316.

immediately passing into Asia. In the end he must enter Asia, but as he could not preach in it, he postponed his entry as long as possible.

In Acts xvi. 1 ff. St. Paul is in Lystra in Lycaonia Galatica, and it is implied in xvi. 2 that he went on to Iconium, which was either the last city in Lycaonia Galatica, or the first in Phrygia Galatica, a long day's journey (30 miles) from the frontier of Asia, and less than 20 miles from the great road to Ephesus. Here St. Paul would naturally have passed into Asia, and I understand St. Luke to mean that, as he found it impossible to preach in Asia, he went round to the south of the Sultan Dagh, through Antioch, to Kinnaborion, and so up to Kotiaion, or perhaps by a road branching off just before Kinnaborion to Dorylaion. Here he was κατὰ τὴν Μυσίαν, and intended to go straight on to Nicomedia—Bithynia can scarcely mean any other town—but being hindered by the "Spirit of Jesus," he turned to the left and went to Troas. I take διῆλθον τὴν Φρυγίαν καὶ Γαλατικὴν χώραν to mean merely that he kept to the south of the Sultan Dagh instead of going to the north of it through Phrygia Asiana, which would have been the more natural route. Probably the reason which influenced St. Paul was the desire to see Pisidian Antioch again, when he found it was impossible to preach in Asia, *i.e.* in Philomelium, to which he would have naturally gone from Iconium *viâ* Laodicea and the main route; for preaching in Asia means preaching along the main road to Ephesus.

This view is, of course, hypothetical, and the evidence at our disposal is quite insufficient to enable us to say exactly which route St. Paul took. The important point is that the phrase, ἡ Φρυγία καὶ Γαλατικὴ χώρα, seems most naturally to refer to Phrygia Galatica in which was Antioch and possibly Iconium. If so, the suggestion is that the Churches in Lystra, Derbe, Iconium, and Pisidian Antioch might naturally be described as Galatian Churches, and in this case the foundation of Christianity in Galatia must be dated in St. Paul's first missionary journey, when he and St. Barnabas visited these towns.

(2) Acts xviii. 22, 23: *καὶ κατελθὼν εἰς Καισαρίαν, ἀναβὰς καὶ ἀσπασάμενος τὴν ἐκκλησίαν, κατέβη εἰς Ἀντιόχειαν, καὶ ποιήσας χρόνον τινὰ ἐξῆλθεν διερχόμενος καθέξης τὴν Γαλατικὴν χώραν καὶ Φρυγίαν στηρίζων πάντας τοὺς μαθητάς* Cf. also Acts xix. 1: *ἐγένετο δὲ . . . Παῦλον διελθόντα τὰ ἀνωτερικὰ μέρη ἐλθεῖν εἰς Ἔφεσον.*

It is clear that these two passages describe a journey from Antioch to Ephesus, covering again the ground which St. Paul had previously gone over. Nor is the first part of the route, which is not described, difficult to identify. St. Paul must have gone from Antioch, through the Syrian Gates, through Tarsus and the Cilician Gates, across Lycaonia Antiochiana, and so to Derbe, where he entered Lycaonia Galatica, and thence through Lystra to Iconium, where he entered Phrygia Galatica; after this he would visit Pisidian Antioch, and finally the reference to the *ἀνωτερικὰ μέρη* probably means that, instead of taking the main road along the south banks of the Lycus and Maeander valleys, he took a smaller road to the north, passing in the end to the north of M. Messogis. When one grasps these facts, the meaning of the change of expression in Acts xviii. 23 from that in xvi. 6 becomes plain. In the latter place, St. Luke says *τὴν Φρυγίαν καὶ Γαλατικὴν χώραν* because he means that one single district was Phrygian-Galatian. In the former place he says *τὴν Γαλατικὴν χώραν καὶ Φρυγίαν*, because he means two districts, namely the Galatic region of Lycaonia, and Phrygia.

Moreover, the fulness of expression in the one case and not in the other is adequately explained by the circumstances. In xvi. 6 St. Paul is at Iconium, and he has the choice between the northerly road to Laodicea and the Phrygian-Asiatic district on the one hand, and the southerly road to Antioch, continuing in the Phrygian-Galatian district, on the other hand. To have said Φρυγίαν here would have been ambiguous, for the whole point was that he stayed in one part of Phrygia instead of in another. Nor would Γαλατικὴν χώραν without further definition have been enough. At Iconium he was on the borders of the Phrygian-Galatian and the Lycaonian-Galatian districts. It is true that the latter would really have been sufficiently excluded by the context; but the point is that St. Luke had just described a check in St. Paul's journey, and the simplest and best style of expression was one which defined the district accurately, and did not leave it to the context to decide whether Phrygian or Lycaonian Galatia was intended. In Acts xviii. 22 the situation is different. If he started from Antioch and went straight ahead, as καθέξης implies, after passing through Lycaonia Antiochiana—and no other route is possible—he would necessarily come to the Galatian district of Lycaonia, and after that to Phrygia—first Phrygia Galatica and afterwards Phrygia Asiana. The route is thus sufficiently indicated, and there was no check at any point to render further definition necessary.

Thus the meaning of the two passages in Acts in which a reference to "Galatian" is found, points to the Churches of Derbe and Lystra as those covered by the expression ἡ Γαλατικὴ χώρα in xviii. 23, and Iconium[1] and Antioch as

[1] Though in the case of Iconium the reservation must be made that it possibly belonged to Lycaonia Galatica (see Appendix I.).

those covered by ἡ Φρυγία καὶ Γαλατικὴ χώρα in xvi. 6. There is nothing in the Acts which need point to any other "Galatian" Churches, and the theories which make St. Paul travel into the middle of the old Kingdom of Galatia are unsupported by the strict interpretation of Acts, and make St. Paul undertake long and dangerous journeys to sparsely populated regions, instead of keeping, as is far more probable, to the great roads and main centres of the Greek-speaking population.

The only weak point in the view here adopted is the insufficiency of inscriptional evidence for the forms used. But this is not a serious matter: the attempt to make St. Luke or St. Paul always use correct official language has been pressed too far. Whether Phrygia Galatica, Lycaonia Galatica, Phrygia Asiana, and Lycaonia Antiochiana were official terms or not, there is no doubt that Phrygia was divided between the Province of Galatia and the Province of Asia, and that Lycaonia was divided between the Province of Galatia and the Kingdom of Antiochus. The districts existed, whatever the official names may have been, and St. Luke's expressions indicate them with sufficient precision. Whether he was using the names which a Roman official writing Greek would have used is a point of secondary interest, and, after all, it must not be forgotten that, so far as there is any inscriptional evidence, it supports the Lucan phraseology.

Turning to the Epistle itself, the question is one based on the consideration of two probabilities. (1) Is it probable that St. Paul made important missionary journeys outside the districts covered by the narrative in Acts? (2) Is it probable that he would refer to the inhabitants of Derbe, Lystra, Iconium, and Antioch as Galatians?

The answer to the first question is, on the whole, in the

negative. It is, of course, true that it is fairly clear from the Epistle that St. Luke only gives the outline of St. Paul's journeys, but it is impossible to see any point in the three great journeys at which a visit to the old Kingdom of Galatia can be interpolated, and there is, therefore, a considerable improbability against any theory which identifies the Galatia of the Epistle with a district outside those which the Acts state that he visited.

To the second question diametrically opposed answers have been given. German writers especially have thought it improbable that the inhabitants of Lycaonia or Phrygia would care to be addressed as Galatians, since their only connection with Galatia was derived from the political arrangements of a conquering nation. But these arguments largely rest on the wholly unproved assumption that the recipients of the Epistle must have been ethnographically Phrygians or Lycaonians, if the Churches of Iconium and Lystra were intended. It is far more probable that they were, or (what is here the important point) preferred to think that they were, Greek or Roman, and identified themselves with Greek and Roman civilization, rather than with the Phrygians, whose name was a synonym for slave, or with the Lycaonians, whose name had become the general title of brigands.

Moreover, one may fairly ask what other generic title than "Galatians" St. Paul could have used, if he was seeking a common name for inhabitants of Lystra and Iconium. The Lystrans were ethnologically Lycaonians, and the inhabitants of Iconium were ethnologically Phrygians. Both were politically Galatians;[1] but was there any other name which could be applied to both?

[1] Jülicher tries to ridicule the suggestion that St. Paul would use the name of

Thus, there is good reason for thinking (1) that Acts refers to the inhabitants of Pisidian Antioch, Iconium, Derbe, and Lystra, as belonging to Galatia; (2) that Acts does not narrate any visit of St. Paul to the old Kingdom of Galatia; (3) that "Galatian" is the term which St. Paul would naturally use to describe these Churches.

Taken together, these facts seem to afford extremely strong evidence in favour of the "South Galatian" view. Nor is this impression weakened by considering the "North Galatian" arguments. I am unable to find that any argument of importance has ever been put forward in support of the "North Galatian" view, except that Acts xvi. 6 must mean that St. Paul passed first through Phrygia and then through Galatia, after he had been prevented from preaching in Asia. This view is subject to the objection that it sacrifices the proper meaning of τὴν Φρυγίαν καὶ Γαλατικὴν χώραν, reads into the aorist participle κωλυθέντες a meaning which, though possible, is not necessary, and makes St. Paul wander wildly through some of the most desolate tracts of Asia, instead of keeping to the main roads and centres of the Greek-speaking population. The first of these objections is remedied by Lightfoot's suggestion, that τὴν Φρυγίαν καὶ Γαλατικὴν χώραν means the country, which was Phrygian before the Galatians conquered it. This is grammatically possible; but it is not likely that St. Luke would have plunged in this way into references to events which had happened two centuries previously.

a province, by saying that no one would refer to the inhabitants of Frankfort-on-the-Main as men of Hesse Nassau. Such arguments are surely valueless. I might equally well say that no one would refer to inhabitants of Natal as Zulus, or of Cape Town as Kaffirs, but might quite well refer to both as South Africans. Both arguments seem to me to darken counsel by specious but false analogies.

Thus the balance of evidence in favour of the South Galatian theory seems to be overwhelmingly strong, and the answer to the question, "Where was Galatia?" must be that it was the Roman Province, and that the Galatians to whom St. Paul was writing were the inhabitants of Pisidian Antioch, Iconium, Derbe, and Lystra.

II. When was Galatians written?

On the South Galatian hypothesis the earliest date for the Epistle is St. Paul's return from his first missionary journey. The choice of a date after this point depends on the view taken of the indications supplied by the Epistle itself. These indications are found in the interpretation of two passages: Gal. iv. 13 and Gal. i. 11—ii. 14.

The Meaning of Gal. iv. 13.

In Gal. iv. 13 St. Paul says: "Ye know that on account of physical infirmity I preached to you formerly." The Greek for "formerly" is *τὸ πρότερον*, and the suggestion has been made, notably by Lightfoot, that this must mean "on the former of two visits"; that is, after St. Paul had been twice to Galatia, and before a third visit. Assuming for the moment that *τὸ πρότερον* must have this meaning, it is important to decide what is its chronological significance. On the North Galatian theory, followed by Lightfoot, it means that the Epistle was written after the visit recorded in Acts xviii. 23, for the visit mentioned in Acts xvi. 6 was the first, and that in Acts xviii. 23 the second, visit to Galatia. On the South Galatian theory the interpretation is less simple. St. Paul visited the Galatian Province for the first time on his first missionary journey, and for the second time on his second journey. Therefore, it would at first seem that Galatians must have been written after the visit on the second journey; but the matter is complicated by the fact that on the first journey St. Paul paid two visits to each of the Galatian Churches, except, perhaps, Derbe, which was the turning-point. Thus, if St. Paul was thinking of the individual Churches rather than of the locality as a whole, he might have said, "the former of my two visits," at any time after the second visit on the first journey; and the first, not the second, missionary journey, becomes the *terminus a quo* for the dating of the Epistle.

But it is much more probable that this view, that τὸ πρότερον means on the former of two occasions, is incorrect. It can equally well be used with no comparative sense, beyond that involved in a contrast between past and present, in the sense of "originally." It is in the "Koine" Greek more common in this sense than in the more classical significance, and in the New Testament this is almost indisputably its meaning in all the ten passages[1] in which it is found.

It is, therefore, more than hazardous to base any theory, or objection to any theory, as to the chronology of Galatians on the view that τὸ πρότερον implies that St. Paul had already paid two visits to the Galatians, for it probably makes no such implication. There is even much to be said for Askwith's contention (p. 75 ff.), that εὐηγγελισάμην in Gal. iv. 13 has more point, if it be supposed that St. Paul, when he wrote, had only once been in Galatia; but the point is too fine to be made the basis of an argument.

[1] John vi. 62; vii. 50; ix. 8; 2 Cor. i. 15; Eph. iv. 22; 1 Tim. i. 13; Heb. iv. 6; vii. 27; x. 32; 1 Pet. i. 14.

The Meaning of Gal. i. 11—ii. 14.

The interpretation of Gal. i. 11—ii. 14 is more difficult, and affords one of the most intricate problems connected with the historical background of the Pauline Epistles. It may be divided into two main questions. (i.) Does St. Paul mean that all the events described took place before the conversion of the Galatians, or before the sending of the Epistle? In other words, does the plan of this section involve his giving a sketch of his relations with the Apostles at Jerusalem up to the time of his converting the Galatians, or up to the time when he wrote to them? (ii.) With what narratives in the Acts can we identify the events mentioned in the Epistle? and, if we cannot identify them at all, when are they likely to have happened?

(i.) The plan of the opening sections of Galatians is to offer a defence against the attacks of Christian missionaries belonging to the Jerusalem or Judaizing party, who had thrown doubt on St. Paul's claim to be an Apostle of Christianity.

St. Paul probably admits in Gal. i. 6 that there was a difference between the gospel preached by himself and his opponents,[1] but he claims that his mission was direct from Christ and God the Father, not from men, *i.e.* not from the Church at Jerusalem. This he states in i. 1, and repeats at greater length in i. 11 ff.: "For I make known to you, brethren, that the gospel preached by me is not according

[1] The exegesis of the verse is difficult: . . . *εἰς ἕτερον εὐαγγέλιον ὃ οὐκ ἐστὶν ἄλλο εἰ μὴ τινές εἰσιν οἱ ταράσσοντες ὑμᾶς, κ.τ.λ.*, may be explained by taking *ἕτερον* and *ἄλλο* in antithesis to each other—and it then becomes a nice question what the two words mean—or by taking *ἄλλο* with *εἰ μὴ* in the sense "nothing else but that there are some who," etc.

to man: for neither did I receive it from man, nor was I taught it, but I received it through a revelation of Jesus Christ." He then goes on to show that this contention, that he has received a direct commission from Christ, not from the Church at Jerusalem, is borne out by his history, and he especially explains the nature of his relations to the Church at Jerusalem during two visits to that city.

The question is whether this plan entailed his giving a sketch of all the occasions when he came into contact with the Apostles of Jerusalem up to the time of his visit to Galatia, or up to the time of his writing the letter. It is clear that it is impossible to dogmatize on this point. It is possible that he did neither the one nor the other, but merely discussed the incidents which had been fastened upon by his opponents as proving his subordination to Jerusalem. It is too often overlooked, in considering this question, that we have to deal with a controversy of which one side only is extant. St. Paul is not writing in a calm scientific spirit for the good of future historians, but is doing his best to pulverize an opponent. Now, in controversy, it is the business of a writer to answer arguments advanced against him, not necessarily to meet them beforehand, and we have no real right to assume that St. Paul discusses every occasion which brought him into contact with the Jerusalem Apostles: he may have limited himself to those incidents which had been attacked. This last point is, in fact, the one which can be advanced with most probability—the incidents dealt with are those which, at least in the opinion of the opposing party, could be used against St. Paul, or, on the other hand, were necessary to St. Paul's purpose of answering attacks.

Thus with regard to the plan of this part of the

Galatians, we can only say that it is intended to answer attacks on the character of St. Paul's apostleship, but it remains more or less uncertain whether he meant to give an account (α) of all his interviews with the Church at Jerusalem up to the time of his conversion of the Galatians, (β) of all his interviews up to the time of writing the Epistle, or (γ) only of those interviews which had been used against him in controversy.

It must, however, be admitted that while all three of these interpretations are possible, there would be more logical force in St. Paul's argument if he gave an account of all his visits to Jerusalem at least up to the time of the conversion of the Galatians, and that this interpretation has therefore a superior probability, if it be found to be consistent with the other factors which influence a decision as to the date of the Epistle.

(ii.) Bearing this conclusion in mind, it is now possible to consider in detail the events narrated in Gal. i. 13—ii. 14. These events can be summarized as follows: (α) St. Paul's life to his conversion (i. 13–16); (β) his action immediately after the conversion (i. 16, 17); (γ) a visit to Jerusalem (i. 18–20); (δ) visit to Syria Cilicia (i. 21–24); (ε) a second visit to Jerusalem (ii. 1–10); (ζ) St. Peter's visit to Antioch (ii. 11–14).

(α) *St. Paul's Life up to his Conversion* (i. 13–16).—In Gal. i. 13–16 St. Paul says, "For ye have heard of my manner of life in time past in the Jews' religion, how that beyond measure I persecuted the Church of God, and made havoc of it: and I advanced in the Jews' religion beyond many of my own age among my countrymen, being more exceedingly zealous for the traditions of my fathers. But when it was the good pleasure of God, who separated me from my mother's womb, and called me through His grace to reveal His Son in me, that I should preach Him among the Gentiles, immediately I conferred not with flesh and blood," etc. This account presents no real difficulty in connection with Acts, which agrees with the Epistle in representing St. Paul as a persecutor up to the time of his conversion. It is true that St. Paul (1–9) says nothing about the sudden vision described in Acts ix., but it is an exaggeration of exegesis to pretend that the phrase "to reveal His Son in me" can be regarded as contradictory to the narrative in Acts.

(β), (γ), (δ). These passages present more difficulty. The sequence of events in Acts and Galatians can best be shown in parallel columns.

ACTS.	GALATIANS.
(1) Visit to Damascus immediately after the conversion.	(1) Visit to Arabia immediately after the conversion.
(2) Escape from Damascus, and visit to Jerusalem.	(2) A "return" to Damascus.
(3) Retreat from Jerusalem to Tarsus in Cilicia.	(3) A visit to Jerusalem "after three years."
	(4) Departure to the "districts of Syria and Cilicia."

The difference between these accounts is obvious, and one cannot entirely escape the admission that either one or both are incomplete or inaccurate. There are, however, two points which are especially worth notice. In the first place, the expression in Galatians, "I returned (ὑπέστρεψα) to Damascus," implies that he had previously been there. It would seem as though St. Paul, for the moment at least, regarded his conversion, or the complex of events of which his conversion was the centre, as having taken place at Damascus, and this more or less corroborates the narrative in Acts, according to which the conversion took place on the road to Damascus, and was followed immediately by a period of temporary blindness passed through in Damascus. In the second place, the statement in Galatians that St. Paul departed to the "districts of Syria and Cilicia" after the first visit to Jerusalem, corroborates the statement in Acts, that, owing to a plot of the Greek-speaking Jews, he was taken by the Christians to Caesarea and sent to Tarsus, his native town in Cilicia.

But the points in which Acts and Galatians wholly fail to corroborate each other are the visit to Arabia and the description of the visit to Jerusalem. With regard to the visit to Arabia, whatever may have been its nature, room can only be found for it if we suppose that St. Luke has telescoped together two visits to Damascus, consciously or unconsciously, and that the events described in Acts ix. 19–25 really cover three years. It should also be noted that the account of St. Paul's escape from Damascus in a basket is corroborated by 2 Cor. xi. 33 ("In Damascus the ethnarch of Aretas the king guarded the city of the Damascenes to take me, and I was let down in a basket through a window"), and is brought into relation with Aretas, the King of the Nabatean kingdom of Arabia. But for the present purpose the question is not of primary importance.[1]

The events at Jerusalem are a more serious matter. The two accounts are best placed in parallel columns.

[1] See further Appendix III. p. 320.

ACTS IX. 26–30.	GAL. I. 18–20.
"And when he was come to Jerusalem he assayed to join himself to the disciples: and they were all afraid of him, not believing that he was a disciple. But Barnabas took him and brought him to the Apostles, and declared unto them how he had seen the Lord in the way, and that He had spoken to him, and how at Damascus he had preached boldly in the name of Jesus. And he was with them going in and coming out at Jerusalem: and he spake and disputed against the Greek-speaking Jews, but they went about to kill him. And when the brethren knew it, they brought him down to Caesarea. . . ."	"After three years I went up to Jerusalem to become acquainted with Cephas, and tarried with him fifteen days. But other of the Apostles saw I none, save James the Lord's brother. Now touching the things which I write unto you, before God, I lie not. Then I came into the districts of Syria and Cilicia. And I was still unknown by face unto the Churches of Judaea which were in Christ, but they only heard say, He that persecuted us once now preacheth the faith of which he once made havoc; and they glorified God in me."

No amount of argument can alter the fact that Acts speaks of a period of preaching in Jerusalem, which attracted sufficient attention to endanger St. Paul's life, while Galatians says that he was unknown by face unto the Churches of Judaea. Considerations which may be allowed to tell on the other side are the possibilities that St. Paul never spoke to any one except the Apostles and Greek-speaking Jews, and that Judaea means "with the exception of Jerusalem." But to most minds this seems very forced and improbable. The general impression made by Galatians is that this visit was a purely private one, during which St. Paul only met St. Peter and St. James of the leaders, while Acts suggests a rather stormy career of preaching in the company of the Apostles and St. Barnabas, who in the Epistles is spoken of as an Apostle (cf. Gal. ii. 9; 1 Cor. ix. 5, 6).

Thus there is a real and essential difference between Acts and Galatians. Probably both documents refer to the same visit, as both place it between St. Paul's departure from Damascus and his departure to Tarsus in Cilicia; but they give divergent accounts of the character of the visit. This is possibly to be explained by defective information on the part of St. Luke, but probably a more important factor is the different purposes for which the two accounts were written. St. Paul is controverting the accusation that he was disloyal to the authorities at Jerusalem, and that he had derived his commission to preach from them. St. Luke is either giving a merely historical account, or is chiefly concerned to show that St. Paul's gospel was not essentially different from that of Jerusalem. St. Paul wishes to show his independence; St. Luke, to make plain his agreement.

The importance of this fact is not so much direct as indirect. It shows that we cannot expect St. Luke and St. Paul to agree closely in their accounts of the same events, and that their disagreement in descriptions is not really any proof that they do not refer to the same things. To what extent this is due to the pressure of controversy

T

influencing St. Paul in one way, and the necessity of omitting irrelevant details affecting St. Luke in another, is impossible to say; the fact remains that when they are relating the same events they sometimes differ so widely that it is only the context which enables us to be sure that they are not referring to different incidents.

(ε) *The Second Visit to Jerusalem.*—This is placed by St. Paul "after fourteen years." It is somewhat doubtful whether he means fourteen years after his conversion, or fourteen years after the first visit. Probably the latter is right (see p. 288 f.), but the point is for the present purpose immaterial. Really important is the omission of any statement as to the reason why he ever left Tarsus and came to Antioch. According to Acts xi. 25, this was at the desire of St. Barnabas, the delegate from Jerusalem, and when St. Paul appears in Acts at Antioch there is no suggestion that he is in any way superior to St. Barnabas; indeed, until the two reach Cyprus St. Paul always is mentioned in the second place. Why did St. Paul say nothing about this? If the account in Acts is accurate it seems admirably calculated to have afforded a weapon for those who maintained that he was subordinate to the Apostles at Jerusalem. One can only suppose that there were some other facts which prevented this incident from being used by St. Paul's opponents, but were either unknown to St. Luke or seemed to him to be immaterial for his purpose. Once more it is plain that one cannot safely assume that either Acts or Galatians gives a complete account of all the occasions when he came into contact with the original Apostles.

The further course of events is most important and difficult. St. Paul says that he went up to Jerusalem, and that various incidents took place. What exactly were these incidents, and to what narratives in Acts do they correspond?

Probably the least confusing manner of dealing with these very complicated and perhaps insoluble questions is to adopt a somewhat artificial division of the material, not entirely justified by the text, and say that there are two problems: (1) the circumcision of Titus, and (2) the interview with St. James, Cephas, and St. John; and it is disappointing, even if honest, to be obliged to admit at the outset that no satisfactorily high degree of probability can be claimed for any solution to either problem.

(1) *The Circumcision of Titus.*—As so often happens in passages which present exegetical difficulties, the text is uncertain. The ordinary text found in all critical editions and in all translations of modern times is: *ἀλλ' οὐδὲ Τίτος ὁ σὺν ἐμοὶ Ἕλλην ὢν ἠναγκάσθη περιτμηθῆναι· διὰ δὲ τοὺς παρεισάκτους ψευδαδέλφους, οἵτινες παρεισῆλθον κατασκοπῆσαι τὴν ἐλευθερίαν ἡμῶν ἣν ἔχομεν ἐν Χριστῷ Ἰησοῦ, ἵνα ἡμᾶς καταδουλώσουσιν, οἷς οὐδὲ πρὸς ὥραν εἴξαμεν τῇ ὑποταγῇ, ἵνα ἡ ἀλήθεια τοῦ εὐαγγελίου διαμείνῃ πρὸς ὑμᾶς.* "But not even Titus who was with me, being a Greek, was compelled to be circumcised, but because of the false brethren privily brought in, who came in privily to spy out our liberty which we have in Christ Jesus, that they might bring us into bondage, to whom we yielded in subjection, no! not for an hour, that the truth of the gospel might continue with you."

This text is found in all Greek MSS. (including אB) except D, but not in the Old Latin version, or in the Peshitto Syriac. It has in so far a claim to recognition that it has not merely much manuscript support, but provides a sentence so impossible to construe and difficult to explain that it invites alteration.

The serious rival to this text is found in D, Irenaeus, Victorinus, Tertullian, Ambrosiaster, Primasius and the Old Latin version: ἀλλ' οὐδὲ Τίτος . . . ἠναγκάσθη περιτμηθῆναι, διὰ δὲ τοὺς παρεισάκτους ψευδαδέλφους . . . πρὸς ὥραν εἴξαμεν τῇ ὑποταγῇ ἵνα ἡ ἀλήθεια, κ.τ.λ., omitting the words οἷς οὐδὲ before πρὸς ὥραν.

Intermediate stages between these two readings are found in Marcion, some Greek MSS. known to Victorinus, and the Peshitto Syriac, who read, οὐδὲ πρὸς ὥραν εἴξαμεν, κ.τ.λ. but without οἷς, and in Jerome's Commentary on Galatians, which reads οἷς πρὸς ὥραν εἴξαμεν without οὐδέ. The question is whether these stages represent emendations of the ordinary text or of that found in D, etc. Undoubtedly, Tertullian and Irenaeus represent an older type of text than anything found, as a whole, in our extant MSS., but in any given instance there is always the chance that they have a purely Western corruption, and that the great MSS. are right. The crucial point of the textual argument is to be found in the reading of the Peshitto and Marcion. This seems to be certainly an emendation; but it may be explained equally well as an emendation of the one text as of the other. If we assume the text of the MSS. to have been the original, it is possible that Marcion and Rabbula (the maker of the Peshitto) struck out οἷς to improve the grammar; if we assume the text of Tertullian and Irenaeus, they may have inserted a negative in order to exclude the exegesis that St. Paul really did "yield in subjection."

It will be seen, therefore, that the real difficulty is not that the textual authorities are equally balanced, but that it is so difficult to see which of the variants is really the *lectio ardua* which explains the others. The question is, Which is more likely to have seemed *ardua* to early scribes, and so to have first invited alteration? Would they have been more shocked by the suggestion that St. Paul had circumcised Titus, or by an anacoluthon in his statement that he did not do so? Personally, I think that they would have been more tolerant of anacoluthon, and therefore am inclined to prefer the text of Irenaeus and Tertullian; but it must be admitted to be a point on which a decision is impossible.

The matter is complicated rather than elucidated by the fact that the verse is, whatever reading be adopted, susceptible of meaning either that Titus was or was not circumcised. The meaning depends entirely on the emphasis placed on the words. "Titus was *not* compelled to be circumcised" is as possible as "Titus was not *compelled* to be circumcised," and the meaning of one is the opposite of the other. Both interpretations (and, in fact, many variations of each type) have often been suggested, but it is unnecessary for the present purpose to discuss them; the truth is that it is quite impossible ever to decide from the actual wording what really happened. This is one of the results which spring from the fact that Galatians is really a letter, dealing with facts which were well known both to the writer and to his correspondents, though not to us. St. Paul was not writing for our benefit, but for the Galatians, who knew all about Titus, and therefore it was unnecessary for him to make plain the fact that Titus had or had not been circumcised—what he had to do was to discuss the importance of the fact.

When, however, we look at the question in this light, no longer as a question of exegesis, but as one of general probability, the point assumes a somewhat different aspect, though it still remains obscure. St. Paul is here defending himself against attack: there is, therefore, a probability that the incidents with which he deals are those which his opponents had used to prove that he was subordinate to the Apostles at Jerusalem. Certainly this is the case with the first visit to Jerusalem, and with the interview with the Apostles on the second visit; clearly these were facts out of which St. Paul's opponents had tried to make capital, and had thus forced him to give his own account of what had happened. If we might assume that this is also the case with the episode of Titus, it would follow that he had been circumcised, that St. Paul's opponents had used this as an argument, and that St. Paul, therefore, found it necessary to explain that, though Titus had been circumcised, it was not under compulsion, but as an act of grace, perhaps of misplaced concession to false brethren, whose true character he did not at the time perceive. At first sight this seems convincing, but it may be argued, on the other hand, with equal plausibility, that the incident of Titus is only mentioned in order to prove that the interview at Jerusalem was not really a permanent submission, as could be seen from the fact that Titus (who was a Gentile) was not circumcised, in spite of the pressure exercised by the false brethren, to whom he yielded only on matters of temporary importance, not on those of principle.[1] Nor is it possible to base a decision between these two lines of argument on our knowledge of what St. Paul is likely to have done. St. Paul argues in his Epistles against the necessity of circumcision, but on the

[1] Or, if another text be followed, "to whom we did not yield even for a moment," or with still another exegetical possibility, "to whom we did not yield even for a moment in any real subjection."

other hand, he circumcised Timothy, who was, after all, a Greek, even though his mother was a Jewess, and we may safely say that no one after reading Gal. v. would ever have expected such a concession to Jewish feeling, though v. 11 ("If I preach circumcision, why am I persecuted?") may be taken as implying that in some way he had given rise to the statement that he did recommend circumcision.

Thus the only possible summing up of the whole point seems to be that a verdict of "not proven" ought to be returned. It is possible to make attractive statements in the spirit of an advocate for either side, but if a judicial attitude is to be observed, no other verdict is conceivable. If, however, I were obliged to take sides, I should say that there is a balance of argument in favour of the view that Titus was circumcised.

(2) *The Interview with St. Peter, St. James, and St. John at Jerusalem.*—The main question here is whether this interview can be placed at the time of the Apostolic Council described in Acts xv., or at that of the visit during the famine described in Acts xi. 30 and xii. 25.

The popular view is the identification of the visit with the Apostolic Council, and the arguments in favour of this view are best set out in the additional note to chap. ii. in Lightfoot's *Commentary*, pp. 123–128. The other view has been defended by Ramsay, Weber, and Bartlett, and still more recently by C. W. Emmet.[1] It will probably be simplest to begin by stating shortly the main arguments for both views, and afterwards discussing them in more detail.

The case for the Identification of the Interview in Gal. ii. with Acts xii.—The main argument for this view will

[1] *Expositor*, March, 1910, reprinted in *The Eschatological Question in the Gospels, and other Studies*, pp. 191 ff.

always be found in the fact that St. Paul's reasoning seems to imply that this interview took place on his second visit to Jerusalem, and the second visit to Jerusalem according to Acts was that in the time of the famine. *A priori* this raises a presumption in favour of the view that St. Luke and St. Paul refer to the same visit, and the *onus probandi* is really on those who deny it.

Secondary arguments in favour of this view are not wanting. It is plain that if St. Paul intended to give an account of the occasions on which he came into contact with the Apostles, it would have seriously injured his argument to omit a visit to Jerusalem. Moreover, two striking parallels can be found between the account given of the second visit in Acts and Gal. ii. These can best be shown in parallel columns :

"I went to Jerusalem with *Barnabas* . . . And I went up by *revelation*."—Gal. ii. 1. "Only they would that we should *remember the poor*, which very thing I was also zealous to do."—Gal. ii. 10.	"There stood one [of the prophets] named Agabus, and signified *by the Spirit* that there should be a famine over all the world . . . and the disciples determined to send *relief unto the brethren* that dwelt in Judaea, which also they did, sending it to the elders by the hand of *Barnabas and Saul*."—Acts xi. 27–30.

Galatians and Acts speak of a visit to Jerusalem made by St. Barnabas and Saul, in accordance with prophetic instructions, and connected with the relief of the poor, and both describe this visit as the second which St. Paul paid to Jerusalem after his conversion.

Such is the main case in favour of the identification of St. Paul's interview with the Apostles with the visit at the time of the famine. To my mind it is extremely strong.

The case for the Identification of the Interview in Gal. ii. with Acts xv.—Lightfoot has stated the case as follows:[1] "The *geography* is the same. In both narratives the communications take place between Jerusalem and Antioch: in both the head-quarters of the false brethren are at the former place, their machinations are carried on in the latter: in both, the Gentile Apostles go up to Jerusalem apparently from Antioch, and return thence to Antioch again. The *time* is the same, or at least not inconsistent. St. Paul places the event fifteen or sixteen years after his conversion: St. Luke's narrative implies that they took place about the year 51.[2] The *persons* are the same: Paul and Barnabas appear as the representatives of the Gentile Churches, Cephas and James as the leaders of the circumcision. The agitators are similarly described in the two accounts: in the Acts, as converted Pharisees, who had imported their dogmas into the Christian Church; in the Epistle, as false brethren who attempt to impose the bondage of the Law on the Gentile converts. The two Apostles of the Gentiles are represented in both accounts as attended: 'certain other Gentiles' (ἐξ αὐτῶν) are mentioned by St. Luke; Titus, a Gentile, is named by St. Paul. The *subject of dispute*

[1] In his *Epistle to the Galatians*, pp. 123 ff.

[2] Lightfoot explains in a footnote that "this is calculated by a back reckoning of the time spent from the Apostolic Council to the appointment of Festus, the date of which is fixed independently at A.D. 66." A modern writer would probably speak less certainly: see Turner's article on *Chronology* in Hastings' *Dictionary of the Bible*.

is the same; the circumcision of the Gentile converts. The *character of the conference* is in general the same; a prolonged and hard-fought contest. The *result* is the same; the exemption of the Gentiles from the enactments of the Law, and the recognition of the apostolic commission of Paul and Barnabas by the leaders of the Jewish Church."

Such are the positive arguments for the two identifications. It remains to compare them, and see which seems to give the best explanation of the facts and to be least susceptible to serious criticism.

It is plain that Lightfoot's argument as to the geography applies equally well to either identification, and that so far as the persons engaged are concerned the representatives of Antioch were on both occasions St. Barnabas and St. Paul. Thus the points which really have to be considered are: (1) the probability or reverse of the presence of St. Peter and St. James in Jerusalem during the famine relief; (2) the character of the meeting; and (3) the result of the meeting. In considering all these points it must be remembered that the task of those who think that the private interview of Gal. ii. took place during the famine relief is to show on the one hand that such an interview is not improbable during that time, and on the other hand that the account in Gal. ii. does not agree with that in Acts xv.; while those who regard this interview as having been a preliminary to the Apostolic Council, have to reverse this process, and show that Gal. ii. does agree with Acts xv., and implies a state of affairs which was improbable during the famine relief.

(1) *The probability of St. Peter's and St. James' presence during the Famine Relief.*—It has to be admitted that St. Luke does not state that these Apostles were present in

Jerusalem, still less that they discussed the nature of the preaching of St. Paul, but this objection really resolves itself into the question of the presence or absence of the Apostles, for it must be remembered that St. Barnabas—the Cypriote—had been sent to Antioch to investigate the preaching of the Cyrenaeans and Cypriotes, and that this visit was his first return to Jerusalem since he had taken the serious step of approving of this preaching and fetching St. Paul from Tarsus to help in carrying it on. If, therefore, the Apostles were present in Jerusalem they must have discussed, at least in private, as St. Paul says in Gal. ii., the nature of this preaching. Thus everything turns on the question of the presence or absence of the Apostles. It is, therefore, desirable to consider the circumstances of the visit to Jerusalem in the time of the famine with somewhat greater closeness.

In the middle section of Acts St. Luke has had to attempt the most difficult task which is ever laid on a historian,—the narration of the history of events in two separate places. The interest passes backwards and forwards between Jerusalem and Antioch.

In xi. 19–30 the centre is Antioch; St. Luke describes how the Cyrenaeans and Cypriotes preached to the Gentiles, how St. Barnabas was sent from Jerusalem to investigate, how he approved of their teaching, and called St. Paul from Tarsus to help in carrying it on, and how at the time of the famine St. Barnabas and St. Paul took relief to Jerusalem. Thus he brings the history down to the time of the famine, which was in 46 A.D.

Then he goes back, takes up the history of Jerusalem for the same period, and in xii. 1–25 describes the death of St. James and the imprisonment of St. Peter, the death of Herod Agrippa I., which took place in 44 A.D., ending with the statement that after this the "word of the Lord increased and multiplied." He then adds a verse (xii. 25) referring to the ministrations of St. Barnabas and Saul, thus bringing the Jerusalem narrative up to the time of the famine, and connecting it with Antiochene section. Whether this verse is intended to represent the beginning or the end of the relief work depends on the text followed[1]—a problem which will never be settled with complete certainty—but it is at least clear that St. Barnabas and St. Paul are represented as in Jerusalem during the period of quiet which followed the death of Herod Agrippa I. This means that St. Peter was out of prison; but the question is whether he was not also out of Jerusalem. This depends on the exegesis of Acts xii. 17, which says that St. Peter ἐξελθὼν (from the house of Mary) ἐπορεύθη εἰς ἕτερον τόπον. It has been argued that this means "went to another town." But the truth seems to be that τόπος is almost exactly the equivalent of "place," and that whether it is "town" or "house" depends entirely on the context. For instance, in Acts iv. 31 (ἐσαλεύθη ὁ τόπος ἐν ᾧ ἦσαν συνηγμένοι) it certainly means either "house" or "room." In the present case the only guide which is given to the meaning is in the adjective ἕτερον. This means "another of two" (Lat. *alter*), and thus connects τόπον with the place from which St. Peter went out. Now, the place from which he went out (ἐξελθών) was the house of Mary, the door of which he had with some difficulty succeeded in having opened. Therefore the strict interpretation of the passage is that he went to another house. There is nothing in the context to suggest anything else. The most probable view, therefore, is that

[1] See Appendix II. p. 317.

St. Peter remained in Jerusalem, and is perhaps supported by the fact that in Acts xv. St. Luke clearly states that St. Peter was in Jerusalem at the time of the Council. It is indeed probable that St. Luke has omitted some, perhaps a whole series, of St. Peter's incidental absences from Jerusalem between Acts xii. and xv., but he shows no consciousness of having taken him out of Jerusalem and never brought him back.

Even if this argument be rejected, it remains clear that St. Luke regards the mission of St. Barnabas and St. Paul with relief for the famine as at all events ending later than the peace of the Church which followed Herod's death, and we certainly have no reason to believe that St. Peter, if he had left Jerusalem until the storm was past, did not return when quiet was re-established. There is, therefore, no justification in the history of St. Peter for the view that he could not have seen St. Paul during the famine visit, and if the identification of the private interview of Gal. ii. with this visit appears to be otherwise probable, no reasonable objection can be made from any theory that St. Peter was not at that time in Jerusalem.

A minor objection of the same nature has, however, been based on the phrase in Acts xi. 30 to the effect that St. Barnabas and St. Paul took alms to the presbyters, not to the Apostles. Hence, it is argued, we must conclude that there were no Apostles in Jerusalem at that time. This objection rests partly on a misapprehension of the difference between an Apostle and a presbyter. The Apostles were the active founders of Churches; the presbyters were the administrative officers of Churches after they had been founded. It is also partly due to ignoring the importance of the narrative in Acts vi., in which St.

Luke describes how the Apostles in Jerusalem were set free from relief work by the appointment of the "seven." St. Barnabas and St. Paul, therefore, would be likely to take alms to the presbyters rather than to the Apostles, but to discuss the nature of their preaching with the latter rather than with the former.

(2) *The Subject under Discussion, and the Character of the Meeting at Jerusalem.*—Lightfoot's statement that the subject of discussion was the circumcision of the converts, and that the character of the conference was in general a prolonged and hard-fought contest, is open to dispute. Certainly the subject of discussion at the Apostolic Council was the circumcision of the converts, and their general relation to the Jewish Law; but this is not exactly the description which St. Paul gives of his conference with the Apostles. He says they had a private discussion as to "his gospel." This is surely a different matter. He had already been preaching to the Gentiles: the question was whether he should continue to do so, and he says that the Apostles agreed that he should go on as he had begun. It is, to my mind, more probable that this represents something anterior to the great missionary activity which called out the protests from Jewish Christians and so led up to the Council. The question of circumcision may have been discussed, but St. Paul seems anxious to give the impression that this was not the question which he discussed at Jerusalem. Moreover, it must be remembered that it is quite doubtful whether St. Paul did or did not allow Titus to be circumcised, and that if a text and interpretation be adopted which means that Titus was circumcised, the matter is really settled—such a concession is unthinkable at the time of the Council, though, perhaps, possible at the earlier date.

Nor is it at all clear that Lightfoot was right in saying that the character of the conference was in general a hard-fought contest. So far as the conference itself is concerned, St. Paul does not hint at any fighting, and the whole idea of contest is based on the doubtful text and doubtful interpretation of Gal. ii. 3. If we follow the most ancient text, that of Irenaeus and Tertullian, St. Paul states that he yielded for the moment, and whether that statement refers to the circumcision of Titus (as I am inclined to believe) or to something else, it is inconsistent both with Lightfoot's description and with Acts xv.

Moreover, it is in any case true that on the main point there is more discrepancy than agreement between Acts xv. and Gal. ii. St. Paul says that he had a private meeting which settled the matter. He does not breathe a word as to this private meeting having been merely preliminary to a public meeting, which had had epoch-making consequences for Christianity, and really settled the question of circumcision; and he observes this silence, in any case curious, in spite of the fact that this same question is one of the two main topics of the Epistle, in which he is at pains to argue the point against adversaries whose leaders had, on Lightfoot's theory, already conceded it to him.

(3) *The Result of the Conference.*—The end of the last paragraph holds equally good as a criticism of Lightfoot's statement that the result of the interview in Gal. ii. was the same as that in Acts xv. So far as St. Paul tells us, the only result of the private interview was that the Apostles agreed that he was doing good work. If they had gone on to draw the—no doubt logical—conclusion that St. Paul's converts were not obliged to be circumcised, surely St. Paul would have said so? The fact is that the result of the

interview was, according to St. Paul, merely that he was encouraged to go on preaching to the Gentiles; which, if the interview be placed at the time of the famine, is what he actually did immediately afterwards on an hitherto unprecedented scale. The result of the Council was that a letter was written to at least some of his converts, disclaiming the necessity of following the Jewish Law, and asking them to observe either the main precepts of the moral law, or a food law. If the three-clause text which implies the former (see pp. 48 ff.) be taken, it is perhaps just possible that this is formally covered by St. Paul's expression, "they imparted nothing to me" (προσανέθεντο), but if the four-clause text implying a food law be adopted, it is impossible to make his words agree with the facts as stated in Acts xv. In either case he is omitting facts of the first importance, and relating those of subordinate importance which led up to them. It is this which, on the hypothesis that Acts xv. and Gal. ii. must refer to the same event, has led so many of the ablest German scholars to regard the account in Acts xv. as wholly unhistorical.

So far the balance of argument seems to be decidedly against the identification of the private interview with the Apostolic Council, and therefore in favour of the suggestion that it took place during the visit to Jerusalem in the time of the famine. It is, however, necessary to examine two important objections which are brought against the latter theory.

(1) *A Chronological Objection.*—In Gal. ii. 1 St. Paul says that he went up to Jerusalem "after fourteen years." If this be taken to mean fourteen years after his first visit,[1]

[1] This view is taken by Lightfoot, Zahn, and Bousset; the other interpretation is followed by Ramsay and McGiffert.

it implies seventeen years after the conversion, and if the famine was in 46–7, this would place the conversion in the year 30, which, though not impossible, is at least very early, though it has been adopted by Harnack. It is possible that St. Paul means fourteen years after his conversion, not after his first visit; this would give 33 as the year of the conversion, and no difficulty would then exist. But it must probably be admitted that this is the less natural interpretation, which ought not to be adopted unless it is quite impossible to fit the other view into the chronology of St. Paul's life. Nevertheless, in view of the other arguments in favour of not identifying the interview in Gal. ii. 6–10 with Acts xv., I am prepared to think either that the conversion did really take place in 30 (31 even is just within the possible limits), or that the fourteen years ought, after all, to be taken as from the conversion; but I feel that this chronological difficulty is real, and the only serious objection to placing the interview at the time of the famine.

(2) *The Objection that such an Interview would have rendered the Apostolic Council unnecessary.*—This objection is best stated by McGiffert[1] in the form that it is impossible to think that St. Barnabas and St. Paul twice went to Jerusalem with the same object, and that from the Epistle it is clear that the main object of the second visit was to secure the recognition of Gentile Christianity. This objection has already been partly discussed; it does not gain strength on examination, for it really assumes all that it ought to prove. The whole point is that the journey described in Galatians ii. had *not* the same object as that in Acts xv. The truth is that St. Paul does not definitely state what the real purpose of his visit was in any

[1] *History of Christianity in the Apostolic Age*, pp. 172 ff.

indisputable manner. What he does definitely say is that his interview with the Apostles was a private conversation, secondary to the main object of his journey; but what this main object was he does not directly state, though he very probably alludes to it when he says that he was zealous to "remember the poor." In fact, a very plausible paraphrase of Gal. ii. would be "I did, I admit, describe my teaching to the Gentiles, but I did not do this with any idea of recognizing a superior authority, and I only discussed the matter in a private conversation, secondary to my main purpose, because I valued the opinion and experience of the men of high position in the Church. They never suggested any change in my method, but only begged me to continue my care for the poor—which was the main object which I had in hand at the time."

The main result of the above discussion is to show a balance of probability in favour of the identification of the "interview" in Gal. ii. with an interview unrecorded by St. Luke during St. Paul's visit to Jerusalem at the time of the famine. Against this has to be set the chronological difficulty. The more popular identification with the Apostolic Council, or more accurately with a conference preceding it, has been seen to be open to many objections, of which the most important are: (1) that Gal. ii. seems to imply that this was St. Paul's second visit, whereas according to Acts it was really his third; and (2) that it is very hard to think that St. Paul would mention a private discussion without mentioning the result of the official meeting. It is now desirable to consider two lines of argument by means of which the attempt has been made to meet these objections.

The only at all satisfactory answer, if Acts be regarded as a trustworthy source of information, is that St. Paul is not describing his visits to Jerusalem, but to the Apostles. This view has partially been dealt with above (pp. 282 ff.). It implies that the Apostles were all absent from Jerusalem during the famine. There is certainly no evidence that they were absent sufficient to render this a positive argument in favour of the identification of Gal. ii. with Acts xv., but, on the other hand, there is no evidence that they were present, and therefore this is a possible answer to the objection, though it must be noted that St. Paul, in describing the object of his visit, does, in fact, say that he went to Jerusalem, and does not say that he went to the Apostles.

Some scholars, however, who maintain the identification of the interview with the preliminaries to the Apostolic Council, are dissatisfied with this method of dealing with the difficulty. They attempt to solve it by postulating more or less serious inaccuracy in the Lucan narrative. Of these attempts the best is that of McGiffert, who maintains that Acts xv., Gal. ii., and the visit in the time of the famine, are all one and the same. St. Luke was misled by the fact that he found in his sources two accounts—one describing especially the philanthropic side of the mission, the other its controversial aspect. These accounts differed so much that he thought that they really belonged to different occasions. There is nothing intrinsically improbable in this suggestion, for early writers were certainly liable to make two incidents out of two varying accounts of the same event. But it has several disadvantages: it avoids the actual difficulty of making St. Paul describe as his second visit to Jerusalem what was really his third, but it removes none of the other objections to the identification of the "private interview" with Acts xv., and adds to them the one serious difficulty—that of chronology—attached to the alternative theory, for the famine provides, on McGiffert's view, the fixed date for this meeting in Jerusalem.

Still more radical is the view of Schmiedel (*Enc. Bibl.*, "Council of Jerusalem"), which represents the mass of advanced German criticism; he thinks that Gal. ii. must refer to the same incident as Acts xv., but that the two accounts are so divergent as to prove that the account in Acts is quite inaccurate in describing an official meeting of the Church, and in imagining the existence of the Apostolic Decrees. According to this criticism there was never either an Apostolic Council or Apostolic Decrees. Some critics of this school go further, and think that the account of a visit to Jerusalem for the relief of the famine is also unhistorical. Such views have, however, of recent years, found less and less support, and are not likely ever to regain their position. It is, however, quite legitimate to use the penetrating and in many ways really moderate criticism of Schmiedel, to show the difficulties of accepting the view that Gal. ii. and Acts xv. refer to the same situation.

To sum up: each of the rival views has its own difficulties. The identification of Gal. ii. with a supposed interview during the time of the famine has to meet the two objections that there is no proof that the Apostles were at that time in Jerusalem, and that it is more difficult to fit into the general chronology of St. Paul's life. The alternative view is liable to the objection that it appears to describe as St. Paul's second visit to Jerusalem, what according to Acts was really his third; and that it makes

St. Paul omit the ultimate decisions of the Council, which were, in any case, most important for the purpose of his Epistle, while giving an account of a private interview which it is assumed had been held previously.

The question is, Which set of objections can be most easily answered? It is here that opinions have differed, and probably will continue to differ: my own view is that the objections placing Gal. ii. at the time of the famine are much the less serious, but I recognize that they are real, and prevent one from claiming the right to feel quite certain on the subject. Probably many of those who take the opposite view would be prepared, *mutatis mutandis*, to say the same.

(ζ) *St. Peter's Visit to Antioch.*—According to the Epistle St. Peter came down to Antioch, and was at first willing to move freely in Gentile circles, but after a time messengers from St. James[1] came from Jerusalem to Antioch, and persuaded St. Peter and the other Jewish Christians to draw back and separate themselves from the Gentile Christians. Against this St. Paul protested, and he quotes the incident here in order to show that he never had accepted any position of subordination to Jerusalem, or had altered the character of his own teaching.

The questions of historical importance are whether this visit of St. Peter ought to be placed chronologically after St. Paul's interview with the Apostles in Jerusalem, and what its relation is to the Apostolic Council of Acts xv.

Lightfoot and Lipsius both think the visit of St. Peter

[1] Or was it only one messenger? The Latin evidence is in favour of *τινά*, not *τινάς*, and ℵBDFG latt. Orig. read *ἦλθεν*, not *ἦλθον*, in the next clause. Origen, who read *τινὰς* and *ἦλθεν*, explained it as meaning that St. James himself came to Antioch.

to Antioch took place after the Council, on the ground that St. Paul is giving a series of events arranged in chronological order. Probably every one will agree that this is the most obvious view to take; but the difficulty has been felt that the incident described is most improbable at that time. In the first place, supposing the Apostolic Decrees were a food law, it is difficult to imagine both St. Peter and St. Paul ignoring them until St. James sent to remind them of the agreement, and almost harder to think either that St. Paul objected to keeping the agreement which he had just made, or, in the alternative, that St. James was trying to insist on more than the Council had conceded; and one or other of these alternatives seems to be necessarily implied. In the second place, if the Council did not prescribe a food law, but agreed to recognize the Antiochene position, which only asked for moral requirements, it is equally hard to imagine that St. James should so soon afterwards have encouraged a movement which, at the Council itself, he failed to support.

These difficulties have led Zahn and Turner[1] to suggest that St. Paul does not here follow the chronological order of events, but passes, after considering the two occasions on which he came into contact with the Apostles in Jerusalem, to deal with the single occasion when St. Peter came down to Antioch; it is not stated definitely that St. Peter did this before or after the events previously mentioned, but historical probability points clearly to an occasion anterior to the Council. In support of this conclusion it is urged that in the previous section St. Paul indicates the chronological order by beginning each sentence by ἔπειτα (i. 18, 21; ii. 1), and that when in ii. 11 he omits to insert

[1] See article on "Chronology" in Hastings' *Dictionary of the Bible.*

ἔπειτα, he implies that he is no longer following the chronological order.

There is a sufficient amount of weight in this reasoning to render the theory just possible; it is, indeed, to my mind, the preferable form of the interpretation which places the "interview" in Gal. ii. in the time of the Apostolic Council. At the same time, it cannot be denied that the straightforward view is that St. Paul is throughout following the chronological order, and that when he says, "But when Peter came," etc., he means that this happened after the meeting in Jerusalem, which he had just described.

It is, therefore, no small advantage for the view that Gal. ii. ought to be placed in the time of the famine, that it avoids all these difficulties. It is then possible to take Gal. ii. as giving the chronological order of events, and at the same time not to read into the account of the "interview" in Jerusalem details only derived from Acts xv. If we confine ourselves to Gal. ii., we know nothing of any agreement as to the conditions of intercourse between Jewish and Gentile Christians. All we know is that the Apostles approved of St. Paul's teaching, and agreed that he should continue to preach to Gentiles, while they kept to the Jews; and, so far as we know, nothing was said as to what the members of the Jerusalem school should do if they happened to be in the province of the mission to the Gentiles. But, if this be recognized, the account of St. Peter's visit to Antioch becomes intelligible. After he had agreed that St. Paul should continue his work on his previous lines, he came to Antioch, and at first fell in with the custom of the Antiochene Christians, and mixed freely with the uncircumcised Gentile Christians who did not obey the Jewish Law. Afterwards, other members of the Church at

Jerusalem came to Antioch, who were shocked at this laxity, persuaded both St. Peter and St. Barnabas to adopt a stricter line, insisted that it was one thing to encourage preaching to the Gentiles, but quite another to derogate from the sacredness of the Law, or to excuse converts from all observance of it, and were stoutly resisted by St. Paul.

Moreover, it is noticeable that this tallies very closely with the account which St. Luke gives of the scene at Antioch before the Council, and the *τινὰς ἀπὸ Ἰακώβου* in Galatians correspond exactly to the *τινὲς κατελθόντες ἀπὸ τῆς Ἰουδαίας* in Acts.

Thus, on the view that the "interview" in Gal. ii. refers to an incident in the time of the famine, this section must be taken to mean that, just before the Apostolic Council, St. Peter was in Antioch, and was somewhat vacillating in the presence of the conflicting claims of the local Church and of the representatives of the Church in Jerusalem. This must have been directly after St. Paul's and St. Barnabas' return from the first missionary journey, as described in Acts.

On this theory, the incident really presents no special difficulties; it falls naturally into place as one of the events which made the Council necessary; that this is historically probable has been recognized by Zahn and Turner, but inasmuch as they still hold to the view that the "interview" belongs to the time of the Council, they are obliged to accept the exegetical improbability that St. Paul has deserted the chronological order of events. The other view, placing the "interview" in the time of the famine, enables us to follow the lines both of historical and of exegetical probability at the same time. Thus regarded, the incident of St. Peter's visit to Antioch is a valuable though secondary argument in favour of the early date of the "interview."

In order to apply the results of the preceding investigation to the date of the Epistle, the main point is to establish the latest date mentioned by St. Paul. As to this it is obvious that three views are possible. (1) On the theory that the "interview" must be placed at the time of the Apostolic Council at Jerusalem, and that St. Paul in Gal. ii. follows the chronological order of events, the visit of St. Peter to Antioch is the latest date mentioned. (2) On the same view, but with the amendment that St. Paul is not following the chronological order, the latest point is the proceedings in Jerusalem immediately preceding the Council. (3) On the view that the "interview" belongs to the time of the famine, the latest date is the visit of St. Peter to Antioch, which must be placed either immediately before, or far more probably immediately after, the first missionary journey, just before the Apostolic Council, when the Judaic controversy was at its height.

Whichever view be adopted—to my mind the third is the most probable—it is clear that this latest date mentioned in the Epistle gives us the *terminus a quo*, before which it cannot have been written. The question which remains is to fix a *terminus ad quem*. This cannot be done even with the same degree of probability as the earlier date: it depends on the view taken of the general plan of the Epistle, and on the consideration of probabilities which appeal with very varying force to different minds. The main lines of discussion may be stated thus: First, it may be argued that St. Paul in Gal. i. and ii. is giving an account of the events not up to the time when he visited them, but up to the time of his writing; in this case the *terminus a quo* established above is actually the date of the Epistle, and we must regard it as written either just before or just after the Apostolic Council, according to the view adopted. Or, secondly, it is possible to hold that St. Paul is only giving an account of events up to the conversion of the Galatians. It should be noticed that for those who hold the South Galatian view—that the Epistle was sent to Pisidian Antioch, Iconium, Lystra, and Derbe—the second of these alternatives is only possible if we suppose that St. Peter's visit to Antioch preceded the first missionary journey. Ramsay seems to have overlooked this point when he argues in one place (*Paul the Traveller*, p. 187) that St. Paul omits the Council of Jerusalem, because it was held after the conversion of the Galatians, and in another (p. 160) that the visit of St. Peter to Antioch took place on St. Paul's return from his first journey, and finally (p. 191) dates the Epistle during St. Paul's visit to Antioch after the second journey. This is inconsistent reasoning; if St. Paul omitted the Council because it was posterior to the conversion of the Galatians, he ought also to have omitted St. Peter's visit to Antioch, and the fact that he does not do so shows that the omission of the Council must be otherwise explained.

Or, thirdly, it may be that he is merely giving an account of the events in his career which played a part in the campaign between him and the Judaizers, either for attack or defence, apart from any question as to their chronological relation to the conversion of the Galatians. The third possibility is, to my mind, the most generally probable, but can obviously neither be proved nor disproved: it is only serviceable in so far as it raises a presumption that if St. Paul omits all mention of events which would certainly have been of use either to himself or to his opponents in the Judaic controversy, this must have been because the events in question had not yet taken place.

The adoption of the North Galatian theory, which holds that St. Paul did not found the Churches in Galatia until his second journey, leaves us free to think that St. Paul, in Gal. i. and ii., describes only events anterior to the foundation of the Churches. In this case, when combined, as it always is, with the identification of the "interview" in Gal. ii. with the Apostolic Council, the North Galatian theory gives us no help in fixing the *terminus ad quem* of the dating of the Epistle. It is necessary to look for other indications. These can be found in one direction only—the connection of the Epistle with that to the Romans.

The relationship of Galatians to Romans is extraordinarily close. It is similar to, though possibly slightly less marked, than that of Colossians to Ephesians, and 1 Thessalonians to 2 Thessalonians. This has been worked out in detail by Lightfoot, in his edition of *Galatians*, pp. 45 ff., and the conclusion which he draws is that, if we are to judge from literary affinity, Galatians must have been written just before Romans. The same view is adopted by Askwith, who does not, however, adopt the North Galatian hypothesis. According to Lightfoot, therefore, Galatians was most probably sent from Corinth, just before St. Paul's last journey to Jerusalem.

On the North Galatian theory this view seems to me to be the most probable,[1] and it is important as drawing

[1] The alternative, which, until the coming of the South Galatian theory, was the most popular in Germany, is that it was written from Ephesus. This view is based on the ideas (1) that the τὸ πρότερον in Gal. iv. 13 implies two visits to

attention to the evidence afforded by the relation of Galatians to Romans.

On the South Galatian theory the position is different. The earliest date to which the Epistle can possibly be ascribed is the one which seems to me the most probable. If we adopt this view the dispute with St. Peter at Antioch is the latest incident mentioned in the Epistle, and St. Paul wrote immediately afterwards, just before the Council, on receipt of the news that the Jerusalem mission, which had caused trouble in Antioch, had also disturbed the Galatian Church. This hypothesis accounts satisfactorily for the absence of any mention of the Apostolic Council and its decrees in a manner which no other hypothesis does:[1] it is, of course, only possible if the conflict with St. Peter be regarded as earlier than the Council. It is best fitted to the view which identifies the "interview" in Gal. ii. with an incident of the visit to Jerusalem in the time of the famine. It is just possible, on the more usual identification of that interview with the preliminaries of the Council, if we suppose (with Zahn and Turner) that the conflict with St. Peter happened earlier, and think that the Epistle was

Galatia—thus the Epistle was written after the visit in Acts xviii. 23—and (2) that it was written very soon after this visit, because St. Paul says, "I marvel that you are *so quickly* removing," etc. (Gal. i. 6). Thus it is thought that St. Paul must have heard of the Galatian defection soon after his arrival in Ephesus, and then wrote the Epistle before writing to the Corinthians.

[1] It is desirable to notice that on the North Galatian theory no theory can explain the absence of any reference to the Apostolic Decrees. If we think that the Galatians lived in North Galatia, we cannot avoid the fact that the Apostolic Council took place, not only before the Epistle was written, but also before the Galatian Church was founded, and it is extraordinarily hard to understand St. Paul's silence as to the decrees. It is, therefore, not surprising that German critics, who hold the North Galatian theory, mostly reject the historical character of the decrees. I must confess that if I held the North Galatian theory I should do the same, and regard the Apostolic Decrees as Lucan rather than historical.

written from Jerusalem during the visit at the time of the Council, but before it had actually held its official meeting as described in Acts xv. But this seems unlikely: if for no other reason, because the way in which Jerusalem is mentioned suggests that St. Paul was not at the time of writing in that city. On this view, then, the Epistle was written shortly before the Council, after St. Paul's return from the first missionary journey. Was it, in this case, written from Antioch? This is the most obvious place, but the objection is that St. Paul refers to Antioch without saying or implying that he was writing there. This is not a very serious objection, but those who feel it to be important can suppose that the Epistle was written at some time during St. Paul's journey from Antioch to Jerusalem described in Acts xv. 3. It is a point in favour of this view that St. Luke's words "they passed through (διήρχοντο) both Phoenicia and Samaria, declaring the conversion (ἐπιστροφή) of the Gentiles." Διέρχεσθαι is the usual word for a journey of propaganda, and St. Luke seems to imply that St. Paul and St. Barnabas went more or less slowly to Jerusalem, gathering adherents as they went. Moreover, if the Epistle was written during this journey it would give a better explanation of the absence of all greetings from a definite Church, and would throw an interesting light on the phrase in Gal. i. 2, "all the brethren who are *with me*," which would be more appropriate as a reference to his companions on the way up to Jerusalem, than as a paraphrase for the Church at Antioch.

Thus, to my mind, the most probable view is that Galatians was written while St. Paul was going from Antioch to Jerusalem, just before the Apostolic Council. It is, however, necessary to point out that the one serious objection to this view is that it does not account for the resemblance of Galatians to Romans, if the traditional date of Romans,—written from Corinth before St. Paul's departure for Jerusalem,—be accepted. The only possible view seems to be that St. Paul wrote Galatians after his return from the first missionary journey during the controversy which led up to the Council; that there was then a temporary lull in the Judaistic controversy, or that the Judaizing propaganda passed over Macedonia and Achaia, and that when it broke out in Rome, St. Paul sent a longer and fuller statement of the arguments which he had used for the Galatians. This is possible: at the same time, there is no other evidence that the controversy had first a lull and afterwards a recrudescence. The choice seems to be between Lightfoot's date, which satisfies the literary problem caused by the resemblance of Galatians to Romans, but fails to meet the historical difficulties raised by St. Paul's silence as to the Council and its decrees, and the theory placing Galatians before the Council, which satisfies these historical difficulties, but fails to meet the literary problem. Personally, I find the historical difficulties greater than the literary ones, and thus prefer the early date, but there will probably always be those who take the opposite position: what is desirable is that the adherents of both views should recognize that there is a real weakness, as well as a real strength, in their own position, and that it is just this weakness which is their opponents' justification. The possibility of another date for Romans is discussed in this connection on pp. 363 ff.

It is, of course, hardly necessary to say that there are other views which demand respect, if only because of the authority which years of study have lent to the names of those who support them, but they seem, on the whole, largely to partake of the weakness of both the theories already mentioned, without having the really strong points of either.

Perhaps the best example of this type is the view advocated by Zahn.[1] He has taken the view which was traditional in Germany among those who maintained the North Galatian theory, that is to say, that the Epistle must have been written soon after St. Paul's second visit to the Galatians,—taking *τὸ πρότερον* in Gal. iv. 13 necessarily to mean "on the former of two occasions." On the North Galatian theory this meant after Acts xviii. 23, but Zahn is a "South Galatian," and therefore regards Acts xvi. 6 as the second visit of St. Paul to the Galatians. Therefore the question resolves itself for him into an attempt to ascertain how soon after this, and at what place, St. Paul is likely to have had news of Galatia. Zahn decides that it must have been at Corinth, and probably before the arrival of Timothy and Silas from Macedonia (see pp. 72 ff.). Thus Galatians is, also according to Zahn, the earliest of all the Pauline Epistles.

In many ways this is an attractive theory, and in Zahn's hands its strong points are made very clear, but it plainly suffers from all the disadvantages of dating the Epistle as contemporaneous with Romans, and also from those attaching to the system which dates it before the Council, for it gives no adequate explanation of St. Paul's silence as to the Apostolic Decrees on the one hand, nor of the close resemblance to Romans on the other. It sacrifices the historical probability that St. Paul would have mentioned

[1] *Kommentar zum N. Testament. IX. Der Brief des Paulus an die Galater.* Cf. his *Einleitung in das Neue Testament*, I. pp. 138 ff.

the decrees had he known them, to the probably erroneous view that τὸ πρότερον must mean the "former of two visits"; and it sacrifices the literary probability that Galatians is contemporaneous with Romans to the supposed necessity of interpreting τάχεως in Gal. i. 6 as "within a few months of my last visit." It is, therefore, so far as I can judge, inferior in probability to either of the other theories.

III.

St. Paul's Opponents among the Galatians.

The foregoing discussion, dry and full of tedious details as it necessarily has been, was essential if any thorough attempt was to be made to fix the position of the Epistle to the Galatians in the history of the Judaistic controversy by a comparison of the chronological data supplied by itself, by Acts, and by Romans. The result has been to show that it may, at the earliest, belong to the period immediately preceding the Council, or at the latest to the last visit of St. Paul to Corinth when he sent the Epistle to the Romans. It now remains to take up a different side of the question, and ask what light the Epistle throws on this controversy itself.

On any view of the date of the Epistle two things stand out clearly. In the first place, there was a divergence of opinion between St. Paul and the Jewish school as to the relation of Christians to the Jewish Law. In the second place, there was an attack on St. Paul's apostolic authority.

The Judaizers clearly maintained that every Christian was bound to observe the Jewish Law, and to be circumcised (cf. especially iv. 21; v. 2; vi. 12). Probably they argued that the promise of the Messianic kingdom was made to the seed of Abraham (cf. especially iii. 16 ff.; iii. 29; iv. 21 ff., in which St. Paul is clearly combating this argument), and that therefore those who wished to belong to the kingdom must become members of the family of Abraham by means of circumcision, and observe the Law which God had given to this family. This kind of teaching had been propagated at Antioch by preachers who were, or at any rate claimed to be, the representatives of St. James, the brother of the Lord, and the head of the Church at Jerusalem. It is extremely important to understand the attitude of mind which this Judaizing teaching implies. But as it is also the theme of the greater part of the Epistle to the Romans, its discussion is better postponed, as is also the consideration of the question whether the controversy with the Judaizers belongs to one period only, or broke out at intervals throughout St. Paul's career,—a question which is of course intimately associated with the respective dates of Galatians and Romans.

Peculiar, however, to Galatians is a subordinate point in the controversy: the accusation made that he was in reality an advocate of circumcision. This is certainly implied by Gal. v. 11, "But I, brethren, if I still preach circumcision, why am I still persecuted?" Clearly St. Paul had done something to give colour to this accusation. Either it must have been his treatment of the episode of Titus, if, as I believe, Titus really was circumcised, or, if a later date be given to the Epistle, it may have been his treatment of Timothy whom he circumcised in Lystra.[1] It is difficult or impossible to discover exactly what the facts were, but it is not impossible that St. Paul did actually recognize circum-

[1] Acts xvi. 3.

cision for Jews, and that at first he was prepared, in the spirit which said, "neither is circumcision anything nor uncircumcision," to admit it as expedient for Gentiles such as Titus, who were otherwise likely to offend Jewish Christians. On the whole, however, the point probably belongs to the comparatively unimportant category of those rather silly accusations of inconsistency which can always be made with some show of correctness against any prominent man. In any controversy the little men are always ready to shout "inconsistency" against the leaders of the opposite side—usually with some degree of speciousness. It never matters very much, for truth triumphs over tactics, and it is not finally hindered by the small mistakes of great men. The controversy in which St. Paul was engaged is in this respect no different from many others.

It is also possible that the danger of a forged letter purporting to be from St. Paul, was present to St. Paul's mind when he wrote at the end of his Epistle, "See with how large letters (πηλίκοις) I have written to you with mine own hand" (Gal. vi. 11). In this case the obvious comparison is to the situation in Thessalonica (see p. 95), but it is clear that the inference is by no means necessary. The whole passage is obscure. Πηλίκοις certainly ought to mean "how large," but it is far from unlikely that it had, in St. Paul's time, a greatly weakened meaning: it is doubtful whether the emphasis ought not rather to be placed on the τῇ ἐμῇ χειρί, and the sentence explained as implying that St. Paul had written the whole letter himself, instead of using an amanuensis. In this case it is unimportant for the explanation of the situation in Galatia. The question can never be cleared up entirely, as the sentence is necessarily as obscure to us, as it was plain to those who saw the original letter.

It serves in this respect to illustrate the true epistolary character of the letter.

Besides this, a bitter attack seems to have been made on St. Paul's personal authority. St. Paul nowhere formulates its character, but we can easily see what it was. His opponents claimed that the leaders of the Church at Jerusalem had special authority; that St. Paul was an Apostle—a delegate—from them, and that if he taught contrary to their commission, his doctrine had no validity. That this was the view promulgated by the Judaizers is as certain as it is, according to St. Paul's evidence, that it was not really based on the actual attitude of the leaders at Jerusalem themselves. Knowing even only the little which we do of the life of Jesus, we can see how such a view may have been justified. The "Twelve," had been appointed by Jesus. He had given them a commission to prepare men for the coming of the Kingdom. They had visibly received the gift of the Spirit. Authority was theirs: and if St. Paul, or any one else, also had authority, he had it only in a secondary degree, because the leaders at Jerusalem had given it to him. It is important to contrast this with the attack made on St. Paul's apostolate at Corinth, for the difference is typical of the Greek and Jewish standpoints. The Jewish mind sought for authority and order. It asked for a properly constituted governing body. The Greek mind, on the other hand, asked for inspiration. Validity for the Jew meant the possession of the proper commission from the proper people, and the delivery of the proper message in the proper way: for the Greek it meant inspiration by the Holy Spirit, the revelation through man of the hidden things of God. Thus, among St. Paul's opponents the Jew said, his mandate is irregular; the Greek, his message is inadequate. No doubt this would be an unjust statement if it were taken as a characterization of all Jews or all Greeks, but it does seem fairly to represent the extremes to which the majority of Greeks and Jews were liable.

The antithesis which is thus implied between constituted authority and the freedom of inspiration goes deeper and lasted longer than the controversies between St. Paul and his opponents on either side. It is, indeed, an antithesis which will never be resolved; it can be traced through all history, and both factors are ultimately beneficial. The use of the factor which emphasizes authority, and demands a proper mandate from the proper source, is to give stability: its abuse leads to stagnation. The use of the other factor, which seeks truth, freedom, and inspiration, is to ensure progress: its abuse leads to anarchy.

LITERATURE.—The best commentaries are those of J. B. Lightfoot, 1865; Th. Zahn, in his *Kommentar zum Neue Testament*, 1905; R. A. Sieffert, in Meyer's *Kritischexegetisch Kommentar über das Neue Testament*, 1899; F. Lipsius, in Holtzmann's *Handkommentar*, 1892; W. Bousset, in J. Weiss' *Die Schriften des Neue Testament*, 1908; and W. M. Ramsay, *Historical Commentary on the Galatians*, 1899. Other important contributions are W. M. Ramsay, *The Church in the Roman Empire*, 1893, and *St. Paul the Traveller and Roman Citizen*, 1895; E. H. Askwith, *The Epistle to the Galatians*, 1902; O. Zöckler, in *Studien und Kritiken*, for 1895, pp. 51–102; V. Weber, *Die Adressaten des Galaterbriefes*, 1900; and the articles in the *Encyclopædia Biblica*, Hastings' *Dictionary of the Bible*, and the *Realencyclopædie für Theologie*, ed. 3.

APPENDIX I

GALATIA, KINGDOM AND PROVINCE

THE population of Asia Minor in the first century after Christ was an extremely complicated mixture of various nationalities, representing different invasions and conquests. One of the lowest strata, representing either an aboriginal population, or one of the earliest invasions, was the Lycaonians, in the district of Lystra, Derbe, and further eastwards. A most recent, but still very ancient stratum, was the Phrygians, who had invaded Asia Minor at the beginning of the first millennium before Christ, or even earlier, and had conquered and settled in the valley of Sangarios, the country near the Hellespont, and the adjacent districts, pressing on as far as Iconium. Originally a fierce and warlike race, they gradually degenerated, and passed under the domination of the Persian Empire, and afterwards under that of Alexander of Macedonia. A disturbed period followed the death of Alexander, and ultimately, after the fall of Seleucus in 281, Antiochus I. became nominal ruler of Phrygia, but was faced with the rivalry of Mithridates of Pontus in the north. Probably the northern part of Phrygia, bordering on Pontus, was more or less completely under Pontic control. At this point, about 278 B.C., a new invasion began ; the Gauls, who had been ravaging all the Mediterranean lands, entered Bithynia, and after some vicissitudes occupied and settled in the north-eastern part of Phrygia, with Ancyra as their chief town. This is the Kingdom of Galatia; its population consisted of at least three superimposed and more or less coalesced strata, Gauls, Phrygians, and earlier inhabitants, perhaps related to the Lycaonians. The history of this kingdom up to the beginning of the second century B.C. is a series of wars and alliances with its neighbours, but in 189 B.C. the Galatian interference with commerce, and the alliance of the Galatians with Antiochus against Rome at the battle of Magnesia, led to a Roman expedition in which, as Livy narrates, an enormous number of Galatians were killed or captured. Further wars with the Pergamene and Pontic kings nevertheless followed, and probably to this period ought to be assigned an expansion of Galatia to the South at the expense of the Lycaonians, probably extending as far as Iconium and Lystra. This is the new territory which Ptolemy calls the "added" land, and Pliny a tetrarchy taken from Lycaonia.[1] The two authorities do not wholly agree, for Ptolemy excludes Iconium, and Pliny says that the tetrarchy included Iconium and fourteen cities; but probably Pliny is right. This explains why, although in 189 B.C. Lycaonia belonged to the Pergamene kingdom, it was not part of the Roman Province of Asia which was made in 133 B.C. out of that kingdom. Nevertheless Galatia

[1] Pliny says (*Nat. Hist.* v. 25), "Hos includit Lycaonia in Asiaticam jurisdictionem versa, cum qua conveniunt Philomelienses, Tymbriani, Leucolithi, Pelteni, Tyrienses. Datur et tetrarchia ex Lycaonia, qua parte Galatiae contermina est, civitatium xiiii urbe celeberrima Iconio." Ptolemy says (*Geogr.* v. 4), Ὑπο δὲ τὰ εἰρημένα ἔθνη διήκουσι Προσειλημμενῖται, ὑπὸ δὲ τούτους οἱ βιζηνοὶ καὶ μέρος Λυκαονίας, κ.τ.λ., while to Lycaonia (*Geogr.* v. 6) he reckons Iconium and six other towns, and to Ἀντιοχειανὴ Derbe, Laranda, and two others. Lystra he does not mention.

was never fully the equal of the Pontic kings in the north, and by 121 Galatia was probably—the point is not quite clear—more or less subordinate to Pontus.

In that year the Romans declared Galatia free—which meant free from Pontus, and practically, if not nominally, under Roman control; but the Mithridatic wars followed, and it was not until 73 B.C. that it was really free from Pontus. In 64 B.C. Pompey reorganized the East. Galatia was placed under three chiefs, and part of the tetrarchy of Lycaonia, including Iconium and Lystra, was taken away.[1] Of the three tetrarchs Deiotarus was the ablest, and in the last two years of his life was the sole King of Galatia. Dreading the horrors of a disputed succession, Deiotarus put to death all his sons but one, but either this son died prematurely or was overlooked, for on the death of Deiotarus in 40 B.C. Antony appointed Castor in his place. Meanwhile Pisidia and the rest of the Lycaonian territory of Galatia had formed part of the Province of Cilicia. Antony now found this arrangement undesirable. It was a disturbed district, and Roman soldiers could not be spared. Antony therefore appointed Amyntas, who had been secretary to Deiotarus, as King of Pisidia and Pisidian Phrygia; Antioch was probably his capital. Similarly, Polemon was made King of part of Lycaonia and Isauria and other districts. His capital was Iconium.[2] Thus in 40 B.C. the centre of Asia Minor was divided between Castor King of Galatia, Amyntas King of Pisidia, with a capital at Pisidian Antioch, and Polemon, with a capital at Iconium.

In 36 B.C. Castor died, and a new arrangement was

[1] In this way Ramsay explains the difference between Pliny and Ptolemy. He thinks that Pliny represents the older, and Ptolemy the later facts.

[2] Strabo, p. 568 ff. 577. Appian, *Bell. Civ.* v. 75.

made. Amyntas was given Galatia, and Lycaonia, which was taken from Polemon, who was moved northwards to Pontus, and the Cilician part of Polemon's kingdom was given to Cleopatra.

The fall of Antony only disturbed this arrangement in so far that Pamphylia and Cilicia Tracheia were added to the kingdom of Amyntas, who finally conquered Derbe, which had previously been an independent stronghold under Antipater. Thus the Kingdom of Amyntas became extremely large and important. Its final extent is indicated on the map facing p. 316.

In 25 B.C. Amyntas was killed, and the Romans decided to take over his kingdom as a new province. Pamphylia, however, was again separated from it, and made into a distinct province, and part of Lycaonia, including Derbe, was given to the Kingdom of Archelaus of Cappadocia. This district went through various changes, but in A.D. 41 a kingdom containing part of Lycaonia and Cilicia Tracheia was confirmed to Antiochus of Commagene, who was given the title of King of the Lycaonians. This kingdom lasted until 72 A.D., when it was absorbed into the Empire. In 41, therefore, the boundary of the Province of Galatia was Derbe, which was restored to it, and Lystra and Antioch had been made into *coloniae* probably because they were important in connection with the dangerous mountain district in which they were situated.

Such is the outline of the history of the change from the Kingdom of Galatia to the Province of Galatia. It will be noted that, except in a strictly ethnological sense, the whole district, including Iconium and Antioch, had been Galatian since the time of King Amyntas.

The name of the whole province was Galatia. This was

at one time disputed by Schürer and others who preferred the North Galatian view; but in the face of the evidence of inscriptions and of Pliny and Ptolemy, they have abandoned this position. The various districts in the province would naturally be described as Galatic, because they belonged to the Galatic Province, but their exact names, and precise proof of them, present many difficulties.

The districts important for the present purpose are those which Ramsay calls Phrygia Asiana, Phrygia Galatica, Lycaonia Galatica, and Lycaonia Antiochiana. The actual evidence for these is as follows:—

Phrygia Asiana is mentioned by Galen, who says . . . Δορύλαι, ἥ ἐστι μὲν ἐσχάτη τῆς Ἀσιανῆς Φρυγίας πόλις. (Περὶ τροφῶν δυνάμεως I), *ed.* Kühn, vi. p. 515.

Phrygia Galatica is probably mentioned in the *Menologium Sirletianum*, "Hi sancti martyres fuerunt sub Diocletiano imperatore in urbe Antiochiae Pisidiae ex regione Phrygiae Galaciae sub praeside Magno," where Galaciae may be emended to Galaticae or Galatiae; Ramsay prefers Galaticae, but Galatiae is palaeographically more probable (A. SS. Sept. vol. vii. p. 562 A.).

Lycaonia Antiochiana is mentioned in CIL v. 8660,[1] an inscription of 166 A.D.; and Ptolemy, v. 6, 17, speaks of Ἀντιοχειανή, though he nowhere supplies Lycaonia as the substantive belonging to this adjective.

This is not very strong evidence, but one must not expect to find overwhelming proof for the details of provincial nomenclature. In any case it is noticeable that the terms Phrygia Galatica, Phrygia Asiana, etc., are exactly parallel in formation to Pontus Galaticus, just as Lycaonia

[1] It should be noted that a widely copied misprint in one of Ramsay's later statements attributes this inscription to CIL. x, instead of CIL. v.

Antiochiana is parallel to Pontus Polemoniacus, both of which names are used by Ptolemy.

That χώρα means "regio" is probably not susceptible of proof: but χώρα is certainly not the usual Greek for "province" (ἐπαρχεία), and the use of the adjective Γαλατικὸς in a political rather than an ethnographical sense is the usual Roman practice. Γαλατία might conceivably mean the land which in the second century before Christ was the Kingdom of Galatia; but the proper title of the province would be ἡ Γαλατικὴ ἐπαρχεία. "The province which is named after the Galatian part of it," and in the same way ἡ Γαλατικὴ χώρα means a district belonging to this province. As Ramsay has pointed out, ἡ Γαλατικὴ χώρα can no more mean "the Kingdom of Galatia" than "the British district" could mean England. It means the district attached to the Province of Galatia, as distinct from a neighbouring district attached to something else.

That "regio" was a name used in Galatia for a district of the province is shown by an inscription from Antioch which mentions a ἑκακοντάρχην ῥεγεωνάριον, discovered by Sterrett, though he found the second word so strange that he was inclined to amend it into λεγεωνάριον.[1] χώρα would be the natural translation of "regio." It only remains to point out two smaller problems connected with Antioch and Iconium.

Antioch was really a Phrygian city: it was called Pisidian because it was close to Pisidia, and Strabo actually called it as such.[2] It was given to Amyntas as King of

[1] Sterrett, *Epigraphic Journey in Asia Minor*, p. 92.

[2] Strabo refers on pp. 569 and 577 to Antioch as ἡ πρὸς Πισιδίᾳ. The meaning of this phrase is shown on p. 566, where he says of Phrygia Magna, ἐν ᾗ ἐστιν ἥ τε παρώρειος λεγομένη Φρυγία καὶ ἡ πρὸς Πισιδίᾳ, κ.τ.λ.

Pisidia in 39 B.C.,[1] and Augustus made it a colonia and the military centre of the district. Strabo's evidence shows that before 20 A.D. the Phrygian character of the country was not forgotten: later on, as Ptolemy shows, it was regarded as Pisidian.

Iconium also was really Phrygian. It is described by Xenophon[2] as the most easterly town in Phrygia, and Pliny also speaks of it as Phrygian. So also in the trial of Justin Martyr Hierax says that he *ἀπὸ Ἰκονίου τῆς Φρυγίας ἀποσπασθεὶς ἐνθάδε' ἐλήλυθα.*[3] During the changes of Roman administration it was usually connected with Lycaonia: thus it went in 39 B.C. to Polemon,[4] not to Amyntas, but in 36 B.C. it passed with part of Lycaonia to Amyntas.[5] It was in this way a border town which politically was probably Lycaonian and nationally probably Phrygian. It is not quite clear whether it belonged to Lycaonia Galatica or Phrygia Galatica. St. Luke, however, seems to regard it in Acts xiv. 6 as Phrygian, for he says that the Apostles fled from Iconium to "the cities of Lycaonica, Lystra, and Derbe." In Acts xvi. 2–6, however, his meaning is less plain. In xvi. 2 he says that Timothy was well spoken of by those in "Lystra and Iconium." Does not this imply that St. Paul was already in Iconium? Then, in xvi. 6 he says that they "passed through the Phrygian and Galatian region." Does this imply that they entered this

[1] Appian says of Antony, *ἵστη δὲ πῃ καὶ βασιλέας, οὓς δοκιμάσειεν. . . Ἀμύνταν δὲ Πισιδῶν, καὶ πολέμωνα μέρους Κιλικίας, κ.τ.λ.* *Civ.* v. 75 ed. Mendelssohn, II. p. 1123).

[2] Xenophon, *Anab.* I. 2, 19.

[3] *Acta Martyrii Justini et Sociorium*, 4.

[4] Strabo, p. 568.

[5] Dio Cassius, xlix. 32, *ὁ δ' οὖν Ἀντώνιος . . . δυναστείας Ἀμύντᾳ μὲν Γαλατίας, καίπερ γραμματεῖ τοῦ Δηιοτάρου γενομένῳ, ἔδωκε, καὶ Λυκαονίας Παμφυλίας τέ τινα αὐτῷ προσθεὶς, κ.τ.λ.*

region after leaving Iconium? If so, Iconium is here regarded as Lycaonian. But the assumption is not necessary. Διῆλθον does not necessarily mean that they only then entered the region.

Probably, therefore, St. Luke ought to be taken as regarding Iconium as Phrygian, and in so far as evidence that Iconium belonged to the region of Phrygia Galatica rather than to that of Lycaonia Galatica. But it would not be wise to press the point. In any case, the argument on p. 259 holds good, that St. Luke's meaning may be that at Iconium St. Paul had to choose between the road going into Phrygia Asiana or that passing through Phrygia Galatica, and that he chose the latter because he found that he would not be able to preach in Asia.

The accompanying map, based on the work of Ramsay, shows the Kingdom of Galatia, the Kingdom of Amyntas, and the Province of Galatia, together with the towns and roads which are important for the history of St. Paul's work.

Those who wish to study further this very complex question will do well to begin by reading the first part of Ramsay's *Historical Commentary on the Epistle to the Galatians*, and his articles on the various towns and provinces in Hastings' *Dictionary of the Bible*, and to look up for themselves the passages which he quotes. The omission of the latter task results in a wholly wrong impression that the matter is, after all, quite simple—which is emphatically not the case.

APPENDIX II

THE TEXT OF ACTS XII. 25

THE text of Acts xii. 25 is so uncertain and so interesting that it cannot be passed by without comment. The text usually printed is Βαρνάβας δὲ καὶ Σαῦλος ὑπέστρεψαν ἐξ Ἱερουσαλήμ, πληρώσαντες τὴν διακονίαν, συνπαραλαβόντες Ἰωάνην τὸν ἐπικληθέντα Μάρκον. But the phrase ἐξ Ἱερουσαλὴμ is uncertain. There are three main variants in the text. (1) ἐξ Ἱερουσαλήμ, found in A 13 69 and many minuscules: (2) ἀπὸ Ἱερουσαλήμ, found in (B)[1] D (E) and some minuscules; (3) εἰς Ἱερουσαλήμ, found in ℵ (B) H L P 61 Syr-hl-mg. Chrys.; together with (4), a subvariant of (2), ἀπὸ Ἱερουσαλὴμ εἰς Ἀντιόχειαν, found in E syr-pesh sah, and many minuscules; and (5) a subvariant of (3), εἰς Ἀντιόχειαν, found in a few minuscules. Variant (1) may be condemned as an Alexandrian emendation of (3) not essentially different in character from (5). It is condemned not only by the weakness of the evidence, but by the fact that ὑποστρέφειν followed by the place whence a return is made, is not elsewhere found with ἐξ in the Lucan writings, but always with ἀπό. The choice, therefore, is really between ἀπὸ and εἰς. Considering

[1] The scribe of B wrote εἰς, but seems to have begun to write ἀπὸ. I think that this shows that ἀπὸ must have been known to the scribe, though it may have been merely a slip, for it is noteworthy that ὑποστρέφειν εἰς Ἱερουσαλὴμ is a common phrase which would come naturally to the scribe's pen, while ἀπὸ Ἱερουσαλὴμ is relatively rare.

the exceedingly important evidence which B gives, the purely manuscriptal evidence is about equally divided. But there is no question but that εἰς Ἱερ. is the *lectio ardua* which explains the others. The natural feeling of any one who reads the whole passage from xi. 27 to xiii. 1, is that xi. 30 describes the arrival of St. Barnabas and St. Paul at Jerusalem, and that xii. 25 ought to describe their departure. This would account for a tendency to change εἰς Ἱερουσαλήμ into some phrase giving the opposite meaning. Ἐξ Ἱερουσαλὴμ and εἰς Ἀντιόχειαν are both attempts to accomplish this purpose; is it not probable that ἀπὸ Ἱερουσαλὴμ is an earlier effort of the same kind? In this case εἰς Ἱερουσαλὴμ must be regarded as the earliest known reading. It remains, however, open to doubt whether it is not a "primitive corruption," which might be explained by Bartlett's suggestion[1] of an original text which said ὑποστρέφειν without any mention of Jerusalem at all, and was erroneously filled up by some scribe who did not pay much attention to the history, but was familiar with the expression ὑποσρέφειν εἰς Ἱερουσαλήμ (cf. Luke ii. 45; xxiv. 33; xxiv. 52; Acts i. 12; viii. 25; xiii. 13; xxii. 17), and was influenced by the fact (though no doubt he could not have formulated it) that ὑποστρέφειν is found in the Lucan writings fifteen times with mention of the place whither (εἰς), and only twice with mention of the place whence (ἀπὸ).

It is, nevertheless, not quite so certain as is often maintained that εἰς Ἱερουσαλὴμ is not the original text. Πληρώσαντες means not so much "after having fulfilled" as "in fulfilment of" (just as ἀσπασάμενοι in xxv. 13 means not "after having greeted" but "with greetings for"), and it is

[1] In the *Century Bible Commentary* on Acts.

possible that St. Luke really meant "St. Barnabas and St. Paul returned to Jerusalem, which was the centre from which St. Barnabas, at all events, had started, in fulfilment of the ministration (which has been already mentioned)." By this means he linked on the Jerusalem-narrative to the Antioch-narrative, and showed, what is historically certain, that the famine came after, not before, the death of Herod. The objection is that, in this case, he does not explain how St. Barnabas and St. Paul come in the next paragraph to be back in Antioch. It is, however, not impossible that he omitted to state that they went back to Antioch, regarding this as obvious: such a view is certainly harsh, but it is too much to say that it is impossible, for it has the advantage of giving a statement of the facts which is historically more probable. The death of Herod was in 44, and the famine was in 46. It is not probable that famine relief was sent from Antioch before the famine, and thus the mission of St. Barnabas and Saul probably took place after the death of Herod. In this case, Acts xii. 25 must be taken merely as a chronological warning, given by St. Luke to show that the famine, which the exigencies of his narrative had forced him to put before the death of Herod, because it belonged primarily to the Antioch narrative, really took place later. It is as though he said to his readers, "You must understand that the incident of the Famine, and the visit of Saul to Jerusalem, to which I alluded when tracing the history of Antioch, must be inserted at this point." Either this view or Dr. Bartlett's seems to me to be preferable to adopting the usual reading (ἐξ), which is so unmistakably condemned by all the rules of textual criticism.

APPENDIX III

ST. PAUL'S JOURNEY TO ARABIA

THE reference in Gal. i. 17 to a visit of St. Paul to Arabia raises several difficulties, which may be conveniently summarized in the questions: (1) Why did he go to Arabia? (2) What does Arabia mean? (3) What is the connection of the incident with the ethnarch of King Aretas (of Arabia) mentioned in 2 Cor. xi. 32?

(1) *Why did St. Paul go to Arabia?*—The usual explanation is that he went away to meditate in the desert, perhaps on Mount Sinai. This exegesis is not impossible, and can be expanded to any length by references to the psychological influence of solitude, and historical parallels to Moses and Elijah. The alternative, which meets with hardly any support at present, is that he went to Arabia to preach the gospel. It is of course quite obvious that certainty on this point is unattainable, but I would urge that on the whole the balance of probability is that St. Paul means to imply missionary activity in Arabia. He is arguing that he received a commission to preach to the Gentiles direct from God, not from man, and that he therefore had no need to confer with man, or to go to Jerusalem, before beginning to preach the gospel. The antithesis is not between conferring with flesh and blood in Jerusalem, and conferring with God in the desert, but between obeying immediately

the commission of God to preach to the Gentiles, and going to some human source in Jerusalem in order to obtain authority or additional instruction. St. Paul's argument seems to me to require the sense "As soon as I received my divine commission, I acted upon it at once, without consulting any one, and began to preach in Arabia." Moreover, it is, to my mind, psychologically more probable that St. Paul, once converted, lost no time before beginning to carry out what he felt to be his duty, but this consideration is too subjective to be valuable, and other minds will no doubt feel differently on the point.

(2) *What does Arabia mean?*—The names "Arab" and "Arabian" were used in ordinary Graeco-Roman language of the Kingdom of the Nabataean Arabs, which in the first century was almost at the highest point of its power under Aretas IV. The best statement on the history of this kingdom will be found in Schürer's *Geschichte des jüdischen Volkes*, I. pp. 726–744.

The point which is important for the present purpose is that the Nabataean Arabs had established themselves by the beginning of the first century as the rulers over a large tract of country stretching from the Euphrates to the Red Sea, with Petra as their capital, and bordering on the Province of Syria. At one time they captured Damascus, but from the time of Pompey this city belonged to the Province of Syria, though even in the second century it was recognized as in some degree Arabian.[1] Their territory was, of course, largely desert, but it contained several towns, of which Petra in the south and Bostra in the north were the most important. When St. Paul says that he went to

[1] Cf. Justin Martyr, *Dial.* 78: Δαμασκὸς τῆς Ἀρραβικῆς γῆς ἦν καὶ ἔστιν, εἰ καὶ νῦν προσνενέμηται τῇ Συροφοινίκῃ λεγομένῃ.

Arabia the impression which he would make on Graeco-Roman readers, in Galatia or elsewhere in the Empire, would be that he went to this Nabataean kingdom, ruled over from 9 B.C. to 40 A.D. by Aretas IV.

(3) *The meaning of* 2 *Cor*. xi. 32 ff.—St. Paul says, "In Damascus the ethnarch of Aretas the king guarded the city of the Damascenes to take me, and I was let down through a window in the wall in a basket, and I escaped from his hands." Apparently this is the same incident as that described in Acts ix. 24 ff., in which St. Luke says that the Jews in Damascus "guarded the gates day and night to kill him, but the disciples took him by night and let him down through the wall in a basket." No doubt St. Paul's own version must be taken as the more accurate, but the reference to the ethnarch of Aretas causes difficulty. It is known that Damascus in the first century before Christ belonged to the Nabataean king, but Pompey gave it to Syria, and the evidence of coins shows that as late as the year 34 A.D. it was Roman. There are, however, no coins from this date until 62 A.D.—in other words, there is no evidence that Damascus was Roman under Caligula or Claudius. The suggestion has therefore been made (and accepted by Schürer) that, at the death of Tiberius, Aretas was made responsible for Damascus. If so, this incident of St. Paul's life must be dated not earlier than 37 A.D., and it is not easy to fit this into the general scheme of chronology. But the whole basis of this suggestion is extremely frail: it consists entirely of the assumption that if Aretas had an ethnarch in Damascus, Damascus was in his kingdom. What are the facts concerning the word "ethnarch"? It came in time, as Schürer says, to mean some one a little more than a tetrarch, and less than a king, but the really important

point is that in the first century it was used as the name of the governor of the Jews in Alexandria.[1] No one concludes from this that therefore Alexandria belonged to the Jews. It is more probable, then, that the ethnarch of Aretas was a representative of the Nabataean king who looked after the Arab element in Damascus, just as the ethnarch of the Jews in Alexandria looked after Jewish interests. In this case the chronological difficulty of the passage is removed.

It is not, I think, impossible to combine the results of this inquiry into a reasonably probable hypothesis. St. Paul immediately after the conversion went into the Nabataean kingdom and preached to the Arabs, perhaps in Bostra. He was not especially successful, but roused the enmity of the Jews, and attracted the hostile attention of Aretas. He returned to Damascus, where both the Jews and the ethnarch of Aretas endeavoured to put an end to his career, but he managed to escape in a basket let down through a window in a house built on the wall.

This view is of course largely imaginative, but it may claim the advantage of giving a reasonable explanation of the difference between Acts ix. and 2 Cor. xi. The objection that St. Luke says nothing about this visit to Arabia of course remains: but it is, I think, sufficiently answered by the fact that St. Luke is only concerned with Christianity within the Empire, and Arabia was outside its limits.

[1] Καθίσταται δὲ καὶ ἐθνάρχης αὐτῶν, ὃς διοικεῖ τε τὸ ἔθνος καὶ διαιτᾷ κρίσεις . . . ὡς ἂν πολιτείας ἄρχων αὐτοτελοῦς. Strabo, quoted in Josephus, *Antiq.* xiv. 7, 2.

CHAPTER VI

THE EPISTLE TO THE ROMANS

THE problems concerned with the Epistle to the Romans may conveniently be divided into three main groups: (1) the critical questions relating to the integrity and destination of the Epistle; (2) the foundation and character of the Church at Rome; (3) the doctrinal and other controversies which called forth the Epistle.

The questions of a purely historical and critical character connected with this Epistle seem at first sight to be few in comparison with those raised by the Galatians and Corinthians. Indeed, if we could take the text of the Epistle as it stands, the question of date, and of the place to which it was sent—points which are so complicated in connection with Galatians—would be so plain as hardly to admit of discussion.

In Rom. xvi. 1 St. Paul refers to Phoebe as the "servant" (διάκονος) of the Church at Cenchreae, the eastern port of Corinth on the Saronic gulf, and commends her to his readers. This is in itself almost enough to justify us in saying that St. Paul was writing from Corinth. Moreover, in Rom. xv. 25–27 there is a clear reference to the "collection" for Jerusalem which St. Paul had made in Achaia and Macedonia.

"But now I go unto Jerusalem to minister unto the saints.

For it hath pleased them of Macedonia and Achaia to make a certain contribution for the poor saints which are at Jerusalem. It hath pleased them verily; and their debtors they are. For if the Gentiles have been made partakers of their spiritual things, their duty is also to minister unto them in carnal things."

From this it is plain that St. Paul has finished the collection and is just starting for Jerusalem. This can scarcely refer to any place except Corinth, and as this agrees so exactly with the inference derived from the mention of Phoebe, there is no reason for the slightest hesitation in saying that the evidence decisively indicates Corinth as the place, and the last visit to Corinth as the time of the writing of the Epistle to the Romans.

Unfortunately, at this point it is necessary to face two problems which disturb this apparently clear indication. In the first place, it is alleged that chap. xvi.—the commendatory letter for Phoebe—was really intended for Ephesus, not for Rome. In the second place, there is clear evidence of the existence of a shorter form of the Epistle, which omitted chaps. xv. and xvi. and made no mention of Rome in chap. i. If this cannot be shown to be a later recension, the argument based on chap. xv. only holds good for the longer text, and the possibility that the short form is the original has to be considered.

Thus, two distinct problems have to be investigated. (1) The destination of chap. xvi. 1–23; (2) the short recension of Romans.

The Original Destination of Rom. xvi. 1–23.

There is no trace of any external evidence for doubting that this section has always belonged to the Epistle. But on internal grounds the double objection has often been made that it is quite unsuitable as a communication to the Church of Rome, and that it bears signs of having really been intended for Ephesus.

The negative argument—that it is unsuitable for Rome—is primarily concerned with the large number of personal greetings which it contains, far larger than in any other Epistle. Is it probable that St. Paul had in a Church which he had never visited more friends than in any other place? Or, if it be thought that this is an unwarrantable inference from the greetings, is it probable that he would have known so many persons in Rome? It must be admitted that there is some force in this argument, even though it is hardly conclusive.

Besides this it must be noted as a secondary argument of a negative kind that Rom. xvi. 17, 18 seems out of place in an Epistle to the Romans. St. Paul says, "Now I beseech you, brethren, mark those who cause divisions and offences contrary to the teaching which ye have learned, and avoid them. For they that are such serve not our Lord Jesus Christ, but their own belly; and by good words and fair speeches deceive the hearts of the simple." By the "teaching which ye have received" does not St. Paul naturally mean his own teaching? And does not the description given of the false teachers fit much more the unethical teaching of "advanced" Christians, such as obtained in Greece and Asia,[1] than the narrow, but certainly ethical teaching of Judaizing Christians against whom Romans is directed? Again, it cannot be denied that there is some force in this argument, though it is not so strong as the

[1] According to the testimony of the Epistles to the Corinthians, the Epistles of the Captivity, and the Pastoral Epistles.

other, because there are some other places in the Epistle which are at least capable of bearing the meaning that there was a tendency to an imperfect appreciation of the ethical obligations of Christianity among some of the Gentile Christians (see pp. 380 ff.), though there is no place which points to a propaganda of this nature, such as Rom. xvi. 17 seems to imply.

The positive argument in favour of Ephesus is based on the mention of Epaenetus, and of Prisca and Aquila.

Epaenetus is described as the firstfruits of Asia,[1]—just as Stephanas in 1 Cor. xvi. 15 is called the firstfruits of Achaia. It is possible that Epaenetus had left Asia; but there is much more force in the description if he was still in Asia, and St. Paul was writing to the Church of which he was the earliest member. At the same time, not much emphasis can be put on this argument, because we know nothing of the history of Epaenetus.

Far more important is the question of Prisca and Aquila. The point is that, although they originally came from Rome, all our information points to the probability that their settled abode at this time was in Ephesus, and that, therefore, when St. Paul sends greetings to them, and to the Church in their house, it is far more probable that he is writing to Ephesus than to Rome.

In connection with this question it will perhaps be best to collect shortly all that we know from the New Testament as to Prisca and Aquila.[2] They are first mentioned

[1] The reading "firstfruits of Achaia" in the A.V. is condemned decisively by the facts (1) that it is not found in any of the best MSS.; (2) that it contradicts 1 Cor. xvi. 15, where the text is undisputed.

[2] It is curious, though probably unimportant, that St. Luke seems always to have written Priscilla, and St. Paul Prisca. It is also remarkable that St. Luke, according to the text of the best MSS., seems always to have written

in Acts xviii. 2, when we read that after St. Paul's arrival in Corinth he "found a certain Jew named Aquila, born in Pontus, lately come from Italy, and his wife Priscilla; (because that Claudius had commanded all Jews to depart from Rome:) and came unto them. And because he was of the same trade, he abode with them, and they carried on a business: for by trade they were tent-makers."[1]

The question may be raised whether they were already Christians, or were converted by St. Paul. As St. Luke makes no statement on the subject, certainty is not attainable, but the probability is somewhat in favour of the view that they were already Christians when they came to Corinth, as Stephanas, not Aquila or his wife, is quoted as the ἀπαρχὴ Ἀχαίας, and from 1 Cor. i. 16 it would seem that Stephanas was a Corinthian.[2] It is true that Aquila is referred to as a Jew, but it is by no means clear that "Jew" was to St. Luke the contradictory of "Christian."

In Corinth they remained until St. Paul's departure, when they went with him to Ephesus (Acts xviii. 18), and they

Priscilla and Aquila—putting the wife in the first place. St. Paul does the same in Rom. xvi. 3 and 2 Tim. iv. 19, but not in 1 Cor. xvi. 19. From this fact the conclusion has been drawn that Prisca was the more important person, either from social standing or from influence in the Church. The supposition has been made that Prisca was a Roman lady who had married a Jew; and Harnack has given much notoriety to the suggestion that she was the authoress of the Epistle to the Hebrews. All these hypotheses are more ingenious than probable, though no doubt there must have been some reason (now irrevocably lost) why Prisca was so often mentioned before her husband.

[1] There are many variants in the text of this passage, though they do not seriously alter the sense. Cf. Harnack's *Über die beiden Recensionen der Geschichte der Prisca und des Aquila in Act* xviii. 1–27 in the *Sitzungsberichte des königl. preuss. Akademie zu Berlin*, 1900, pp. 2–13.

[2] Zahn, however, thinks that he must have been converted in Athens, which was also in Achaia, since he was the "firstfruits," and St. Paul's preaching in Athens was not wholly unsuccessful; still, Athens plays so small a part in the early history of Christian Achaia that I think St. Paul probably meant Corinth.

were still in Ephesus when St. Paul wrote 1 Corinthians, as he refers (1 Cor. xvi. 19) to the Church in their house; indeed, if the tradition preserved in the text of the group of Graeco-Latin MSS. (DEFG), in 1 Cor. xvi. 19 could be trusted, he lodged in their house at Ephesus (see p. 143). Thus it would appear that they had settled more or less permanently in Ephesus. Finally, in 2 Tim. iv. 19 greetings are sent to Prisca and Aquila at Ephesus. It is of course doubtful whether 2 Timothy is a genuine Epistle of St. Paul, but at the least this reference points to the existence of a tradition connecting Aquila with Ephesus, for the Epistle is certainly intended to convey the impression that it was written from Rome to Ephesus, and if it be genuine it shows that about eight years after their first arrival in Ephesus Aquila and his wife were in that city.

Thus, apart from Rom. xvi. 3, all the evidence suggests that Aquila and his wife settled permanently in Ephesus, and this gives real support to the theory that Rom. xvi. is actually a short letter of commendation given to Phoebe for her use in Ephesus, not in Rome. It is not very probable that Aquila and Prisca left their settled home in Ephesus soon after St. Paul had written 1 Corinthians, that a year later their house in Rome was the centre of a Church, and that they later on returned to Ephesus, and once more took up the same position in the Christian community.

This argument is not lightly to be set aside, and if Rom. xvi. 1–23 were a loose fragment, with no context, I do not doubt that it would have been regarded as quite certainly a letter sent to Ephesus to commend Phoebe. The difficulty is in explaining how in this case a commendatory note (for it is really nothing more) to Ephesus, ever got into the Epistle to the Romans. This difficulty has led to many attempts at a fresh analysis of the greetings, intended to show that they really point to Rome, and to more or less ingenious efforts to find traces of Prisca and others in the early history of the Church of Rome.

The general analysis of the greetings has drawn attention to the fact that there is more evidence for the various names in inscriptions from Rome than in those from other places, and considerable weight has been attached to this point by those who support the Roman hypothesis. I doubt, however, whether they are quite justified in their conclusions. Our knowledge of Roman inscriptions has been, until recently, much greater than that of those in other places, and as our information has grown, the number of names which really are peculiar has decreased. It is true, as Lightfoot pointed out,[1] that many of the names in the salutations can be paralleled in Roman inscriptions referring to the household of Caesar, but these inscriptions are not contemporary, and most of the names are found in other places as well as Rome. For instance, without any full research into the *Corpus Inscriptionum*, a glance at Thieme's *Inschriften von Magnesia am Mäander und das Neue Testament* shows that Stachys and Philologus, both of which Lightfoot regarded as rare, and therefore adding weight to his argument, are found in inscriptions in Magnesia[2] and in the island of Thera.[3] The mere fact that many of the names in the greetings in Rom. xvi. are found in Roman inscriptions connected with the imperial household is of very little weight unless it can be shown either that the names in question are, as a whole, so rare that their combination in the greetings, and again in the imperial household can

[1] *Epistle to the Philippians*, pp. 171–178. [2] See Thieme, *op. cit.* p. 41.
[3] I Gr. xii. 3. 339, 671, 1527.

only be explained by their reference to the same persons, or that there is some reason for making this identification on other grounds. The former can certainly not be maintained; there is perhaps more ground for supporting the latter view.

This support is found in connection with the "household of Aristobulus," and the "household of Narcissus."[1] It is suggested that the phrase translated "the household of Aristobulus"—*οἱ Ἀριστοβούλου*—means the slaves in the Imperial household whom the Emperor inherited from Aristobulus, the grandson of Herod the Great. This Aristobulus is known to have lived in Rome, and to have been a friend of the Emperor Claudius.[2] The suggestion is that if, as is probable, he was dead by the middle of the first century, he had bequeathed his slaves to the Emperor, and that they were known as Aristobuliani—*οἱ τοῦ Ἀριστοβούλου*—in the Imperial household. This is possible, for it was not uncommon for slaves to pass in this way into the Imperial household, and to have a distinctive name. But, of course, it is pure assumption. There is no proof either that such Aristobuliani existed, or that Aristobulus left his slaves to the Emperor. A stronger case, of the same kind, can be made out for an identification of the "household of Narcissus." There was a well-known freedman named Narcissus who was put to death by Agrippina at the beginning of Nero's reign.[3] It is suggested, with much probability, that after his death his slaves were confiscated by the Emperor. This is quite likely, and, if so, these slaves would be called Narcissiani. There are, however,

[1] Rom. xvi. 10 f.

[2] Josephus, *Bell. Jud.* II. 11, 6; *Antiq.* xviii. 5, 4; xx. 1, 2.

[3] Cf. Tacitus, *Ann.* xi. 29–38; xii. 1; xiii. 1; Suetonius, *Claudius*, 28.

two objections to this theory, though neither is fatal. In the first place, Narcissus is quite a common name; in the second, there is no proof that *Narcissiani* must be translated into Greek as οἱ Ναρκίσσου. Words like *Herodiani* were transliterated directly. Would not St. Paul have said οἱ Ναρκισσιανοί if he had meant Narcissiani? It seems to me more probable that οἱ Ναρκίσσου means "the family of Narcissus," and that it refers to some living person named Narcissus.[1] At the same time, there is undoubtedly force in the contention that it is remarkable that in the Imperial household, among which we know that there were Christians,[2] it should be possible to show that there may probably have been at this time two sub-groups connected with the names of Aristobulus and Narcissus. My own feeling is that if it were certain that Rom. xvi. 1–23 really was sent to Rome, I should regard it as probable that οἱ Ἀριστοβούλου and οἱ Ναρκίσσου should be explained in this way. But I feel less prepared to accept this exegesis as a decisive argument in favour of the Roman hypothesis, when this is in dispute.

The attempt to find definite traces of Prisca and others in the early tradition of the Roman Church, is chiefly the work of de Rossi, the famous investigator of the catacombs in Rome.[3] He maintained in the first place that the Church of St. Prisca, on the Aventine hill, was founded on the site of the house of Prisca and Aquila. De Rossi was a very great man, but here it cannot be said that his arguments are impressive. It is sufficient to say that there is no real

[1] So Ambrosiaster thought. He describes Narcissus as a "Presbyter" (see Souter's *Ambrosiaster*, p. 199). This at least shows that if the Narcissus in Romans was the freedman, no tradition survived in Rome.

[2] Phil. iv. 22.

[3] *Aquila e Priscilla et gli Acillii Glabrioni* in the *Bull. di Archeologia Cristiana*, 1888, pp. 129 ff. See also Sanday and Headlam's *Romans*, p. 418.

evidence at all for proving that the site of St. Prisca's was that of the house of Prisca and Aquila, and no evidence for thinking that the church was called SS. Aquila et Prisca before the eighth century.

A far more serious argument was based by de Rossi on the *coemeterium Priscillae* in the catacombs. It is apparently probable that this cemetery was originally that of the Acilia gens, and Priscilla was a common name among the women of this gens. Thus it is suggested that the cemetery of this family was called after their distinguished member, Prisca the wife of Aquila. Dr. Hort[1] goes further and thinks that as Prisca is usually mentioned before her husband she may have been of more distinguished birth than her husband. Why not go further still, and suggest that Aquila was a freedman of the gens Pontia, in which Aquila was a common name? Is it not possible that ποντικὸν τῷ γένει is a misunderstanding of this fact? It seems to me that such suggestions are dangerously fanciful, and that there is not really any sufficient evidence for connecting the *coemeterium Priscillae* with Prisca the wife of Aquila.

Similar use has been made of the presence of the name of Ampliatus in inscriptions in the cemetery of Domitilla.[2] The name is found twice: but it is not uncommon, and though these inscriptions show that in the second century there were Christians of that name in Rome, there is not much reason for thinking that the Ampliatus mentioned by St. Paul must necessarily have lived there.

The same can also be said of Nereus. This name is celebrated through the Acts of Nereus and Achilleus,[3] who

[1] *Romans and Ephesians*, pp. 12–14.

[2] De Rossi, *Bull. di Archeologia Cristiana*, 1881, pp. 57–74.

[3] See *Acta SS. Nerei et Achillei* by H. Achelis in *Texte und Untersuchungen*, XI. 2.

according to the legend were eunuchs in the household of Domitilla. The name is quite common, and the Acts seem to contain much legend and little or no history.

Apart from the tradition of the Epistle there is thus a comparatively weak case for the Roman hypothesis. Still, the fact always remains that Rom. xvi. 1–23 is an integral part of all MSS. of the Epistle which we now possess. Thus the earliest tradition which we have connects it with Rome, not with Ephesus. This is not everything, but it is a great deal. Probably it is enough to prevent the Ephesian hypothesis from ever being unanimously accepted, and rightly so, for it can never be proved fully. Still there seems to me to be a distinct balance of argument in favour of Ephesus, though I must admit to vacillation on the question, and I should not like to say that I shall never come back to the Roman hypothesis. To some extent I have been influenced by the growing conviction that the text of the *Corpus Paulinum* is not always the same as the text which St. Paul wrote. If, as seems to me certain, 2 Corinthians is a combination of parts of two letters, whose union has left no trace in the textual tradition, clearly there was an important interval in the history of the text of the individual letters, and of the small collections of Pauline material made by individual communities, before the *Corpus Paulinum* was defined and its text established.

If the Ephesian hypothesis be adopted, it is clear that Rom. xvi. 1–23 must be regarded as a letter of introduction sent by St. Paul to Ephesus for Phoebe, a servant of the Church at Cenchreae, the eastern port of Corinth. Whether it was sent by St. Paul on the eve of his departure to Jerusalem must remain doubtful. There is nothing in its contents to help us, but it is at least the most probable moment, unless we assume that St. Paul visited Corinth again after he was set free in Rome.

The importance of the question in relation to the history of the Epistle as a whole can naturally only be discussed after the more serious problem of the existence of a short recension has been dealt with.

THE SHORT RECENSION.

The proof of the existence of a short recension of the Epistle resolves itself into the treatment of the textual evidence for the reference to Rome in the first chapter, and of that for the two last chapters. It is probably best to begin by showing why there is reason to believe that there was once a text which omitted the two last chapters, and then to go on to give the reasons for thinking that this shorter form contained no reference to Rome.

The most widespread evidence for the omission of the two chapters can be found in the ordinary Latin chapter headings (or *breves*) given in the Codex Amiatinus of the Vulgate and in many others (Berger, *Histoire de la Vulgate*, p. 357, mentions at least 48). This system gives Romans as divided into 51 chapters: the last but one (No. 50) is entitled, *De periculo contristante fratrem suum esca sua, et quod non sit regnum dei esca et potus sed justitia et pax et gaudium in spiritu sancto.* This clearly covers Rom. xiv. 15–23. The next and last (No. 51) is *De mysterio dei ante passionem in silentio habito post passionem vero ipsius revelato.* This equally clearly covers Rom. xvi. 25–27 and nothing else. In other words, it implies a text of the Epistle which ended with chapter xiv. *plus* the doxology which we usually read at the end of the Epistle.

Moreover, corroboration is not wanting that this conclusion is just. There is found in some MSS. a sort of concordance or harmony of the Pauline Epistles, which arranges under reference to the chapter numbers the parallel passages which deal with the same questions. The references to Romans are usually missing; but it is possible that the full text is preserved in a MS. at Murbach (*Codex Morbacensis*) which gives 43 headings from Romans. These are given according to the Amiatine chapter divisions, and the two last are *Quod regnum dei non sit esca et potus, ad Rom. L., ad Cor. pr. XI.*, and *De abscondito sacramento a saeculo, ad Rom. LI., ad Eph. IX., ad Coloss. III., ad Tit. I., ad Hebr. II.* This can scarcely be explained except on the hypothesis that a short recension was used. There is, it is true, some ground for thinking that possibly Corssen is wrong, and that the Murbach MS. is not the original form of the *capitulatio*, but a later edition of it. The reason for this is that whereas the other MSS. omit all reference both to Romans and Hebrews, the Murbach MS. contains both. The references to Hebrews are probably an accretion, and it is open to argument that the same is true of Romans. It is not, however, necessary to discuss this point here,[1] for in any case, whether the Murbach MS. represent original *capitulatio* or an interpolated version of it, it is based on a short text of Romans.

For myself I cannot see any possible answer to this argument, and the attempts of Zahn and Riggenbach to maintain that the Amiatine system of *breves* is defective have

[1] Those who find the point important should read not only Corssen's articles, *Zur Überlieferungsgeschichte des Römerbriefes* in the *Zeitschrift für die N.T.-liche. Wiss.*, 1909, 1 and 2, but also Dom Donatien de Bruyne's *Une concordance biblique d'origine pélagienne* in the *Revue Biblique*, 1908, pp. 75-83.

little or no strength.[1] It is not as though the Amiatine system was only found in a few MSS.; those mentioned by Berger are probably not a twentieth of the whole number, and there seems to be no reason to doubt the obvious conclusion drawn from the facts by a whole series of scholars, who have agreed in thinking that the Amiatine system of *breves* points to a short recension, though they have differed widely enough in their explanation of the fact.

It is obvious[2] that the Latin version implied by the Amiatine *breves* is not the Vulgate, but is ante-Hieronymian. Further traces of the existence of the short text can be found in Latin in Cyprian, and in Tertullian.

In the case of Cyprian, the evidence is merely the dangerous *argumentum e silentio*, but is a strong example of its kind. In his *Testimonia* he gives a collection of texts from every possible source, arranged according to their community of meaning, so as to serve as an arsenal of proof texts for various dogmas. It is certainly a fact that he does not clearly quote anything from chaps. xv. and xvi. of Romans, and each must judge for himself whether this can be accidental. The main point is, that in *Test.* III. 68, 78, 95, Cyprian musters the passages enjoining the duty of avoiding heretics, under the three headings; **68.** *Recedendum ab eo qui inordinate et contra disciplinam vivat,*

[1] Zahn, *Einleitung in das neue Testament*, i. 280 f. (3rd ed.), and Riggenbach in the *Neue Jahrbücher für deutsche Theologie*, 1892, pp. 526 ff., on *Die Textgeschichte der Doxologie Rom.* xvi. 25–27. The Murbach text of the "concordance" can be found in Vezzosi's edition of the works of J. M. Thomasius, i. 489, the Amiatine *breves* in Tischendorf's edition of the *Codex Amiatinus*, pp. 240 ff., and the shorter form of the concordance or *capitulatio* on pp. 237 ff.

[2] This was first pointed out by Lightfoot (*Biblical Essays*, p. 362), who drew attention to the fact that section 42, *de tempore serviendo*, implies a reading (τῷ καιρῷ instead of τῷ κυρίῳ in Rom. xii. 11) which Jerome expressly condemns. See also further in Riggenbach, *op. cit.* pp. 531 ff.

2 Thess. iii. 6. **78.** *Cum hereticis non loquendum*, Tit. 3 10 f., 1 Joh. ii. 19, 2 Tim. ii. 17. **95.** *Bonis convivendum malos autem vitandos*, 1 Cor. xv. 33. Why does he not quote Rom. xvi. 17: "Now I beseech you, brethren, mark them which are causing the divisions and occasions of stumbling, contrary to the doctrine which ye learned," etc.? It is instructive to note that in the spurious *De Singularitate Clericorum* (Cyprian, ed. Hartel, appendix, p. 212), 2 Thess. iii. 6 is quoted, and a few lines further down Rom. xvi. 17, which shows how naturally any one who knew Rom. xvi. would have used it in this connection. It seems to me exceedingly probable that Cyprian had the same short text as the Amiatine *breves*, and that this text must be provisionally regarded as having obtained in Africa in the third century.

Going still further back, the evidence of Tertullian is, if anything, stronger; for not only is there the same *argumentum e silentio* in the fact that he nowhere quotes chaps. xv. and xvi., but in *Adv. Marcionem*, 5, 13, he quotes Rom. xiv. 10, and says that this verse comes *in clausula*, *i.e.* in the closing section of the Epistle. It is true that he is contrasting the end with the beginning, and Hort (cf. Lightfoot, *Biblical Essays*, p. 335) argued that this need not imply the absence of the two last chapters. This might be admitted if it were not for the other evidence for a short recension; as it is, the natural interpretation of the facts is that Tertullian, like Cyprian, used a short text of Romans. Moreover, though it be true that the *argumentum e silentio* is much less strong in the case of Tertullian than in that of Cyprian, because he quotes so much less, it is noteworthy that Rom. xv. and xvi. are so full of passages opposed to the doctrine of Marcion, that it is suggested (by Sanday and Headlam, and by Corssen) that the short recension is a Marcionite production; yet Tertullian never alludes to these passages, either to throw at Marcion or to comment on his excision of them—and he was by no means disposed to pass over Marcion's emendations (real or supposed) in silence, even though he endeavoured to answer the heretic out of his own text.

Thus there is good reason for believing that, in Africa, in the second as well as in the third century, the Epistle to the Romans was used in a short text which omitted chaps. xv. and xvi. The Amiatine *breves* were made for a similar text, and suggest that this recension was closed by the doxology which we usually read in Rom. xvi. 25–27.

It is, however, improbable that the Amiatine *breves* represent an originally African text. Riggenbach has shown that in the summaries given the text of the Epistles is sufficiently closely followed to enable us to identify its character. It is not African, and it is not Vulgate; but represents the European type which was current in Italy before the days of Jerome. Thus we have European as well as African evidence for the short recension.[1] It is at present impossible to say whether there was originally one or more Latin versions; so that we do not know whether this agreement between African and European Latin ought to be taken as representing one or two Greek originals. It is, however,

[1] I can hardly think that the short recension was used in Rome itself: can we regard this as suggesting that the "European version" is, in origin, not Roman? Or shall we perhaps find that the "European" Latin ought to be divided into two, a Roman and a non-Roman, and that the *Breves* belong to the non-Roman type? There is a real difficulty here, and I do not see a satisfactory solution on any hypothesis yet known to me. To regard the *Breves* as Marcionite is the simplest suggestion, but the other objections to this view seem to me to be too great.

in any case certain that the evidence takes us back to the second century.

Another witness, but a suspected one, to the same short text, is Marcion. For our knowledge of this fact we are indebted to Rufinus' translation of Origen's Commentary on Rom. xvi. 25–27. He says, *Caput hoc Marcion, a quo scripturae evangelicae atque apostolicae interpolatae sunt, de hac epistola penitus abstulit; et non solum hoc, sed et ab eo loco ubi scriptum est omne autem quod non est ex fide, peccatum est* (xiv. 23) *usque ad finem cuncta dissecuit.* The meaning of this passage is one of two. Clearly it implies that Marcion removed the doxology altogether (*abstulit*), but there is room for doubt as to what he did with the rest of the Epistle. What is the meaning of *dissecuit*? The obvious meaning, which is nearly always adopted, seems to be "cut away," but the objection, first made, I think, by Hort, is that this is not the true meaning either of *dissecuit*, or of the Greek (which it may be supposed to represent) διέτεμεν; it ought rather to be translated "separated off."[1] This argument gains strength if we try to distinguish between *abstulit* and *dissecuit*. It is, perhaps, impossible to decide the point; if *dissecuit* be used loosely it means that Marcion cut away not only the doxology, but also Rom. xv. and xvi.; if it be taken strictly it means that Marcion separated Rom. xv. and xvi. from the rest of the Epistle, and cut out the doxology which came at the end of chap. xiv. Probably the former view is right, and the difference between *abstulit* and *dissecuit* is to be explained as merely due to a desire for variation.

[1] Zahn (*Einleitung*, i. p. 280) thinks that *cuncta dissecuit* means that Marcion "hat alles . . . zerschnitten, durch Ausmerzungen zerstümmelt." But this does not seem to me to be at all a natural interpretation of the Latin, and still less of the presumable Greek, πάντα διέτεμεν.

No MSS. in any language preserves the short recension. Corssen, it is true, thinks that in a certain limited sense this may be claimed for the group DEFG or rather for their ancestor *Z* (see Appendix I.). He argues that the character of the text in Rom. xv. and xvi. differs from that in the other chapters to such an extent that the only possible solution is that the scribe of *Z*, or of an ancestor of *Z*, used two exemplars, of which he followed one for Rom. i.–xiv. and the other for Rom. xv. and xvi. In this case it would be probable that the former exemplar belonged to the short recension, and that the scribe passed on to the latter MSS. because he knew that a long recension existed, and he had the usual scribe's preference for the longer text. It would, however, be wrong to regard this as quite decisive, for though the argument is quite reasonable, it is too complicated to be wholly final. Moreover, the complete analysis of the text is still unedited. So far as I can see, Corssen is right, but the proof of his thesis demands a rather fuller treatment than he or any one else has yet given to it.

Apart, however, from direct MS. evidence, the traces of the textual influence of the short recension are tolerably plain.

In the Epistle to the Romans as it stands at present in critical editions the arrangement of the contents of the last three chapters is as follows : (1) Rom. xiv. 1–23 is devoted to the question of the propriety of observing a distinction between lawful and unlawful food ; (2) Rom. xv. 1–13 continues the argument on more general lines ; (3) Rom. xv. 14–33 is chiefly concerned with St. Paul's plans for the future ; (4) Rom. xvi. 1–20^{a} is a list of greetings to members of the Church to which he writes, and a commendation of

Phoebe of Cenchreae; (5) Rom. xvi. 20^{b} is a benediction; (6) Rom. xvi. 20–23 is a postscript of greetings from companions of St. Paul; and (7) Rom. xvi. 25–27[1] is a closing benediction. It is clear that there is no serious break in thought between xiv. 23 and xv. 1, and that the doxology is in its correct place at the end of everything. Yet in the Antiochene text, represented by the great majority of Greek MSS., the doxology comes not at the end, but between chaps. xiv. and xv. Moreover, it is certain that this represents an early text, which was adopted, to use Westcott and Hort's expression, by the "Syrian Revisers," because we have the distinct evidence of Origen that this reading was that of some of the texts which had not been corrupted by Marcion: *In nonnullis etenim codicibus post eum locum quem suprà diximus, hoc est Omne autem quod non est ex fide peccatum est, statim cohaerens habetur Ei autem qui potens est*, etc., though he was also acquainted with others which put the doxology at the end of the Epistle, and, like modern critical editors, believed that this was the right place for it. The same text was used by Chrysostom, Theodoret, Oecumenius and Theophylact, so that, leaving out the Latin version for the moment, it would seem as though the Eastern text originally had the doxology after chap. xiv., and that in Alexandria it was moved to the end of chap. xvi., though in the time of Origen the MSS. known to him still differed on the question.

The history of the Latin text on this point is not easy to follow, owing to our almost complete ignorance of the Old Latin text of the Epistle. The known facts, however, seem to be these; there were in the Latin versions before Jerome three types of reading: (1) with the doxology at

[1] Rom. xvi. 24 is omitted by the R.V. and all critical editors.

the end of the Epistle, found in D and used by Pelagius and Ambrosiaster, possibly owing to Alexandrian influence ; (2) with the doxology after xiv. 23, found in Codex Guelferbytanus and a fragment at Monza [1] $\left(\text{cod. } \frac{1-2}{9}\right)$, and (3) without any doxology, used by Priscillian and found in FG and Cod. Ambrosianus E 26. It is also probable that *Z*, the archetype of the Graeco-Latin MSS. DEFG, ought to be added either to the second or third of these categories.[2]

The most probable solution of these facts seems to me to be that the earliest type of Old Latin had the doxology after xiv. 23 and that the texts of Priscillian [3] and Ambrosiaster represent Spanish and Italian attempts to emend an obviously difficult reading. It is, I think, an illustration of the fact that, with the exception of the Alexandrians, the Greeks were less apt to be struck by textual difficulties than the Latins.

It is now possible to sum up the probabilities of the case with regard to the doxology. It is very unlikely that this was originally anywhere else than at the end of the Epistle, wherever that was [4] : therefore all the MSS. which

[1] For the fullest statement of the facts about this MS. see Dom Bruyne, *Des deux derniers chapitres de la lettre aux Romains*, in *Revue Bénédictine*, 1908, p. 423 ff.

[2] See Appendix, pp. 414 ff.

[3] The agreement between Priscillian and FG suggests that *Y*, the archetype of FG, may have had Spanish elements, and possibly this may even be true of *Z*, and would account for the agreement with Spec. to which Corssen has drawn attention. D is, I fancy, more like the text of Lucifer and of Ambrosiaster than was that of *Z*, but the question requires investigation.

[4] Zahn, it is true, in his commentary (see esp. pp. 620 ff) argues that the doxology is really best in place between chaps. xiv. and xv. But I cannot see that he succeeds in explaining away the break which it then makes in the text. I agree that, on transcriptional grounds, xiv. 23 is the most probable place for the doxology, but I regard this as only possible if we assume that it belonged

insert it after xiv. 23 are really evidence for the existence of the short recension, and confirm the witness of Tertullian, Cyprian, and the Latin *Breves* and *Capitulatio*.

Moreover, it is not probable that the doxology belongs to the long recension, or rather to chap. xvi. of the long recension. For, if we assume that it did so, we have to imagine that its presence in the short recension is due to the fact that some scribe, who knew both the short and the long recensions, took the doxology—and the doxology only—from the long recension in order to add it on to the short recension. This is exceedingly improbable; and even more improbable is it that, if the doxology had been found at the end of the long recension, it would ever have been taken out of its place and put in the middle of the connected argument of chaps. xiv. and xv. Thus the assumption that the doxology belonged originally to chap. xvi. in the long recension renders it impossible to explain either (1) the short recension *plus* the doxology, or (2) the long recension *plus* the doxology after xiv. 23.

On the other hand, if we assume that the doxology really belonged originally to the short recension, or to one form of the short recension, and the long recension had no doxology at all, but ended with the "Grace" (or with a postscript after the "Grace," according to the view taken of the textual question of the "Grace"), the textual history

originally to the shorter recension. Zahn is perhaps right in believing that the "Grace" originally came in xvi. 24 only. It has been displaced in the long recension when the doxology was moved from xiv. 23 to xvi. 25. It is curious to note that Dom Bruyne is rather inclined to think that the "Grace" originally preceded the doxology in the short recension. It appears to have done so in the Monza MSS. The matter is complicated, but not sufficiently important for the present purpose to warrant the rather long discussion of details which would be necessary to deal with it fully.

seems to admit of a reasonable reconstruction, as the result of attempts of scribes to combine these two forms. The simplest method was simply to add on to the complete short recension the added matter of the long recension, *i.e.* chaps. xv. and xvi. This was the method that the Antiochene text adopted. It had the disadvantage that it made the doxology appear to be intrusive and in an impossible position. An attempt to remedy this was the method of passing from one text to the other before the doxology: this would give a text indistinguishable from the original long recension, and is found in Priscillian and probably in *Z*, the archetype of DEFG. A third course taken in Alexandria, or at least in circles known to Origen, consisted in moving the doxology to the end of chap. xvi., and this was also adopted by Pelagius, Ambrosiaster, and Jerome.

The most important conclusion from these results is that there are no longer extant any pure MSS. either of the short or of the long recension. It is of course obvious that the short recension does not exist now, as no extant MSS. omit Rom. xv. and xvi. Similarly, the existence of the doxology is the proof that the long recension has been, at least so far, contaminated with the short recension. The only possible witnesses which we have to the pure long recension are the MSS. known to Jerome which had not the doxology, and possibly also those used by Priscillian.[1]

In any case, though many of the details are uncertain,

[1] It is, however, quite possible that Priscillian's text is really the short recension without the doxology, but with the addition of chaps. xv. and xvi. The same thing is true of *Z*, and in this case is certain if it be true as Corssen thinks—I believe rightly—that there is sufficient textual difference between the text of Rom. i.–xiv. and xv.–xvi. in *Z* to show that a different archetype was used for xv. and xvi. (see above, p. 341).

and the history of the text is obscure, there is, I think, sufficient evidence to justify the statement that in the second century there was a short recension of Romans, and that traces of the process of its gradual abandonment in favour of the long recension can be found in the third and fourth centuries.

It is now necessary to go on to show that the short recension probably omitted the reference to Rome in i. 7 and i. 15. For these omissions there are three direct witnesses: Origen, Ambrosiaster, and Cod. G—here probably representing the archetype *Z*.

The evidence of Origen is given directly in Cod. Athous Laurae 184, a MS. which E. von der Goltz discovered in 1897[1] to contain a text of the Epistle to the Romans made from the lost Greek of the commentary of Origen. This MS. gives, it is true, the words ἐν Ῥώμῃ in Rom. i. 7 and 15, but the scribe has been honest enough to add a note to the effect that this was not in his original, τοῦ ἐν Ῥώμῃ οὔτε ἐν τῇ ἐξηγήσει οὔτε ἐν τῷ ῥητῷ (*i.e.* the section of text at the head of the comment) μνημονεύει. The unexpressed subject of this sentence[2] is of course Origen. Von der Goltz is, however, probably mistaken in thinking that this reading is not confirmed by the Latin text of Origen made by Rufinus. It is true that the words in dispute come in the text, but as Lightfoot pointed out long ago in *Biblical Essays*, p. 287, the comment does not imply them.

It is possible that Origen knew MSS. containing the

[1] E. von der Goltz, *Eine textkritische Arbeit des zehnten bezw. sechsten Jahrhundert*, in Gebhardt and Harnack's *Texte und Untersuchungen neue Folge*, ii. 4, 1898.

[2] The same note, but without any explanation, is found in MS. Bodl. Roe 16 (Cod. Paul. 47).

words ἐν Ῥώμῃ, but it is at least certain that he preferred to follow others which omitted them.

The evidence of Ambrosiaster is contained in his commentary.[1] He says, according to the existing MSS., "'omnibus qui sunt Romae in caritate (v.l. dilectis) Dei vocatis sanctis,' quamvis Romanis scribat illis tamen se scribere significat qui in caritate dei sunt." It is difficult to avoid the conclusion that the comment here implies a different text from that printed, and that Ambrosiaster's Bible omitted ἐν Ῥώμῃ and read ἐν ἀγάπῃ (or in caritate) instead of ἀγαπητοῖς. This view is taken not only by Zahn but also by Lightfoot,[2] and the fact is notorious that in patristic commentaries the Biblical text has often been regularized by scribes who are betrayed by the comments which they did not understand and therefore copied faithfully.

The evidence of G agrees exactly with that of the commentary of Ambrosiaster, that is to say, it reads τοῖς οὖσι ἐν ἀγάπῃ Θεοῦ. It is probable (see Appendix) that this was the reading of *Z*, the archetype of DEFG. If, as is probable, the reading of D was τοῖς οὖσιν ἐν Ῥώμῃ ἐν ἀγάπῃ Θεοῦ, this provides an exact parallel to the text of the MSS. of Ambrosiaster, just as G is a parallel to the commentary of Ambrosiaster. The same reading is also found in the Vulgate MSS. Amiatinus and Fuldensis.

[1] According to the information supplied to Prof. Zahn by Dr. Brewer, who is editing the text of Ambrosiaster for the Vienna Corpus, there are in existence three recensions of this commentary (cf. the parallel features in the text of the *Quaestiones*, mentioned by Souter in his edition in the same Corpus). These are apparently all the work of "Ambrosiaster" himself; but in the passage quoted, the only difference is that 1 and 2 read *dilectis Dei*, 3 *in caritate Dei*. All three read *in caritate* in the comment, and *dilectis* is probably merely textual corruption (see Zahn, *Comm.* p. 616.)

[2] *Biblical Essays*, p. 288.

Thus we have early evidence in Europe and in Alexandria for the omission of the words ἐν Ῥώμῃ. African evidence, on either side, I have been unable to find. This is, however, quite sufficient to prove the early existence of a recension which did not mention Rome. But was this recension the long or the short recension? I believe that it must have been the short recension, because the Latin version used by Ambrosiaster is textually closely related to the version used in the Latin *Breves* which are one of the primary witnesses to the short recension. Moreover, *Z* appears in the evidence both for the short recension and for the omission of ἐν Ῥώμῃ. Origen, Tertullian, Cyprian, and Marcion remain. As to Tertullian and Cyprian, it is unknown whether they did or did not read ἐν Ῥώμῃ. Marcion's reading is also unknown. Origen used a text omitting ἐν Ῥώμῃ, yet possessing Rom. xv. and xvi.; but the evidence which he gives as to the doxology shows his text was not that of the pure long recension, but a contaminated form, so that the omission of ἐν Ῥώμῃ may be an eclectic reading from the short recension quite as probably as one from the long recension. Thus there seems to be a great preponderance of evidence in favour of connecting the omission of ἐν Ῥώμῃ with the short recension.

The result of the preceding rather long and tedious inquiry seems to establish the fact that in the second century there was in existence a short recension omitting chaps. xv. and xvi. and the mention of Rome, and probably ending with the doxology. Indeed, there is, strictly speaking, earlier evidence for the short recension than for the long. I do not know of any quotations from Rom. xv. and xvi. in writers of the second century, whereas Marcion and

Tertullian both seem to have used the short recension. It would, however, be wrong to base any serious argument on this fact, because the chapters in question were not likely to be quoted. Moreover, there is no reason to doubt the Pauline authorship of chap. xv., which is closely connected with chap. xiv. Thus there is no justification for any theory that chap. xv. is a later, non-Pauline, addition to the original short recension. Nor is it easy to think that chap. xv. was written by St. Paul for some other purpose: the connection of thought between Rom. xiv. and xv. is far too clear. Otherwise, the most attractive theory would be that just as 2 Corinthians represents two or more fragments of Pauline letters, which were pieced together and thus formed one letter in the Corpus Paulinum, so also Romans consists of one main document with a few fragments of Pauline letters, found in the Roman archives perhaps, pieced on at the end.

This theory seems to me to be rendered improbable so far as Rom. xv.[1] is concerned by the clear connection in thought between it and Rom. xiv. It would perhaps be too much to call it impossible, but it does not seem to do justice to all the facts. Thus we have to face the existence of the long recension as genuinely Pauline, in the sense that St. Paul is responsible not only for the words, but also for the arrangement of the contents, and that he meant chap. xv. to be the continuation of chap. xiv.

How, then, is the existence of the short form to be explained? Two main theories are possible: (1) St. Paul wrote the long recension, and some one else issued the short recension later on. (2) St. Paul himself wrote both,

[1] The question of chap. xvi. is of course separate.

issuing the letter in two forms, either simultaneously or successively.

At the present time the former of these theories is the more popular, and it is widely held that the short recension was made for dogmatic reasons by Marcion.

THE MARCION HYPOTHESIS.

This hypothesis, that the short recension was made by Marcion, has been best defended by Sanday and Headlam, Corssen, and von Soden.

Sanday and Headlam argue that Marcion excised chaps. xv. and xvi. because they, or rather chap. xv., contained passages contrary to his teaching. "To begin with," they say (p. xcvii.), "five of these verses (*i.e.* Rom. xv. 1–13) contain quotations from the Old Testament; but further, ver. 8 contains an expression—λέγω γὰρ Χριστὸν διάκονον γεγενῆσθαι περιτομῆς ὑπὲρ ἀληθείας Θεοῦ—which he most certainly could not have used. Still more is this the case with regard to ver. 4 (ὅσα γὰρ προεγράφη εἰς τὴν ἡμετέραν διδασκαλίαν ἐγράφη), which directly contradicts the whole of his special teaching." The point is that Marcion rejected the general Christian view that the Old Testament was a special revelation from the supreme God, whom he distinguished from the God of Creation worshipped by the Jews, and did not recognize that Christianity was in any sense the legitimate outcome or fulfilment of Judaism. In order to support this theory he altered the text of the Gospel of St. Luke and the Pauline Epistles, which constituted his Scriptures, accommodating them to his teaching.

Corssen uses a somewhat different argument. In the

first place, he argues that the doxology cannot be regarded as Pauline, and is tainted with Marcionism. Therefore, even if it be true that it did not figure in the text of Marcion's edition, it must be regarded as the product of the Marcionite Church, and thus the short recension, which contained the doxology, must be regarded as the work of Marcion. Probably this reasoning, in spite of its ingenuity, will make few converts; but much more importance belongs to another argument which Corssen also set forward, not knowing that he had, in the main points, been anticipated by Dom de Bruyne.[1] This is the fact that the Latin prologues to the Epistles, which are found in many Vulgate MSS. including many of those which have the Latin *Breves*, are undoubtedly of Marcionite origin. Thus it is impossible to argue that it is incredible that Marcion should have so much influence on the canonical text; for, although there is no sufficient ground for connecting the Prologues and the *Breves*, it is nevertheless a suspicious fact that they should be found, at least partially, in the same MSS.

Von Soden's[2] advocacy of the Marcionite hypothesis is bound up with his general position, and it is probably desirable to state this in outline, as, owing to a variety of reasons, his book on the text is not yet widely read (at all events in England), even by those who are interested in textual criticism.

He thinks that in the fourth century there were in existence three main types of the text of the Epistles, to

[1] In the *Revue Bénédictine* for January, 1907, pp. 1 ff., *Prologues Bibliques d'origine Marcionite.*

[2] *Die Schriften des Neuen Testaments in ihrer ältesten erreichbaren Textgestalt*, i. 3, pp. 2028 ff.

which he assigns the symbols *K*(οινή), *H*(σύχιος), and *I*(ερουσαλήμ). The *K* type corresponds more or less to Westcott and Hort's *Syrian* text and is subdivided into K^c and K^r. It is found in the mass of MSS., and K^r is the Greek text of the Middle Ages. The *H* type covers both the *Neutral* and the *Alexandrian* texts of Westcott and Hort's system. It is best represented by ℵBACH Ψ 17; of these manuscripts ℵB are the most important, both being descended from a common archetype (not much older, but better than either), called by von Soden δ^{1-2}. The *I* type is subdivided into the three families, I^a, I^b, and I^c; of these, I^a is best represented by the Graeco-Latin MSS.[1] DEFG, I^b by the "Origen" MS. found by von der Goltz[2] on Mt. Athos (von Soden's α 78, not known to Tischendorf), and I^c by various MSS. which had never hitherto attracted special attention. Of these three families, I^a is no doubt the best, though I^b has often valuable readings. It seems natural to think that, just as *K* is Westcott and Hort's *Syrian* text, and *H* the *Neutral* and *Alexandrian* texts, so *I* is Westcott and Hort's Western text; but this is only quite partially true, for von Soden rejects many readings in DEFG as due to the influence of the Old Latin, which he regards as earlier than *I*, whereas Westcott and Hort think that the Old Latin and DEFG belonged to the same type.

Turning from MSS. to patristic evidence, the *H* text was used in Alexandria by Athanasius and Cyril, the *I* text in Palestine by Eusebius, Cyril of Jerusalem, and, with less accuracy, by Epiphanius, and the *K* text in Syria by Theodoret and Chrysostom. In the same way the Bohairic

[1] See Appendix, pp. 414 ff.

[2] See p. 346.

version represents the *H* text and the Syriac Peshitta the *K* text.

This only takes us back to the fourth century, and so far it is probable that von Soden's results will prove in the main to be sound. His view does not seriously differ from Westcott and Hort's: both he and they recognize the existence of three great types of text, and von Soden has enriched our knowledge of the various MSS. of a later date to an enormous extent without impugning this classification. The difference begins when we try to go further. Neither Westcott and Hort nor von Soden can find evidence for the *K* text earlier than the fourth century, and both agree in thinking that it is connected with the recension of Lucian, but whereas Westcott and Hort think that Lucian made use of two older texts, the *Neutral* and *Western*, roughly corresponding to von Soden's *H* and *I*, von Soden thinks that the two types *H* and *I* are co-ordinate recensions, made in Alexandria and Palestine respectively, and that the three, *H*, *I*, and *K*, are all based on the same text, to which the symbol is given of *I-H-K*.

So far as the Epistles are concerned, von Soden thinks that this *I-H-K* text can be traced in the quotations of Clement of Alexandria, Irenaeus, Tertullian, and Origen, and in the European and African Latin versions. At the same time, there are many places in which *I-H-K* (as reconstructed by a comparison of the three separate texts, *I*, *H*, *K*) is deserted by these authorities. He thinks that this is generally due to the influence of Marcion's text.

His method is to take Zahn's reconstruction of Marcion's text, and to compare it with the texts of the separate authorities for the *I-H-K* text. He then arrives at the conclusion that in many of the places where the separate authorities desert the true *I-H-K* type they agree with Marcion. Especially is this the case with the Old Latin, with the special readings of I^1 (*i.e.* the archetype of DEFG) and with *K*.

In view of these considerations it is not wonderful that the Marcion hypothesis with regard to the short recension is exceedingly popular, and I should hesitate to say that it is an improbable view. At the same time, there are certain objections which are perhaps too little noticed.

In the first place, if it be conceded that the "short recension" omitted ἐν Ῥώμῃ it is necessary to show that Marcion cut these words out of his text. It is, therefore, argued that Marcion desired to convert the Epistle into a general treatise on Christian doctrine, and in pursuance of this plan omitted all local references. Unfortunately, the recently discovered Marcionite Prologues overthrew this theory. From these it is plain that he described the Epistle as "to the Romans" in the usual way. This is of course no proof that Marcion read ἐν Ῥώμῃ in i. 7, but it at least shows that he did not try to treat the Epistle as a general treatise. Therefore, supposing that Marcion used the short recension, it is, so far as the omission of ἐν Ῥώμῃ is concerned, more probable that he used it because he found it already existing, than that he manufactured it.

Moreover, in the Marcionite Prologues there is a difference of reading between the various manuscripts as to the place from which Romans was sent. The majority say from Corinth, as is the usual tradition, but some say from Athens. Corssen is inclined to regard the latter reading as original, and I believe that he is right, for it is easy to understand how Athens came to be altered to Corinth, but the reverse process is unintelligible. The tradition naming Corinth is generally recognized to be an obvious and correct deduction from chaps. xv. and xvi.; if this be so, is it not probable that the tradition mentioning Athens is based on a text, known as it is to have existed, which omitted these chapters? In this case it would seem more likely that Marcion, the author of the Athens tradition, used the short recension because he found it already in existence, than that he fashioned it for the first time. If he had known—even though he rejected—chaps. xv. and xvi. he would surely have chosen Corinth rather than Athens.

More important, however, than the question of ἐν Ῥώμῃ is that of chaps. xv. and xvi. An answer has to be given to Sanday and Headlam's theory of Marcion's omission on doctrinal grounds, to von Soden's textual theory, and to Corssen's argument about the doxology.

Sanday and Headlam. In one sense this argument is unanswerable. It cannot be denied that chaps. xv. and xvi. contain statements to which Marcion would have objected. But this truth is beside the point if it be possible to show that the short recension existed so widely at such an early period that it cannot be due to the doctrinal excisions of Marcion. If it be true that the short recension was used by Tertullian, can it be purely Marcionite? This view is only tenable if we accept the theory, which has many advocates, that the existence of a Pauline canon is altogether due to Marcion. But this seems to me inacceptable because I believe in the genuineness of the Ignatian Epistles, and it seems on the whole probable that the authority of the Pauline Epistles is recognized in them. Moreover, the recognition of the scriptural character of the Epistles is found in 2 Peter, and is one of the most important reasons for rejecting its Petrine authorship; but can 2 Peter be later than Marcion? Thus, while admitting that Marcion might have produced the short recension for doctrinal reasons, it seems to me possible to go behind this argument, and claim probability for the view that the short recension existed, before or at the same time as Marcion, in Catholic circles.

Von Soden. With regard to von Soden's position it is necessary to state a theory of the history of the text which may be taken as an alternative to his view. The starting-point is the same as his, the existence in the fourth century of three recensions, but it is plain that three recensions may represent three attempts at standardizing a great variety of local texts, and that the suggested *I-H-K* text may never have existed. It is well to remember that we have to deal with two separate questions; the original text of each individual Epistle, and the original text of the canonical collection of Pauline Epistles. Of course, the former is what we desire, but it is quite certain that it is not what we possess, and we can only reach it by establishing, as a preliminary, the text of the canonical collection or collections of Epistles.

The first question, therefore, is whether we possess traces of one or more collections of Epistles. Our main guide here must be the order of Epistles, though any indirect information which can be gathered as to the text has, of course, an important bearing on the point.

The earliest collection of which we can establish both the order and contents, is that of Marcion—

(1) Galatians
(2) Corinthians
(3) Romans
(4) Thessalonians
(5) Laodiceans (= Ephesians)
(6) Colossians
(7) Philippians
(8) Philemon

Little if at all later in origin is the list in the Canon of Muratori—

(1) Corinthians	(6) Thessalonians
(2) Ephesians	(7) Romans
(3) Philippians	(8) Philemon
(4) Colossians	(9) Titus
(5) Galatians	(10) Timothy

It also appears probable that this list, though it contains the Pastoral Epistles, draws a distinction between them and the Epistles to the Churches, not in the sense that their authenticity was doubted, but as though the Epistles were divided into two groups according as they were intended for Churches or persons. According to the generally received opinion, this represents the canon of the Church in Rome before the end of the second century.

Going on a little later, and passing from Rome to Africa, Tertullian probably supplies us with a similar, but still distinctly different, list, so far as the following Epistles (of which alone we can speak with certainty) are concerned—

(1) Corinthians	(4) Thessalonians
(2) Galatians	(5) Ephesians
(3) Philippians	(6) Romans

The position of Colossians and the Pastorals cannot be determined, though there is no reason to doubt that Tertullian knew them. Probably this ought to be taken as the African canon, and though the order of Cyprian's Bible cannot be accurately determined, it at least appears from the order of the quotations in the *Testimonia* that Corinthians was probably the first and Romans the last of the "Epistles to Churches."

Moving from Africa to Alexandria, the nearest approach

which we can find to a list of the Pauline Epistles before the end of the third century is in Origen, who seems to give the order—[1]

(1) Corinthians	(4) Thessalonians
(2) Ephesians	(5) Philippians
(3) Colossians	(6) Romans

Finally, in the fourth century in Alexandria, we find Athanasius insisting, with an emphasis which suggests opposition, on the order which is found in the great uncials,[2] and was made familiar by its adoption in the ecclesiastical texts of the fifth and following centuries. The small variations, some of which are probably due to the influence of earlier orders, are not important for the present purpose.[3]

Moreover, we find that this variety of order in the list of the Epistles is accompanied by variations in the text, and the most natural conclusion is that we have to deal with various collections of the Pauline Epistles, so that if we confine ourselves to the reconstruction of the text of the *Corpus Paulinum*, as distinct from that of the separate Epistles, we have to recognize that there never was any single "original" text, but that various Churches had their own collections, each with its own text. No doubt from the beginning there

[1] Here again it is necessary to add that of course there is no suggestion that Origen was unacquainted with the other Epistles, but merely that we cannot say in what order they came in his Bible.

[2] It is hard to realize at first that there seems to be no evidence for this order, with which we are so familiar, before the fourth century. Probably it was part of the textual and critical revision which the New Testament underwent, chiefly, but not exclusively, at the hand of Alexandrian scholars, in the fourth century.

[3] All the facts given above are discussed fully in Zahn's *Geschichte des Neutestamentlichen Kanons*, ii. pp. 344 ff., but I cannot think that he is successful in reducing all the early lists to one original collection.

was an interchange of documents, and thus each text influenced the others in turn.

The reconstruction of these local texts is probably impossible, except in a few details. Marcion's text is sometimes recoverable, and so is Tertullian's, but we cannot claim to know anything about the second century text of Rome or of Alexandria. When, however, we find Marcion and Tertullian apparently agreeing in using the short recension of Romans, it seems more natural to accept this as evidence that the *Corpus Paulinum* in Carthage and that used by Marcion agreed on this point, than to suggest that Tertullian, whose *Corpus* was, as the order shows, quite independent, borrowed on this point from Marcion. The order of the Epistles shows that the Catholic *Corpus* or *Corpora* were from the beginning distinct from that of Marcion.

Corssen. The main point of Corssen's theory, apart from the Marcionite prologues, which have already been discussed, is the doxology. He presents two propositions: (1) that it is not genuine; (2) that it is a Marcionite addition.

That it is not genuine I am inclined to accept. It is true that there are various doxological passages in the Epistles, but none of such length, and none at the end, after the salutations. Moreover, Corssen's arguments seem to me very powerful. St. Paul, no doubt, preached that the "mystery" of Christianity had been unrecognized in past ages; but he nowhere else says that it was never announced. There was "a veil on the faces" of the Jews when they read the Scriptures, and their meaning was hidden from them, but the writings of the prophets were a revelation spoken by God. The Israelites had not understood, but God had not kept silence.[1] Thus it is scarcely true to argue, as Sanday and Headlam do, that the doxology can only be rejected by those who reject the Epistles of the captivity and the Pastoral Epistles. The doxology goes beyond and even is contrary to anything in any Epistle.

But to admit that the doxology is probably not Pauline does not take us all the way to regarding it as Marcionite. In the first place, we have the definite evidence of Origen that Marcion did not have the doxology, and presumably he was speaking of the Marcionite text of the third century. In the second place, the facts concerning the order of the Epistles suggest an alternative theory.

It is generally recognized as a characteristic of scribes that they were inclined to add doxologies at the end of the books or collection of books which they copied. If, therefore, the doxology is not genuine, it is possibly to be attributed to this cause, and if so it is most probable that it arose in some collection of Epistles in which Romans was the last. Now, it is remarkable that the Muratorian Canon suggests that the Epistles were divided into two groups, letters to Churches and letters to persons, and that both in this list and in those of Tertullian and Origen, the last Epistle in the group of letters to Churches is Romans. This is not the case in Marcion's collection, and the suggestion is obvious that the doxology was the close of the Catholic collection of letters to Churches. If Marcion knew it he left it out because he recognized it as not part of the letter, but it is quite probable that he really had, from the beginning, a different collection. It is surely a striking combination of facts that (1) the doxology belongs to the short recension;

[1] See Corssen in the *Zeitschr. für N.-Tliche Wissenschaft*, 1909, p. 32 ff.

(2) Doxologies generally come at the end of books; (3) Tertullian probably had the short recension; (4) the canon of Muratori shows that a distinction was made between letters to Churches and letters to persons; and (5) in Tertullian's Bible, as well as in the canon of Muratori and in Origen's Bible, Romans is the last of the letters to Churches.

To say that these facts afford a proof would be ridiculous: we are on the very borders of the history of the canon, and certainty is unattainable. All that can be said is that evidence points in the direction of one hypothesis rather than another, and I submit that, on the whole, and with our present knowledge, it points away from the Marcionite hypothesis and in favour of the primitive existence of a short recension, which originally belonged to a Catholic Corpus, closed by a doxology, in which it was the last of the Epistles to Churches.

Alternatives to the Marcionite Hypothesis.

Of these there have been many, but for the most part their days have been few and evil, and they now are interred with but short epitaphs in the pages of Zahn's *Einleitung*.

One of the simplest which deserves attention was supported by Bishop Lightfoot.[1] He thought that St. Paul may have made the short recension himself in order to give a general account of his position in the controversy between Jewish and Gentile Christians. To this theory the decisive objection is the improbability that any one who was not animated by dogmatic prepossessions, as Marcion

[1] *Journal of Philology*, 1869–71. Reprinted in *Biblical Essays*, pp. 287 ff.

is supposed to have been, would ever have split the Epistle at xiv. 23.

The natural divisions are after xi. 36; xiii. 14; or xv. 13. Moreover, it is doubtful whether it is on general grounds so likely that an originally local letter was turned into a general treatise, as that the reverse took place.

Perhaps more attention ought to be paid to the possibility that the short recension is the original form of the text which was afterwards expanded. This view was suggested, in a complicated and somewhat fantastic form, by E. Renan in the introduction to his *L'apôtre Paul*, and was decisively criticized by Lightfoot in the essay just mentioned. Yet, after all, Lightfoot only answered Renan's form of the hypothesis, and a hearing may be asked for a simpler one, as an alternative to the popular Marcionite hypothesis.

The main features of the problem which must be taken into account are two: (1) there was, from as early a time as evidence on textual points reaches, an Epistle to the Romans which stopped at Rom. xiv. 23, with or without the doxology, and without any reference to Rome in chap. i.; (2) nevertheless, chaps. xv. and xvi. are clearly genuinely Pauline, and are never found except as a continuation of the other chapters. I suggest that it is not impossible that the short recension represents a letter written by St. Paul at the same time as Galatians, in connection with the question of Jewish and Gentile Christians, for the general instruction of mixed Churches which he had not visited. It had originally nothing to do with Rome. Later on he sent a copy to Rome, with the addition of the other chapters to serve, as we should say, as a covering letter.

The arguments in favour of this hypothesis may be formulated somewhat as follows. Assuming that St. Paul first wrote an Epistle which in i. 7 read, τοῖς οὖσιν ἐν . . . ἀγαπήτοις θεοῦ, κλήτοις ἁγίοις (or possibly ἐν ἀγάπῃ, κ.τ.λ.), and ended with xiv. 23, what are the probabilities as to its date, the place from which it was written, and the community to which it was addressed? Dealing with the last point first, it is clear that there is nothing whatever to justify us in singling out any one community, though the general indications point to those hitherto unvisited by St. Paul, in which Jewish and Gentile Christians came into contact with each other. We have to deal with a general Epistle, devoid of address or of greetings. Those are exactly the same phenomena as are found in the best text of Ephesians. In that Epistle there are no greetings, and the words ἐν Ἐφέσῳ are omitted by the critical editors, and the generally received explanation is that it (which we call Ephesians, and Marcion called Laodiceans) was originally designed exclusively for neither of these Churches, but was a circular Epistle, in which the name could be filled in according to circumstances. As companion letters to Ephesians we have Colossians and Philemon, and it would seem that Ephesians is the general Epistle to the Christians in Asia, Colossians an Epistle to a special Church in that province, and Philemon a private note to an individual Christian either in Colossae or a neighbouring town.

The connection in thought between Ephesians and Colossians is scarcely plainer than that between Romans and Galatians, and if we take the short recension the parallel is almost perfect. Why should it not be, then, that "Romans" was originally a general Epistle written by St. Paul, at the same time as Galatians, to the mixed Churches which had sprung up round Antioch and further on in Asia Minor? In that case we should have another instance of St. Paul's custom of writing a general Epistle, and supporting it by a series of letters to the separate Churches, or groups of Churches, in the district for which it was intended.

The strength of this position can be best seen if we suppose that all copies of the long recension had been lost, and that we only possessed the shorter form. It cannot be doubted that in this case we should have been unanimous in saying that the Epistle belonged to the same period as Galatians. No one would have suggested that it was written after 2 Corinthians and sent to Rome. Even if the superscription "to the Romans" had existed, we should have said, as is, *mutatis mutandis*, so commonly said in connection with Ephesians, that this only means that the archetype of existing MSS. comes from Rome; and it would have been popularly argued that "Romans" means "Roman citizens," not necessarily inhabitants of Rome, and that it was probably used by courtesy of many who were not actually citizens.

Thus if we were justified in assuming that the short recension was the original form of the Epistle, the theory that the Epistle is a general letter contemporary with Galatians, and directed to the Gentile Christians in general, would have very strong arguments in its favour.

Unfortunately this is just the point which we cannot assume without argument. As Sanday and Headlam pointed out long ago, no theory is satisfactory which does not recognize the organic connection between Rom. xiv. and xv.; there is a definite line of argument which runs on from one to the other, and this continuity, which justifies the argument that texts inserting the doxology between the two chapters really point to the existence of the short recension, also proves that no hypothesis is satisfactory which fails to do justice to its existence. Sanday and Headlam argued that this must mean that the long recension is prior in origin to the short recension, and up to the present this view has held the field. If, therefore, the priority of the short recension is to be rendered even a subject for discussion, it is necessary to produce some theory which will nevertheless account for chaps. xv. and xvi., and their organic connection with the preceding chapter.

Such a theory would be that St. Paul had sent a copy of the short recension to Rome from Corinth, and added the last chapters as an expansion of the practical exhortations, and as greetings to the individual members of the Church. A more or less imaginative reconstruction of the circumstances would be the following: St. Paul was in Corinth, on the point of departure for Jerusalem, and, influenced by the information of Aquila and Priscilla, sent a copy of his "Anti-Judaistic Letter" to the Roman Christians,[1] adding at the end a few more paragraphs continuing the thoughts of his original writing, probably because Aquila had told him that this was desirable.

The only objection that I can see to this hypothesis is that St. Paul ought to have described in his covering letter the contents of his enclosure. It is true that this would have been more natural, especially if he had been using modern paper and envelopes. But I take it that what happened was that St. Paul told a copyist to make a copy of the "short recension," and then dictated the remainder. If the Romans wished to know any more about the form of the document, they must ask the bearers.

[1] If, after all, Rom. xvi. 1–23 was really sent to Rome, the desire to give an introductory letter to Phoebe no doubt also played a part, inducing him to write to a Church which he had not yet visited; but I doubt if this section really belongs to Romans, and therefore must make no use of this argument.

The history of the Epistle after it reached Rome is, in any case, a problem which can never be solved with certainty, yet on the theory of the priority of the short recension, we can form quite as possible a reconstruction as the Marcionite hypothesis. The growth of the *Corpus Paulinum* is practically unknown to us. All that we know is that in the second century the process of collecting Pauline Epistles was going on in more than one place, so that in one locality there was one order, in another something different. That is to say, at an early period Churches began to exchange copies of St. Paul's Epistles, not because of their intrinsic value as letters, but because they were Pauline. It was for that reason that the Epistle to Philemon came into the canon. Considerably earlier than this must have been the time when the letters were copied, not simply because they were Pauline, but because they dealt with important subjects. During this time no Epistles are more likely to have been copied than Romans—in the short form—and Ephesians, and as a matter of fact there is no Epistle, except, perhaps, 1 Corinthians, which is so well attested in the sub-Apostolic period as these two. During this period the short recension of Romans would be more likely to attract attention than the longer form, though in Rome the latter would naturally be perpetuated. Probably to this period must be assigned the genesis of the collection of "Epistles to Churches," ending with Romans, and the addition of the doxology. As soon, however, as the emphasis of interest came to fall not on the contents, but on the authorship of the Epistles, the tendency was to copy and circulate everything which was Pauline, and so the longer texts made in Rome with the addition of the "covering letter" would be more popular, and the original form of the "long recension" would come into circulation, copies of the short recension would be amplified by the addition of the fresh material, and the complicated textual process described on p. 345 would begin. A parallel to this process may probably be found in 2 Corinthians. The internal evidence is here much stronger than it is in Romans, but, on the other hand, there is no trace of any textual evidence. It is perhaps interesting to ask why the textual tradition should be less strong in the case of 2 Corinthians, than in that of Romans. Probably the answer is to be found in the independent circulation of the short form of Romans, and in the fact that 2 Corinthians seems to come into general use much later than 1 Corinthians. Dr. Kennedy suggests that it did so only after the Epistle of Clement drove the Corinthians to look at their archives and find various fragments of an almost forgotten correspondence.

That the theory which is here suggested, as to the history of the Epistle to the Romans, can never become more than a possible hypothesis, is of course obvious, nor would I venture to claim that it has any self-evident probability. But the fact that a "short form" did exist in the second and third centuries is certain, and has to be dealt with somehow.

The Marcionite hypothesis is of course a simpler view, and in so far deserves the preference which it enjoys at present, but the alternative will demand serious consideration from those who do not think that so general a depravation of the text by Marcionite influence is entirely probable. This, then, is the point which at the moment ought to be studied by those who desire to carry research further; is it reasonable to suppose that the text used by the anonymous maker of the Latin *Breves*, by the text behind the

Antiochene recension, and by Tertullian,[1] was influenced by Marcion? In other words, a serious attempt must be made to deal with the facts and theories presented by von Soden. To do this will require much fresh research, and I must rest content with saying that if he prove to be right, the correctness of the Marcionite hypothesis as to the short recension will become overwhelmingly probable. But if it be shown that the influence of Marcion on the text of the Epistles was not so great, the Marcionite hypothesis becomes improbable, for the evidence for the short recension is too wide and too early. In this case the hypothesis of a short form, written by St. Paul, earlier than the long recension, contemporary with Galatians, and not intended for Rome, must be seriously considered; and such an hypothesis has of course the advantage of, to some extent, freeing the Epistle from the objections that it is improbable that St. Paul, at the end of the quite different controversy at Corinth, should have worked over on a larger scale the arguments used in Galatians, and sent them to a Church which he had never seen. If St. Paul really heard from Aquila that the Judaizing Christianity was making progress in Rome, he is quite likely to have used over again an Epistle which had formerly been of use in Syria, but he is not so likely to have re-modelled in a new and more elaborate form arguments which he had once used in Galatians in the course of a controversy of which there is no trace in Corinth.

It is now necessary to return once more to the question of Rom. xvi. 1–23, and ask what its relation is to the

[1] That is, of course, if it be conceded that Tertullian used the short recension. Opinion is likely to differ on this point. Personally, I believe that the balance of evidence inclines in that direction, but it is not decisively clear, and others take a different view.

problem of the short recension. It was seen above that this section is probably Ephesian, and this fact adds to the complication of the situation. Of course, if this conclusion be wrong, there is no difficulty :[1] the section is part of the long recension, and helps to explain why St. Paul wrote to Rome. But if the conclusion reached be right, how did the section in question find its way into the long recension?

To this question no answer seems possible. Anything—in itself improbable—may actually have happened to bring together the Ephesian letter and the long recension, but it is idle to guess on a point as to which we have no evidence. All that we know is that the evidence points to Ephesus for Rom. xvi. 1–23 and to Rome for the rest of the long recension. Whether the junction was made in Rome or in Ephesus or somewhere else will always remain uncertain.

The result of the foregoing discussion has been to show that the original destination and date of the Epistle is not so certain as it at first seems, and it may fairly be charged with belonging to that unsatisfactory though necessary class of investigations which raise problems which cannot be solved. What remains clear is that the long recension, probably without Rom. xvi. 1–23, was sent by St. Paul from Corinth to Rome, and that it belongs in the main to the same controversy as Galatians,—that with Judaizing Christians, though it also contains some allusions to the

[1] I wish I could honestly have reached the result that it is wrong. The whole question of the short recension is much more easy—on my hypothesis—if Rom. xvi. 1–23 was really always part of the longer recension and a truly Roman Epistle. Therefore, I should be delighted to be convinced that the Ephesian destination of Rom. xvi. 1–23 is a mistake, but at present I am unable to put aside the force of the arguments in its favour.

struggle with the "spiritual" Gentile Christianity which is the background of the Corinthian Epistles.

It is, therefore, necessary to ask in more detail what was this Judaizing Christianity, and what was the history of the foundation of the Church at Rome.

II. The Church at Rome.

There was throughout the nineteenth century much controversy as to the nature of the Roman Church. Was it originally Jewish or Gentile? The traditional view was that it was Gentile. Baur,[1] however, attacked this view, and maintained that it was primarily Jewish. This contention was taken up and elaborately defended by Mangold,[2] and remained the prevalent view in critical circles until Weizsacker[3] returned more or less to the older view, and was only ready to recognize a Jewish element in the form of proselytes.

The points in which a Gentile origin is implied for the readers of the Epistle are the following: (1) In Rom. i. 5, 6 St. Paul says that he is an Apostle "to all the Gentiles . . . among whom ye are also," etc.; and in Rom. i. 13 he expresses the hope that he may "have some fruit in you also, even as in the rest of the Gentiles."[4] (2) In Rom. xi. 13 St. Paul says, "But I speak to you who are Gentiles."

These two passages are definite proof of the existence of Gentiles in the Church, and as they are mentioned with

[1] *Paulus*, i. 343 ff.

[2] In 1866 in *Der Römerbrief und die Anfänge der römischen Gemeindes*, and in 1884, in *Der Römerbrief und seine geschichtliche Voraussetzungen.*

[3] *Apostolische Zeitalter*, Ed. 2, pp. 407 f.

[4] The word here and in i. 5 is τοῖς ἔθνεσι, which regularly means "Gentiles." In Jewish Greek the Jews are ὁ λαός, and the Gentiles are τὰ ἔθνη. It is curious that the R.V. translates the first passage as "nations."

such emphasis in the opening salutations, they must have been an important party.

A Jewish origin, on the other hand, is implied in passages in which St. Paul, by using the first person plural, seems to assume a Jewish nationality for his readers as well as for himself. The chief of such passages are: Rom. iv. 1, "What shall we say that Abraham, our forefather according to the flesh, hath found?" Rom. vii. 6, "But now we have been discharged from the Law, having died to that wherein we were holden"; Rom. ix. 10, "Isaac, our father."[1]

There is no sufficient answer to the arguments based on these texts. The existence of both elements in Rome must be recognized, and therefore it is now generally conceded there was a measure of truth in both the earlier contentions.

The reason for this *rapprochement* is not merely the consideration of definite allusions in the Epistle. It is on general grounds so probable that all early Christian communities were based on converts from the synagogue, and from the God-fearers, who were more or less loosely connected with the synagogue, that any other suggestion would need strong evidence before it would deserve consideration.

Especially is this true of a city like Rome, in which both elements were numerous. The Jews in Rome had already a long and interesting history[2] by the time that St. Paul wrote. There was probably a settlement of Jews early in the first century before Christ, but it first attained

[1] A list of other arguments with the objections to them, on either side, is given in a concise manner in H. Holtzmann's *Einleitung in das neue Testament*, pp. 235 ff. Those given above are only those which seem decisive.

[2] For more detailed information and references to special books, see Schürer, *Geschichte des judischen Volkes*, Ed. 4, iii. pp. 57–67.

really large dimensions when Pompey in 63 B.C. brought an enormous number of Jews to Rome as prisoners of war, who were sold into slavery.[1] Many of them, however, were set free, as they proved unsatisfactory as slaves, owing to their inflexible adherence to the Law. They then settled on the other bank of the Tiber, where a colony of Jews existed until 1556, when they were brought across the river to the spot which is still known as the Ghetto, though it was abolished as such after the incorporation of Rome into the Italian kingdom. There were also originally other colonies in Rome, in the Subura, and the Campus Martius. The numbers of these settlements must have been very great, for though Tiberius appears to have tried to abolish them, in consequence of frauds committed on a certain rich proselyte lady named Fulvia,[2] he seems to have failed, even though he drafted four thousand into the Sardinian police in order to put down the brigands, "et, si," says Tacitus, "ob gravitatem coeli interiisent, vile damnum." Later, after the fall of Sejanus, Tiberius became more friendly to the Jews, and the colony was firmly established in the time of Caligula, when Philo came to Rome on behalf of the Alexandrian Jews. Claudius began by being tolerant, but later on the riots of the Jews (see p. 374 f.) led to the decree of banishment which is mentioned in Acts xviii. 2. Probably this decree proved impracticable: it is not easy to banish a population of many thousands if it sit still, unless measures of deportation on a large and expensive scale are carried out. Certainly there is no hint in any

[1] It seems to me probable that this treatment, so reminiscent of Nebuchadnezzar, is at least partly the origin of the half-apocalyptic custom of calling Rome Babylon.

[2] She was induced to subscribe largely towards the Temple, and her subscriptions were never forwarded to Jerusalem. See Josephus, *Ant.* xviii. 3, 5.

writing that the Jewish colony was seriously diminished, though a scholiast to Juvenal[1] says that many of them went to Aricia.

Thus there were probably few Gentile cities in which Jews were so numerous as in Rome, and no doubt they would be some of the first to hear of Christianity.

A mixed community is therefore the type which would naturally be expected, and as this type is also indicated by the definite allusions in the Epistle,[2] we have no reason for doubting its accuracy. We have, however, but little information as to the foundation of this Church.

All that we know with certainty is that it was in existence before St. Paul wrote. It is therefore clear that one or more Christians had already made their way to Rome, and had met with some success in propagating their faith. If Rom. xvi. 1–23 be really an Epistle to Rome, and if the suggestion be right that "those of Narcissus" and "those of Aristobulus" can be identified with the slaves of the freedman Narcissus and of Aristobulus, the member of the Herod family, we can go a step further, and say that the circle of Christians in Rome included some of the Imperial slaves, and that St. Paul is referring to them when he speaks in Phil. iv. 22 of "Caesar's household." If, as seems to me more probable, this section of Romans was intended for

[1] Juvenal, *Sat.* iv. 117, "Dignus Aricinos qui mendicaret ad axes," and the scholiast (quoted by Schürer) says, "qui ad portam Aricinam rite ad clivum mendicaret inter Judaeos, qui ad Ariciam transierant ex Urbe missi."

[2] To some extent this statement must be modified if the view be adopted that the short recension, which contains all these allusions, was originally sent, not to Rome, but to some other Gentile Church in the neighbourhood of Antioch. But the modification necessary is slight and unimportant. Probably all early Gentile communities were mixed with a strong Jewish-Christian element. All that the "short recension" theory necessitates is the theory that St. Paul recognized that the situation in Rome resembled that in Antioch.

Ephesus, this argument cannot be used. It remains true, on the authority of Philippians, that when St. Paul was in Rome there were Christians in the Imperial household; but it becomes open to doubt whether these converts to Christianity had been made by St. Paul or existed before his arrival.

There are only two other pieces of evidence in really early writers which throw light on the question. The first of these is the evidence of Aquila and Priscilla. If they were Christians when St. Paul first met them, they must have been converted before they came to Corinth. The point is, of course, open to question, but St. Luke says nothing about their conversion, and as a rule (though not always) he mentions the conversion of important people by St. Paul. The narrative in Acts seems to imply that Aquila and Priscilla were already Christians when St. Paul went to stay in their house.

The second point is the curious evidence of Suetonius [1] as to the causes which led to the banishment of the Jews from Rome. He says of Claudius, "Judaeos impulsore Chresto assidue tumultuantes Roma expulit." This is no doubt the decree referred to in Acts,[2] in consequence of which Aquila and Priscilla left Rome. There are two difficulties in connection with this narrative.

In the first place, some doubt has been thrown on the statement that Claudius actually banished the Jews, because Dio Cassius simply says that Claudius prohibited their meetings and societies.[3] This point is, however, not

[1] Suetonius, *Claudius*, 25.

[2] Acts xviii. 2.

[3] Dio Cassius, lx. 6: τοὺς δὲ Ἰουδαίους πλεονάσαντες αὖθις ὥστε χαλεπῶς ἂν ἄνευ ταραχῆς ὑπὸ τοῦ ὀχλοῦ σφῶν τῆς πόλεως εἰρχθῆναι, οὐκ ἐξήλασε μεν, τῷ δὲ δὴ

really of great importance for the present purpose, as it is clear that in any case some change of regulation was made adversely affecting the Jews. Much more important is the question of the meaning of "Chresto" in Suetonius. The most probable view must surely be that there is some connection between it and the word "Christ" in the sense of Messiah. The spelling "Chrestus" instead of "Christus" is quite common, and is without any importance.

If this be so it is difficult to avoid the conclusion that the "constant tumults" among the Jews were due to Messianic controversy, and there is no reason for thinking that this cannot have been due to Christian propaganda. Against this it is argued that Chrestus is a common slave name, and that he was probably the actual leader of some political trouble. The point cannot be settled; but personally I think that it is extremely probable that we have here a reference to the first introduction of Christianity into Rome and the opposition of the Jews. If so, the evidence of Suetonius, of the Acts (with the suggestion that Aquila and Priscilla were Christians before they reached Corinth), and of the Epistle to the Romans, all points in the same direction, and indicates that there was a Christian community in Rome during the reign of Claudius (41–54 A.D.) and probably at least as early as the year 50.

Probably it is quite impossible to go any further or to identify the Christians who first brought Christianity to Rome. The later tradition is of course well known. According to this St. Peter was Bishop of Rome for twenty-five years, and was martyred in 67 A.D. He therefore reached

πατρίῳ νόμῳ βίῳ χρωμένους ἐκέλευσε μὴ συναθροίξεσθαι, τάς τε ἑταιρείας ἐπαναχθείσας ὑπὸ τοῦ Γαίου διέλυσεν.

Rome in 42. This tradition is found in Eusebius' *Chronicon* in which (in Jerome's version) the arrival of St. Peter in Rome is attributed to the year 42 A.D., and his death to 67. Probably the tradition is derived from Hippolytus.[1]

The line of argument by which "radical" critics dispose of this tradition of St. Peter's presence in Rome is unsatisfactory. In the first place, they argue that the evidence is insufficient; and the statements in I Peter, Clement of Rome, Ignatius, Hippolytus, Eusebius, and others are explained away or dismissed as not authentic. Of course, the evidence is not demonstrative—if it were a hanging matter I should not claim a verdict—but for the question in hand it seems to me to raise a real presumption in favour of St. Peter's presence in Rome, and because the evidence is, as every one admits, insufficient to give certainty, to claim that, therefore, the opposite conclusion ought to be accepted, is to ignore the limitations and the method of historical research. Mathematicians and jurists may look for the attainment of demonstration; historians can only hope for the establishment of probability.

In the second place, they argue that the whole tradition of St. Peter's presence in Rome was invented in order to account for the Roman teaching as to St. Peter's primacy in the Church. This is, of course, not in itself impossible. Tradition is as often the child as it is the parent of doctrine. But neither tradition nor doctrine come quite spontaneously into existence, and a theory is scarcely probable which leaves both hanging, as it were, in the air without any means

[1] The whole question is mixed up with that of the early lists of bishops, from which the idea of a twenty-five years' episcopate for St. Peter is probably derived. See the discussion, which is the basis of all modern investigation, in Harnack's *Chronologie der altchristlichen litteratur bis Eusebius*, i. 70–230 and 703–7.

of support, which is in reality the net result of "radical" criticism with regard to St. Peter in Rome. For what is the basis of the Roman doctrine of the primacy of St. Peter? "Thou art Peter, and on this rock will I found My Church," is the obvious answer. To those who accept this text as authentic it is a sufficient answer, and they are entitled to argue that we have here the doctrinal source, combined with the metropolitan rank of the city of Rome, which produced the tradition of St. Peter. But the irony of the situation is that "radical" critics, as a rule (and here I believe that they are probably right), regard this text as one of the late Mathaean additions to the original Marcan text. But, if so, why was it added? To support, they say, the Roman tradition of the episcopate of St. Peter, *i.e.* his presence in Rome. But it has been argued that the tradition of St. Peter's presence in Rome is the result of the Roman doctrine of St. Peter's primacy. This is perilously near a *reductio ad absurdum* of the whole argument, and is clearly an illegitimate reasoning in a circle. It is permissible to explain the tradition as due to the doctrine, or the doctrine as due to the tradition, but it is not permissible to argue in both ways at once, and it is this logical crime of which "radical" criticism seems sometimes to be guilty. The truth is that with the rejection of the authenticity of "Thou art Peter," the last reason has also been rejected for doubting the tradition that St. Peter was in Rome. If "Thou art Peter" is a Roman invention, it was invented because St. Peter was already recognized as historically connected with Rome.

It is, therefore, very difficult to doubt that St. Peter was in Rome, and that he played a prominent part in the early history of the Christian Church. But it is quite a different thing to say that he was actually the first to preach in that city, or that he reached it as early as 42 A.D. Against this two facts must be set. In the first place, the release of St. Peter from prison[1] in Jerusalem seems to be synchronized by St. Luke with the death of Herod, which was not earlier than 44 A.D.; in the second place, if it be the case, as I believe, that St. Peter visited Corinth soon after St. Paul left it, the suggestion certainly is that *c.* 52 A.D. he had not yet reached so far West as Rome. Nevertheless, these arguments are not conclusive, and personally I am not at all convinced that St. Peter was not the founder of the Roman Church—perhaps he came to Corinth from the West—but the evidence is insufficient in either direction. In any case, it seems to me much more doubtful than is generally admitted, whether any great importance ought to be attached to St. Paul's silence as to St. Peter in Epistles which were presumably written to or from Rome.

An adverse argument has sometimes been found in Rom. xv. 20. Here St. Paul says that he has made it his aim "so to preach the gospel, not where Christ was already named, that I might not build on another man's foundation." From this it has been argued that St. Paul would not have gone to Rome if it had been St. Peter's foundation, and that in some way the Roman Church must have been his own foundation, probably because it had been established by his own converts. This exegesis is incorrect. St. Paul clearly implies that the Roman Church was another man's foundation, and that he had hitherto refused to preach in such places where others had made a beginning; this was the

[1] According to traditional exegesis the ἕτερον τόπον to which St. Peter went, after his release, was Rome. This is not justified by the text, and is clearly an after-thought. See p. 284 for a disscussion of the meaning of τόπος.

reason why he had never yet been to Rome. "Wherefore," he says, "I was greatly hindered (ἐνεκοπτόμην τὰ πολλά) from coming to you." The "you" implies that the Church was some one's else foundation, and the "wherefore" explains that this was his reason for not coming. He then goes on to explain why he now proposes to depart from his principle: there is now "no place left for him in these districts," *i.e.* from Jerusalem to Illyria. Thus with a proper exegesis the meaning of this passage is that the Church of Rome was founded by some one else, and the question will always remain, why not St. Peter?

III. The Controversial Motives of the Epistle.

In some ways the Epistle to the Romans stands midway between Corinthians and Galatians. Corinthians is concerned almost exclusively with the problems which arose in a Gentile city in which a Greek-thinking population accepted Christianity. Even though there was a Jewish element in Corinth, it belonged to a Judaism which turned its face to Greece rather than to Palestine. Galatians, on the other hand, is almost exclusively concerned with the controversy between the more liberal Christianity supported by St. Paul and the stiff Judaistic Christianity of Jerusalem. But Romans, as compared with the other Epistles, has more of the Greek element than Galatians, and more of the Judaic element than Corinthians. There is, however, a further distinction: the specially Greek elements are clearer and more important in Corinthians, and their treatment in connection with those Epistles leaves it here only necessary to add a few details. On the other hand, the Judaizing element controverted by St. Paul is much more exhaustively discussed than in Galatians, and the full treatment of the general point of view which it implies falls naturally into place at this point. These considerations justify a division of the present section under the two heads of (1) Gentile problems, and (2) Judaic problems.

(1) *Gentile Problems.*—So far as these are concerned, the general situation at Rome, as manifested by the practical problems which arose, was apparently much like that in Corinth, except that there was not the same controversial and partisan tension; the result is that we can see the details much less clearly, for St. Paul is not forced to define and distinguish with the same careful exactitude. But three points stand out, in which there is a marked resemblance to the situation in Corinth.

(*a*) *A Tendency to dispute as to the Relative Value of "Gifts."*—This is the background of Rom. xii. 3–21. It strikingly resembles the more detailed exposition in 1 Corinthians, both in the actual statements and in the manner in which it passes into a general discussion of virtues which ought to be found in a Christian community. The most important verses for the present purpose are 3–8: "For I say through the grace given unto me, to every man that is among you, not to think of himself more highly than he ought to think; but to think soberly, according as God hath dealt to every man the measure of faith. For as we have many members in one body, and all members have not the same office; so we, being many, are one body in Christ, and every one members one of another. Having then gifts differing according to the grace that is given to us, whether prophecy, let us prophesy according to the proportion of faith: or ministry, let us wait on our ministering: or he that teacheth, on teaching: or he that exhorteth, on exhortation:

he that giveth, let him do it with simplicity: he that ruleth, with diligence: he that sheweth mercy, with cheerfulness." It is plain that this passage is a short and general description of the problems dealt with at length in 1 Cor. xii.–xiv.

(β) *A Difference of Opinion as to Food.*—This question is discussed by St. Paul in Rom. xiv., and is continued in a more general manner in Rom. xv. What is clear is that that there was a strict party which limited the food lawful for Christians, and a more liberal party which imposed no restrictions. Between these parties there was some ill feeling. "One man," says St. Paul, "hath faith to eat all things: but he that is weak is a vegetarian." Obviously the liberal argument was that all things were indifferent in themselves. This is implied by St. Paul's admissions. "I know, and am persuaded in the Lord Jesus, that nothing is unclean of itself," and "All things indeed are clean." He recognizes that the liberal view is, in itself, correct, though he argues (1) that it does not justify those who have any scruples,[1] (2) that it is not justifiable in practice to offend the prejudices of the weaker brethren.[2] It is clear that this implies very much the same type of thought and practice as is found in 1 Corinthians, and the liberal party must have had the same standpoint as the "spiritual" party in Corinth.

It is more difficult to identify the stricter party. The points which are clear are that they (or some of them) abstained from meat and wine, and that they observed "days," [3] which in this context can scarcely mean anything except "fast and feast days." [4] Whether however they were

[1] Rom. xiv. 14, 20, 23. [2] Rom. xiv. 13, 15, 21.

[3] Rom. xiv. 2, 21, and xiv. 5 ff.

[4] It is obviously impossible to say whether these were the weekly fast days,

Jews or Gentiles, and what was their doctrine, is impossible to settle finally.

The oldest view is that the strict party were Judaizers. The serious objection to this view is that the Jewish Law objected to various forms of food, but was neither teetotal nor vegetarian. A popular view among later critics has been that the strict party was Essene. Here, again, the objection is that there is no evidence that there were Essenes in Rome, and that though Jerome ascribes vegetarianism to them, this is not supported by the evidence of Philo and Josephus.

A different solution is sought by others in a reference to the vegetarian ascetics mentioned by Seneca. This is, of course, not impossible, but there is no evidence that these ascetics observed special fast days. The truth appears to be that the question is insoluble. We know that there were both Jews and Gentiles in the Roman Churches, and we know also there were "strict" and "liberal" Christians: but whether these divisions coincided or crossed each other, we do not know. Only on general grounds can we support one or the other view, and on these grounds it is more probable that they crossed each other.

It remains to notice that there is no trace that the question of food was connected with the belief in demons, and the consequent danger of things offered to idols, as it was in Corinth. It does not, however, follow that this element was absent. The *argumentum a silentio* from St. Paul would be here peculiarly dangerous.

(γ) *A Low Standard of Morality.*—A tendency to moral and ethical laxness is probably indicated by Rom. iii. 7.

which the Jews in some circles observed on Mondays and Thursdays, and the early Christians (cf. the *Didache*) transposed to Wednesdays and Fridays.

"If the truth of God abounded to His glory by my lie, why am I still judged as a sinner, and not, (as we are traduced, and some affirm that we say,) Let us do evil, that good may come?" but it is most clearly part of the implication of the sixth and twelfth chapters. For instance, the question at the beginning of Rom. vi., "Shall we remain in sin, that grace may abound?" and the warning in vi. 12, "Let not therefore sin reign in your mortal body," are not only the reply to a Jewish propaganda which regarded Gentile Christianity as ethically insufficient, but are directed against Gentiles who were really inclined to adopt an unethical view of Sacramental Christianity. It is clear that just as some Corinthians had argued that, because they had been baptized, and partook of spiritual food and drink, they were safe, and might do anything they liked, so also some of the Gentiles to whom St. Paul sent Romans, seem to have argued that Baptism carried with it the privilege of salvation, without the responsibility of morality.

The same implication is clearly made in Rom. xii. 1, 2: "I beseech you, brethren, by the mercies of God, to present your bodies as a living sacrifice, holy, acceptable to God,—your spiritual (λογικὴν) service. And be not conformed to this world, but change your nature (μεταμορφουσθε) with the renewal of your mind (τοῦ νοός), to prove what is the will of God—that which is good, and acceptable and perfect." The suggestion here is clearly made that the Gentile Christians were in danger of insufficiently recognizing the moral and ethical requirements of the new spirit[1] which they had received.

From Rom. vi. it is obvious that this unethical view of

[1] This is, I take it, the meaning of the ἀνάκαίνισις τοῦ νοός. It is another variant of the καινὴ κτίσις of Galatians and 2 Corinthians.

Christianity, with its accompanying evils, was connected with Baptism, in so much as St. Paul argues that its obligations have been misunderstood. At the same time, this—the question of the ethical obligations of the Sacraments—is the only point which he treats as in any way controversial. For the rest Baptism and its significance was common ground to him and all other Christians, and he only refers to it as the basis—not as the subject—of controversy. For this reason the direct references to Baptism in the Epistles, essentially controversial as they are, are few and short; but they are for that very reason extremely important, and it has seemed best to bring them together and to discuss them at this point.

The most simple and primitive conception of Baptism is that of a cleansing from sin. This is clearly referred to by St. Paul in 1 Cor. vi. 11, "Ye were washed, ye were sanctified, ye were justified in the Name of the Lord Jesus Christ, and in the Spirit of our God." But it appears that the "cleansing" is here not regarded as in any way purely negative or preparatory; it is closely connected with the more positive conception of the gift of being "made holy," and of receiving the Spirit, and it is important to notice that it is directly bound up with "the Name" of the Lord.

Still more clearly is the idea of the gift of the Spirit through Baptism to be found in 1 Cor. xii. 12: "For as the body is one and has many limbs, and all the limbs of the body, being many, are one body, so also is Christ. For in one Spirit were we all baptized into one body." The whole argument in this chapter is that the Christians, whatever may be their obviously differing gifts, are united by the fact that they are all the separate channels by which the one Spirit, who for St. Paul and his hearers is scarcely, if at all, distinguishable from the risen Christ, manifests Himself in the Church. St. Paul says that the relation between Christians and the Spirit is actually parallel to the relation between "limbs" and "body," and by this he does not mean anything merely symbolic or allegorical. The unity of the Spirit did not mean to the first Christians an intellectual unanimity in matters of controversy, or ecclesiastical organization, but a common inspiration by the same Divine Spirit, which was different from anything to be obtained by natural means.

The same kind of idea, though here expressed in terms of "the Lord" instead of in those of "the Spirit," is found in Rom. vi. 3. "Are ye ignorant that all we who were baptized into Christ Jesus were baptized into His death? We were buried with Him through baptism, into death, that like as the Christ was raised from the dead through the glory of the Father, so we also might walk in newness of life." In the same way in Gal. iii. 27 he says, "As many of you as were baptized into Christ did put on Christ." Baptism is here clearly indicated as effecting the union with Christ, and there is no reason for trying to minimize the force of this fact. Baptism is, for St. Paul and his readers, universally and unquestioningly accepted as a "mystery" or sacrament which works *ex opere operato*; and from the unhesitating manner in which St. Paul uses this fact as a basis for argument, as if it were a point on which Christian opinion did not vary, it would seem as though this sacramental teaching is central in the primitive Christianity to which the Roman Empire began to be converted.

There were apparently three factors which were regarded as essential. The Water, the Name, and the Spirit, though the last gives rise to some difficulty. The water was the actual "efficacious sign" used in the mystery; the Name was the power which enabled the water to be used in this way; and the Spirit was the Divine life (or living being?) which made a "new creature" of the initiate.

The importance of the water to the mind of a Gentile of the first four centuries was by no means a simple conception, and may have varied in different circles. The idea of washing corresponds to the idea of removing sin and any other impediment to initiation; but the idea of "life" was also frequently bound up with the idea of water, especially flowing or "living" water,[1] and Tertullian [2] regards it as a commonplace that there was an affinity between water and spirits, for just as evil spirits haunt springs, and thus make men "nympholept," so also the Holy Spirit (as was the case at the Creation) is especially connected with water. The idea is not the modern one of symbolism, which was almost unknown to the ancients, but rather that the water was really the instrument by which the act of initiation was performed. The same thing, *mutatis mutandis*, could be shown of other initiatory rites in which blood or oil was used instead of water.

The water, however, was insufficient in itself. It was necessary to use it in the power of the "Name."[3] The underlying conception is one common to almost every early religion.[4] Certain beings are supposed to have

[1] In early Christian literature (*e.g.* the *Didache*) ζῶν is the technical name for running water, and its use was enjoined, if possible, in Baptism.

[2] *De Baptismo*, especially chapters 3–6.

[3] There is a dispute as to the original Christian formula. At a very early time the formula of Baptism was "in the name of the Father, of the Son, and of the Holy Spirit," but the evidence of Acts, supported by other subordinate arguments, suggests that the most primitive formula was "in the name of Jesus," or "in the name of the Lord." See further *Encyclopaedia of Religion and Ethics*, vol. ii. pp. 380 ff.

[4] Cf. also 1 Cor. i. 13, "Were ye baptized *in the name* of Paul?"

supernatural power over the forces of nature, and over the spirit-world which in the ancient view of the universe was sometimes identified with, sometimes distinguished from, natural phenomena. Now, not only these beings themselves could use this power, but also all those who knew how to make use of their name, with which their authority was bound up. This is the origin of all magical formulae of exorcism, and it seems to me impossible to deny that the formula of Baptism belongs to the same category.

Psychologically, the use of names in magical formulae is extremely interesting, and shows why the doctrine was so universal. One of the most frequent uses of exorcism was the cure of what we now should unhesitatingly diagnose as nervous trouble. In these cases nothing is so likely to succeed as treatment in which the patient believes. "Suggestion" and "faith" are the most important therapeutic agents known; it is comparatively immaterial whether the patient's belief is reasonable; what is important is that he should believe it unhesitatingly. This condition was admirably fulfilled by the old "magical" exorcism: the patient believed in the power of the "name," and recovered. It seemed strong evidence that the cure was really effected objectively by the "name." The reason why we are justified in rejecting this view is the fact that no formula and no name can claim an exclusive or consistent record of success, and that whereas cases are frequent in which a cure has been effected by "faith" or "suggestion" without a magical formula, there is no sufficient evidence of cure by a magical formula without "faith" or "suggestion."

The "Spirit" was the result of Baptism. Such, at least, seems to have been the normal view, shared by St. Paul. It is, of course, true that St. Paul says a great deal about "faith" and very little about Baptism. But it is equally true that he speaks so much about the one, and so little about the other, because the one was disputed and the other was not. "Faith" was, no doubt, the necessary preliminary to Baptism, and was the condition of salvation. I imagine that this conception was probably common to the Hellenist mysteries, and was probably not really disputed by Jewish Christians: the reason why it was controversial was that the latter thought that faith ought to include the acceptance of the Jewish Law, and the Gentile Christians, with St. Paul, believed that the acceptance of Jesus as the Redeemer was sufficient to justify initiation into the Christian mysteries. At the same time, it is probable that there were from the beginning exceptional instances in which the signs of possession by the Spirit preceded the act of Baptism. In this case logic would have suggested omitting Baptism as unnecessary, but human nature loves regularity, and probably Baptism was nevertheless administered. Moreover, it is doubtful whether the gift of the Spirit was connected with the act of Baptism in the strict sense of the word, or with the "laying on of hands," of which St. Paul does not speak except (and it is very doubtful if the reference is to Baptism) in the Pastoral Epistles. The evidence of Acts points to the connection of the Spirit with the act of "laying on of hands,"[1] and we have not really sufficient evidence to be certain of St. Paul's position. Without anything further one would say that he connects the Spirit directly with Baptism; yet he says nothing at all comparable to the clear statements in which Tertullian connects the Spirit with the water, and nevertheless, when it becomes necessary to be

[1] Cf. especially Acts viii. 12 ff. and x. 47 ff.; the point is discussed at greater length in the *Encyclopaedia of Religion and Ethics*, vol. ii. pp. 282 ff.

precise, Tertullian is quite positive that the gift of the Spirit comes from the laying on of hands immediately after the catechumen rises up out of the water, not from the water itself. Thus there is here a difficulty; but, if we take Baptism in the wider sense as possibly covering also a rite of laying on of hands, there is no reasonable doubt but that the primitive Churches to whom the Epistles were sent regarded the Spirit as the gift received in Baptism.

So far, I do not feel that there is real room for doubt; even though it is impossible to ignore that many critics of the highest standing among Protestant theologians would deny the soundness of the views enunciated, and maintain that primitive Christianity was not centrally sacramental. Such theologians believe that a purely symbolical and subjective doctrine of Baptism and other sacraments is not only desirable for the present day, but also true to primitive thought. I incline to the view that this position has received its death-blow from the modern study of the history of religions; and the theologian of the present and future will be obliged to distinguish more clearly than his predecessors between the primitive origin and the permanent validity of the various factors of thought and practice which constitute historic Christianity.

To return to the historical question: it is, as has been said, extremely probable that the world of Christianity to which the Epistles were sent held strongly sacramental views of Baptism. It is easy to understand that such a presentment of Christian Baptism offered no obstacle but rather a great attraction to Gentile converts: it was precisely parallel to the teaching and practice to be found in the Hellenistic Mysteries in general. In them in exactly the same way the initiate was washed with water (sometimes also with blood); in exactly the same way use was made of the magic power of a name or some other formula; and in exactly the same way the result was regarded as salvation, or new birth, and was explained as due to the union of the initiate with the god. Moreover, it is equally easy to understand the danger, which was the starting-point of this discussion, of an unethical [1] conception of sacramental grace, and the constant efforts of the Church from the beginning to deal with this evil [2] can be clearly traced in the later Christian literature.

Strictly speaking, the establishment of these facts is all that lies within the province of this book; but a serious problem is just over the border. It is quite plain that a sacramental or even magical view of Baptism would be an attraction to Gentiles: it was exactly what they expected to find in religion. But did the same view obtain among the Jewish Christians, and in what relation does it stand to the teaching of Jesus?

It is quite possible that these problems are insoluble, but it is permissible to indicate in outline the kind of theory which seems to be the most probable.

In the first place, it is very doubtful whether we can lay down any fixed rules about Jewish Christians. But reducing the question to the stricter type of Jew, it seems, on the whole, probable that they regarded Baptism primarily as a part of the eschatological preparation for the coming of the Kingdom. Whether they can be said to have regarded it

[1] "Unethical" and "magical" are not synonyms: in the scientific sense of the word much Christian sacramental doctrine was and is magical, but it is not necessarily unethical.

[2] The beginnings of an attempt to follow out this line of thought will be found in an article on the *Shepherd* of Hermas in the *Harvard Theological Review* for 1911, and in the article on *Early Christian Baptism* in Hastings' *Encyclopaedia of Religion and Ethics*.

sacramentally or not is difficult to say; certainly there was some difference between the Jewish and the Greek view, but it is often over-stated.

The relation of Baptism to the teaching of Jesus is still more obscure. There is very little on the subject in the Gospels, and nothing which is not open to grave doubt. Personally, I believe that St. John the Baptist preached a Baptism for the remission of sins, and that the custom was kept up perhaps by Jesus,[1] and certainly by His followers, who added the Christian formula. At the same time, the apparent confusion in the earliest documents as to the relation between Christian Baptism, the Baptism of John (which seems to have been connected with the Messiah), and the gift of the Spirit may possibly (it is far from certain) point to an original conflation of two things. The point is very obscure, and any one who can clear it up a little more will do good work, but we can see enough, if we trust our documents, to show that Baptism is probably a primitive Christian rite, practised by the immediate hearers of Jesus in Palestine, and that even if it were not a "mystery" or "sacrament" to them in quite the Greek sense, it was sufficiently nearly so to render inevitable and natural its adoption as a "Mystery" in the earliest Gentile circles, and among the more "Greek-minded" Jews in the Diaspora.

(2) *Judaic Problems.*—The main problem for Jewish Christians was, of course, that which is conveniently summed up as the Judaistic controversy, but before discussing this, it is desirable to notice another small question which seems to have affected the Jewish rather than the Gentile Christians. This concerns the relation of Christians to the civil powers,

[1] On one occasion Jesus almost (but perhaps not quite) implies that the Baptism of John was from heaven. How far does that take us?

and, though there is room for some hesitation, it seems to be best explicable in connection with Jewish thought.

This point is without parallel in the Epistles to Corinth. In Corinth, so far as we can see, there was no tendency to disregard the magistrates of the Empire, and St. Paul rather protests against a tendency to make use of the Roman courts in case of quarrels among Christians. But the implication of Rom. xiii. is that there was a disposition to disregard the magistrates—the "powers that be"—and to resist their decrees. The whole chapter is clearly directed against this tendency.

It is easier to see that this is the case than to know what conclusions ought to be drawn from it. If it is regarded as certain that Romans was originally written to Rome, it is possible that purely local circumstances may sufficiently account for the facts. There was undoubtedly a lawless disposition among the Jews at this time, who, for whatever reason, had been "assidue tumultuantes." It is not impossible that St. Paul was afraid that the same spirit would spread to the Christians. But there is another possibility which deserves attention, and is especially important if it be thought that "Romans" was originally written for Syrian or Cilician Christians. This is the belief in a "Messianic war."

It is impossible to discuss at length this intricate question,[1] but certain main points are important and tolerably certain. There was a general belief among the Jews that the Messianic Kingdom would be inaugurated by means of a war. As to the nature of this war opinions differed. There was one party which maintained that it

[1] The best monograph on the question is the very interesting treatise of Dr. H. Windisch, *Der Messianische Krieg und das Ur-Christentum*.

would be carried out by the miraculous and unaided efforts of the Messiah. Another party thought it would be the work of Jahveh Himself. Still another placed all the emphasis on a supernatural conflict with evil spirits. But politically the most important was the view that the Kingdom must be prepared for by the victorious effort of the pious in a rebellion against the enemies of Israel, and it was held that in this rebellion supernatural assistance would be given at the proper moment. It was not a warfare under the leadership of the Messiah, but a warfare in preparation for the Messiah. As Windisch has pointed out, this is the real difference between the rising of Judas and the earlier propaganda of the Zealots on the one hand, and the rebellions of Theudas and of Bar Kochba on the other. But obviously the distinction between a Messianic war under the leadership of a Messiah, and a Messianic war in preparation for a Messiah, though historically important, is politically negligible, and the repressive methods of the Romans differ in degree rather than in kind from those which any conquering nation of our own time would adopt.

What was the relation of Christianity to this movement? There seems to me little doubt but that the teaching of Jesus was directly opposed to that of the Zealots, and with but slightly less certainty I should feel inclined to argue that the Zealot teaching is the background against which we ought to place such sayings as "Resist not evil," "Love your enemies," etc. No doubt they were intended to have a wider application, but they were spoken with a special meaning. The Zealots said, "The Kingdom will not come unless you prepare the way by waging war on the enemies of Israel." Jesus said, "Not so: the 'Anavim,'"—the "poor" of the Psalms—"are the true guide; in your suffering, not in your victory, do you gain your lives, and final salvation is with him who suffers to the end." Like all one-sided generalizations, the statement that the preaching of Jesus was anti-Zealotic[1] would be an exaggeration and a distortion. Yet it contains an important element of truth. There is, however, another side to the question. Neither Jesus nor His disciples contemplated taking up arms, but they probably did believe that the existing kingdom, that of Rome, would be destroyed in the final catastrophe which would inaugurate the Kingdom of God. In this sense Jesus, as the Messiah, really was the rival of the Emperors, and it is easy to see how hard it would be to persuade a Roman, especially a magistrate, that Christians were nevertheless not meditating a violent revolution. They could not deny that they expected the annihilation of the Roman power, and the sovereignty of their own Master, in consequence of a Messianic war. Who would believe them when they said that they only meant a supernatural war, and that they themselves did not propose to take part in it?

When we realize this it is easy to understand that there was a double reason for St. Paul's advice that Christians should obey the "powers that be." On the one hand, there was the necessity of proving by the evidence of deeds that the Christians, though believing in the speedy Parousia of the Messiah, did not intend to hasten his coming by a rebellion, such as the Zealots advocated. On the other hand, there was probably (though this cannot be proved) the danger that Christians might be infected with the Zealot spirit, and think that they could combine the belief that

[1] And for that reason the presence of a Zealot among His followers was deserving of mention.

their Master was the Messiah with the Zealot view that His Kingdom could only be established by the self-sacrificing and warlike enterprise of His followers.[1]

It is now time to consider the main controversy between St. Paul and Jewish Christians of the strict Jerusalem school—the so-called Judaistic controversy—and the clearest method is to begin by considering what was in all probability the point of view of the ordinary Palestinian Christian in the middle of the first century.

In the first place, such a Christian accepted the "good news" which Jesus had preached, so far as he understood it. What this "good news" was we can find in the Marcan narrative and in those passages of Matthew and Luke which belong to Q; it is summed up in Mark i. 15: "The Time is fulfilled, and the Kingdom of God is at hand; repent, and believe the good news." The εὐαγγέλιον here is clearly the announcement which has just been made—"the Kingdom is at hand." This was the message of Jesus with regard to the immediate future; His message with regard to the present was equally definite: "Repent, otherwise the Kingdom is not for you, and believe what I tell you." This message was accepted by His followers; they did believe that the Kingdom was at hand, and they did repent. They also went a step further, and they identified the Jesus who announced the coming of the Kingdom with the Anointed King who should judge, reign, and rule in the Kingdom when it came. I do not doubt but that in doing this they had the authority of Jesus. It seems to me certain that Jesus did regard Himself as the future Messiah, or, to put it somewhat differently, as the

[1] Some aspects of the Crusades are a curious and belated example of a fervid Christianity with Zealot principles.

Messiah in personality though not yet in function. Nevertheless, this was not part of His general message which He proclaimed publicly, it was the secret which He shared with disciples. However much it be true that the centre of the gospel of the first Christians was "the Messiah is Jesus," it is equally true that the centre of the gospel of Jesus was not this, but "the Kingdom of God is at hand, believe it, and repent." He went through the villages of Galilee, He preached on the hillside and by the shore of the lake, and He went up to die in Jerusalem, not to convince men that He was the Christ, but to call them to repent, to amend their evil lives, lest when the Kingdom came they should be left in outward darkness. His gospel was eschatological and ethical—all the more ethical because it was eschatological—but it was not Christological in the sense that it did not, as Christian preachers did from the beginning, make the identification of the Messiah with Jesus the central point of teaching.

Why, in the mind of a Jew, was repentance so necessary if the Kingdom was coming? Because the Kingdom was to be the inheritance of the righteous: sinners would be excluded. In the Kingdom there would indeed be no more sin, for the condition of nature lost by man at the beginning of history would be restored, and this belief can be amply illustrated from Jewish literature.

In *Enoch* there is no exception to the view that righteousness will be a characteristic of the members of the Kingdom. "And I will transform the earth and make it a blessing, and cause My elect ones to dwell upon it, but the sinners and evil-doers will not set foot thereon." [1] Or, in an earlier passage, "And all the children of men shall

[1] Enoch xlv. 5.

become righteous, and all nations shall offer Me adoration and praise, and all will worship Me, and the earth will be cleansed from all corruption, and from all sin, and from all punishment and torment," etc.[1]

So also in the *Testaments of the Twelve Patriarchs* in the great prophecy of Levi of a priestly Messiah : "In his priesthood sin shall disappear, and the lawless (ἄνομοι) shall fall into evil, but the righteous shall rest in him." [2]

Still more clearly in the *Psalms of Solomon :* "And he shall purify Jerusalem in sanctification, as at the beginning, . . . and in the midst of them there is no unrighteousness in his days, for all are holy (ἅγιοι),[3] the Lord Messiah is their King." [4]

It is unnecessary to multiply references : probably no one will ever dispute the fact that the Jewish conception of the Kingdom was that the righteous would enjoy it, and that it would be free from sin. But who were the righteous ? And how could a sinner become righteous ? To these questions also Jews had quite definite answers.

The righteous were those who kept the Law of God. No doubt there were differences of attitude towards the Law. At the one extreme there was the purely formal legalism against which Jesus so constantly protested, but at the other there was the truly spiritual appreciation which speaks through the Psalms and Prophets, and as the *Testaments*

[1] Enoch x. 21 ff.

[2] *Test. Lev.* xviii. 9. I have followed the text of *e* in reading καταπέσουσιν rather than καταπαύσουσιν. It seems to give the right meaning, and the evidence of *e* is always important. Whether, as Charles thinks, the following words ought to be omitted (also with *e*) seems to me doubtful. I cannot see that the parallelism is clearly against them. See Charles' *Greek Text of the Testaments of the Twelve Patriarchs*, p. 63.

[3] Note that this is St. Paul's favourite designation for Christians.

[4] *Pss. Sal.* xvii. 33-36.

of the Twelve Patriarchs and many of the *Sayings of the Fathers* show, was still a force in Judaism. We are too apt to forget that the Pharisees and lawyers who are held up to reprobation in the New Testament were only one side of Judaism. The question, therefore, which the Jewish Christian was obliged to put to himself was whether the teaching of Jesus abrogated the Law, or called on him to be "righteous" in his careful observance of it. Obviously he decided that the latter was the right answer. It is difficult for us to reconstruct his position fully, because the Gospels are either the product of Gentile, not Jewish, Christianity, or at least of Jews who had adopted Gentile thought, and the position of Liberal Judaism in the Diaspora. Nevertheless, we can see even now that the Jewish position was not wholly unjustified. Jesus had inveighed against the Pharisees: but had He not claimed that the "righteousness" of those who would enter the Kingdom must be greater than theirs? Had He not said, "Till heaven and earth pass away, no jot or tittle shall pass from the Law"? Had He not said, "The scribes and the Pharisees sit in Moses' seat: do therefore and observe whatsoever they say unto you, but do not according to their deeds; for they say, and do not perform"? What was the meaning of His advice to the rich young man, "Thou knowest the commandments," if He did not mean that the righteousness which leads to life is to be found in the Law? It is easy enough for us to say that such questions imply a narrow and unintelligent attitude; but the question of the attitude of Jesus to the Law has never yet been satisfactorily discussed in the light of modern researches into the Synoptic Gospels. It is, however, tolerably plain that such a discussion, when it takes place, will lead to the recognition of the fact that the Judaizing Christians had something to say for themselves when they claimed to be the interpreters of the mind of Jesus.

Thus "the righteous" meant for the Jewish Christian those who observed the divinely given Law, and were opposed to sinners who neglected it. But the problem which had especially to be faced was how a sinner who had neglected the Law was to be set free from sin. Here also the Jew naturally thought along the lines of his inherited theology. More than one factor can be distinguished. In the first place, there was the doctrine, which finds an especial emphasis in Ezekiel, that by repentance, that is to say, turning back and observing the Law, righteousness can be obtained.[1]

This view is common to all Jewish thought,[2] but it does not stand alone. Alongside of it is the doctrine that former sin must be cleansed away. Sometimes, as in some parts of Ezekiel, there is the view that present righteousness cancels and abolishes past sin, but more frequently a doctrine of purification was added. This purification was by sacrifice and lustration, or ceremonial washing, and it was thought that part of the preparation for the Messianic Kingdom would be a general purification. This idea is expressed clearly in such passages as Ezek. xxxvi. 25: "And I will sprinkle clean water upon you, and ye shall be clean, from all your foulness, and from all your idols will I cleanse you." And in Enoch x. 20 the duty is given to Michael of

[1] It is not without importance that the word for "repentance" in the Old Testament is usually שרב, which means a change of conduct. It is generally translated in the LXX by ἐπιστρέφειν, but in Ecclesiasticus xlviii. 11 it is apparently represented by μετενόησεν, and in the later translations the ἐπιστρέφειν (or ἀποστρέφειν) of the LXX is usually replaced by μετανοεῖν. See Windisch, *Taufe und Sünde im ältesten Christentum*, p. 8 ff.

[2] Cf. Ez. xviii. 21 ff.; Isa. i. 16; Ps. xv.; Ecclus. xvii. 25; *Test. XII. Patr.*, *Reub.* 4, etc.; cf. Windisch, *op. cit.* pp. 8–34.

cleansing the earth from sin.[1] The preaching of St. John the Baptist is obviously connected with this doctrine. He announced the coming of the Kingdom, and offered a baptism of purification from sin in combination with his message of repentance, of turning back to the paths of righteousness. This view was taken over by the Christians, and in Jewish Christian circles Baptism was probably regarded as the "Messianic" purification necessary for entering into the coming Kingdom.[2] The incident in Acts xix. 1–6 when St. Paul met Christians who had been baptized with the Baptism of St. John, seems to be the proof that in some circles, which must have been Jewish in origin, there was no Christian Baptism as distinct from that of St. John the Baptist.

It is now necessary to consider another element in the situation, partly connected with the Jewish doctrine of sin, partly with that of the Messianic expectation. Alongside of the view that sin consists in disobedience, and righteousness

[1] An interesting problem is raised by this passage in connection with the place of Michael in this passage by the strange confusion which obtains in the *Shepherd* of Hermas between Michael and the Messiah. The last word has by no means been said on the history of the figure of Michael: the best introduction to the subject is W. Lueken's *Michael, eine Darstellung und Vergleichung der jüdischen und der morgenlandisch-christlichen Tradition vom Erzengel Michael.*

It should be noted that Charles assigns this function to Gabriel, as he regards the reference to Michael as an interpolation. I cannot see that there is sufficient reason for this emendation.

[2] To Gentile Christians Baptism had from the beginning a somewhat different aspect. It was the entry into the Kingdom, in the same sense in which the Mysteries gave entry into eternal life. It was a "regeneration to eternity." It is even probable that some Jewish circles had similar views, for parallel phrases were used of the Proselytes; but, on the whole, it is probably true that to the Jewish mind the emphasis was on the concept of cleansing, and to the Gentile on that of "regeneration." There is a real difference between the two, even though in practice they no doubt always had a tendency to coalesce, and when we distinguish them clearly we introduce a sharpness of contrast which is not historically justifiable.

in obedience to the Divine Law, there was the parallel doctrine that sin was due to evil spirits, and righteousness to a holy spirit. The former view found its historical justification in the story of the Fall, and the latter in that of the intercourse between women and angels (Gen. vi.), and is the more usual in the Apocryphal literature.

The complement of this view of sin was the belief that part of the work of the Messiah would be the destruction of the evil spirits and the inspiration of the members of the Kingdom by the Holy Spirit. This view is found in some passages in the Old Testament in connection with the last days, and it was, apart from this eschatological view, developed in the Diaspora, as may be seen in Philo.[1] According to him, purification from sin is accomplished by the Spirit. So far as man is really under the control of the Spirit he is sinless, and Philo explains the sins of the "perfect" by the curious theory that the Spirit is, as it were, occasionally absent. In Philo this "spiritual" view is associated with a strongly ethical theory of repentance, not essentially different from the usual Jewish one, but it is easy to see that in circles which went further than he did, the "spiritual" view might become quite unethical in practice, and might explain the existence of Jews in the party of the πνευματικοὶ described in the last chapter (pp. 222 ff.). It was part of the bridge between Judaism and Hellenism.

There can be no question but that Christians, certainly not excluding Jewish Christians in Jerusalem, regarded themselves as having received the Spirit, and were inclined to give an eschatological significance to this fact. It is not less certain that they also regarded themselves as, for this reason, holy and righteous. The question of the

[1] See especially Windisch, *Taufe und Sünde*, pp. 61–70.

position which they assigned to Baptism in this connection is more doubtful (see pp. 384 ff.). The evidence of the Acts suggests that there may have been a difference of opinion from the beginning as to whether the gift of the Spirit was directly given in Baptism or separately. But in some circles the doctrine certainly obtained that the Spirit was given in Baptism, and Christian Baptism was regarded as differentiated by this from the Baptism of St. John.

The really important point in this complex of facts is that there was in this way a double series. (1) Looking at the facts of life from the point of view of Law, sin was regarded as the transgression of the Law, righteousness as the observance of the Law, and repentance as the change of conduct from transgression to observance. (2) Looking at the facts from the point of view of spiritual experience, interpreted in the language which explained it as due to the influence of spirits and demons, sin was regarded as the power of an evil spirit, righteousness as the power of a holy spirit, and repentance as the passage from the control of one to that of the other.

Probably no school of Judaism thought exclusively from either point of view; but the Palestinian Jew was more inclined to take that of Law. Thus to such a mind a belief that Jesus was right in His message, "The Kingdom of heaven is at hand, Repent!" and that He was right in His belief that He would be the King in the Kingdom, made him all the more anxious to "repent"—to turn round—and to observe the Law, and in this way to secure the righteousness which was essential for members of the Kingdom.

But a Jew of the Diaspora, and still more a Gentile convert to Christianity, took the other line. To him his "righteousness" was secured by the possession of the Spirit, not by the works of the Law. When he was contradicted on this point he began to go still further, to ask pertinent questions concerning the history of the Law, and to react against its claims. To do this successfully he had to explain more fully what faith and righteousness were, and what the Law was, and this is the task which St. Paul attempts in Rom. i.–viii. and in the dogmatic parts of Galatians. The minute exegesis of these passages is extremely difficult, but in the main the meaning of St. Paul is tolerably clear. He is arguing that the Law did not and could not give righteousness, that this contention can be proved alike by the history of Israel and by individual experience; that, on the other hand, the Christian who has the Spirit has obtained righteousness, and that the true interpretation of the prophetic history of Abraham shows this to have been always the intention of God.

Moreover, if we look a little more closely, we can reconstruct, even though only in dim outlines, some of the objections which the strict Jewish Christian, in his turn, alleged against the positive side of this "spiritual" conception of righteousness, and cognate questions. These objections lie behind some of the questions which St. Paul puts, half rhetorically, in the course of his argument in the earlier chapters of Romans, and they can be reduced to three main propositions. (1) The "spiritual" conception of righteousness was unethical. It encouraged men to sin by the promise of an abundance of pardoning grace. (2) It ignored the special position of the Jews as the people of promise. (3) It failed to recognize the Law as Divine.

The former of these propositions is clearly adumbrated in such passages as Rom. vi. 15: "What then? shall we sin because we are not under law but under grace?" or still more plainly in Rom. iii. 8: "Why not, (as we be slanderously reported, and as some affirm that we say,) Let us do evil that good may come?" Obviously the background of these questions is the contention by Jewish Christians that their opponents were preaching an unethical and even immoral gospel. We have seen already that the history of the Thessalonian and Corinthian communities shows that the Jewish Christians were so far right that in purely Gentile circles there was a danger of Christianity being regarded as a means of obtaining eternal life by sacramental means, devoid of ethical obligations.

The second proposition of the Jewish Christians, that the position of the Jews was not recognized, and their privileges set aside, is the background of some "asides" in the earlier chapters of Romans; for instance, Rom. iii. 1, "What advantage then hath the Jew?" but is especially treated in chaps. ix.–xi.[1] To a Jew this was of course a matter of really vital importance. It was held that to the family of Abraham special blessings had been given and promised, and the Christian Universalism seemed to deprive these promises of all real meaning.

One must admit that, from his point of view, the Jewish Christian was perfectly correct. Neither by St. Paul nor by later Christians was the Jewish position answered in any manner which could possibly shake a Jew's conviction.

[1] The question has sometimes been raised whether this section is the genesis of the whole Epistle, or, on the other hand, whether it is not really independent of the rest. Personally, I cannot see the justification for either question. The Epistle is often difficult to interpret, but each part of it seems to correspond to some tendency among the Jewish Christians, and as a whole it is perfectly intelligible as a contribution to the controversy described above; indeed, I would add that only as such is it intelligible at all.

The Jew was right when he maintained that the Old Testament in many places made promises to the Jews and excluded the Gentiles, and that the writers of the Old Testament meant this. Exegesis was on the side of the Jew: but exegesis is a poor thing when it conflicts with the facts of experience, and these facts were on the side of the Gentile. He had received the Spirit; and therefore a doctrine which excluded Gentiles was condemned by experience. The really logical attitude for Christians to have adopted would have been to deny the validity of the argument from the Old Testament,[1] but instead of doing this they impugned the Jewish exegesis.[2] Probably it was just as well that they did so: Christianity had need of the Jewish ethical element to balance the dangers of the Gentile movement, and too radical a break with the Jewish view of the Old Testament might have been disastrous.

The third objection of the Jewish Christian dealt with the question of the Law. Was it not true, he said in effect, that the Law had been given to the Jews as a Divine instruction in the way of righteousness? It ought to be observed. If not, what was the Law? Here, again, there was probably a difference of opinion between Jews in Palestine and those in the Diaspora as to the binding character of the Law on all nations. It is easy to understand the position which argued that the Law was eternal —as Jesus Himself seems to have said—and that it was

[1] Later on Marcion did so; but his heretical opinions tended to confirm opinion against him.

[2] It is impossible to read the Epistle of St. Barnabas or the *Dialogue* of Justin Martyr with Trypho without feeling that, regarded from the point of view of actual historical correctness, the early Christians are at their worst when they are dealing with the Old Testament, and, though it is a shock to our feelings to have to admit it, it cannot be denied that the arguments from the Old Testament in St. Paul's Epistles are not essentially different.

universal. Against this was the narrower view which regarded the Law as purely preparative for the Kingdom, and only valid for the Jews, and until the coming of the Messiah. According to the one party, the Law and the Promise were identical: the Kingdom would be the rule of God, under whom the Law would be perfectly obeyed. According to the other, the Law was later than the Promise, and was only *ad interim* until the Kingdom should come. Moreover, although in one sense the Kingdom was still future, Christians were already—even though proleptically—members of it, and lived under its conditions as ἅγιοι, holy. They had passed beyond the sphere of the Law.[1]

St. Paul appears in Romans to have definitely accepted this narrower view of the Law. The greater part of the opening chapters are devoted to supporting it, and controverting the stricter Jewish position. He did not deny the Divine origin or purpose of the Law, as his Judaizing opponents accused him of doing,[2] but he asserted that they mistook the nature and scope of this Divine purpose.

These are the main elements of the dispute about the Law and Righteousness, which was the most important, or at least the most obvious element of the controversy between the stricter Jewish Christians and the more liberal Jewish and Gentile Christians of the Diaspora. But there seems to have been another important element which

[1] It is, of course, obvious that this sort of argument led directly to the identification of the Kingdom and the Church, and to the view that the life of Jesus was a preliminary parousia, the "first coming" of the Messiah, an idea originally quite foreign to Jewish thought.

[2] It is doubtful whether there were any Christians who really did reject the Law, as distinct from limiting the scope of the Law, until Marcion: but it is possible that he had predecessors of whom we know nothing, and that St. Paul was in this respect not the extremist which he is sometimes painted.

demands attention. It is quite plain that St. Paul is arguing in many places in Romans that the death of Jesus was important for the salvation of the individual Christian. It is unnecessary here to ask precisely what this importance was, for such an inquiry belongs rather to the exegesis of the Epistle; but from the controversial emphasis laid upon it is clear that St. Paul was contending for the truth of teaching which was disputed by his immediate opponents, the Judaistic Christians, and it is desirable to find out, so far as possible, what was the attitude of those who—to speak somewhat loosely—saw no "atoning" work in the death of Jesus.

The Jewish doctrine of the Kingdom of God[1] did not include that of a suffering Messiah. The doctrine of a Messiah was a complex of originally separate factors. Probably the original idea of Messiah was merely that of the anointed King who reigned over Jahveh's people.[2] Perhaps in monarchical periods there was no further development. Later, probably under Babylonian influence, prominence was given to the belief in a heavenly "Man" who would ultimately appear to inaugurate the kingdom, and this figure was conflated with that of the original royal Messiah. This process appears to be complete in the Book of Enoch, and it is very doubtful whether Jewish thought in the first century or later ever added new elements.

Nevertheless, the material for a new element already

[1] Indeed, it seems sometimes not to have included a Messiah at all.

[2] Modern researches have thrown a curious light on this question. It is not clear what was, according to ancient conceptions, the relation between kingship and divinity, but certainly they were closely connected. In some places probably the king was the god, and the god was the king (cf. J. G. Frazer, *The Origin of Kingship*). Clearly this is of great importance for the history of the early stages of the Messianic belief among the Jews, but it has not yet been fully worked out.

existed in the Old Testament, in the figure of the Ebed Jahveh or the Suffering Servant, who appears in Isaiah liii. and cognate passages. Here there is undoubtedly the idea of vicarious suffering; but whatever the origin of the figure may be, there is a complete lack of proof that Palestinian Jews ever connected it with the figure of the Messiah.[1]

Under these circumstances what is likely to have been the meaning attached by Jewish Christians to the death and resurrection of Jesus? On general principles one would expect to find that the Resurrection was regarded either merely as the proof that the Christian view of Jesus was correct, and the Divine confirmation of His message, or as the means whereby He had attained (or, possibly, resumed) the heavenly nature of the "man" who was to appear at the coming of the Kingdom as the divinely appointed King. There would be no suggestion that the Resurrection had a personal importance for individual Christians, for it was not expected that the individual Christian would die before the coming of the Kingdom. This is exactly what is implied by the speeches in the early chapters of Acts. The Resurrection is always referred to as evidence for the truth of the message of Jesus, and the correctness of the Christian view of His Messianic nature.

In the same way it is on general principles probable that the Crucifixion was in such circles regarded merely as one of the long list of crimes against the Messengers of God, of which the Jewish nation was guilty. This, again, is exactly what we find in the discourses in the early chapters of Acts. "Him," says St. Peter on the Day of Pentecost, "being delivered up by the determinate counsel and fore-

[1] Cf. H. Gressman, *Der Ursprung der Israelitisch-jüdischen Eschatologie*, pp. 301–333.

knowledge of God, ye by the hand of lawless men did crucify and slay, whom God raised up, having loosed the pangs of death, because it was not possible that He should be holden of it. . . . Let all the house of Israel therefore know assuredly that God hath made Him both Lord and Messiah, this Jesus whom ye crucified."[1]

Quite in the same spirit St. Stephen says at the end of his speech, "Ye stiffnecked and uncircumcised in heart and ears, ye do always resist the Holy Spirit; as your fathers did, so do ye. Which of the prophets did not your fathers persecute? and they killed them which shewed before the coming of the righteous one, whose betrayers and murderers ye are now become."[2] Clearly St. Stephen did not regard the death of Jesus as differing in quality from that of the prophets whom previous generations of Jews had murdered.

It is true that the matter is not so simple as the foregoing statement would make it appear: the question remains how far the Jews of the first century may have seen the power of an atoning sacrifice in the death of the prophets and of the righteous in general. This question really belongs largely to the province of Old Testament exegesis, and I hesitate to speak on a subject so far outside the limits of my own knowledge, and apparently so far from having been settled by expert study, but my impression is that it is quite probable that some such teaching did exist, and that it was especially connected with the Suffering Servant of Isaiah liii. and cognate passages. If so, this would provide a natural bridge for the development of Christian teaching as to the death of Jesus. It appears to me quite likely that

[1] Acts ii. 23–24. Cf. with this passage Acts iii. 14 ff.; iv. 10; v. 28 ff.; x. 39.

[2] Acts vii. 51–53.

in limiting[1] the atoning efficacy of a martyr's death to the one case of the Christ, and in enhancing its importance, Christianity was narrowing, even though heightening, a doctrine of which the Jews had already learned the rudiments.

At the same time, however much importance may ultimately be attributed to this side of Jewish teaching, it is quite clear that all the evidence which we possess shows that some Jewish Christians were not in the least inclined to see in the death of Jesus a unique atoning sacrifice, just as it is equally clear that St. Paul did assign this value to it.

It is for this reason that in Romans, devoted as it is to dealing with the views of Jewish Christians, St. Paul is at such pains to explain the real meaning of the death of Jesus. If there had been no difference of opinion on the subject St. Paul would not have been at such pains to argue it out, any more than he argues out the fact of the Resurrection, or of Baptism. The Epistles are not academic treatises, and we may be sure that when St. Paul is at pains to discuss a point at length it is because he knew that it was disputed.

It remains to ask why Gentile Christians were more ready to find a special significance in the death of Jesus. That this was the case is sufficiently proved by the fact that St. Paul never discusses the point in writing to them. It is inconceivable that he did not preach this doctrine, and it must have been accepted by them without any demur or surprise. Why did they believe easily what Jewish Christians hesitated to accept? Because such teaching agreed exactly with what they expected to find in any form of religion. The death of the god, and its intimate

[1] If they really did so; here, again, there is, I fancy, real need for a fresh investigation into the history of the Catholic doctrine of martyrs.

connection with the Mysteries by which the initiate shared in his risen life, is as central in Hellenistic religion as it is peripheral or outside the periphery in Jewish religion. This does not mean that there was any "borrowing" from one of the Mystery Religions, but that this conception was in the air of Hellenistic thought, and a Greek, when he became a Christian, naturally continued to think along the lines already familiar to him. The spiritual experience of Christianity was no doubt the same among Jews and Greeks, but when it was a question of translating this experience into the language of the intellect, and stating its connection with the historical fact of Jesus, His life and death, each thought in the manner familiar to him.[1]

Such seem to be the main outlines of the general picture of Christian life revealed by the Epistle to the Romans. Perhaps the really surprising point is, that it should appear that the Judaic problems were, on the whole, more important than the Gentile problems. To some extent this fact is modified if the hypothesis (see p. 362) be adopted, that the short recension of Romans was originally sent to Churches in the neighbourhood of the Syrian Antioch at the time of, or before, the Council of Jerusalem. In that case it is easily intelligible why Judaic problems were the most important, and why the Gentile problems

[1] I would deprecate attempts too nicely to distinguish between the value of Greek and Jewish thought; neither are the same as our own, which is partly the offspring of both, partly something really new. The important point is that human religious experience, and human intellectual thought are both imperfect and both progressive; each generation is constantly engaged in a process of re-adjustment. One of the first duties of the theologian is not to confuse separate things. Religious experience is valuable in proportion to its spiritual elevation. Theological expression must, above all, be true to logic, historical research demands fidelity to fact, and—πρὸς ταῦτα τίς ἱκανός;

seem to be less developed than in Corinth. It is, moreover, easier to understand why there is no reference to the Apostolic Decrees, though if these represent a moral law, not a food law, there was in any case no special reason why they should be quoted. Still, even if this hypothesis of an early date for the short recension be adopted, we have to face the fact that St. Paul thought it desirable to send a copy to Rome, and this must mean that there was a stronger Judaic element in the Roman Church than in Corinth.

It is desirable to note precisely what is the import of this fact. It does not imply that there was a majority of Jewish Christians in Rome, but that there were Jewish Christians who preached strongly the position of the Jerusalem school of thought, and did not accept the teaching of the liberal Antiochene movement. This propaganda was clearly in existence in Galatia, but there is no trace of it in Macedonia (in the Epistles to the Thessalonians) in which St. Paul's enemies were Jews, not Jewish Christians, or in Corinth, in which, though his opponents may have been of Jewish nationality, they belonged not to the Jerusalem school,[1] but to an exaggeration of

[1] I do not think that St. Peter, even if he was in Corinth, can be regarded as belonging to the Jerusalem school. He was, according to the evidence which we possess, if we treat it fairly, much more in real sympathy with St. Paul. A scarcely justifiable use has been made in this connection of the phrase in Galatians that St. Paul "withstood him to the face because he was κατεγνωσμένος." That only means "clearly wrong," for though κατεγνωσμένος may no doubt be translated by a stronger expression, this would be untrue to English idiom. Languages have different methods of contradiction: writing in English I have begun this criticism of a view which I reject by calling it "scarcely justifiable"; had I been using Dutch, I should probably have said, "zeer ten onrecht," or in German "ganz falsch." I would ask those who build much on Galatians, whether they have never described any one as "clearly wrong," who in the main, or afterwards, belonged to their own party?

the Antiochene movement. It is probable that in Philippians we can see signs of the presence of the Judaizing school in Macedonia at a later date. The importance of these facts is that they suggest that whereas the Antiochene movement was the first to establish itself in Macedonia and Achaia, the Jerusalem propaganda passed over these districts and went first to Italy. No doubt "Antiochene" Christians were soon met with in Rome, but the important point is that if we regard Christianity as making its way across Europe in two waves, the Antiochene wave seems to have been highest in Achaia, while the Jerusalem wave reached its height in Syria and Italy, and passed by, at least relatively, the intervening districts of Macedonia and Achaia.

LITERATURE.—General information will be found in the introductory sections of the commentaries of Meyer, Holtzmann, Leitzmann, Zahn, and Sanday and Headlam. For the problem of the short recension the most important contributions are the articles of Corssen and de Bruyne quoted on p. 336. For the question of Baptism indispensable books are W. Heitmuller's *Taufe und Abendmahl bei Paulus* and *Im Namen Jesu*.

APPENDIX

THE TEXTUAL EVIDENCE OF THE GROUP DEFG

THE evidence of the group DEFG as to the short recension is important, and complicated. The MSS. of the group, and their relations to each other, are as follows :—

D is *Codex Claromontanus*, of the sixth century, in the Bibliothèque Nationale in Paris. It is a Graeco-Latin MS., written colometrically, not in stichoi, that is to say, the size of the lines is regulated by the sense, not by the number of the letters. It represents two MSS., not merely a text with a translation, but the Greek text belongs to the same type, on the whole, as the original of the Old Latin version, though it has almost certainly been accommodated in many places to a more usual type. It is also famous for possessing the so-called Claromontane stichometry, one of the oldest lists of canonical books, representing, according to Harnack, an Alexandrian document of the fourth century. It was in modern times first used by Beza, who says that it came from the monastery of Clermont Beauvais.

E is *Codex Petropolitanus* Muralti xx., formerly belonging to the convent of St. Germains in Paris. When the convent was burnt the MS. was bought by Dobrowski at the end of the eighteenth century, and taken to St.

Petersburg. It is a copy of D made in the ninth century, and is only valuable in places where D is no longer extant.

F is *Codex Augiensis*, of the ninth century, a Graeco-Latin MS. formerly the property of the monastery of Augia Dives or Reichenau, and now in the library of Trinity College, Cambridge. The Greek text greatly resembles that of G, but the Latin is that of the Vulgate written in a separate column and not between the Greek lines.

G is *Codex Boernerianus*, of the ninth century, a Greek MS. with an interlinear Latin translation of an Old Latin type. It was probably written by an Irishman in the Monastery of St. Gall, and is now in Dresden. The text belongs to the same type as D, but is inferior in value and has been much more contaminated with the usual type of late text.

The most important points in connection with these MSS. are concerned with the relations subsisting between F and G, and those between D and the archetype of F and G.

The relationship between F and G. There has always been a dispute among critics whether F is a copy of G or of the archetype of G, and it is not even now possible to say that any general agreement has been reached. The only way in which such a point can be settled is by a comparison of the places where there are differences of reading. If two MSS. make the same mistakes it is certain that they are closely connected, but it is not necessary to conclude that one is a copy—indeed, absolute proof of this point is almost impossible. If, however, the mistakes can be arranged in two classes, (α) those common to both MSS., and (β) those found in one alone, and the second can all be explained most naturally as mistakes made by the scribe of the second MS. in copying the first, the case for a direct derivation of one from the other is very strong. If, on the other hand, it appears that the MS. which is suspected of being a copy has nevertheless the right reading in some places where the supposed original has a mistake, then the theory of a direct derivation must be abandoned in favour of a common ancestry, unless it can be shown that these right readings are natural corrections made by the scribe. For instance, if it be found that a MS. which is supposed to be the original of another reads ἀνθώπῳ instead of ἀνθρώπῳ, nothing is proved by the fact that the supposed copy has correctly ἀνθρώπῳ, because the correction is obvious. It will, however, be seen that the application of this canon of criticism is very much more difficult than its statement, for who is to decide as to the limits of "natural corrections of obvious mistakes"?

This is just the point on which everything turns with regard to G and F. There are a number of places in which G and F have mistakes in common, and a much smaller number where F has a right reading against a mistake in G. Zimmer believes that all of this latter class are "natural corrections of obvious mistakes" in G, while Corssen thinks that this explanation fails, and that F and G are two copies of the same original, G being the more accurate.

It is impossible to reproduce the arguments of these two scholars, for they turn on the nice consideration of a number of small points. Personally, I think that Corssen is right, and that F and G are independent witnesses to a common archetype, *Y*.

The relationship between Y and D. On this point there is less theoretical difficulty. It is generally recognized that D is a better example of its type than *Y*, but there are sufficient places in which *Y* seems to have the family reading as against D to show that D is not the archetype of *Y*, but that D and *Y* are the representatives of a common ancestor, *Z*.

The reconstruction of *Z* is not yet complete, and is one of the most obvious needs of textual criticism. But Dr. Corssen's researches have gone some way to establishing various interesting points. He thinks that *Z* represents a Graeco-Latin edition of the fifth century, written in *cola* (*i.e.* in lines arranged according to the sense, rather than merely according to a fixed number of letters), and that it represents largely the European or Italian type of Latin found in Ambrosiaster and Victorinus. This result is supported by Dr. Souter's investigations (*Ambrosiaster*, in *Texts and Studies*, p. 214), which show that the text of D is especially close to that used by Lucifer of Cagliari in Sardinia.

In working out the problem of the text of *Z* the ideal would be to publish an edition of the three MSS. D, F, G with a reasoned critical commentary establishing the text of *Y* and of *Z*. Until the time when this edition appears it is necessary to attempt to anticipate its results for individual passages.

For the present purpose two such passages are necessary: (1) The words ἐν Ῥώμῃ in Rom. i. 7 and 15; (2) the Doxology.

(1) ἐν Ῥώμῃ *in Rom.* i. 7 *and* 15. The facts are these: G reads—

ΠΑCΙ ΤΟΙC ΟUCΙΝ ЄΝ ΑΓΑΠΗ ΘЄΟU ΚΛΗΤΟΙC ΑΓΙΟΙC
omnibus qui sunt in caritate dei vocatis sanctis.

As F does not exist at this point, we must assume that this was the reading of *Y*.

D is not fully extant—the MS. begins with the words κλητοῖς ἁγίοις, but *d* (the Latin version of D) reads *qui sunt Romae in caritate dei vocatis sanctis*, with a sign against *in* referring to a marginal note which has perished. Tischendorf

2 E

thought that this note was probably a reference to the Vulgate reading *dilectis* instead of *in caritate*, but E, the copy of D which is later than D, and has adopted all the corrections in it, reads πᾶσιν τοῖς οὖσιν ἐν Ῥώμῃ, κλητοῖς ἁγίοις. It is therefore more probable, as Zahn suggests (*Commentary*, p. 617), that the note stated that ἐν ἀγάπῃ was an alternative to ἐν Ῥώμῃ, and E has acted on this and chosen ἐν Ῥώμῃ. In this case the evidence of (D)E goes to support the omission of ἐν Ῥώμῃ, which must be credited to *Z* as well as to *Y*; and it remains an open point whether *Z* may not even have omitted ἐν ἀγάπῃ Θεοῦ as well as ἐν Ῥώμῃ. But this last point, on which no final decision is possible, is not nearly so important as the establishment of the fact that ἐν Ῥώμῃ was not in *Z*.

In i. 15, where the words ἐν Ῥώμῃ recur, G omits them, and is probably to be regarded as the representative of *Z*, though D F have been accommodated to the usual text.

The Doxology (*Rom.* xvi. 25–27). Either *Z* omitted the doxology altogether, or it placed it after xiv. 23. This result is reached by the following considerations. D has the doxology at the end of the Epistle, but F omits it altogether, and G leaves a blank space. It is clear that *Y* either omitted it or placed it after xiv. 23. The blank space in G may point to the scribe's objection to the position of the doxology in xiv. 23, in spite of the fact that he found it there in his exemplar, or to his knowledge of the fact that xiv. 23 was the usual place in which to insert it, in spite of the fact that it was not there in his exemplar, and therefore he did not feel justified in inserting it. In any case, *Y* did not insert the doxology after xvi. 23. The question therefore only remains, whether D or *Y* best represents *Z*. While admitting that there must always be an element of doubt on the subject, I think that *Y* must be regarded as transcriptionally more probable; the doxology is obviously in a more natural place at the end of the Epistle, and the tendency must have been to move it from xiv. 23 to xvi. 23, rather than the reverse. The fact that the Antiochene text as a whole kept to xiv. 23 is no answer to this fact, but merely shows that the Antiochene text preserved, on this point, an early text.

Whether the text of *Y* really had the doxology at xiv. 23, or omitted it altogether, is more doubtful. I am inclined to think that there is a slight balance of probability in favour of omission: the tendency of scribes was to invent and insert doxologies and other liturgical additions, not to omit them, and therefore the omission is transcriptionally slightly the more probable reading.

The question remains whether, supposing that *Y* omitted the doxology, it did so because it disturbed the sense, or because it was already omitted by *Z*. Here unfortunately the evidence will not take us, and it is useless to indulge in guesses.

Dr. Corssen, however, argues that the text of *Z* in chaps. xv. and xvi. belongs to a different archetype from the rest of the Epistle. His argument is that in these two chapters there are almost as many singular readings which may be attributed to *Z* as in all the other chapters put together. On this point he seems to be right, and though of course his explanation of the fact is not the only one possible, it is a plausible theory that behind *Z* was a copy of the Epistle which omitted chaps. xv. and xvi. and ended with xiv. 23, with or without the doxology, and had no reference to Rome in the opening verses of the Epistle. But the scribe of *Z* was acquainted with the tradition which had the concluding chapters, and he added them from another MS.

If this be so, the archetype of *Z* must have been a pure copy of the short recension. This result, though, of course, it cannot be regarded as certain, is important as evidence for the short recension, and also is textually important as tending to show that in the text of the group representing *Z* the considerable differences from the other early uncials are really due to its representing a different collection of Epistles.

CHAPTER VII

CONCLUSION

THE purpose of the preceding pages has been to discuss the critical questions which belong to the "introduction" to the earlier letters, and to throw some light on the general background of thought and practice which is so important a factor in explaining the motives leading to the origin of the Epistles.

With regard to the critical questions, two points have been omitted. No treatment has been offered of the actual chronology of St. Paul, as distinguished from the relative chronology of the Epistles. Nor has anything been said as to the authenticity of the earlier letters.

As to chronology, it has seemed better to postpone its treatment until the later Epistles are dealt with, in which connection I hope to discuss the whole question. So far as the earlier Epistles are concerned, the more or less fixed point is the famine of *c.* 46 A.D. The first missionary journey began soon after it, from which a rough reckoning can be made of the time occupied by the various journeys, and each Epistle dated according to the point in the journey to which it is assigned.[1]

The genuineness of the Epistles which have been discussed has, with the exception of 2 Thessalonians, been

[1] See especially the article on "Chronology" in Hastings' *Dictionary of the Bible*, by C. H. Turner.

assumed without discussion. This has been done because I believe, in common with the enormous majority of all who have studied the question, that the authenticity of these documents, and their comparative freedom from serious interpolations, is quite unassailable by any reasonable criticism, and the best argument in favour of this view is the fact that, assuming the authenticity of the Epistles as genuine letters written by St. Paul, it is possible to place them satisfactorily against a background of thought and practice consistent with what we know of the first century.

It is, however, common knowledge that the authenticity of the earlier Epistles was rejected by W. C. van Manen, and respect for the memory of my predecessor at Leiden, coupled with the recognition that truth is not always on the side of the majority, impels me to give a short statement of my reasons for disagreeing with his teaching.

The really serious arguments which are brought forward by those who reject the Pauline authorship of these Epistles are: (1) they are not really letters but theological treatises in the form of letters; (2) they presume an impossibly rapid development in Christian doctrine; (3) they imply a writer who has no resemblance to the historical St. Paul described in the Acts. These three arguments call for further consideration.

1. So far as the argument that the Pauline Epistles are not really letters is not a confusion of thought it seems to mean that the Epistles are theological treatises, for which the writer desired to claim superior authority by attributing them to an Apostle. Largely, however, it is really based on nothing but a confusion of thought.

There are really two distinct questions. First, whether the documents in question are properly described as letters;

secondly, whether they were, whatever may be their proper description, written pseudonymously. The former question is actually very insignificant, but it has obtained a spurious importance, because it is sometimes so stated as to suggest that, if it could be shown that the documents in question are treatises in epistolary form rather than letters, they must necessarily be spurious—which is absurdly illogical. The really serious question is whether the theory of pseudonymity gives a satisfactory explanation of the Epistles.

The suggestion is that the letters are the work of a circle of "Pauline" writers in the second century, who put into epistolary form a series of treatises dealing with the main points of Christian doctrine, and serving as manuals for ecclesiastical instruction and liturgical reading; their survival no less than their composition proves that they represent a dominant type of Christianity. That is in itself a possible and reasonable hypothesis: but does it correspond to the known facts? In treatises of this kind the greatest emphasis is laid on the most important points; we ought to be able to reconstruct from the documents a tolerably good picture of the main doctrines of early Christianity. Many such attempts have, of course, been made, notably in Pfleiderer's *Paulinismus*,[1] and have profoundly affected modern theology. But what is the outcome?—the monstrous result that no further trace of this alleged Paulinismus can be found anywhere except in Marcion, and that the question can be raised in vain, "How is it that the Gentile Christianity in Asia, Greece, and Rome became so

[1] Pfleiderer, of course accepted the greater Epistles as genuine; but he always handled them as theological treatises, and in so far he was naturally the forerunner of the Dutch school, who saw—as he did not—that if the Epistles are treatises they represent a Christianity which is not that of the first century. Therein I entirely agree; but the mistake is in ever regarding them as treatises.

thoroughly unpauline? Where did 'Paulinismus' survive, except in Marcion?"[1] There is no answer, for though critics have sought long and carefully they can nowhere find their "Paulinismus," but have to be content with tracing a faint and occasional influence in isolated passages. This is the *reductio ad absurdum* of the whole argument; it is impossible to believe that in the second century some unknown persons forged a series of letters which, by hypothesis, represented their own views, not those of the historic Paul, that they were so influential that these documents were soon accepted as Holy Scripture, and that simultaneously the Paulinismus, which the letters represent and were written to encourage, disappeared from off the face of the earth, and left scarcely a wrack behind.

The theory does not work: the historical facts are not intelligible at all on the hypothesis of forged letters supporting a system of Paulinismus. But they seem to be quite satisfactorily intelligible if we accept the Epistles as genuine letters, dealing with definite questions, and implying a background which in the main is recognizable as possessing precisely those features of which we have a more developed form in the second century. Treat the Epistles as letters; recognize that in letters the subjects discussed are not those on which all parties are agreed, but those on which there is difference of opinion, so that the really central points are not those which are supported by argument, but those which are assumed as generally believed, and it will appear that the Christianity of St. Paul did not really differ from that of the Catholic Church as we find it at the beginning of Christian history.[2]

[1] Harnack, *Lukas der Arzt*, p. 101.

[2] I was much interested lately to hear the *obiter dictum* of one of the foremost

I submit that this is strong evidence in favour of the authenticity of the Epistles, and of the general correctness of the view of the "background of the Epistles" which has been taken in the preceding chapters.

2. A second line of argument is that the Epistles represent a much greater amount of development than can possibly have taken place before the second century. The answer to this contention is twofold. In the first place, the "Urchristentum" with which the Pauline Epistles are compared is a figment of the imagination. According to the extreme radical school of criticism, we possess no documents of the first century or even of the early second century. The Urchristentum which they postulate has no documentary evidence, on their own showing. It may, indeed, in one sense, be admitted that they understate the case with regard to development; if the original early Christianity had had the character they suggest, it could never have produced the early Christian literature; but instead of concluding from this that no early Christian literature is genuine until the second century, that even then it is grossly interpolated, and that all the evidence of Tacitus, Suetonius, and Pliny is a forgery, it might be well to ask if it is not possible that the fault lies in the conception of early Christianity. In the second place, critics of this school seem to under-estimate the speed at which development takes place in a young movement. A comparison with

representatives of the Dutch school to the effect that the Epistles were imbued with the Catholic spirit, and (it was implied), therefore, could not be primitive. The Dutch school represents a keen and independent criticism of the Protestant view that Catholic Christianity is a degenerate form of Primitive Christianity. It sees that the Epistles belong to Catholic Christianity, and argues that they are, therefore, late. The true conclusion is that Catholic Christianity is, therefore, primitive.

the history of the Salvation Army, or of Babiism in Persia, in the nineteenth century shows that so far as the general possibilities of development are concerned the most suspected parts of the Pastoral Epistles, to say nothing of the earlier Epistles, might well have been written within thirty years of the Crucifixion.

3. A far more important argument than either of the preceding is that the historical St. Paul, who is revealed by the Acts, could never have written the Epistles. Apart from the critical question, whether the Acts ought to be preferred to the Epistles, this objection really means that the Epistles cannot have been written by a Jew of the first century. Now it must be admitted that it is very hard to believe that the Epistles could have been written by the Rabbinical Jew whom critical fancy has read back from the Talmud into the first century; and if we accept the criticism which identified the Judaism of the first century with that of two centuries later, van Manen's criticism is not only proper, but perhaps unanswerable. So far, however, from its appearing to be true that all Jews, or even all Pharisees, in the first century were of the later Rabbinical type, it is becoming more and more plain (α) that we know comparatively little about the various parties, sects, and tendencies in Judaism before the fall of the Temple; (β) that many Jews, especially in the Diaspora, were of a liberal and ethnicizing disposition. There is a general tendency to discount Friedlander's work on Judaism, and probably he may have exaggerated his case, but the quotations in his writings cannot be wholly brushed aside, and even though many of them be inaccurate, there is enough amply to cover St. Paul, and to show that his letters might well have been written by a Tarsiote Jew of the first century. It is true that St.

Paul in the Acts says that he was a pupil of Gamaliel, but the importance of this fact may be over-estimated. For this view two reasons may be alleged ; in the first place, supposing that it is quite certain that St. Paul was, before his conversion, a strict Pharisee, it does not follow that the change which his thoughts underwent did not include a change to the more liberal point of view with which he surely must have been acquainted in Tarsus and elsewhere. In the second place, it does not follow that pupils always follow the doctrine of their teachers. Saul of Tarsus may have been a pupil of Gamaliel, and been profoundly affected by him, and yet have afterwards succumbed to other influences. We do not always follow all the opinions of our teachers, and it would be scarcely suggested that our books are not authentic because they do not agree with the teaching which we received at our Universities or Theological Colleges.

For these general reasons it seems to me that the attack on the authenticity of the Epistles has completely failed. It is unnecessary to go into further details ; those who desire more will find that the works of Deissmann and Clemen have dealt faithfully with all the arguments which were brought forward by van Manen.[1] His premature death removed the possibility of his making any full rejoinder ; one cannot say what he would have written had

[1] The most important literature on the subject is : W. C. van Manen, *Paulus* and his article on " *Old Christian* " *Literature* in the *Encyclopaedia Biblica ;* and R. Steck, *Der Galaterbrief*, impugning the authenticity of the Epistle ; and A. Deissmann, *Bibelstudien* and *Neue Bibelstudien* (translated in a single volume as *Bible Studies*) ; Th. Zahn, *Einleitung*, i. pp. 108 ff. ; C. Clemen, *Paulus, sein Leben und Wirken*, i. pp. 6–114. This section is valuable not only for its own merits, but also for its full reference to other literature. I believe that there is also a full treatment in Knowling's *Witness of the Epistles*, but this book has not been accessible to me.

he lived; but none of his followers have shown any power of refuting the German scholars who criticized his position.

However important critical questions may be, they are merely preliminary; and the main purpose of the preceding chapters has been to discover the general characteristics of the Gentile Christianity in the Churches to which St. Paul wrote. The necessity for discussing critical and literary problems has lengthened the process, but it is, after all, the world of religious life and thought implied by the Epistles which is really important. Of this world each Epistle gives us a glimpse: it is never a clear vision, but enough is revealed to show that, in spite of local differences, the general background is in the main the same. It is, moreover, a background very different from that of our own time, and it is, therefore, desirable to give a little space to a concluding discussion of the permanent importance of the principal points.

As was said in the second chapter, the circle of Gentiles who accepted Christianity was chiefly that of the God-fearers, who were already imbued to some extent with Jewish ideas, as well as with the general conceptions of the Mystery Religions which were practically the only cults which were really alive at that time. Thus, quite apart from the influence of Jewish converts, there were from the beginning Jewish and Graeco-Oriental strains in early Christianity, and the difference between various communities is partly to be explained as due to the varying proportions in which these strains were mingled, and the consequently varying point of view from which the original Christian preaching[1] was regarded.

[1] That this factor also affected Church organization is probable, but there is

The general basis of Christian life seems to have been the assurance of salvation, the belief that this salvation was obtained by the "mysteries" or sacraments, through which the believer was united to the Redeemer-God Jesus, and the expectation that this same Jesus would speedily come to destroy the power of evil and establish the kingdom of God on earth. The point in this complex which was debated was the relation of sacramental salvation to ethical and moral obligation; the Greek element was, on the whole, liable to ignore the necessity of moral life, and to regard the mysteries or sacraments as magical, while the Jewish element introduced a legalistic conception of morality and regarded obedience to the Law as the source of salvation. Looked at in this way, we can see that the problems faced by St. Paul in Corinth and in Rome or Galatia, are really very closely related. It is in each case the relation of ethical to sacramental religion which is the central question, and the difference in the Epistles is due to the fact that while in the more purely Greek circles at Corinth the danger was an unethical sacramentalism, in Rome, under the influence of Jewish propaganda, an unspiritual and legalistic conception of morality was the more prominent evil.

The task which we have to face is not that of giving an *exposé* of St. Paul's arguments against his opponents, or of proving the undesirability of a religion which is unethical on the one hand or legalistic on the other. The former I hope to discuss more fully on another occasion, the latter is so generally recognized as to require no further

so little evidence as to organization at the time of the earlier Epistles that no definite information of importance can be gained, The most important point is the evidence of the litigious tendency in Corinth (see pp. 131 ff.).

exposition. It is more important to direct attention to the psychological basis of the two types of imperfect Christianity which are revealed in the background of the Epistles.

It will be convenient to refer to the two types as Greek and Jewish; such a nomenclature is of course unfair, if it be pressed, for many Greeks had the finest ethical perception, and many Jews were deeply spiritual, but it does not inadequately represent the weak sides of the two nations.

The Jewish type of religion is connected with a special way of regarding life. According to it life is a series of acts; it is conduct. Now, it is often very hard to do what is right, and thus for the Jew the primary importance of religion is that by its means man obtains information as to what he ought to do—he is given a law. It makes, for the psychology of the question, no difference whether this law be given once for all in an inspired code, or communicated by degrees directly or indirectly. The point is that men wish to know what to do, and religion tells them. Such men think in terms of action or conduct. Their conception of salvation as well as that of sin and repentance is expressed in the same terms. Sin is, to such persons, wrong-doing; and this definition remains true, whether they do or do not add the qualification that it must be conscious wrong-doing —the act of choice which sees the good and takes the evil. Repentance, again, is (as the Jew always was inclined to express it) a "turning back and walking in the right direction," and a state of safety or salvation is that which is reached by the man who walks in the way of the Lord, and "doeth that which is lawful and right." It needs no argument to show that for such a type institutional religion appeals in so far as it offers a code of righteous conduct by which "he who doeth it shall live," and personal religion is valuable so far as it is a means whereby help is obtained in the difficulty of choosing the right and rejecting the wrong course of action.

The Greek type, on the other hand, regards life as "being" rather than conduct. What a man is, not what he does, is important. Obviously, this affects the whole series of religious ideas. For such men sin is not doing wrong, but being wrong. It is, with such a conception of life, possible never to do anything wrong, and still to be the greatest of sinners; for sin is a leprosy of the soul, which is deadly in itself, even though it never manifest itself in action. Repentance similarly is not a change of conduct, but rather the desire for a change of nature; and salvation is a new nature, or "regeneration," a "new creation" or a transfiguration to a different being. Obviously, for such natures religion is valuable in so far as it offers, either as an institution or as the result of personal communion with a higher power, the means of obtaining, here or hereafter, this "new life," which ensures salvation, and brings us nearer to the ideal which we sometimes see and never attain.

That these two types are rarely found in an unmixed state needs no demonstration. A purely "Greek" or purely "Jewish" form of experience is exceptional, and therefore the foregoing statement is unduly sharp, and neglects the existence of a long series of intermediate types. Nevertheless, most people are inclined to one or the other extreme, even though their natures contain some degree of mixture of the other sort.

Each type has its own strength and weakness. The "Jewish" type develops a high morality, but it is liable to degenerate into a hard legalism, and to give rise to hypocrisy and self-righteousness. Allowing for the usual inaccuracy of generalizations, it is the source of all that is best and all that is worst in Protestant Puritanism.[1]

The Greek type, on the other hand, takes a deep and sympathetic view of life; it recognizes that life is something more than a series of acts, that human nature, as it is, is unsatisfactory, and longs for some new development which will raise it to something higher. Its strength is spiritual; but in some natures it is accompanied by a somewhat feeble sense of morality, or of right and wrong as such. Thus, there is often a danger of moral failure, a tendency to despise conduct, and to think slightingly of "mere morality."

To some extent, these two types are the same as William James's, or rather F. W. Newman's, "Once born" and "Twice born."[2] The "Jewish" type is "once born." It seeks for no change of nature. The Greek type is "twice born"; it is dissatisfied with its nature and seeks (and obtains) in religion a "new birth." Or to use a different nomenclature, also from William James, the "Jewish" type is in the main the "healthy-minded" and the "Greek"[3] is the "sick soul." The ethical, "Jewish" type of nature can quite well be contented with things as they are. The

[1] Not, of course, of all Puritans. Indeed, I imagine that the leaders of Puritan movements have sometimes belonged to the other type; but the average Puritan has always been inclined to lay great stress on conduct, to regulate it according to a code, and to be distinctly intolerant and unintelligent towards other people.

[2] William James, *The Varieties of Religious Experience*, pp. 80 ff. James calls attention to and quotes from F. W. Newman's *The Soul; its Sorrows and its Aspirations*, 3rd ed., 1852.

[3] I am quite prepared to believe that this statement would be ridiculous if applied to classical Greek religion; but it seems to be true of the Greek elements in early Christianity. The truth is, of course, that in Christian times the word "Greek" had gained a different connotation, and a Greek was more Oriental than Hellenic in his religious feelings.

spiritual "Greek" can scarcely be happy before he has gained access to a new life. Until he has done this he is a "sick soul," though the degree of his suffering may vary from occasional unrest to the greatest agony of spirit. The classical description of his experience in the New Testament is Rom. vii.–viii.; for St. Paul, though by blood a Jew, was by nature a "Greek," who had passed through the misery of the "sick soul" to the peace of the "twice born."

When we consider the facts in this way it is fairly clear why the religion of the Greek tends to become a "Mystery Religion," and that of the Jew a "religion of legalism," while the ordinary "mixed type" of man combines something of each. More difficult is the question why the "Mystery Religions" really succeed in supplying by means of their sacraments the regeneration which is sought. For that they are actually successful is not open to dispute.

The theory which has been dominant in Christianity may be called the sacramental theory. According to this God has ordained various acts which the Christian must perform under various conditions, and if he does so he will receive a blessing of Divine grace which he would not otherwise obtain, and which cannot be gained in any other way.

The difference between this and Magic is that a Sacrament implies that the worshipper obtains certain benefits by fulfilling a covenant made with him by God, while Magic implies that he obtains them because he knows how to compel the deity to grant them. The difference is real,[1] but not superficially obvious, and in every age has been ignored or misunderstood by the adherents no less than by

[1] My impression is that, in this sense, many of the heathen Mystery Religions had, by the first century, ceased to be magical and become sacramental.

the opponents of Catholic Christianity; so that it is true both that to many uneducated Catholics the Sacraments are merely Christian magic, and that the educated Catholic is justified in protesting that the true orthodox doctrine is not magical.

Much more confusion of thought has, however, been produced by the feeling that "magic" is a delusion, and therefore that sacramental religion, which is, at the least, akin to magic, must also be a delusion. This reasoning fails to distinguish between the facts which the sacramental theory seeks to explain, and the theory itself.

The facts of experience, to confine the question to one side of research, are that certain persons habitually receive the Sacraments of the Church and habitually are conscious that they derive benefit after doing so. On this is based the theory that they derive this benefit because they receive the Sacraments. It is held that it is *propter hoc* as well as *post hoc.*

The theory is, of course, open to argument: it is impossible to deny the efficacious working of sacramental religion, but whether the sacramental theory is correct or not is a matter of evidence. If the Catholic theory of Sacraments prove in the end to cover all the facts, and to be the only theory which does cover them, it will in the end be universally accepted, and the more it is discussed the sooner will this end be reached. At present, however, the difficulty is that Catholics argue too much as though "Catholic" experience really were "universal" experience, and up till now no final answer has been given to three anti-Catholic statements.

First, there exists in contemporary Protestantism a body of Christians, who can produce the same experiential evidence of "grace" as can the Catholic Church, and do not attribute it to the Sacraments, which some of them reject entirely. It is, for instance, hard to deny the evidence of spiritual life among the Quakers in England, and yet they have neither Baptism nor Eucharist.

Secondly, the student of religions is inclined to dispute the exclusive claim of the Christian Sacraments on the ground that the same claims can be substantiated by other Mystery Religions. This is a comparatively new point, but it is likely to obtain increasing importance in the discussion of this subject.

Thirdly, the students of psychology suggest to us that there is a rival explanation in the facts of "suggestion" and in the working of the "subliminal consciousness" which seems to be in a marked degree the seat of religious life.

To discuss these points at length would be outside the province of the present book, but it is probably safe to say that they serve to indicate the main lines which research into sacramental religion will follow in the immediate future.

To return to history. One of the most important factors in the development of early Christianity was the preponderance of the "Greek" or "twice born" type in the first generation, and the gradual increase of the "Jewish" type (though not of Jewish nationality) in those which followed. That the first generation should be "Greek" is obviously natural; it is the "sick souls," not the "healthy minded," who wander in the search for help in religion. The latter are not irreligious, but they generally remain in the cult in which they were born, or if they change it is for intellectual or social reasons. Thus in all new religious movements the first generation is usually "Greek," and "twice born." The majority of mankind, however, belongs rather to the other type, and therefore, as Christianity grew older, the second generation, born in the Church, began to be more and more "Jewish," "healthy-minded," and "once born." The fact is of enormous importance for the history of doctrine. It explains why the Church so soon adopted a "law," almost as strict and quite as externalized as anything the Synagogue ever knew. It also explains how Christian doctrine, which was originally the expression of religious experience, came to be regarded as a model to which all experience must conform, and its centre was shifted from the soul to the intellect. But to deal with these facts is the office of the historian of a later period, and I must not here pursue their study any further.

It remains to consider the eschatological element. There is at present much controversy among theologians as to the amount of eschatological teaching which can really be traced back to Jesus Himself. Personally, I think that the Synoptic Gospels give us a correct account of the facts, and I see no reason for the excision of Mark xiii., or of parts of it, as a Jewish interpolation. But it is unnecessary to discuss this point, for probably no one denies that a strong eschatological expectation, that the Parousia of the Messiah was imminent, was one of the most fundamental parts of early Christianity. The critics who deny that this view was that of Jesus may possibly be right, but at all events the Synoptic Gospels were largely written to prove the opposite, and whether we trust the Evangelists [1] or not as to their

[1]. It is to my mind a most remarkable fact that many scholars who haggle and dispute over the exact meaning of an obscure phrase in the Gospels, spend an infinity of trouble in discussing the precise Aramaic of the phrases used by Jews, and are shocked at the suggestion of doctrinal corruption in the text, are nevertheless quite ready to believe that the disciples wholly misunderstood Jesus and that the eschatological expectation of the first Christians was not

report of Jesus' teaching, they are absolutely contemporary evidence as to the view of the first Christians, and the indirect testimony of the Epistles supports them.

It is quite certain that the first Christians expected the immediate coming of the Kingdom, and they believed that Jesus would be the anointed King, the representative of God, in that Kingdom. This is what was meant by saying that Jesus was the Messiah. So far there is probably no dispute among students of the New Testament. Nor is it disputed that this belief is found in the Pauline Epistles; the point which is seriously doubted is whether it is central or peripheral. That it was absolutely central to the average Gentile Christian in, for instance, Corinth, I do not believe; for the centre of Christianity for him was the Sacraments rather than the expectation of the Parousia, even though the latter was a very prominent part of his creed. On the other hand, for a Jewish Christian, the expectation of the Parousia was probably quite central. I believe that it was so for St. Paul himself, and the reason why there is comparatively so little in the Epistles on the subject is because it was not a subject for controversy among Christians, but an undisputed hope, which all cherished. St. Paul found it necessary to devote pages of argument to the discussion of the Law, as against Jewish Christians, and to that of "Spirits" as against Gentile Christians, but he never stopped to argue that "that day" was coming,—this was a common element of belief. Similarly, he never gives any reason to Thessalonians or Corinthians for believing in the Parousia; he only assures them that death—which they had not expected

based on His own sayings. If the Gospels are trustworthy, let us trust them, and if not let us confess our ignorance. The choice is not between eschatology and ethics, but between history and myth.

—could not exclude Christians from the company of Christ when He came. The manner and the consequences of the Parousia were open to further discussion. The fact that it was imminent was generally conceded.

Most of the foregoing statement is generally accepted; nevertheless, there is a strong tendency among theologians to dislike the eschatological element in early Christianity, to under-estimate its importance, and to reduce its dimensions by a free use of the critical knife. The reason for this tendency is worth consideration, because the process of discussion is the best means of emphasizing the real nature of eschatological thought, and showing that much of the reluctance which is shown to accepting the fact of its early importance is based on a misconception of its implications.

Perhaps the antipathy to a full recognition of early Christian eschatology may be summed up in two propositions: (1) Eschatological hope is, and was, an illusion; (2) eschatological thought is unethical. Of these the first is a half-truth, the second is wholly untrue.

The eschatological expectation of the first Christians has undoubtedly been falsified by history. They expected that Jesus would return within their lifetime, and that the Kingdom of God would be established by a dramatic catastrophe, abolishing sin, suffering, and death, and raising to life the righteous dead. That did not happen: in the sense that the Christian hope of the Parousia was disappointed, the eschatological expectation was an illusion. Nor is it possible to say that the Christians were only wrong as to the time. There are, it is true, still some Christians who cherish the hope of a "second coming"; but there are many more, though they are largely a silent majority, to whom this hope is altogether strange. I do not doubt but that they are right. The eschatological hope of the first Christians, in the exact form in which they held it, has undoubtedly been falsified; there is no reason to suppose that it will be fulfilled in some inexact form, and the more we study the history of religions, the more plainly we can see that the eschatological prognostication of a dramatic judgment of the world, the sudden inauguration of a Kingdom under the rule of the Messiah, and the change of human nature to an original, but lost, perfection, is a legacy from older speculations, and has no real claim to our acceptance. As a prophecy of the future the eschatological hope has not been justified, and all that distinctly belongs to it, in that sense, has to be given up. There is nothing gained by attempting to gloss over this fact. As a prognostication of the course of history Christian eschatology has proved to be an illusion. It does not in this respect differ from other prognostications.

Nevertheless, to consider the matter from this point of view alone is narrow and erroneous. An eschatological expectation is strange and repulsive to many minds at the present, because they do not see that it is much more than a prognostication of the course of history: it is the last chapter in a complete view of the universe—a catastrophic *weltanschauung*—which stands directly opposed to the evolutionary system which we all usually employ. It is opposed to the strong points of the latter, but it is also opposed to its weak points.

The strong point of an evolutionary *weltanschauung* is that it does justice to the elements of progress, of continuity, and of consequence in the universe. There is no difficulty with an evolutionary system in recognizing that the whole of history is a progress of steadily increasing complication,[1] or in showing that this formula can be applied with considerable justice to the spiritual and intellectual as well as to the material and economic sides of life.

But progress, continuity, and consequence are not the only elements in life. There are also present catastrophic factors. On the one hand, progress—which is life—is apt after a period of scarcely perceptible growth to burst out into a sudden efflorescence of production by which more seems to be accomplished in a single generation than in the fifty which preceded it. So it happened in the domain of art in the time of Pericles, and so it has happened in our own time in the domain of natural and mechanical science. In such an efflorescence there is something catastrophic, which is usually overlooked by the votaries of evolution. On the other hand, degeneration—the passing away of life from institutions and nations which have served their purpose—is apt to end in a cleansing conflagration of disaster. So it was in the fifth century in the Roman Empire, and in such a conflagration there is always something sudden, decisive, and catastrophic, which overwhelms what has previously seemed to be the strongest and best elements of the existing organization of society.

It would be unfair to say that an evolutionary *weltanschauung* cannot do justice to this catastrophic element in history: in the hands of its masters it can be made to express this as well as the elements of steady and consistent

[1] If the earlier writers had seen this as clearly as their successors do, we should probably have been all talking about involution rather than evolution. The two things have come to mean the same: it is evolution so far as it is a movement from an original type, it is involution so far as it results in something containing, not so much anything new, as old elements involved in each other, and reacting on each other in ever-increasing complexity.

growth. But it expresses them with more difficulty, and in the hands of smaller men frequently does not express them at all. The catastrophic *weltanschauung*, on the contrary, expresses admirably the catastrophic element in history, but at the expense of other sides. It recognizes and explains the value of the sudden efflorescence, of the "golden ages" of history, and does equal justice to those great conflagrations of disaster which are necessary to cleanse the world from its accumulation of putrefying degeneration, or—to use a more Biblical metaphor—to burn up the chaff, and prepare the threshing-floor for the next harvest.

If the eschatology of early Christianity be regarded in this way as part of a *weltanschauung* rather than as a prognostication of the future, all questions of illusion or anything of the kind are seen to be beside the mark. No view of the universe, or *weltanschauung*, is perfect: it is an attempt to see as much as possible of the facts of life from one point of view. But although some points of view are better than others, it is certainly not at present possible to see all the facts from the same point of view, nor can it be denied that different facts can be best seen from different points. Few really large landscapes can be seen completely from a single point. The fact that the traveller has to move from point to point, and from each point sees something new, is not regarded as proving the desirability of never moving, nor, because the accidents of one point of view may produce an appearance which the greater facilities of another point show to be an illusion, is any one prepared to argue that the first point has no advantages.

So it is with an eschatological *weltanschauung*. It provides us with a point of view from which we see certain features of life—the catastrophic features—to the greatest advantage; other elements—the slow, constant progress—we cannot see at all; and others again—the probable course of future history—we see distorted and in a false perspective. It is therefore, on the whole, a good thing that we have moved on to another point of view, and generally adopted the evolutionary *weltanschauung*, which enables us to see to advantage what was formerly obscured. But we should not forget that in losing the disadvantages, we have also lost the advantages of our former position; it is not necessary to deny what we could see there; and it is certainly desirable to reflect that a prognostication of the course of history based exclusively on evolutionary thought, is quite as certain to prove a distortion and an illusion as that which was once based on a catastrophic or eschatological foundation.

The objection that an eschatological gospel is unethical is often made, and more often implied. It must in the first place be claimed that, even if this were true, it would not justify the historian in arguing that therefore early Christianity had not an eschatological gospel. Our business is to interpret our evidence, to find out what the witnesses really do say, not to make them say what we wish that they had said. Nothing has retarded the progress of research into the history of early Christianity more than the subconscious feeling that the first Christians cannot have been really influenced by ideas foreign to the thought of the present generation. It is an unkind parody of the truth to say that much "Liberal" criticism has gone on the system of thinking that its own special brand of Protestant theology is identical with the Gospel of Luther in the sixteenth century, and of St. Paul in the first: it is an unkind parody, and the men against whom it is directed have taught us all ten times more than any other school of criticism, nevertheless, there is just a sufficient element of truth in it to point a warning to ourselves.

But, as a matter of fact, it is not in the least true that an eschatological gospel is or must be unethical. The earliest Christian gospel—that of Jesus Himself—was two-fold: (1) The Kingdom is at hand; (2) Repent. The first half is eschatological; the second half is ethical. Of the two most ancient sources in the Synoptic Gospels Mark is inclined to emphasize rather the eschatological side, and Q the ethical side, but both contain both elements. The fact is that, so far from eschatology being unethical, ethical teaching of the highest kind can be given better in the terms of an eschatological *weltanschauung* than in the language of evolution. The Sermon on the Mount, which may be taken as the typical example of Christian ethics, is not a code which can be applied directly and simply to our ordinary daily life. It is impossible not to resist evil, it is undesirable to lend, distrusting no man, and it is ruinous to give to every one who asks. You cannot base a code of conduct on the literal observance of the Sermon on the Mount, if society is to continue, and human nature remain as it is. That is exactly the point; early Christianity assumed that society was not going to continue, and that human nature was going to be changed. With that assumption Christians were in a position to see and to appreciate the absolute principles of life at its highest. The effect of their eschatological belief was that they were enabled to see ethical problems in isolation —in an unnatural isolation, if you like—and to reach nearer to reality than they could ever otherwise have done. That "the world is passing away" and the "Kingdom of God is at hand" was the very clear and vivid eschatological belief of the first Christians, and it enabled them to produce an ethical gospel which is permanent, just because it can never be a practical code for the world as it is, but is the eternal possession of the children of the Kingdom.[1] That is what the eschatological assumption rendered possible. The evolutionary assumption [2] has not yet proved equally valuable in enabling us to state the law of spiritual life, as distinct from economic and social life. This is not to deny that in other respects evolution is probably an hypothesis much nearer the truth than was the eschatological hope, or the catastrophic *weltanschauung*.

The marked contempt shown in so many liberal circles for anything to do with eschatology is as little justifiable as would be a similar attitude on the part of a soldier to the bows which were used at Creçy. We cannot afford to despise or to patronize the arms by which our fathers won their victories, even though we do not propose to use them ourselves. It is more desirable to ask what were actually the disadvantages and advantages to the early Church entailed by the eschatological point of view.

Some disadvantage there certainly was: the eschatological hope was the main reason why Christianity stood apart from the general life and culture of the Roman

[1] The truth about the ethics of the Gospels seems to me best expressed in paradox. It was an "interim" ethic, for the Kingdom of God was coming in which it would be impossible to love one's enemies, because there would be no enemies left. It was an absolute ethic, because it expressed principles derived from the world of reality, not from the imperfect society in which we live.

[2] It is unnecessary to remind those who know anything of the history of physical science that the value of an assumption for experimental purposes does not depend on its actual truth. The truths of physical laws have often been established by experiments involving assumptions either known to be mathematically untrue, or afterwards to be so.

Empire, and the Dark Ages, in which the Empire fell but the Church remained, are partly due to this cause. It is always lamentable when any large part of the best men are excluded, or exclude themselves, from the public service of organized society. This is what happened with regard to Christians in the Empire, and it was not entirely and only the fault of the Empire. Moreover, the mass of Western Christianity stood largely apart from the best culture and the best philosophy.[1] Of coursc it would be unfair to say that this was the wholly fault of Christian teachings. Primarily, it was due to the defect of character in the best intellectual life of the day which made men shrink from anything new, and from the sterner side of religious or ethical truth. But, secondarily, it was due to an unjustifiable tendency on the side of Christians to regard the whole fabric of society as irredeemably evil and its culture as sinful.[2] It cannot be doubted that this was largely due to the eschatological hope which made men regard the Empire and the whole of existing human society as doomed to a speedy extinction by the judgment of God.

On the other hand, the eschatological hope worked for good in two ways. Christianity began during a time of efflorescence. The first century was the efflorescent period of law and organization which produced the Empire. Roughly speaking, this period was the culminating point of seven hundred years of preparation, and it lasted rather less than two centuries. By the second century the signs of

[1] It is impossible to read Plutarch on the subject of Isis and Osiris and contrast him with Justin Martyr's Apology for Christianity and not feel that intellectually Plutarch stands higher.

[2] There were, of course, exceptions on some points. Justin, for instance, says that Socrates was inspired by the Logos, but by no means all Christians admitted this.

decay were obvious, with startling rapidity the process of degeneration set in, and the catastrophic fall of the culture of the Empire followed. The one thing which survived to be the source of another civilization was the Church; and the Church survived largely because her eschatological hope had kept her from entirely identifying her life with any single form of social organization.

Nor was this the only way in which the eschatological hope, illusion though it was as a prognostication of the future, worked for good in the development of Christianity. The first Christians had expected the coming of a Kingdom —of a state of society—in which everything would be different, and this expectation enabled them to accept a method of life and a series of commands which were only permanently possible if society underwent a radical change. It is true that society did not undergo a radical change, and that the main problem for the succeeding generations of Christians was to accommodate to a society which showed no signs of passing away beliefs and doctrines which had been based on the expectation of its transitoriness. Instead of entering a new world, Christians found themselves busy with the task of improving the old one. Not only is this true, but it is one of the most important factors in early Church history; on the success with which the readjustment was made depended the existence of the Church. Nevertheless, it is equally true that the driving power which enabled the Church to succeed was largely due to the expectation which she had once cherished. The Messianic Kingdom, its laws and its teaching, ceased to be an expectation, but survived as an ideal. Though men gradually ceased to look for the coming of a Kingdom in which sin, suffering, and death would miraculously be abolished, they never wholly forgot that they had enjoyed the vision of the time when these things would happen, and they pressed forward to make the world in which they were living correspond somewhat more closely to the city of God which they had seen.

I. INDEX OF SUBJECTS AND PERSONS

D

E

F

Q

R

S

II. REFERENCES TO PASSAGES QUOTED